STREET PEOPLE

INVISIBLE NEW YORK MADE VISIBLE

OTHER BOOKS BY DAVID J. BOOKBINDER

What Folk Music Is All About
Paths to Wholeness
52 Flower Mandalas
52 (more) Flower Mandalas
The Art of Balance
Street People Portfolio

OTHER BOOKS BY TRANSFORMATIONS PRESS

Metaphysical Tales
Vienna ØØ
O Amazonas Escuro
The House of Nordquist
Maison Cristina
Cotton Moon

STREET PEOPLE

INVISIBLE NEW YORK MADE VISIBLE

DAVID J. BOOKBINDER

TRANSFORMATIONS PRESS

ISBN: 9781736984734

Library of Congress Control Number: 2022908021

Published in Wenham, Massachusetts by Transformations Press.

Phone: 857-264-0312
Email: info@transformationspress.org
Web: transformationspress.org

Printed in the United States of America.

For Linda, who got me started
and Gene, who kept me going

A portfolio of the photographs and illustrations in this book is available at phototransformations.com

Contents

Foreword

We don't need philosophers or physicists to tell us that time is elastic and wrinkled. We experience it vividly — those times that stretch out into every corner of our consciousness and rise monumentally above the flat ticking of our historical clocks, those times that are incredibly charged emotionally and bursting with meaning. Times like the seventies in NYC.

1970s New York was a mecca for artists, writers, and musicians drawn to its vibrant energy and creative possibilities. It was also a place of grinding poverty and urban decay, where crime and violence were everyday realities and hope danced with despair. In *Street People: Invisible New York Made Visible*, David J. Bookbinder exposes the grit and splendor of a city at its most raw and real. Words and pictures combine to create a graphic testament to this time, this place, and to the haunting people who inhabited it.

Prowl the nighttime streets with Margie — the drag queen who inspired more than fifty works by Andy Warhol — and Romeo, part-time mugger, full-time philosopher, and king of the corner of West 98th Street and Broadway. Set up shop at the crack of dawn with Morris Kavesh as he assembles Manhattan's oldest newsstand, then spend the day with the denizens of his street corner society. Slip downtown and ride shotgun with amateur pimp and prostitute Frankie and Cookie on their first night out. Cross the bridge into Brooklyn to bear witness to Edward, the self-appointed Second Coming of Christ, here to bring down destruction on the human race.

Bookbinder was there as a perceptive and adventurous young man, an aspiring journalist with a notebook and a camera. He delivers the street in the wholeness of its violence, its sexuality, its poignance, in portraits so vivid that they fairly leap off the page and into our psyches. There, lodged like the earworms of old songs we've half forgotten, they summon memories we didn't know we had, sympathies we have suppressed. Bookbinder's people are alive, eloquent in testimony of their humanity, unforgettable. He gives them to us for our astonishment and admiration, for our reflection — a gift of great value to take in, to live with, to understand, in all their grotesqueness and their beauty, as we go from page to page with a growing sense of wonder.

The past is embedded in our present, in us. It may be grand, it may be inglorious, but it is inescapable, and the great danger is to forget it. Remembering, Carl Jung posited, is absolutely essential to a full development of the psyche. The same is true of a culture. To fail to remember is to be dangerously stunted.

In *Street People*, we remember. This book joins such classics as Agee and Evans' *Let Us Now Praise Famous Men,* Hubert Selby's *Last Exit to Brooklyn,* and Lou Reed's *Walk on the Wild Side* in its timeless portrayal of life on the margins. Experience this strikingly illustrated account of New York City's forgotten people. Witness invisible New York made visible.

- Eugene K. Garber

MANHATTAN

Margie

I always been attracted to beautiful womans. I admire them. Not sexually — a woman don't arouse me, don't get me on — but I always like to be like one. I always like to be a beautiful chick.

When I was a little boy, five or six years old — that's as long as I can remember — I always want to be a little girl. I used to daydream a lot, you know? I used to go to bed and I say, 'Oh, my God! I wish that when I wake up, I wake up in the morning a woman.' Ah, to wake up as a woman in the morning ... When my family would go visiting, and they would sit in the parlor on the rocking chairs, I always used to sit on the men's laps. So devilish! I used to sit on the men's laps, just to feel them.

In school, the other boys call me sissy, and I was always fighting. But in a way I was lucky, because I always hang around with the girls, and they stick up for me. Most of the boys — you know how *cruel* they could be — they try to make fun out of me, try to beat me up or something, and the girls always *chase* 'em away. We were real pals. I always get along with the girls, and I always was with the group of girls. That's the only way I could go through school. Although it was hell. It was really horrible, I can tell you.

My parents feel terrible about me, especially my mother. I was to a psychiatrist, and he told me that I identify with my mummy, because my father die when I was five or six years old. But I don't believe that. I was raised up by my mummy, and I grew up loving my mother so much, but I think it was a case of hormones, an imbalance of hormones. Whatever it was, as long as I can remember, I always been attracted to boys, instead of being attracted to girls. Sexually, you know?

—

I'm 29 — no, let's be truthful, I'm 33. And I been draggin' since I was 14 years old.

I was a pretty child: a teenage, gay, homosexual child. And I run away from my parents in San Juan, Puerto Rico, when I was 14 years old, and I join a company of female impersonators called the Little Parrot. It's like the Jewel Box Revue here, but they were all Spanish-speaking — you know, Puerto Rican.

I didn't have no previous experience of the stage, but I meet the owner of the club — he's a Puerto Rican singer, and he's gay — and he was interested in me because I was so young and so cute, and that was what the people went to see: young, really cute boys in drag — dressed as a woman. It was a gay club, frequented by mixed people. Many people went there for this reason or that: just to have a nice time, or to laugh at the faggots, or to see how they dress, or to ooh and ahh. You know, 'Ooh, how good they look! Like a woman! How could that be a man?' and such and such. I could remember I do a dance called La Samba. I dress up as Carmen Miranda, with a full headdress with fruits and feathers and a bra and the whole costume, and I *tico tico te, tico ta*: I dance to the whole number. They announce me as 'Mr. or Mrs. Carmen Miranda.' That was my hit solo number. And then there was the chorus.

So, that was my first stage appearance. I spend about four years there: 14, 15, 16, 17, 18. Then, I meet a tourist from New York. He was gay. He was old. And he was president of a bank from Fifth Avenue or Park Avenue or somewhere around there. He fell for me and I fell for him, and once, when I went out of the club, we went to bed.

After that happen, I run away with him to New York. He pay my fare and he bring me to 74th Street between Amsterdam and Columbus. It was a nice, furnished, big, big room. He came and visit me twice or three times a week, and he give me an allowance so I could have my clotheses and food and everything. I was a kept woman! That's the way I start, really, prostituting myself.

I didn't knew his true identity, 'cause he was living with his aging mother, as he told me, on Park Avenue. I know he was filthy rich and everything like that, but I didn't know anything about his life. I was too innocent to care much about all those things. But after a while, something went wrong. Once, when he came to visit me, I went through his wallet and I reached his true name and his phone number, and where he work and such and such. So, I call him at home. Because I love him. I love him.

I didn't have no idea of blackmail or nothing like that, but something in his mind make him panic, and after that he refuse even to see me at all — he cut all ties. His reputation, his bank account, and maybe even more things stop him from being seen with me or from having a closer relationship, because he was gay and nobody knew he *was*.

I try to find work as a female impersonator. By the time I come here, 72nd Street was swarming with queens, with gay people, and I meet a very great female impersonator whose name was — whose name is, because she's still living — Baby Martell. She introduce me to another very famous female impersonator named Bruno Le Fantastique, and she find me a job working at the Club 82, Fourth Street and Second Avenue.

I work there for, let's say, six months. That was on the chorus line, because I didn't have too much training as a dancer. After that, I got in trouble with the owner. Head feathers and a rhinestone necklace disappear. Somebody say I did it. I did not. They couldn't prove it was me, anyway. But, that was the end of it.

Since then, I have been dressing as a woman daytime and night-time and going out with mens. Some of them know if I am a woman, some of them do not. Sometimes, they are surprised — I have been close to get killed twice or three times.

—

First when I left the club, I try to act butch, to dress like a boy. I don't have no money to live by myself, so I go to live with my sister — I used to have a sister living in the Bronx. She find me a job in a um-brella factory — some kind of paper flowers or something — and I was making $60 a week. Every Friday, I got $60, my paycheck.

On weekends, I went downtown to 42nd Street for movies and this and that. One time, I meet this beautiful guy — not beautiful guy, I mean I meet this *guy* — and he told me, Did I want to go out? Did I want to go up with him to his house? Understand, I was hip to the homosexual scene already. I was 19 or 20 years old, and I wasn't in drag, I was dressed as a boy, with blue jeans. But I know that tricks favor blue jeans — cowboy-style blue jeans, and sometimes rough corduroy pants. So, when this gentleman ask me if I could go up to his house, and he said, 'I'll give you $15 just for a good time,' I guessed he was gay.

He took me to the Edison Hotel. We went up, he serve me a drink, and after that we went to bed. And, it was very common, you know? We get our clotheses off and we go in the bed and we start to caress each other and he said, 'How do you want to do it, in the sixty-nine position?' So we do a sixty-nine position: He suck me off and I suck him off. That was my first real trick. For him, I don't feel nothing at all, just friendship like when I meet a person. But I went with him because he offered me $15.

Of course, we were in bed not for more than half an hour, and after that, he said, 'I want to see you every Saturday.' (It was Saturday night.) So, I keep meeting him for four or five Saturdays more. Then I keep going to 42nd Street, and I start going with some others and they pay me more and more — twenty or twenty-five, $40. I was making more money turning tricks than I was in the factory, so I quit the factory and I move away with another queen, a friend of mine, on 42nd Street. Now, she's a sex change.

—

For ten to fifteen years since then, I been doing the same thing. I walk the street, and most of what I do is car hopping.

I sleep in the daytime. I wake up around four or five o'clock. If I have to go visiting somebody or I have to go shopping, sometimes I go in drag, sometimes I go as a guy. I can dress as a guy and you wouldn't recognize me, that's for sure. Not even my landlord. He thinks it's two people living in the same apartment! And I say, 'That's my sister.'

I work from six to six: six o'clock at night to six o'clock in the morning. Friday and Saturday are the best nights, 'cause Friday I always make — sucking and fucking flat, without pickpocketing and robbing — I make a hundred, a hundred and twenty-five. Friday and Saturday, I never make less than $80 a night.

So, A car stop, I go inside the car and sweet-talk the driver: 'Do you wanna go out? What do you want, a french? Do you want a nice blow job? Do you wanna fuck? What do you want?' Most of them are afraid of fucking a whore in the pussy, because most of them are married — they're afraid of catching *something*. So most of them go for blow jobs. That's all the girls you see on Broadway do: they offer a blow job for $15, and they say, 'Well, if you want a good time, fuck and suck, I give you a good time for $25.' And then they also rob them.

Most of them, especially some of the black ones you see parading up and down, they are on hard drugs, and some of them have pimps. That's something I don't have to worry about myself. I take speed sometimes — I love speed because it give me a lot of energy — but I'm not on hard drugs and I don't have a pimp, so I don't have to rob. But, I have done it many times, too, so in a way I'm talking about myself.

So, the girl go in the car, and she sit close to the guy who's driving, and she start playing with his dick, kissing him here and here and here, and then they park, especially on Riverside Drive on a dark, dark spot, or in a few dark parking lots. The first thing the guy do is to unbuckle his pants and pull them all the way down to his knees. He open his legs so we can go to work on him, start frenchin' him, and he just lay back and start enjoyin' his french, still sitting in the driver's seat. But the girl is sucking his cock and sucking his balls and at the same time she is going through his pockets and through his wallet.

I do that, too, especially if he's not hip to it, like so many tourists in the summertime are not hip to it. But many of them *are* hip to it. They keep their money in the back seat of the car, with lock and key, so it's impossible to do it.

When I am working, I put my mind on the $10, because that's what I charge for a nice blow job. So, I don't care if the dick is good, big, small, whatever size it is or how it looks like or anything. I ask — everybody ask — for the money first. And when he give me a $10 bill, I put it in my panties or in my brassiere, and after that, we perform. It doesn't last more than ten minutes or fifteen minutes, if the guy is not drinking.

Once, I went with this guy and he *was* drinking and he couldn't come, so I said, 'I'm sorry, but for $10 I can't be sucking you all night long.' So he give me $10 more. And, he couldn't come, in the end. I try to open the door to get out, so he grab me by the hands and we start fighting, 'cause he want the money back. Then he grab me by the neck and he almost choke the *life* out of me. He almost killed me! He was furious, because he couldn't come, and he wanted to come so badly. And it wasn't my fault, anyway.

That's one of the times I almost died. When he saw that I start going limp, he just open the door and speed away. But I still keep the $20. He didn't run away with my $20.

—

Men are not offering more than $10 for blow jobs, and they are not offering more than $15 for a blow job and a fuck. That's why every prostitute in town is trying to rob them, honey. They go through their wallets, and many of them get killed. Many prostitutes get killed. Drag queens appear killed in some parking lot. Men kill prostitutes in bed. You read that in the press every day, and I hear it through the grapevine. In this more or less ten to fifteen years that I got doing this, they have killed many of my girlfriends.

My roommate was killed by a trick because she used to take them. She used to get a very close bra, then between the bra, she keep a hunting knife. So, when she was sucking his dick, she get the knife and put it on his balls and say, 'All right, give me all your money or I'll just stick the knife on your balls.' So most of the guys get panicked. But this one didn't panic. He got a gun, and he said, 'Well, you stick that knife on my balls and I blow your brains out.' So, she wasn't ready, the queen wasn't ready enough just to *stab*. He was quicker than she was and he knock her down with the butt of the gun. He hit her in the head and she laid down back, and he shot her three times in the stomach and then threw her body on 11th Avenue and 52nd Street. They found her there. And they call her family and her sister give her a nice burial, and that was the end of Miss Bridget. She was 20 years old. They never grab the guy who kill her. I know what happen because another queen, whose name is Liza, was in the same parking lot as our girl, and she saw more or less what happen. She was with a guy, and they keep quiet while all this rumble was going on because they don't want no trouble, and no part of it.

Then one time another one of my girlfriends went with a man who was a sex maniac, and she was sucking his cock and he got a knife and he stab her in the back and just open the door and throw her in the parking lot. It happen, you know. It could happen to me as any of those girls, there are so many of them loose.

If I can rob somebody and I know he's safe, like I pick one of his pockets without him knowing nothing about it, then I will. But if I know something can be dangerous, if the guy is bigger than I, then I'm not gonna do it.

When I go with a man in a car I always grab his hands. I make believe I'm caressing him, but I'm searching him to see if he got any gun or anything. I always look in the back seat, and I got quick reflexes, and I'm always looking in his hands, so in case he try to do something, I can open the door and run away. But anyway, you never know when it's gonna happen. Could happen any time.

—

I been in jail three times.

They catch me twice for prostitution. The first time, I was standing on the corner trying to make some money, Eighth Avenue in
midtown, and this guy stop. He never look like a police, he look like
the guy next door. And he say, 'Come in, honey. I'm gonna have a nice
time with you. I give you $15 for a quick french.'

I say okay and I jump in the car. We park in the parking lot, and I
say, 'Okay, give me the $15.' But when he got his wallet out, what he
showed me was his badge and his gun. He was undercover policeman!
So, they give me thirty-five days for that on Riker's Island.

Jail wasn't that good, honey, because they have the homos in a special section, you know? They don't have them in the general population. They send everybody who sign a paper who says 'I'm a homo'
to this special dormitory, and they got around a hundred and fifty-five
people in there. And you can't have sex with a real — you know, queens
like me like to have a real *butch* type — I don't like to go with sissies
like myself! So, it wasn't that good. But, it wasn't that bad. It could be
better, of course.

—

Now, you can see almost five bitches on every corner on Broadway
around here, from 96th Street to 72nd Street all the way down. They
are not staying on the corner, they are parading up and down. You can
tell them, honey. They are car hopping.

Broadway is getting more and more of the girls and queens from
around Times Square, because Times Square is getting too hot. A lot
of police is *patroolling* around, and they are operating at least seven
or eight mini-wagons. They walk around and they pick up the prostitutes and the drag queens and the drunks for loitering, and they keep
you all night long. You sleeped all night long on a hard bench in jail,
and you can't make a penny — they keep you out of circulation for the
night. And it happen every night: They catch you seven nights a week,
seven nights a week they catch you. Because they catch me three times
in a *row*.

Since then, the only time I go to Times Square is when the guys
from New Jersey come there after they got out of work at four o'clock
in the afternoon. They have to go home, so they ride around Ninth or
Eighth Avenue. I work there from about four-thirty or five to six or

sometimes seven, 'cause the mini-wagon start picking people up around eight o'clock.

Say I have great luck. I make some money there, and then I move to the East Village, Second or Third Avenue. If it's too hot there — the police say, 'Move! Move! Move! Move, or we'll lock you up!' — then I move out to the West Village. If the West Village is too hot, then I move to Sixth Avenue. If Sixth Avenue is too hot, then I stay around Broadway, around here, because this is my neighborhood, and they can't pick me up for loitering since I live right here on 95th Street.

That's why they call us streetwalkers, honey. That's the right name, streetwalking.

—

I think, if I ever got something done, I will have the titties. Just that. Big breasts, my breasts. Because my main attraction is to attract the men, you know. To attract the men, a nice face, I can do it with hair and makeup. Powder and makeup and makeup and powder make a woman look what she ain't! But, with a nice pair of breasts, any man is attracted.

Now, I got very small hormone breasts. You have to go to a doctor for that, Dr. Jones on Fifth Avenue. They give you a shot for $10, a shot of estrogen every week, especially on Mondays. And then, I'm wearing a little bit of pad, foam rubber. My breasts are not big enough, honey. Right now, they are just on the working stage. But I'm planning to have them be completely big. I'm saving to have them with silicone.

I'm not interested in becoming a woman because I know myself and I'm not a transsexual, more or less. You got a transsexual, she thinks she's a woman trapped inside a man's body, but in fact, I'm really more of a transvestite. I'm just interested in having sex with nice men I dig, you know?

I been with girls. I have made love to girls. Like, I have met many guys, especially this trick I have, he's from Westchester, and every time I met him, he wants me to introduce him to this girl. I always introduce him to a girl, any girl in the street I know, and we go to bed: the girl, me, and him. And, I used to suck her pussy, and I used to fuck her, too, and the only thing he do while we're doing that is, he just jack off, and he hide under the curtain and make believe he's a Peeping Tom. I understand that clearly: He's got a Peeping Tom complex, or something like that. But, I'm doing it for the money, 'cause he always spend $40, $50 for it. For pleasure, never have I done it.

For money I do anything, but for my own personal pleasure, I prefer to have sex especially with Negro mens, especially with beautiful Negro mens, and get a nice fuck and get a nice love with them. I don't have no steady boyfriend, but I got friends, some friends that I go with once in a while. I enjoy sex. It satisfy me, really. A good fuck make me come oh, fantastic!

—

You will never be too old for drag. I have seen drag queens ... I know a drag queen, Bruno Le Fantastique, she's more than 84 years old, and she keeps dragging all the time, and she got an act that she dress half a man and half a woman, and she's still entertaining, and she know how to sew. I know how to sew a little bit, too, so if I have to go to work, really *work* for a living, not to *starve*, I can go looking for sewing for some kind of job. But I'm planning to drag until I die. You know, for the rest of my life.

There's no age for drag, that's for sure. I have seen persons 70 years old and I have seen them with full-face surgical makeup and hair and they look 45, 40 years old. Younger, younger, and younger. That's something. There is no age for drag. I mean, that's my opinion. You can think different.

—

The most important thing for me now is making enough money this summer. I'm planning to spend all this summer out, and that's when I'm tricking flat. I'm saving my money so in the spring I'm leaving.

Right now, everybody's looking for something. All my girlfriends used to work in drag at the 82 Club. There is no more place for them. The Jewel Box come once a year, and all I can do is a little bit of comedy, a little bit of dance. But where? There is no place.

What really is getting on us now are the go-go girls. Now they are recruiting them even for Alaska. Two girlfriends of mine — they are transsexuals, they got the boobies, but they don't have the pussy done yet — they get the penis taped back and the hair combed down, and they pass the test: They thought they were cunt! They're in Alaska now, making $200 a week just for go-going in those bars over there.

I got a girlfriend, now, she's in Tijuana. I never been there, but I think it's next to or close to California. She's what you call a transsexual, too. She got the breasts made, but she don't have the pussy yet. And she's working as a stripper and she's stripping and she's turning tricks, just turning tricks galore. Oh! She's making money, and she says the money now is in Tijuana. So that's where I'm going for in the spring, honey. As soon as I found my money, I'm leaving New York and going there. I hope so, you know. If I don't get killed by a trick or a sex maniac in a car! Then if everything go good for me in Tijuana, I stay there, 'cause that's what I want: some money. And there is no money in New York, that's for sure.

—

If somehow I could do anything I want, something I think I should do is just to become famous, just to show up my family, 'cause I been rejected by them because I was a homosexual. They disown me and everything since I run away, since I was 14 years old.

I got two brothers — my father died, my mother is still living — and they never like me. I know where they live and I know everything about them by some friends of mine in San Juan. They are both married. One of them is a sergeant of policemens in San Juan, and the other one work as the director of a school in San Juan. And my dream shall be, even if I don't want, really, to go through the pain and the hassle and the aggravation of being a sex change — because now, if I get all the money to do it, I could go to a hospital right here in Yonkers and they make me more gorgeous as that woman in the Playboy magazine, with my pussy, my titties, my nose, my sex change *complete*.

And then after I got my sex change, I will fly to San Juan and I will seduce both of my brothers and go to bed with them and let them fuck me and I suck them, and then I will stand in front of them and tell them, 'I'm your brother Harry, honey. How do you like it?'

Yes, that's what I should do! How I should love to do that! 'I'm the little brother you used to beat because he was a faggot, remember me, honey?' They will die, yes ...

—

Oh, honey, I think our time is up, darling. So, when you want to have me again, let me know when. You know where to find me.

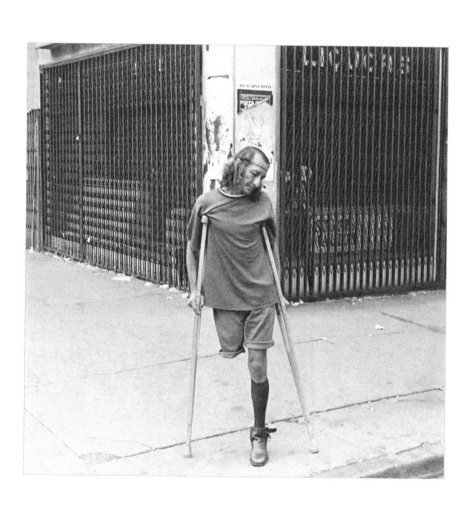

Romeo & Muñeca

Every night, beginning about eight, they gathered at the corner across from our building, leaning on any available car, hanging out by the phone booth, making occasional forays to the bodega down the block for cigarettes and beer, or to the pizza parlor for Italian ices. Sometimes, coming home late in the evening, I would see two or three scuffling. At first, I crossed the street or veered wide to avoid them, but after a while I saw that the fights were mostly good-natured — they were just goofing on each other, clowning and chatting in Spanish and English. Soon, I was nodding to them or saying "hi" as I walked by.

One night, a tall, fair-skinned redhead caught my eye. Her long hair, lit by the streetlight, glistened. Leaning on the front bumper of a deep blue Pontiac, dragging on a cigarette, she seemed, somehow, the center of the rough activity taking place around her.

I wanted to take her photograph.

I had been taking pictures again for some months, after a lapse of several years. In part, I was influenced by my roommate Henry, who had converted the kitchen pantry into a darkroom. But I understand now that there was more to it: From behind the camera, I did not have to experience, so directly, what I saw.

A couple of evenings later, I decided to approach her. People of indeterminate sex wandered in and out of the area. I walked up to the redhead. "I'd like to photograph you," I said. "Just for myself," I quickly added.

Immediately, a petite, blond transvestite hopped off the hood of the car she'd been sitting on, set her hands on her hips, and began to strut about between me and the car, tracing a small circle on the sidewalk, grinding and grunting in a grotesque parody of seduction. She stopped about a foot from where I stood and pulled up her blouse, exposing a flat, hairless chest. "You wanna take a picture? Take a picture of this!" she said. Another queen, more shapely, spat to one side and blurted out, "You suck my dick and have somebody take a picture, and *fuck* you!" They all laughed as she staggered away, indignant.

"See you later," I said, and walked — with what I hoped was a casual step — across the street and into my building, thankful I had been able to conceal at least some of my unease.

—

It was two weeks before I approached them again, and this time I was with Henry. Like me, Henry was a recent arrival in New York, here to make his mark. We had been talking about teaming up on a book project, he the photographer, I the interviewer and writer. When I told him about my encounters with the transvestites on the corner, he said he'd like to come out with me one night to talk with them.

I was reluctant to work with Henry. He was pushy and obsessive, and I was afraid he would dominate the partnership, as he often tried to do in our roommate relationship. Also, although he had lived in New York several months longer than I, he seemed even less savvy about the darker corners of this city.

Still, there were advantages to working with him. He was a more experienced photographer and, importantly, he was also brazen enough to pull things off that I could hardly even imagine myself doing. Take the way he was with women. Henry approached them on the street, on the train, in the supermarket — anywhere he might find them. Where I might risk a faint smile, Henry came on strong, with a line about their beautiful hair or striking eyes, and how he would *love* to photograph them, and would they be interested in coming to his studio? Though his boldness often irked me, I thought it might come in handy in the line of work we were considering.

I also sensed in him a subtle vulnerability. I was fairly confident that even though, at every turn, he might *like* to have everything go his way, he would push me only as far as he could without endangering our tenuous friendship.

—

For several minutes, Henry and I had been speaking with Muñeca, the tall, pale redhead I had approached before. Henry was doing most of the talking. He was laying it on thick, telling her she looked so interesting, how great she would be to photograph, that the pictures would be very ... dignified, of course. I had seen him use this tactic with the women he lured to our apartment, with mixed results. It was hard to predict how it would play out this time.

The others around us were clearly amused, making comments like, "Oh, come on, Muñeca, you'll be a fashion queen!" But Muñeca herself spoke infrequently, and when she did, her voice was soft, her words almost overwhelmed by the din of Broadway.

At last Henry finished his pitch. Muñeca smiled, then shook her head, tucking her chin to her chest like a sleeping bird. "I don't know," she whispered. "You'll have to ask my husband, when he comes back. He's the man. You'll have to ask Romeo."

"Will your Romeo be back soon?" Henry asked.

"I don't know for sure when," she said, "but yes, I think soon."

We decided to wait. Muñeca stepped away to talk with the others, but she didn't seem to mind us hanging around.

A few minutes later, a smooth, deep voice from behind us snapped, "Hey, you want somethin'?"

We spun around. Facing us was a muscular young man in a brown tank top, his broad lips twisted into a snarl. Before either Henry or I could respond, his left hand went to the pocket of his jeans. There was a glint of flashing steel.

We froze.

"It's okay, it's okay, Romeo." A plump woman who had been talking with Muñeca came up behind him and laid her hands on his shoulders. "It's jus' those guys I tol' you about, the ones that wanted to take the pictures."

Romeo shook back and forth like a dog on a choke chain, freeing himself from her grip. He glared first at her, then at Henry and me. Moments that felt like minutes passed. The chaos of the corner receded, a movie fading to black.

Muñeca sidled up to him and put an arm around his waist. He relaxed into her embrace, his mouth softening to a tight smile. "Hello," he said. "I'm Romeo, and this is Muñeca."

We nodded like a pair of ventriloquist's dummies.

Romeo's knife hand still hovering near his pocket, his eyes still hard, he held out a hand to Henry, then to me. His grip was strong and I could feel the calluses on his palm.

"Very nice to meet you," Henry said.

Romeo gestured toward the plump woman who had intervened and to the wiry young man now standing beside her. "And this is Carmen and Joey," he said.

Henry and I introduced ourselves. I explained that I was a writer and an amateur photographer. Henry described himself as "a professional photographer" — his ambition, though at the time he was still working as a photographer's assistant. We were interested, I said, in doing a book about people on the West Side, people we met on the street. We wanted to portray their lives, their stories, their problems, in words and in pictures. I told Romeo that we meant him and Muñeca no harm — just the opposite, in fact — and that we had only been talking with her about taking her picture and interviewing her. "Of course," Henry added, "we would like to talk to you, as well."

Romeo nodded, crossing his arms in front of his chest, taking us in. "Uh-huh," he said.

"You'll find we're very friendly," Henry said. He flashed Romeo his come-hither smile. "You didn't have to pull your knife on us."

Romeo nodded again, looked us over once more, and set his hands on his hips. "Yeah, well, I just don't want nobody messin' with my woman, that's all."

He pushed himself onto the hood of a car and leaned back against its windshield, arms behind his head, surveying his domain. Then he smiled, almost grinned.

"They told me there was these two guys messin' with Muñeca, so I come runnin', but Carmen told me about you. You want to know about the corner? No big deal, I can tell you."

I sat on the car opposite Romeo and returned his smile. With an open hand, I gestured toward the cluster of people around us. "Can you tell us about your friends?"

"Sure," he said. "Carmen and Joey over there, they're some straight friends that we know. But then Mona, the one that had his arm around my wife, he is butch queen. He feels like a woman, he has a husband who fucks him and so forth, he's a woman in his own way, but he dresses like a man."

He pointed out a husky queen sipping a beer from a paper bag. "That one, her name's Eba. She hustles by car right here on Broadway. She was hustling the other night and three men — you know, supposed to be hard men who don't like faggots — took her in the park and raped her." He shook his head. "They're supposed to be so *hard rock* — you know, 'I wouldn't fuck a man for nothin' in this world' — but yet, they took her in the park and raped her."

"Terrible," I said.

By now Henry had joined me on the trunk of the car. I sensed him sizing everyone up, framing images in his mind's eye.

Romeo nodded. "Now, that fat boy over there sucking on the Italian ice?" he said. "Willie, that's his butch name, but we call him Wilma. He's basically gay. He has no desire for a woman, he feels like a woman, and he's felt this way all his life. He's never even had a piece of pussy. I tell you, some people are *born* that way.

"He has sex with men, he has his boyfriend and everything, but he won't be going into drag or nothin' until he moves away from his family. Why? Because a lot of gay people don't have no family, you might say. Their family might live right across the street, and yet they don't wanna accept them no more. Like, my father, he's gay himself, but yet if he walked right by here, right now, he would act like he didn't even know who the hell I was."

Henry checked his watch. I could see he wanted to get back to the business of arranging a photo shoot. We both had to be up early the next morning, but I wanted to hear more. As Romeo warmed to the conversation, I fumbled for a more personal way to connect. "It must be hard," I said, "I've had some pretty bad trouble with my father, too."

"Yeah," Romeo said, "but, like, it's not just that. Just being gay, it's hard. A lotta people are basically against gay people, for no reason at all. They just don't like 'em, you know?"

I nodded again. I did know, or at least I wasn't completely in the dark. My college roommate, Sam, had been president of the local Gay Lib, and I'd gotten to know his history and that of many of his friends.

"But, gay people are more happier than straight people," Romeo went on. "When you go to a gay party, everybody's dancing — high, high, high, everybody's together. And they're easier to get along with. They take life for what it's worth: 'This is life and that's great and I'm gonna enjoy it.' You see? Because when you're trying to be something or get something and you have to work for it, you appreciate it more. But then of course, it isn't always like that. One minute you can be happy as all outdoors, and the next you can be at each other's throats. People have been killed in gay life."

He paused, as if to let that sink in. His sharp eyes moving between Henry and me, he continued. "In most gay situations, you are their family, you're everything. They usually depend on their friends or their lover to give them the love of their mother, father, brothers, and sisters. With a woman, you would try to build a home for her so that she would raise your children there, right? You would be looking forward to that. With a gay person, makes no difference where you live or how you live, just as long as you're together and it's workin' out. Even as they get old, they still depend on each other. It's much harder."

He looked down, briefly, then gazed at me with a pained intensity.

"You gotta understand that these are people, too. Each and every person has a different way of acting and a way of feeling how they want life to be. Just like you're all straight people, but you have a different way of thinkin' and doin' and livin' and so forth — it's the same with them."

A mischievous smile crossed his face. "There is crazy gay people, though, I'll tell you that much," he said. "Like, Monic and Victor, this guy and this queen who live together like me and Muñeca. Since they been together — almost a year — he has stabbed her three times, and she has stabbed him three times. And both of them are no good. They're junkies and they take downers and methadone pills and they drink all day. But yet, they're happy. You couldn't take Monic and Victor apart for nothin' in this world."

Romeo told us of "the queens who shouldn't be queens," like Lengy, whom he had met one night at the Gilded Grape. She had broad shoulders and thick, muscular arms. He went home with her once. "She had titties, but she had a tattoo of a ship going across them, and a tattoo of "MOM" on her arm." She had been in the service, and afterwards had decided to become a queen.

The same thing with Cricket, who used to be a boxer. "You know how she looks like in a dress?" Romeo asked. "Still like a boxer." He shook his head. "There a lot to it."

I nodded, taking it in. This was not the Gay Lib world that Sam had introduced me to.

Romeo continued his crash course on gay life as he knew it. There were the sadists, who liked to beat people. And the bars in the Village, where guys came in with leather suits and wigs. "Of course, there's money in that, from the hustling point of view. If a guy wants to beat you, he's gotta pay a lot for it." Romeo had done that for money. "I believe in trying everything at least once, because you never understand anything unless you've tried it yourself. Experience is the best teacher," he said.

"You got high-class gay people, you got low-class gay people, middle-class gay people, and some that just don't care," he observed. "And then you have these trash gay people."

He described a section of Central Park he could take us to, right then if we wanted, where we would see nothing but men walking around. All night long, they had sex with different people, changing from one to the next just for the hell of it. "That's really sick," he said. "That's low, low class. But yet, they could live in some fancy building and everything. That's just their bag, they dig it." He'd been around there. Not to do anything, but he was told about it, so he said, "I'm gonna go see for myself. And I couldn't believe it. There were over a hundred men in one section of that park."

—

While we listened to Romeo hold forth, the sky had darkened, the air had grown uncomfortably cool, and the traffic along Broadway had thinned. Most of the corner regulars had also drifted away.

"And what about you?" Henry asked. "You like to have sex just with men? Forgive me if I'm too abrupt, but I don't know much about these things. I've only gone with women."

Romeo sat up on the car hood and hugged his knees. He chewed his lower lip and shook his head.

I was afraid we would lose him.

But I underestimated his patience. Like a school teacher speaking to a child who has failed to understand an assignment, he explained, "I like women *and* men. But I have no thrill for anything that looks like a man or has hair on his face or anything. I'm still a man, I'm considered a man. Muñeca attracts me because she looks like a woman. You might say it's my eyesight: I *project*, I see her as a woman, not as a man. Where, if I was to go with a person that looked like a man and he wanted to see me as a woman, he'd just look and see, 'Damn, you're not a woman!'"

I nudged Henry to try to get him to back off, but he pressed on. "And the sex," he said, "is it actually anal sex?"

Romeo gripped his knees so hard the veins on his hands stood out. He took a breath and let it out slowly.

I cut in. "Maybe that's too personal," I said. "It's fine if you don't want to talk about that."

"It's okay," Romeo said, "it's cool." He turned to Henry. "Look, it would be just like if I was to have sex with a woman. I have nothing to do with the front part of *her* body and she has nothing to do with the back part of *mine*. You understand what I'm saying? It's like, *I fuck her*, you understand? And that's all there is to it, just like you would be with a woman: You fuck the woman."

"Yes," Henry said, "but a woman has a pussy."

"Yeah ..."

"And Muñeca doesn't have a pussy, right?"

Was gay sex unknown where Henry came from? I was sure that at any moment Romeo would tell us to get lost.

But again I underestimated Romeo's patience — or perhaps his desire to be heard. He drew another deep breath and sighed. Leaning in, he whispered, "But she has an ass."

Henry nodded. "Ah," he said.

"Look," Romeo said, "I don't do anything that you might say is in the feminine point of view. I don't suck no man's dick, I don't get fucked in my ass, nothin' of that sort. Let's not put it vulgarly, but, more or less, that's the woman's part. You see what I'm saying? But I'm putting it nicely." He looked over his shoulder and put on a little boy smile. "I don't want to upset nobody's nerves."

Muñeca, silent as a cat, had joined us. She scowled at Romeo, and I felt a momentary chill, like passing through a cold spot in the ocean.

"Are you upset?" I asked Muñeca.

"He's all right," she said, her eyes tracking her feet as they rearranged the trash alongside the curb.

"All right?" Romeo asked. He hopped off the car. "All *right*? I thought you loved me, baby. Now I'm 'all right'?"

They faced each other, a foot apart, Romeo's hands on his hips, Muñeca slouching but still half a foot taller than him. (Only later did I learn that "muñeca" is Spanish for "doll.")

Muñeca's gaze stayed fixed on her shoes. Romeo laughed, but a hint of uncertainty lingered. Then Muñeca raised her eyes to meet his, and she smiled. Romeo put a hand on her shoulder, lifted himself on his toes, and kissed her on the forehead. They embraced, effecting a repair.

"We should get going," I said. "Can we meet again?"

"You can come to my studio," Henry said. "I have lights and background paper so we can do a proper portrait. And we can also take photographs in your home."

Romeo frowned. "It's not a home, it's a room," he said. "But you can come there."

Henry, as always pushing boundaries, asked if he might also take pictures of Muñeca "in the half-nude, so you could see that what looks like a woman is actually a man." Romeo said no way to that, and Henry, to his credit, dropped it. We agreed to meet them on the corner in two days, at eight o'clock.

As we were saying our formal goodbyes, goodnights, and nice-to-have-met-yous, Carmen stormed over in a huff. She'd just had a dispute with Willie/Wilma, the chubby 17-year-old Romeo had pointed out earlier.

"That fat elephant over there tried to *read* me," she said, pointing with her heavy arm. "I said, 'You *wish* you had my body.' I said, 'You don't have nothin' to offer, so what're you talkin' about, stupid?' I just said to her, 'You got meat on top of meat.' That's true. That's what she's got. *He*, rather. He. That's all he is, is *he*."

She was met with embarrassed silence all around. "Well," I said, "We'll be going now. See you Thursday, okay?"

"Goodbye, Muñeca," Henry said, bowing slightly and smiling. "It was a pleasure to meet you." Muñeca nodded and returned his smile. Despite its insincerity, this silly, formal gesture seemed to restore the mood.

As we headed back to our building, I fretted about our next encounter and what I would say to Henry about how we should conduct the interviews. But before I had a chance to say anything, the kid who worked in the pizza shop jumped in front of us.

"Let me tell you," he said, standing with his legs spread, hips jutting forward, hands pulling apart his inner thighs, "a guy's ass is *better* than a girl's pussy. That shit is *tight*, bro!"

—

Neither Romeo nor Muñeca was on the corner when Henry and I got there Thursday night, and after half an hour, we returned to our apartment to call them. Fortunately, I'd gotten their number.

Henry made the call. Muñeca picked up the phone, but turned it over to Romeo when she heard it was us. Something had come up, Romeo told Henry, and they wouldn't be able to make it. "Would you be able to do it sometime over the weekend?" Henry asked. Romeo thought they could. Henry arranged for us to meet them Sunday night.

But Romeo and Muñeca were not on the corner when we arrived on Sunday, either. I was angry with myself for not somehow finding a way to cement things that first night, but I was also at a loss for what I might have done. Henry and I told each other this was the kind of thing we would probably just have to get used to with "these kinds of people."

Just as we were heading back to the apartment again, Romeo showed up. He apologized for being late this time and for leaving us hanging the time before. "Me and Muñeca got some new grass," he said, "and we got so wiped out we forgot all about the appointment. I guess you were afraid we'd skip out this time, too, right?"

"Not at all," Henry lied.

Romeo looked as if all the air had been let out of him. "What's up?" I asked him. "Are you feeling all right?"

He sighed. "I got a call from my father today asking me to meet him in the park," he said. "I hadn't seen him for weeks, so I said, 'Damn, I want to see what's happening with him. Maybe he's got something nice he wants to say or maybe he understands me. Maybe I can get to see him more often, get back together with my family.' But I waited all day around the fountain in the park and he didn't even show. I just came from there now."

Romeo stood with his hands in his pockets, his round, smooth face pulled into a sorrowful mask. "That's tough," I said. Then, "How old are you?"

"Nineteen."

Despite my own innocence of his world, I had the benefit of a few years' experience. "You know how I told you that things were bad between me and my father?"

"Yeah?"

"Well, they got better, after a couple of years."

"Yeah, well," Romeo said, "it's already been a couple of years."

I could find nothing more to say.

Henry asked, cautiously, "If it's still all right, we would like to photograph you and Muñeca tonight. Is it still all right?"

Though his nerves were frayed, Romeo managed to pull himself together. "Sure, man," he said, forcing a smile. "That's cool. That's what I'm here for."

We walked the block and a half to their hotel slowly, not saying much. By the time we arrived, Romeo's mood had brightened, the swagger back in his step. Somehow, our presence seemed to cheer him up. I was glad of that, for his sake and ours. It offset the uneasiness I felt about prying into their lives.

—

Judging from its recessed, canopied entrance and the red and blue stained glass windows in its lobby, their hotel must have been something to see, thirty or forty years earlier, but now it was just a cut above the neighborhood's welfare hotels. It was reputed to be a transvestite hotel. In the shops and stores on the Upper West Side, I had

28

seen many of what I'd presumed were its occupants. The more overt queens I recognized. Others, like Muñeca, I likely mistook for women.

Romeo led us into a rickety elevator that smelled of urine and cigarette butts, then down a litter-strewn corridor and through the brown doorway to their room. The hallway had a worn-out, claustrophobic feel to it, and their room, though tidy, felt oppressive for the first few minutes we were there. Muñeca, her long hair tied back in a pony tail, a floral print dress under her paisley apron, was frying pork chops, and the heat and smoke added to the closeness of the atmosphere.

The only light came from a bare bulb on the ceiling. The room was painted a dull, uneven green, and scarcely large enough to hold their single mattress, an old-fashioned dresser, a wooden arm chair, and an apartment-sized refrigerator, on top of which rested the two-burner hot plate Muñeca stood before. There was a blurry snapshot of the two of them stuck in the frame of the mirror above the dresser. Other than the photograph, there was nothing decorative on the grease-stained walls but a few discolored prints and a portrait of Jesus, on which was superimposed in white, block letters the words DIOS BENDIGA NUESTRO HOGAR — God Bless Our Home. The prints looked as if they belonged to the place; the portrait was Muñeca's. The bathroom, which they shared with several other families, was in the hall.

Henry began to set up his equipment. I sat on the bed. Romeo pulled the arm chair up beside me, and we began to talk.

Romeo said that although only Muñeca was working right then and they were having a hard time scraping together $35 each week for the rent, they had been trying to get a bigger room. The landlord would tell them, "It'll be ready next Wednesday," but when Wednesday came, "It'll be ready next Tuesday" was his story. When Tuesday came, he promised it would be ready in a week. This had been going on for four or five weeks. "Monday, we're gonna get it," Muñeca said, slapping a pork chop on a plate and handing it to Romeo. I moved over on the bed, and she sat with us, too.

—

She was born in Puerto Rico but moved, with her family, to Syracuse, New York, when she was 12. She was 27 now. She wanted to be a woman all her life, as long as she could remember, but she didn't start dressing in drag, growing her hair long, or taking hormones or anything until after she moved to New York. That was five years ago. Her parents, she said, didn't mind when she was "just a little butch," but they hated the way she was now that she was a queen. She had recently told her mother, "If you don't accept me the way I am, then it will have to be like you don't have a son. You will have to forget about me."

She worked in a factory in Queens, assembling cables. She'd worked there since she'd moved to the city and had been hired as a man. "Gay life," she said, "is more free here than upstate. It's more quiet there, more conservative. That's why I like to live here."

At 16 she had quit school to go to work, and she'd been working ever since. She never hustled. Once, she wasn't working for three months, and she was collecting unemployment insurance, and it was $30 for the room and $20 for food and nothing for clothes or anything else, and sometimes she would go to bed hungry, but she would never go out on the street and sell her body. "For myself," Muñeca said, "I don't like it. I prefer to work." Nor would she steal. "The only thing Muñeca would steal," Romeo told me, "is flowers. And that's the God's truth. Flowers. Not money, not food, or anything. Just flowers."

Someday, she hoped to have enough money to complete her sex change. She really wanted to do that. And then, if she had money beyond that, she would like to buy a house, and give some money to her mother and her family, and give some other money to a church or wherever — to the poor people. "Because I always think about other people, too. I never think only of myself." And any money that was left after that, she would keep to live, to buy everything she needed and to have enough to survive, herself. With her man.

—

Romeo was born in Manhattan and grew up in Manhattan and the Bronx, "and a very small part in Queens." His twentieth birthday was next month. His father was part black and part American Indian, his mother German and Puerto Rican. "So I ain't nothin'. Hah! I'm a little bit of everything, you know?"

He dropped out of high school — Bronx Science ("You had to have honors to get in, but I was on the honor roll all through high school") — two months before he was to graduate.

Now he was collecting unemployment insurance. "There's no basic category to really make money by," he said. "It's kinda hard, 'cause first of all, you gotta have such a great education, somethin' worthwhile. And then the trades — well, usually, so many people are takin' a trade that it's not worthwhile takin' one in the first place. So, I just basically look for a job and hope it works out and I make my money. When I get old, I'll get my Social Security benefits or whatever. Right now, it don't make much difference." He had worked in restaurants mopping floors and washing dishes. He could cook. He loaded and unloaded trucks. He worked for a sanitation project in New Jersey. "Basic things, nothing elaborate, nothing high class. Hah! Nothin' that anybody couldn't do if they put their mind to it."

He also used to fight for money. People bet on him against another guy, and he got paid for it. "I used to take martial arts — Kung Fu, like that — and always in my neighborhood there was a person that was supposed to be more tougher than the other one, so about every weekend, we used to get together and have somebody from our block fight somebody else. Somebody would come that I didn't even know, and I would fight him. Crazy."

That was when he was 17. When he was in high school, the thing he wanted most to be was a psychiatrist, "to understand people's problems and maybe find a way or explain to them a way they could help themselves." Maybe someday he could do that. "Maybe when I'm 45 years old, I'll be in some school studying psychiatry. Hah!" He last worked for a city laundry. But "they started a job shortage here in New York," so since then he got his money however he could.

For a while, he was into hustling. Stopped working, said to himself: "Wow, I gotta make me some money." He knew a few things about it, so he went out and tried it. But he stopped when they threw him in jail one time. Some bimbo set the cops on his tail — claimed Romeo had robbed his house, just because he wouldn't spend the night for $35. "Thirty-five dollars! Hah! Everybody knows, in business that's no price." Romeo heard the guy had put a warrant out on him. When he ran into him again, they ended up squaring off. "I hit him in such a nice way that it ripped his nose to one side." That's when the cops picked him up.

"I don't hustle no more," he said, "but ..." he looked around, and his voice dropped to a whisper, "sometimes I go late at night with a few friends and take a couple of people off. Seriously. We don't do it every day, but, you know, when things really get tight ... That's truthful. I don't mean to lie." He showed me how he did it, coming up and choking from behind. "We don't hurt 'em or nothin', though," he assured me.

Muñeca had been washing dishes and straightening up while we talked. I asked her how she felt about what Romeo did. She hesitated, and Romeo spoke for her. "She feels that if that's what I gotta do to make money, more or less to do it. She can't stop me, because I'm the man, and if I wanna get out there and make some money, I can make it, right? I don't like to always be asking her for things. I like to have my own."

—

They met three months ago, at the Gilded Grape. According to Romeo, most of the other gay bars in the city wouldn't allow a female impersonator in. "The police consider a queen a hazard," he explained, "because she feels like a woman. But when she goes to the women's bathroom she doesn't go for the same reasons I would, to see a piece of pussy or something. She goes to pee like anybody else."

They had lived together roughly two out of the past three months, on and off at first, and then steadily. In the beginning, Muñeca was living on 101st Street, but she was married to a guy named Daniel and seeing Romeo on the side. She dug him and he dug her, and one day, she told Romeo she was thinking about leaving Daniel. It wasn't because of Romeo exactly, she told him, but because she didn't want to be with Daniel anymore. "And since I found somebody else I could understand and who could understand me," Muñeca said, "I told him why don't we see if we could get it together?" Romeo was agreeable to that.

So, one day Romeo would stay with Muñeca, and another time he would stay with some people he knew. Daniel was working on Long Island then, anyway, so he wasn't around. Then Muñeca got into a jam where she had to collect unemployment insurance and she couldn't hold the rent for the room. Whenever Romeo got money, he'd run it to her, but she said to herself, "Well, I'm not gonna stay with Daniel, I might as well get a cheaper room." And that was that for Daniel. Muñeca moved downtown, to 48th Street between Ninth and 10th Avenue.

Romeo, meanwhile, was living with another queen by then, and seeing Muñeca on the side. "That's the way it's done, you know."

Romeo hadn't seen Muñeca for a little while. When he finally went to see her, he figured she was still living on 101st Street. But then he couldn't find her. He couldn't find her for a whole week, so he did the next best thing: he met somebody else. He started rapping with Michelle, and they got very tight together, and pretty soon Romeo started living with her. And Michelle was Muñeca's best friend.

After a while, Muñeca moved back to the Upper West Side. One day, Romeo was breezing through the block and somebody told him, "Muñeca just moved down here again and she don't want to see you. She hates your guts." Naturally, Romeo asked, "Why does Muñeca hate my guts?" And this somebody said, "Because she found out you was livin' with her best friend."

So Romeo stayed out of sight for a while. Then one day, he was running out of the subway, expecting to go to somebody's house, and bam! He ran right into who? Into Muñeca.

He said, "Oh, hi, Muñeca. How you feel?"

She said, "Uh-huh. You been around here hiding from me, trying to keep out of my way. I ain't going to fight with you. Are you happy living with who you're with?"

"What do you mean by that?" Romeo said. He was playing dumb. But Muñeca told him she'd heard the dirt. People had told her. So Romeo came right back and said, "It's workin' out all right."

And that really got to Muñeca. She told Romeo that she really loved him and wanted him to come back with her. If he wanted to. "It's up to you," she said.

He decided to.

But things were rough in the beginning. Muñeca started in arguing every day about her best friend: What was Romeo doing with her? Was he messin' with Michelle when he and Muñeca first met? She wouldn't believe anything he had to say. Plus, she would argue with Michelle whenever they ran into each other on the street. One day, she said she was gonna go *cut* Michelle.

Finally, Romeo up and left and went back with Michelle. But then he and Michelle got into some pretty heavy shit themselves, fighting and so forth, and Romeo broke up with her and came back to Muñeca. "Now, I'm not goin' nowhere, no time," he said.

Muñeca was married to Daniel for four years before she met Romeo, but she loved Romeo, now. "And I don't give a damn about the other one. I already changed." She hoped she and Romeo would stay together for a long time. She would even like them to adopt children someday, after she got her sex change. "I love kids," she said.

—

Kids turned out to be something of a sore point. The three of us had been sitting together for quite some time, and despite our differences, we had developed a feeling of comradery. I turned to Romeo and asked, "What about you? How do you feel about adopting kids?"

I was surprised by his frown. "Well, I don't expect to adopt any," he said.

I turned back to Muñeca. "Do you think that'll be a problem?"

She tucked her chin to her chest. "Well," she said, "I mean ... I don't think we would, if he don't want them. But for myself, I would like to."

By this time, Henry was through setting up his equipment. We started the photo shoot. I assisted Henry, holding lights and placing umbrellas to get the shadows just so. I'd never seen him work before. He really did have remarkable skill. Leaning into his camera, he posed Muñeca at the hot plate; then the two of them sitting on the bed, her head on his shoulder; then each of them alone, she coy and reticent, he pensive, somber, but with a wry look in his eyes.

Henry shot several rolls. "Professional snapshots," he called them. They were his specialty. "Good," he said, as he instructed them to move this way or that. "Excellent. Very good. Beautiful."

—

After the shoot, Muñeca made coffee. Their friend Carmen (who, as it turned out, lived down the hall with Joey) dropped in. She and Muñeca spoke briefly in Spanish. On her way out, Carmen asked Romeo what he told us about her.

"That you're a straight friend of ours," he said, "a straight person who's a friend. It would make sense, wouldn't it? That's what you are." We all laughed.

After Carmen left, I asked about their other friends. "I work with straight people," Muñeca said. "But, I don't got too many friends. Well, I got a lot of gay friends, but not too close. I'm associated with them, you know — we're not really friends." Most of Romeo's friends, the people he grew up with, didn't even know he was gay. "They wouldn't understand what was happenin' with me if I was to tell 'em, anyway," he said. "They would still be my friends, but every time I see them, they would *read* me, you know? 'Damn, man, get yourself a woman.' They try to put you down, try to make you stop it."

Muñeca got up again to finish cleaning. Henry and I continued to sit with Romeo on the bed. "Why did you become gay?" Henry asked.

Romeo paused before he answered. "Everybody has feminine traits in them," he said. "I'm not trying to degrade anybody or so forth, but everyone has it. They say, 'He's a faggot' because he admires another man, but I'm sure you have looked at another man and said, 'Damn, he does look good. I wish I had his features.'"

Henry and I agreed we had.

"What happened to me," Romeo went on, "is that I went with a woman, you understand? I got married, I had a child ... My wife just fucked over me and she hurt me. I'm not saying that all women are alike, but, you know, once you love a woman once, you have no desire to love another woman again. And then, too, there's the way it was with a lotta girls. I could get many a girl, I had a lotta raps and what not, but the majority of them were just fulla shit. They expected the *world*, you know? I mean, I'd be with these girls, you had to take 'em out every Saturday or else you couldn't kiss 'em or something. Sick broads." He laughed. "Right? I'm sure you've been through that. So I tried the next best thing: gay life.

"Now, gay life, I understand because why? My father is gay. But he is butch queen: He's a man, but he feels feminine, then he don't feel feminine. My mother died when I was small, so that's what made *him* go gay. So many reasons ...

"I've been in gay life about three years, but I've messed with it all my life because he raised me, and he's always been around other men who were gay and they bother you and fuck around with you. I was his son, I was living with him, so I always dealt with it. But yet he doesn't understand why I'm gay because I used to be straight."

Romeo grinned. "Truthfully speaking, when I first went to the Gilded Grape, my father took me there, and I thought they were all women. So he let me go ahead and be my little bad self and I rapped to somebody who sounded like a woman, looked like a woman, had titties and everything, and I went up to her house, started schemin' with her — kissin' her and so forth. After a while I reached down there and she said, 'You know what you're doing, right?' And I said, 'Yeah, I know what I'm doing,' and I went ahead. Then I said, 'Oh, shit! What's that?' and she said, 'You don't know what I am? I'm a man.' So I said, 'But you got titties!' Then she said, 'Yeah, they're real,' and I said, 'Let me see.' And she picked up her shirt and I saw the chest and I said, 'Well, I can't understand it. What's happening?' So, she said, 'Well, I don't got time to explain to you. Do you wanna fuck with me or not?'"

He went on: "I have one brother, and he's butch queen, and he's going into drag soon. He's younger than me. But, I'm trying to stop him, for what reason? Because he's young. He's had his girlfriends and so forth, but he hasn't really — like me, I haven't really checked out life for what it's worth, but I've had my experiences and I feel like this is what's good for me now. At times I say, no, I don't want to be in this life, and then I say yes. But then him, he's not definite on it. He says he wants to be a woman, but yet, you know ... it's just not him. You understand what I'm saying? It's just not him.

"Me, I could change my mind tomorrow. I could just happen to be standing somewhere and a young lady'll stop me and say, 'What time is it?' and so forth. You never know how life is gonna change tomorrow. I might not even be alive tomorrow. But, as far as I feel now, this is the way I want to live. I'm satisfied. I'm happy. I live my life straight. It's no big hassle.

"What I see in the future, hoping to predict, is that I start working while Muñeca's working and we get, probably, an apartment and furniture and so forth and get ourselves together good. I mean, if we're supposed to be living straight, this is no place to be living for the rest of your life. I sure don't wanna live here, anyway."

By then it was close to ten o'clock. Henry packed up his lights and cameras and I put away my tape recorder. We planned to reconvene at our place, and hoped to finish our work with Romeo and Muñeca that night. Neither of us had as much time to give to this project as we might have liked.

Henry asked Romeo and Muñeca to get dressed up as if they were going out for the night, and then to come over to our place to have their pictures taken in a studio setting.

"Do you have time to do that?" I asked Romeo.

"We got all the time in the world," he said.

Henry wanted to see what they'd be wearing. Romeo showed him a pair of shiny, bright-red pants and a matching sleeveless body shirt. "That's fine," Henry said. "Very, very nice." But they couldn't find anything suitable for Muñeca to wear. She said she had only one nice dress, and she had no shoes or stockings to match. "I don't want to look funny, you know," she said. She wanted to wear overalls instead, but Romeo wouldn't allow it. They whispered together. It looked to me like they were arguing.

"She can get something together," Romeo said.

We told him we'd meet them at our place in half an hour.

—

What happened next took Henry and me totally by surprise.

When Romeo and Muñeca failed to show up on time again, we decided to walk back to their hotel and try to hurry them along. But on the way, we ran into Romeo, decked out in the fancy clothes he'd shown Henry back in their room. We waved to him, but he didn't wave back. We met him half-way down the block.

"That bitch won't come," he muttered. "I just come to tell you. I know I promised you and everything, but you're just gonna have to forget it."

"What happened?" I asked.

"She kept saying she had nothing to wear, right? I'd pick up a dress or a skirt or something like that and she would say it was no good. Then I told her, 'You're supposed to be a drag queen, right? Look like a woman? But you don't do nothing to make yourself look good.'"

Muñeca started to cry. She said Romeo didn't love her anymore. Romeo said Muñeca was hanging on him too much, and what did she mean about adopting kids? They argued back and forth for a few minutes, and then Romeo walked out — for good, he said. He was on his way downtown.

"Where are you going to stay tonight?" I asked him. I wanted to offer to let him stay at our place, but I was wary of what Henry might say about that.

"Oh, you can live anywhere in New York," Romeo said. "You didn't know that? You just gotta be in the right place at the right time, and you meet the right person," he snapped his fingers, "and there's a new home for you. You see all them fags coming up and down Broadway? Just give 'em a little wink, and I've found myself a new home. By the time I get downtown, I'll have something. Tomorrow I move my things out, I have a new place to live, maybe a whole new relationship."

"I feel like this is all our fault," I said. "I feel terrible about it."

Romeo shook his head. "A lot came out that should've come out a long time ago. It ain't your fault," he said.

We tried to persuade him to come up to our apartment and call Muñeca to try to patch things up. (Our motives, I confess, were mixed. We still wanted those pictures.) It's just a quarrel, we said. Don't worry about it. You know how women are. We'll call her in a little while, and you'll talk to her, and everything will be just fine.

"All right," Romeo said at last, "but it won't do no good to talk to her."

In fact, it did no good even to try, since Muñeca didn't pick up the phone. But Romeo stayed for Henry to take more photographs, and then remained half the night to talk.

—

Beginning with my anguished mother, who made me her confidant when I was a child, for as long as I can remember, people have talked to me about themselves.

Perhaps it's because I am much more likely to listen than to speak. Or maybe it's because I see myself as a stranger in a strange land, and they pick up on my curiosity about what makes them tick. Whatever the reason, all my life, people have entrusted me with their pain, their hopes, their dreams, and sometimes even with their deepest, darkest secrets.

Romeo was no exception.

While Henry tended to his photo equipment, Romeo and I moved to the kitchen. I made him a cup of tea. And I listened. With little prompting beyond an occasional nod, grunt, *um-hmm*, or an easy question, he told me his story.

He began with Muñeca.

—

Muñeca's gotta get herself together, man. Because anything I do, I gotta be free to do it. I try to enjoy each and every thing I do. And she ... she lives in a *dry* world. She lives like the whole world has collapsed around her and she's just driftin' along. She told me that now that we broke up, there's nothin' for her left in the world. She said she's gonna kill herself. But, a lotta people say that and don't do it. Not Muñeca. She wouldn't kill herself — no way. She's got too much to live for, too much to look forward to.

She's good people in many ways — there's nothing wrong with her heart — but the way she acts, even conversations that we have, it don't make it, man. I can't live with somebody that's *quiet* all the time, and that's basically what Muñeca is: quiet. She'll laugh and joke with her friends and they say, 'Oh, wow, we had a beautiful time with Muñeca today.' I say, 'Not with me.'

Carmen told me Muñeca was scared to laugh and joke with me, but why would you be scared? That's kind of ignorant. Even if she were to tell me, 'You're an ugly fat slob' or something, I'd probably tell her something in return and we'd just throw things at each other and laugh it off. It's fun, sometimes, to goof on each other. But she doesn't even take time for that.

When I first met Muñeca, she was always laughing and joking. There wasn't nothing we couldn't sit and discuss. It was nice! It's really a drag now. We used to go to the park every day and have fun. Now, all we do is leave the room and go to the corner, and go from the corner back down to the room. Ugh! We could go to Central Park, walk around in there, have fun like we used to. Damn. She acts like, if the world's coming to an end tomorrow, she's gotta take time to pray.

Everybody says it's me. They say, 'She loves you with all her heart.' But I don't feel that way. She expects for everything to happen overnight — for us to get a big apartment and all this — so she can show the other queens that I stayed with her the longest and look how great we are together. You understand what I'm sayin'? That since I had this reputation of not staying with all those other queens for more than a week, two weeks, she figured none of them worked out. But now that I've stayed with her the longest, she's in a hurry to get a big, fabulous apartment with all new furniture and then to show it off. You know, like when you get a new car? You say, 'Check this out. Ain't this nice?'

I'm not tryin' to impress nobody. I just wanna get with somebody that I don't have to go through changes with. I just wanna work, be cool, and be able to at least get along with the person or be able to have a conversation with 'em. If it don't work, it don't work. I don't got forever to keep trying with her. When you really find somebody who wants to make it with you, you stop.

I think life would be much different if a lot of people would think about bein' sincere about what they're doin', you know what I mean? Be sincere. If this is what you're gonna do, do it. If you're gonna be with somebody, be with 'em, but be sure. But, it's kinda hard to be sure. There's a lotta if's and but's and why's, causes and so forth ...

Crazy, man. I'm talkin' about everybody has this problem. I'm not speakin' of gay people in general.

—

Though I'd expected Henry to join us, he had apparently decided that his work for the night was done. I put out the few snacks we had — pretzels, peanuts, bits of cheese — and made Romeo and myself a second cup of tea.

I asked Romeo about his past, about what he was doing before he met Muñeca. Romeo settled back in his chair, sipped his tea, and continued.

—

I got married when I was 17. I used to play handball with my wife's brother, and I met her through him. We got to be very close friends and I loved her a lot and everything, and then one day I said, 'Will you marry me?' and she said yes.

Then about two weeks after I asked her to marry me, she said, 'I'm pregnant.' I said, 'Oh, thanks.' Oh, God, no way, I couldn't believe it. So that delayed the marriage because I had to pay money for the child to be born into the world. Then Mandy — that was my daughter — started growing up, and then we went ahead and got married. Nothing elaborate, but it was a nice wedding.

I was married to her about a year and a half, but we was gettin' more apart from each other by, let's say, eight months after we were married. We were, like, less together. Her mother told her that she couldn't get along without her, so I had to live in the building her mother lived in, and she was more with her mother than with me.

My wife is 27. But she had the mind of a 16-year-old. She really had nothing to look forward to, and she acted like a baby. I mean, damn, man, I was workin' for the city and we had our own place, the furniture was new, I had credit, I was still in night school. I was really *makin'* something out of myself. But when I found out it wasn't gonna work out between us, it's like she snatched the rug from under me and I just fell on my face.

I used to believe in God very strongly. I'll tell you why I don't anymore. If you pray to Him, He's supposed to give you what you want, right? Well, a lot of times I prayed for something — basically speaking, on my wife and my daughter — and I didn't get it.

You see how I am now. I prayed the whole world that we wouldn't get broken up, or that now that we were broken up, that we could get back together and get a more better understanding.

Then, I heard my daughter died. I said to myself, 'Oh, God, why can't you say it's not for real?' You know, let somebody come up to me and say, 'Oh, they was just bullshittin' you, man. You wanna go see Mandy?' But it didn't happen like that. Somebody who I thought hated my guts came and told me that my daughter died.

From the way Paco told me — that's my wife's cousin — the baby grew up somewhat good, and she was playing in the street and the mother wasn't payin' no attention. A guy with a car hit her, and just a short *smack* like that could kill her instantly, why? Because she's a baby. I was told two or three months after it happened, when she was buried and everything.

Damn, that night I was like a maniac. If you was walkin' around and you seen me ... I met a trick that night, somebody to make money by. I ripped him off, I beat the hell outta him. I wanted to take it out on the world. Somebody'd come and talk to me: 'Fuck you! I don't wanna talk about it.' Very e-vil. Then I said, 'Why didn't my father tell me?' He went to the funeral and he didn't even let me know what was happening.

I loved that girl more than anything in this world. When me and my wife broke up, after we were apart two months, I kidnapped Mandy, and she was with me having fun each and every day. Then my wife found out where I was living and she had me locked up for kidnapping. But she didn't press any charges. She just wanted Mandy back.

Strange, huh? But you see, I knew that my wife wouldn't turn around and raise Mandy herself or just get one guy and stay with him and they would raise her. She would be showing Mandy father after father after father, getting together with different guys over and over again, and before you knew it, Mandy's gonna get used to the facts of it and she's gonna turn out to be a little whore or something. So it's probably better she got killed anyway, because they wouldn't give her to me or to my family.

—

Even what I do now, and the things that I've been through, knowing that my daughter died and everything, I think about it and I call up and try to talk to her, but she acts like she's talking to a stranger. I say, 'Hello, can I speak to Rhonda?' and she says, 'Who's this?' I say, 'Romeo,' and she says, 'Oh. What do you want?' Like that. Then I say, 'Well, how you been doin'?' and she says, 'Why is it your concern?' I say, 'Are you going with somebody else now?' She says, 'Even if I wasn't, I don't wanna see you.' What a conversation! I say, 'Sorry to bother you,' and hang up.

If I see her on the street, she acts like she don't know me, and if I get too close to her, she'll scream or run. I'm not gonna hurt her, I just wanna talk to her. But she wants me to stay away. She figures if she screams I'll say, 'Wow, she's gonna get me in trouble, so I better get out of the way!'

I ran after her for the longest time. I would say if she was to take time to think about what I was tellin' her, then she would see the point and come back to me. But she loves her mother too much. That was one of the basic things why we broke up. No chance of me getting back with her.

—

I feel I could get along with a woman again. Of course. But it's the point of getting the right one. I don't want to get a nothing, you understand? I want to be with somebody who's really worthwhile being with, even if it's in gay life.

The only thing that gay life really strikes me against is the point that you couldn't basically have a family. It would be mostly you and whoever you're with. I dig children. I'd like to have my own. Even if Muñeca was to get her sex change, I don't want to adopt nobody else's children. Why should I, when I can have my own?

Of course, just because she couldn't give birth to a child doesn't mean *I* couldn't have one. I know girls that don't necessarily love me, but they wouldn't mind just giving the child to me because they know that I would take good care of it. Maybe they want to have children, but they don't want to support them. Or they want to see them whenever they want but somebody else could raise them. Or they just want to see what their children would look like. You know, there's a lot of sickies — I've been around a lot of 'em. Damn!

But, two gay people raisin' a child? More or less, I don't even dig the point of us raisin' a child together, because imagine a child growing up thinking this was a woman all the time, never knowing the fact of what it was? Damn. One day findin' out? You wouldn't dig it, right? All the time he thought that was his mother, and to find out he's a man? Shit! That would automatically put me through some changes, man.

—

I'm thinkin' about what I'm gonna do now.

If I could do anything, I would like to go back to school. I couldn't believe it when I stopped. I started working two jobs and I didn't think about how I was messin' myself up. Then the next thing I knew I said, 'Hey, man, I'm supposed to graduate this year.' So I said, 'I'll go back to school and I'll try to make it up again.' But then I said, 'A whole year again before I graduate?' Forget it. I couldn't take the year again — they'd call me 'super senior.' So I lost all interest, and I said, 'Look, I'm working, and I got a daughter and a family to support.'

Now look at me. I wish I had finished. But then, just that paper's not no good no more. A long time ago, if somebody had a high school education, they could get almost any job, but now you gotta have at least two years of college …

If I was working right now, I would just say fuck it and get myself a room somewhere uptown and stay by myself and get to know people of my age bracket, because, you know, almost entirely the queens I've been around are a lot older than me. Just get myself a place and stop tryin' to make it with people, tryin' to get it together with somebody. Shit. Just let it come to me. If it don't come, it don't come.

But, if I'm gonna be in school, I'm gonna meet other people, and eventually I'm gonna meet somebody that's on my level, got my kinda mind or whatever. Male or female. I can always find somebody else, very easily. I'm truthful: I know I'm not ugly. Even if I *was* ugly, even an ugly man can find someone to like him, no matter how bad he looks.

New York City has a lotta sad stories. I've heard other people tell me some stories about their lives and you say, 'Damn, did that happen to a person and they're still out here?' Look at the majority of the black population. They got twelve and thirteen kids in one family, they're on welfare, the kids are dirty and bein' bit by rats and livin' in the slums and all this. That's a pretty rough life. And the father's a wino, the mother's a whore and the kids gotta cook for themselves. You didn't know about all those things? So how could my life be that bad?

To me, I feel that life is life and take it for what it's worth, and today you'll be happy, tomorrow you'll be sad. It's still life. Why should I kill myself over petty shit, right?

—

After Romeo left, I had a sleepless night.

My intention had been to be an ambassador of the unseen and the unheard. Now I wondered if I was doing more harm than good; the risk of exploiting the very people I'd hoped to elevate weighed on me. Henry had no such misgivings. The transvestite world excited and intrigued him, both as an artist and a voyeur.

It was difficult for me to reconcile our differences. Much as Henry and I had triggered a breach between Romeo and Muñeca, our interaction with them had also deepened a fault line between us.

—

The next night I saw Romeo and Muñeca at the corner, sitting together, arms around each other, as if nothing had happened. Romeo did seem a little on edge. As I approached them, his eyes said "Be cool."

A week or so later, Romeo came by our apartment to pick up the prints Henry had made from the photo shoot. He also asked us if we wanted to buy any of the jewelry he'd recently stolen. Henry bought a watch.

A couple of weeks after that, I saw Carmen in the laundromat. She told me Romeo had gone back to the Bronx.

I bumped into him a few months later at the hot dog stand in the Columbus Circle subway station. He asked me about the project with Henry, and I told him we weren't working together anymore. Romeo said he'd gone back to school and was living with his wife again. "How're you getting by?" I asked. He winked. "You know how I make my living, man," he said.

I saw Muñeca for the last time just before I left 98th Street and Broadway. She told me she'd moved to 97th Street, and that she was fine. But she was wearing a little more make-up, then.

All the News That Fits

I lifted my head from my desk, rubbed my eyes, and yawned. How long had I been asleep? Just past noon. Not so long. I wondered, habitually, whether there was any point to all of this, then shuffled into the kitchen for another cup of coffee.

I emptied the kettle and watched a half-drowned cockroach scurry along the sink bottom. I'd grown accustomed to the gloominess of this place and the drunken super's threats, and Henry and his women hogging the bathroom in the morning, but I hoped never to get used to roaches in my coffee. I washed it down the drain and off to oblivion.

In the Cold War between myself and the cockroaches, I acknowledged that as long as the lights were out, the kitchen and bathroom were no man's land. But I had my limits, and when the bugs exceeded them, I sometimes went to lunatic extremes.

The night before, I'd been working late on another round of job applications, typing in the kitchen so as not to keep Henry up. With each passing hour, the roaches grew bolder, until they disregarded both the kitchen light and my presence. I managed mostly to ignore them: Détente. But when one tumbled from the ceiling onto my head, it crossed a line.

I shook the thing to the floor and squashed it, then mussed my hair, in case another was lodged there undetected.

And I declared war.

I leapt from my chair. The roaches crawling on the walls and furniture I slapped at with my hands, and with my feet I crushed those that crept across the scarred linoleum. Next, from beneath the sink, I grabbed a can of insecticide and sprayed the cracks and corners where the vermin hid, directly targeting any that ran from cover. I watched with satisfaction as the dying turned on their backs, slowly wiggling their legs like tiny, ugly sea anemones.

The stove I saved for last. I'd known for months that it was Roach Central, their breeding ground, a cockroach Eden. "Well, you little fuckers," I said out loud, "those days are gone."

I lifted the grates, laid down a toxic stream under each burner, lit all four and the oven, and turned the flames up to full.

In seconds, the first roach wriggled from beneath a front burner. I flicked it into the flames. In less than a minute, cockroaches were crawling from every orifice. With my right hand I swatted at them dementedly with a rolled-up magazine, while with the left I flattened any bugs that made it to the sides of the stove. I stomped the refugees that escaped to the floor, heedless of my downstairs neighbors. This was no time for niceties.

The rout of the roaches went on for twenty or thirty minutes, and then their exodus ceased. Battle worn and dazed, I shut off the burners and the oven, swept up the corpses, and turned off the light. Walking down the dark hallway to my room, I imagined for a moment I could hear the spirits of the dead crying out for revenge. That night I woke from a dream in which my bed was crawling with bugs.

I had landed in this roach-infested apartment after two years adrift. Post-college, I'd spent six months on a farm in Central New York, and then a miserable winter in Buffalo doing construction and renovation, living with Ruth in a tiny one-bedroom apartment whose only source of warmth was a space heater in the kitchen. That spring, Ruth returned to New York City. Two months later, I followed her there.

The idea of writing for a living came to me during a sleepless night a few days after I arrived. All that day, I'd fruitlessly scanned the Help Wanted postings in the Sunday *Times*, finding only jobs I was not qualified to do. As a poet and construction worker, a life in New York seemed destined to fit me like somebody else's suit — the pants too short, sleeves too long, the lapels of the jacket too wide, the colors wild and strange. If I were to survive I needed to narrow my focus. To specialize.

It was a resume-writing exercise that led me to journalism. The concept of a resume was alien to me, but the exercises on how to "color my parachute" were unexpectedly helpful. Writing deep into the night about my talents, skills, and interests intrigued me more than trying to stretch my education, experiences, and achievements out to a full page, and these exercises led me to their intended purpose: identifying a career for which I was temperamentally suited, and which I would likely find engaging, perhaps for a lifetime.

For this conclusion I should have thanked the author. That I had come to it in the worst location in America to begin a career as a reporter, during the highest period of unemployment in decades, was not his fault.

The few people I was loosely connected to in the field — one just finishing Columbia's journalism program, the other a distant cousin at the *New York Times* — alerted me to the likely futility of my chosen career path. Both had been kind enough to show me around their respective environments, each in its own way representing the acme of the field. Both also advised me to leave this city, move to a small town, and try to establish a foothold as a freelancer for the local paper. In this scenario, I would slowly work my way through ever-larger venues until, years down the timeline, I'd assembled enough clips and experience to try for a job at the *New York Post* or *Daily News*. Unsaid was what it would then take to write for the *Times*.

All of this made sense, but I had a compelling reason — Ruth — to stay in New York. So against all reason, but encouraged by the parachute-book author and my own naiveté, I continued to believe that perseverance would win the day.

—

When I returned to the scene of the crime the next morning, I heard Vivaldi seeping through the door of the kitchen pantry, where Henry, I imagined, was printing nude photographs of his latest conquest. The kettle whistled. A small waterbug the color of dark chocolate floated from the ceiling to the kitchen table and expired beneath my thumbnail, its shell emitting a tinny *rrk*. Sounds of the city. Sounds of my home. I poured hot water into a mug, spooned in sugar and instant coffee, added milk, and returned to my room.

I slid the typewriter I'd borrowed from Ruth's brother into place on the makeshift desk I had assembled from orange crates and a plank scrounged from a dumpster. I arranged stacks of envelopes and resumes and a list of companies to apply to, then looked over what I'd written prior to the Battle of the Roaches.

Too meek.

"If you don't blow your own horn, nobody else will," Arthur, the old journalist who ran the stock photo agency I'd worked at for a year, had often told me. And though I resented the bastard for firing me, I thought there was wisdom in what he'd said. I ripped the previous night's letter from the typewriter, crumpled it, and rolled in a fresh sheet of paper. Of course, even when you *did* blow your own horn, there was no guarantee anybody would hear it.

I was halfway through yet another cover letter when shouts from the street broke my concentration. Craning my head out my bedroom window, I could see only a sliver of Broadway, so I ducked into Henry's room, the only place in the apartment not facing an airshaft, for a better look.

A band of shouting men, women, and children, most of them holding signs and banners, was moving past our building. I couldn't make out what they were saying or read their signs, but I sensed a story.

For several months, I'd been eking out a living as a stringer for a couple of Manhattan weekly papers. Though the pay was meager, every story, I hoped, would bring me one step closer to becoming Jimmy Olson at the *Daily Planet*. Armed with a steno pad in one hand and camera in the other, in seconds I was fumbling with the locks on the door.

Just then, Henry emerged from the darkroom. Bleary-eyed, he called to me. "David!" he said, in his booming, cheerful voice. "How are you doing?"

I forced a harried smile. Whatever he wanted would have to wait. "Look, I'm in kind of a hurry. There's a march or something going on outside, and I want to check it out. I'll talk to you later, okay?"

"Of course, David," he said, his face unreadable, his tone flat. I pulled open the door. Halfway out, I asked, "Is your darkroom free tonight? Can I use it?"

Henry smiled. "Of course, David, you can use it if it's free," he said, which seemed no answer at all.

I stifled a sigh. "I'll see you later," I said, and shut the door behind me. I took the five flights two steps at a time.

Outside, the light blinded me momentarily and I had to shield my eyes. From further down Broadway, I heard the surge of dozens of voices chanting, "Strike, strike, against the hike! Strike, strike! Don't pay the hike!" and, in informal counterpoint, "Jobs, yes! Cutbacks, no! Racist layoffs gotta go!" The subway fare, I remembered, was supposed to go from 35¢ to 50¢ in a day or two.

I wrapped my camera strap around my wrist, stuffed my notepad into my back pocket, and patted my chest pocket to make sure I had a pencil or a pen. Good to go.

As I caught up to the march, I looked for somebody to tag along with and fill me in. Running beside the more slowly moving line of marchers reminded me of the disorienting sense of motion of an express train overtaking a local.

In my mind's eye, I was framing still images and mini-movies: A woman in a denim hat holding a banner that read, Fight Back Jump the Turnstiles Don't Pay, with a young boy walking a few steps in front of her displaying a cardboard placard reading simply JOBS! Two

51

women walking side by side, one with a sign that read AMNESTY FIGHT DEPORTATIONS, the other WORKERS' POWER, neither of which seemed relevant to the protest now underway. Toward the front of the line, a young, curly-haired man with wire-rimmed glasses, hollering into a microphone, his too-loud voice emerging from a megaphone on the shoulder of a Black man several feet away, as if through ventriloquism. "Westsiders!" the voice proclaimed, "Join the march against the hike! Show the crooks who's boss!"

From my brief run, I could already feel sweat trickling down my chest. I stopped for a second to catch my breath. Leaning against a rusty gray Chevy, I focused my camera on the marchers as they moved past the viewfinder. I clicked the shutter, warming up my reflexes. A heavy girl in a tie-dyed red T-shirt scowled at me.

I soon reached the front of the line. At the head of the march was a petite young woman with pale white skin and dark hair. Her eyes seemed angry, but otherwise, I couldn't help noticing, she was stunning. She held a megaphone in one hand and supported half of a large banner in the other. On the opposite end of the banner was another woman, a little older and nearly as homely as her partner was attractive. Visually, they contrasted in a way that, if I could frame it correctly, might go nicely with the story I was already composing in my mind. I considered rushing ahead so I could get them walking toward me, but instead made a mental note to photograph them when we stopped moving, if the opportunity arose.

I slid into place beside a skinny, freckle-faced man who carried a placard that read, DOWN WITH IMPERIALISM WE NEED SOCIALISM, which seemed reasonable enough to me.

"What's going on?" I asked him. I pulled my pad from my back pocket, prepared for a quote.

"We're gonna stop the fare hike," he explained. "We're gonna jump the turnstiles and show the pigs who's boss!"

The energetic woman holding the young man's free hand leaned across him, and in a half shout she added, "We're going to picket the unemployment office, and then we're heading uptown to jump the subway turnstiles at 103rd Street. C'mon!" she beckoned, smiling. "Join us!"

I asked her who was sponsoring the march, my notepad again at the ready. She frowned. "A coalition of groups of workers and the unemployed," she said, her tone gone cold.

"I saw a banner back there about the Progressive Labor Party," I persisted. "Are they part of it? I need to know," it occurred to me to explain, "because I'm writing a news story about it."

She took a moment to reply. "Just say it's sponsored by a coalition of workers and the unemployed. It's not accurate to say it's just a PL thing. Honest."

I thanked them both and ran on to the unemployment office a couple of blocks ahead, a location I knew well. Leaning against a pale green VW bus, one foot braced on the bumper, I focused my camera on the marchers as they walked toward me. I felt calm and professional, pleased at the competence I'd developed. Now if only I could find a job ...

The crowd formed itself into a line, and then an oval that rotated slowly on the wide sidewalk in front of the unemployment office, the protesters chanting their slogans in an endless loop.

I'd taken several shots by the time I heard, behind me, a harsh, amplified female voice calling out, repeatedly, "Strike, strike, against the hike! Strike, strike, don't pay the hike!" While I was preoccupied with the picketers, the demonstration's organizers had set up a platform on the bed of a dented pickup. The voice belonged to the pretty woman I had seen at the head of the march. Beside her, silent, her less attractive partner pointed the loudspeaker toward the crowd. The banner they'd held was gone, the composition no longer intriguing.

The pretty woman stopped chanting. Her features hardened, her face faceted like a cut gem. "Friends! Comrades! Fellow workers! And members of the unemployed!" she said. "You know why we're here — I don't have to tell you." She told us anyway. "We're here because the fascists who run this city are getting ready to stick it to us again! We're here because the union leaders and the politicians are trying to screw us again! We're here to put a stop to this exploitation!"

She paused, apparently for applause. A few people clapped or stamped their feet, but the picket line mostly moved in silence, encircling itself. She went on: "Every day you read about layoffs, and some racist taking advantage of the situation. You read about politicians *raising* their salaries $10,000 a year, when a lot of us don't even *make* $10,000 a year. You read about the city's financial crisis. Who created that?"

She waited for us to answer. No one replied. She continued: "And now they tell us they're going to raise the subway fare. They don't even *ride* the train! *They're* in trouble, and their system is in trouble. They want us to pay for *their* mistakes. They want to put our money in *their* pockets. But we're not gonna let them get away with it!"

She paused again for applause, and this time it came more readily. She introduced the first of several speakers. "They'll be talking to you about what's been going down. They're people like yourselves, workers and the unemployed," she said, extending her arms toward us.

She handed the mike to a scruffy young man in blue jeans and a plaid shirt. With his dirty-blonde mustache and few days growth of beard, he looked like every left-wing radical I'd seen speak at the university student union during the many antiwar rallies I'd attended there. He described himself as "a city worker and a member of the Committee Against Racism." He was, he said, the first of half a dozen men and women who would enlighten us today.

When each speaker took the stage, I tried to capture the gist of what he or she said, and to get at least one potential quote, but as the presentation dragged on, I found it hard to pay attention. I was weary of hearing complex problems reduced to slogans. I asked myself: Where is this story's hook? Is there a story here at all?

As my attention drifted away from the speakers, I noticed two patrol cars parked across the street from the unemployment office. I also saw, dotted throughout the crowd, four or five cops.

I walked over to the cop nearest me, a tall, pale man with reddish hair and sleepy eyes who looked only a few years older than I was. Irish, I thought. Kowalski, his nameplate read.

"Excuse me," I said, "can I talk with you a minute?"

"What do you want?" Kowalski replied.

"I'm doing a story on the rally," I said, brandishing my notepad. "What do *you* think about it?"

The young cop sighed. "As long as it's peaceful," he said, "they can talk all day."

I wrote this down, as inconspicuously as I could. "How about the fare hike?" I asked him. "How do you feel about *that*?"

"Personally," Kowalski said, "I don't agree with it." He shrugged. "But what are you gonna do?"

This seemed a more promising line of questioning, but I had no chance to pursue it. "Kowalski!" somebody hollered. A cop halfway across the street motioned *c'mon* with his hand.

"I gotta go," Kowalski said. "What I said there's off the record, by the way," he added, tipping his thumb toward my notes.

Right.

The crowd fidgeted. I turned toward the pickup truck. The pretty woman had stepped up to the mike again, her face now a mask of outrage. "We'll show the bosses and the bankers they can't make us pay!" she shouted. "Let's go!"

The picketers cheered and the chanting resumed: "Strike! Strike! Against the hike!" With surprising speed, the now much larger group formed itself into a phalanx that spanned the sidewalk and adjacent lane of Broadway. Then, slowly, it began to creep uptown, rippling like a caterpillar on the hot pavement.

Across the street, the two patrol cars likewise began to move.

—

Though my income from freelancing was meager, the fare hike meant little to me personally — I rode the train no more than a few times a week. And although I understood what the increase would mean for the working poor, I'd developed a personal aversion to the subway.

In my year of commuting to a job in midtown, the train had transformed from novelty (Buffalo had no subway system) to oppressive routine: cramming myself each morning into cars jammed to capacity with other bodies of all races, nationalities, colors, sizes, shapes, ages, smells, and economic backgrounds, then reversing the ordeal each evening.

On the platform, waiting for my train, I'd learned to position myself just to the side of the entrance as a car squealed to a stop. On a very good day, this trick got me a seat, but mostly I rode to my unrewarding job sharing a hand-hold with two or three others, each of our bodies pressed against different parts of each other's, our

collective mass swaying and lurching through the intermittent darkness, with no escape from the belchers and farters and off-key whist-
lers, from boom boxes, screeching babies, or smokers sneaking in a
quick one.

I hated most getting off at Times Square, the too-cheerful conductor singing out "Let 'em off, Let 'em off! Step lively, step lively!" when
it was all any of us could do to keep our footing as our hodgepodge of
sweaty flesh flowed onto the platform.

Sometimes, foolishly, I would fight back, bracing my arms against
the open doorway, holding up the crowd pressing on me until a few
inches cleared and I could step onto the platform with human dignity.
I knew that pushing back was a dangerous thing to do, but in those
brief, triumphant moments, I didn't care.

—

Now I was part of another collective mass united by subway
oppression, and they, too, were willing to fight back with their bodies.

I wound my way to the front of the march again, this time much more slowly. The ribbon of chanting, angry people continued its spread across Broadway, blocking traffic and pulling bystanders into its midst like a snowball rolling downhill. "C'mon!" some of its members said to people watching from doorways and side streets, "Let's go! Strike against the hike!" Others cried out in Spanish, "¡No paguéis! ¡No paguéis!" On its trek to the unemployment office, the crowd had been excited but orderly. It was frenzied, now, and the intensity of this frenzy increased with each step we took toward the 103rd Street station. Meanwhile, across the street, the two patrol cars rolled along, their pace exactly matching the marchers' steady uptown crawl.

As we neared the station, I tried to anticipate what would happen when we arrived, drawing on my experience with protest marches against the draft and the Vietnam War. In what seemed a likely scenario, the cops, aware of the group's intentions, would amass at the station entrances on either side of Broadway and block them with patrol cars or scooters, allowing passengers to leave but preventing the marchers from entering. Carried away by the fervor of the crowd, I also indulged an alternate scenario: The cops, some of whom likely resented the fare hike as much as the demonstrators did, would not intervene, and we would gain entrance to the Promised Land, toll free. I flashed briefly on darker scenarios — I had just seen *The Day of the Locust* — but the frenzy of the crowd had engulfed me, too, and I brushed these aside.

Our group had doubled in size by the time we traversed the thirteen blocks from the unemployment office to the station. The marchers now spread across the width of Broadway, an impromptu collective of men, women, and children united in a common cause. The two patrol cars had paced us all the way to 103rd Street.

Remarkably, as I'd predicted in scenario number two, the police did nothing when the still-chanting mass funneled down the stairways and into the station. Nor did they act as half of the group jumped the turnstiles. Still at the head of the parade, I was among them. Even if I'd wanted to resist jumping the turnstiles, as I had resisted my fellow commuters, to do so would have been suicide.

I stood six feet inside the turnstiles, surrounded by a hundred marchers shouting slogans, stamping feet, and pumping fists, urging the others to join us. Their cries of victory vibrated the stagnant air. We had stormed the gates and made it to the Promised Land. But what now? We had nowhere to go and nothing to do with our triumph.

Subway patrons emerged from the depths of the platform. Startled, their egress blocked by the crowd, most quickly scurried back from where they'd come. A few panicked. I noticed an old woman backed against the tile wall, trembling.

Marchers continued to pour in from the street, the younger men and women jumping the turnstiles, then turning to assist the older members of the group and the children so they, too, could join us. Everywhere, there was the savage rush of victory and the giddiness of celebration. I had felt nothing like this since we shut down Cornell University in the spring of 1970.

This victory celebration, however, was premature. Shouldering their way through the protesters who had not yet jumped, half a dozen cops, each with his nightstick in one hand and the other on his holstered gun, blocked the turnstiles. Their appearance was so sudden and unexpected, it was as if they had been transported there by some futuristic technology.

Their arrival instantly altered the state of our subterranean world. The flow of people over the turnstiles halted. Half the marchers now stood behind the blue-suited barrier, the other half outside. Looking at these six cops, I asked myself, Why *now*? Why wait till *now*?

The cops held their line, nightsticks across their chests poised to lash out at anyone who defied them. The pull to recombine the two halves of the severed crowd felt irresistible — yet nobody moved and nobody made a sound. For five minutes, the tension in the air was as tight as steel cables stretched to their limit.

Then the silence broke. "Strike, strike, against the hike!" marchers on each side chanted, but also, in increasing numbers, "Let them through!" from within the confines of our side of the human barrier and, "Let us through!" from outside it. The pressure, already at the redline, built toward a breaking point, the mutual attraction now literally irresistible.

And the barrier buckled.

A young man with a banner pushed through the first few rows of demonstrators between him and the turnstiles. In a bold maneuver, he attempted to pole vault between two of the cops stationed there. As if it were an afterthought, one of the officers thrust out his arm and caught the would-be vaulter in mid-leap, smashing him to the floor. The two men struggled, the outcome uncertain until a cop at an adjacent turnstile joined in. Together, they subdued the agile demonstrator.

Now it was the cops' victory that was short-lived. Those nearby immediately started to chant, "Let him go! Let him go!" The crowd descended on all three, like players in a football game pouncing on a fumbled ball.

En masse, people surged toward the unmanned turnstile. A few more demonstrators jumped across, then moments later, dozens rushed the thin blue line. Outside the turnstiles, fights broke out between cops and demonstrators, some of the latter pushing past the cops while others hung onto their billy-clubbed arms, preventing them from delivering their intended blows. From inside, demonstrators pummeled the cops' backs.

The police held their positions for a few more seconds, but they were vastly outnumbered. Just as it seemed certain the crowd would overwhelm them, one of the cops broke free of his assailants. He unholstered his gun, and in that moment, the state of our world changed again.

Someone shouted, "Look out!" and somebody else, "Guns!" Then dozens of people screamed in a cacophonic expression of terror. Pressed in on all sides, I watched, trying to raise my camera to my face, but I was shoved along toward the exit doors as, in unison, all of us seemed to grasp what would happen if bullets were fired inside the concrete vault of the station.

I thrust my camera above the crowd and got off one blind shot before I was nearly swept off my feet. It captured a moment I cannot forget.

The cops penetrated the churning, panicked crowds on both sides of the turnstiles. One grabbed a young Black man, threw him against the station wall, and put a gun to his head, then handed him off to another cop. Gun still drawn, he ran on to the exit door, his expression an embodiment of fury and determination.

After the crowd thinned, I moved against the wall and edged toward the remaining cops to take another picture. But I had over-estimated the frames left in the camera. I was out of film.

As if I'd been in a fugue state, I found myself on the street without quite knowing how I got there. The dense, late-summer air roiled with the screams of sirens. Police cars, scooters, and motorcycles all converged on the intersection, scattering people as they drove through the crowd, which had swelled to fill the entire intersection and also spilled down both ends of 103rd Street.

I'd never seen that many cops in one place. I lost count at twenty patrol cars, and the motorcycles and scooters were too numerous, and moved too quickly, for me to catalog. The last police vehicle to arrive was a bus full of cops in full riot gear.

Dozens of men in uniform spilled out of patrol cars and the riot bus, then charged into the melee. They dispersed through the crowd, chasing demonstrators, wrestling them to the ground, dragging them into patrol cars. I noticed on their collars the emblems of three different police precincts. We had been inside the station for no more than ten or fifteen minutes. How had they come so quickly?

There was nowhere safe to stand. I shifted my location frequently to avoid being bowled over. Leaning against a mailbox, I watched as two cops tackled a young man, pinned him to the street, and hand-cuffed him. One of them dragged the man, still struggling, toward a patrol car.

Before the cop could stuff his prisoner into the back seat, the pretty woman who had introduced the speakers at the rally charged toward them. With her purse, she hit the cop on his back and arm in an effort to free her comrade. In what felt like slow motion, the other cop, a balding, burly guy in his late thirties, pulled back his nightstick and hit her square across the face, knocking her to her knees. I recognized him from the rally as the guy who'd called to Kowalski.

I stood paralyzed as I watched the woman stagger to her feet, blood trickling down her cheek, her face already swelling from the blow. The cop grabbed one arm and she shielded her face with the other as she tried to wriggle free. He raised his club and brought it down on her again. She fell to the ground, then rose and, stunned, shaking, somehow broke away and fled across Broadway.

I found myself moving toward her as the two cops from the patrol car, joined by two more, brushed past me, forcing their way through the shifting crowd. I ducked bottles and cans thrown at the cops as the young woman pounded on the closed door of a shoe store. A salesman let her in, but her respite was brief: Moments later, he also admitted her pursuers.

A Black man ran past me, two cops close behind. I recognized him as the man the cop in the station had subdued at gunpoint. He had apparently escaped in the confusion, but his freedom short-lived — they captured him seconds later and pinned him against a bright red Volkswagen. A third cop joined in, and all three started hitting the Black man with their nightsticks, battering his head, chest, and legs while he attempted, futilely, to parry their blows with a wooden pole still attached to a shredded placard.

I glanced down 103rd Street. Chaos had spread far down the block. As much to see what was happening there as to get away from what was happening *here*, I trotted toward Columbus Avenue. I felt my eyes tear, my chest tremble, my palms drip with sweat, as fear and excite-ment merged into one fight-or-flight response.

A few yards down the street, a man who appeared to be no older than me, with long hair and neatly patched jeans, shouted, *"Stop!"* I turned to face him and found a pistol pointed at my chest. "Clear out! Get off the street!" he yelled, waving the gun wildly, his other hand holding a badge, terror in his eyes. I recognized him from the rally, too. Undercover cop? I didn't stay long enough to find out. Heart pounding, I ran back into the crowd, as if there I would find refuge.

I wanted to flee the scene and return to the safety of my Sisyphean job-hunting task, but though I had not managed to capture them with my camera, the images of cops pulling their guns in the station and beating people in the street were imprinted on my mind's eye. Where fear had set up shop, righteous anger was moving in. In those parachute-coloring exercises I'd written soon after I'd arrived in New York, I had told myself that trying to set things right was my purpose and that journalism was my means. I couldn't turn my back on that now. Horror gave way to a sense of mission — that this was a story I must tell *and* show — and I looked around for somewhere to buy another roll of film.

I ducked into a drugstore across Broadway where half a dozen people were waiting out the storm. "I'm a reporter," I said to the white-haired clerk. "I need a roll of Tri-X 400." I loaded the cartridge into my camera before I left the building.

Back on the street, the barrage of cans and bottles had ceased, and most people had moved out of harm's way, huddling in doorways and under awnings. Some, however, had regrouped, a few still carrying banners and placards. A deep voice called for us to march to the precinct station on 100th Street and Columbus Avenue. Now committed to following the story to its conclusion, I again fell into line.

At the corner of 100th and Amsterdam Avenue, I spotted a phone booth and split off from the marchers. Not only did I have a story, I realized, I also had an opportunity. I had pictures. I had notes. I may have been the only writer actually on the scene. I decided to call my cousin at the *Times*.

I fished through my pockets for a dime and found only a quarter. It wouldn't fit in the slot, which I saw was jammed. Should I try to find another phone? Rejoin the march? While I struggled to determine my next move, a man in a corduroy jacket rapped urgently on the phone booth door. "I need to use the phone," he said. "I'm a reporter. I'm with the AP."

"This phone doesn't work," I said, intimidated by his credentials but also determined to call in my story. "I'm a reporter, too. I'm trying to get through to somebody at the *Times*." I noticed he had no camera. "I've got pictures of the riot," I told him.

The AP reporter frowned. "You're distorting things," he said angrily. "You don't know what you're talking about. That wasn't any riot. It was a disturbance, that's all."

Bullshit, I thought but didn't say. I decided to bluff my way through. "Look, I don't care what you want to label it. I've gotta call it in. You can use the phone when I'm done."

I dialed zero and explained to the operator that I was at a broken phone and had to reach "my editor" at the *Times*. "There's a riot going on," I said, "and none of the phones nearby is working. Can you put me through?" Though she seemed dubious when she asked for the number and I told her I didn't have it, the operator agreed to make the connection. "Just call the main number," I said.

The *Times* switchboard operator put me through to my cousin's extension.

"Slater," he said.

"Richard?"

"Yes. Who is this?"

"This is David Bookbinder. Remember me?"

"Oh, hello, David, what can I do for you? How are you coming along?"

"I'm doing okay. Look, I haven't got much time. I'm over near the police station at 100th Street and Columbus, the 24th precinct. There was a demonstration against the subway fare hike and it turned into a riot. The police were beating people. I saw the whole thing. I can write a story or just give you the information."

"Hold on a minute. Let me check." I heard muffled voices on the other end. I noticed that the AP reporter had departed.

"David?"

"Yeah?"

"I just talked with the city desk. We've got it covered. There's a reporter and a photographer already on the way."

"On the way? But I was there for the whole thing," I reiterated. "I saw it all."

"We've got it covered," my cousin said more firmly. "Thanks, anyway, for calling."

I could think of no further argument. "Okay," I said. "I'll talk with you another time."

I headed back toward the police station, adrenaline spent and, with it, my sense of urgency. Except for those moments when I'd faced a gun, the whole experience now had a dream-like quality.

Still, I had my mission to complete. I caught up with the marchers outside the police station, where a new demonstration was already in progress.

Many of the protesters and organizers from the unemployment office rally were there, marching again in an endless loop with, miraculously restored, their banners calling for jobs, amnesty for immigrants, and — anachronistically — a strike against the hike. Now they paraded before a much smaller number of bystanders and the disapproving glares of the two dozen cops in hard hats and heavy boots who blocked the entrance to the station.

By then, the TV and radio crews had arrived. "What's going on?" I asked a TV reporter.

"Press conference," he said.

Would they, I wondered, let me in without a press pass? I pulled out my notepad and pencil, approximating the look of a reporter as best I could, and filed in with the TV-2 crew. Nobody asked for an I.D.

I'd never attended a press conference, but I found it anticlimactic. One of the cops who had tried to block the demonstrators at the turnstiles, a lieutenant with a cut lip, gave the array of microphones and cameras thrust in his face a much different account from what I had just witnessed. He said thirteen cops had been injured and seven people were arrested. He didn't mention that half of us had successfully jumped the turnstiles. He didn't mention that demonstrators had been beaten until I asked him whether any were hurt, and then his reply was, "Nobody was badly injured." This, he said before he left the room, was "a minor disturbance, quickly handled by the police, with appropriate use of reinforcements to prevent a greater problem."

That's *their* story, I thought, as I walked away, disheartened.

I left the reporters to their news outlets and the demonstrators to their demonstration and headed home through streets littered with broken bottles and trash. I thought of the AP reporter, the team from the *Times*, the other bastions of journalism, the best of the best, who were covering this story. Of some consolation was the hope that someone in that room would set the record straight, even if it couldn't be me.

—

That evening, I met Ruth for dinner in Chinatown and told her everything. On the way home, at the newsstand around the corner from my apartment, I picked up the late edition of the *Times*, the *Post*, and the *News*. In the kitchen, I put on a pot of tea and, with the roaches looking on, scanned each paper cover to cover.

A story on an inside page of the *Times* mentioned a "disturbance at the 103rd Street IRT station," along with brief accounts of other "disturbances" throughout the five boroughs. The story repeated the lieutenant's account of injuries to policemen and demonstrators arrested; it provided no further details. The *Post* and *News* had nothing at all. If the AP reporter had found a phone and called in his report, neither paper had deemed it worth the space to publish it.

I was stunned and disillusioned. These were my role models, my idols, the hoped-for endpoint of my nascent career. "We've got it covered," my cousin had told me twice. I understood, for the first time, the true meaning of the *Times'* motto, "All the News That's Fit to Print." I set aside the three newspapers and, along with them, my naïve fantasy of what it meant to be a reporter for a major news outlet.

—

During another sleepless night, I re-examined the direction my writing and photography should take, and my life along with it.

The following morning, I wrote my account of the events I'd witnessed and sold it to a local paper, *The Westsider*. The people in my neighborhood, at least, would know the score.

Of course, a lot of them already did.

-30-

Morris Kavesh, Newsstand Man

Imagine a man 5' 10" inches tall, barrel-chested, strong-limbed and hardy. Imagine him in summertime, sitting on a milk crate behind an improvised bench, reading the paper or arguing while you try to pay for your *Daily News*.

Or, again, in mid-December: Find him hunched over, a knit cap on his head, warming his fingers on an electric heater while snow drifts over rumpled copies of *El Diario*, *Jewish Week*, and *Modern People*.

Or in April, amidst spring showers: See him crouched in the doorway of Congregation Machzeh Avruhom shul, blue plastic slicker shielding him from rain, handing out papers that lie beneath plastic sheeting, the edges of the piles of newsprint darkening as moisture seeps toward their centers.

Now imagine him, summertime again, posed before three stacks of the Sunday *New York Times*, each half as tall as he is: hands in pockets, red apron hanging from his neck, shirt undone, proud as anything.

Imagine him at the corner of West 98th Street and Broadway, beside Sloan's supermarket, and imagine him there long before anybody ever thought about Sloan's.

Imagine Morris Kavesh, newsstand man.

Opening:

It is 6:30 a.m. and, for the first time since I moved to the Upper West Side, I hear birdsong in the morning. Morris Kavesh walks carefully across the street, arriving at the pile of *New York Times* in front of what will become his newsstand just in time to meet the *Daily News* delivery. He's wearing a light blue fedora, red sneakers, a white shirt, and green work pants.

"Not a long story, don't give me a long story, but where'd you buy that hat?" the *News* delivery guy asks. Morris cocks his head and tips the hat. The delivery guy laughs and says something I can't make out, then ambles down Broadway toward the donut shop.

I ask Morris if he'd like me to help him set up. He shakes his head. "You will get in the way."

"Okay," I say. I step aside and watch him unlock the metal door to the shul. "I'm going for coffee. Can I pick something up for you?"

Morris shakes his head again. "I send someone later."

In the donut shop, a bum asks me for 20¢. He sways slightly and there is alcohol on his breath. The store manager overhears. "Stop bothering people. Get out!" he says.

"Let me finish," the bum says. "I paid 25¢ for this cup of coffee."

"You didn't buy that," the manager says, "somebody bought it for you. Get out of here!" And he gives the bum the bum's rush.

When I return to the newsstand, Morris has already set out three makeshift benches, assembled from planks and wooden crates. On them, he piles tall stacks of the *Daily News* and the *New York Times*. He stores the planks and crates in the hallway behind him, between the men's and women's toilets for the shul. Every morning he constructs his newsstand from these time-worn boards and boxes, and every afternoon he disassembles it and stores it in the hallway.

Morris cinches up his belt and puts on his vendor's apron, one of several I've seen him wear. This one is red, from Fortune magazine. The text imprinted on it reads: Can we interest you in a small Fortune?

Someone from shul — it sounds like Rabbi Steinberg, but I'm not sure — calls to him in Yiddish. Morris replies in kind.

A truck drives up to deliver the *Voice*. In the next few minutes, more news trucks appear, and delivery men drop off the *Wall Street Journal, Jewish Press, El Diario*.

The balding, bespectacled owner of the cleaning shop next door unlocks the black accordion gate and pushes it aside.

The flow of customers and passersby migrating to the subway, two blocks down Broadway on 96th Street, begins.

"They all go to the subway," Morris explains. "They don't tell anything." And indeed, I had done exactly that every morning for more than a year, when I took the train to midtown for a job at a stock photo agency.

The newsstand's first customer is a short, dark-haired man. He plucks a *Daily News* off the stack and hands Morris a dollar bill. "Fifteen cents," Morris says, and gives him a subway token and 35¢ in change. "I buy $20 in tokens every morning. Better than cash."

A man in a tallis and yarmulke, about 60, comes down from the shul, his footfalls echoing in the hallway. He tells Morris to put weights on his papers. Morris is rushing to complete the newsstand's assembly, sorting papers, positioning wire milk crates behind them. "I have not time," he says.

But a moment later, a breeze lifts the edges of the topmost papers on Morris's stacks, and he fetches the weights from just inside the entrance to the shul. As Morris bends over to set them on the stacks of newspapers, the man with the yarmulke comments, "You're losing your pants, you cocksucker. For that, you *have* to have time."

A man in a beige leisure suit grabs a *Times* and offers Morris a token. "Yes," Morris says, reaching into his apron for 30¢. "See?" he says, glancing at me. "Better than cash." Morris pays that token forward to his next customer in her change. She looks at it for a second and laughs. "Okay," she says, and heads down Broadway with her *Daily News*.

In what seems like no time at all, the stillness of the early morning has been breached, and Broadway's bustling with men and women on foot, on bicycles, and in cars, hurrying off to work.

Two men from the shul, wearing black felt hats and topcoats, come down and kibbitz briefly with Morris in Yiddish. One buys a copy of the *Jewish Press*, the other a Hebrew-language paper. "Moishe," I hear, followed by more conversation in Yiddish, a language I cannot understand but that recalls the many Sundays I spent at my grandparents when I was a boy.

A lady with a fur hat and a white dog buys the *Times*. "You want token?" Morris asks.

A man in jeans and an army coat buys the *Daily World*.

I scan the burgeoning array of papers spread out on the bench: *Village Voice, Jewish Press, Wall Street Journal, The National Insider, Good Times, People, Enquirer, El Diario, Jewish Week, Jewish Journal*. In the rack he's hung from the shul's outside wall are a couple of copies each of *Civil Service Leader*, a Russian paper, *Il Progresso*, and the *Daily World* in Hungarian, Italian, and Polish.

Morris rummages through a cardboard shoebox and pulls out a pair of scissors. "Now I have my tools," he says. He puts on a light jacket and somehow, in the process, almost drops his pants.

He yanks them up. Turning to me he says, "*Now* I send a fellow for coffee."

"*Times*, please," I hear from behind me.

"Yes!" Morris says.

Origins ...

People say my newsstand next to Sloan's. I was here before Sloan's. I say *Sloan's* next to *me*!

My mother established this business. My stand here since 1928. Sloan's wasn't here. Was here a big restaurant, Fleisher's Restaurant, very fancy, like Tip Toe Inn used to be here on Broadway once before. Fancy restaurant. Was four partners, or three partners. One was my cousin, second cousin. So, when my mother came to America ... Before she came, because she was married in Mexico ... My mother was a widow ... Ach! Well, it's a whole story.

So ... my mother was here, and one of our cousins who live in Canada came to visit her. He told my mother that another cousin here has a restaurant. My mother asked, maybe the cousin can give a job to my brother who came to America with her?

So ... my brother, Nathan, work here in Fleisher's Restaurant. A lot of people go in there, a lot going to the subway. My brother says, 'Mother, why don't you put a newsstand here.' So my mother ask permission of my second cousin, and he says, 'Yes, you can put it.' And that's what.

I was not in this country — I came 1930. When I came in here, was Depression time. Four years I was in Brooklyn, working in laundry, busboy, factory. I struggled for my life, here in America.

That time, newsstand was open up to twelve o'clock at night. There was no television, no radio — people used to buy papers. Before I came, my brother and everybody helping. Then my brother got married. My mother could not be alone here, so I start to work with her — that's why.

Since then, 1934, I work with my mother. When I was first here, *Daily News* delivered in horse and wagon. Horse and wagon! Now they have a hundred-fifty trucks.

Moonies:

Morris scurries out onto the street to toss the morning's accumulation of trash into a passing garbage truck. The driver hollers out the window, "Good morning. You got a *TV Guide*?"

Morris tells him, "No, it didn't come. I'm sorry. I have it by ten o'clock."

Three Moonies are sweeping the sidewalks. They wear white jump suits with Reverend Moon buttons on the front, America the Beautiful and red, white, and blue insignia on the back. I talk with one, a thin, curly haired young man who says his name is Benjamin. He leans his broom against a street sign and hands me a brochure, an invitation to Reverend Moon's upcoming Bicentennial celebration in Yankee Stadium. (I later attend.)

"They were here a week ago," Morris tells me.

"We come out every day," Benjamin says.

He turns to Morris. "Hi, how are you today?" he asks.

"All right," Morris replies. "Couldn't be any worse!"

We all laugh.

The man he sent to the donut shop a few minutes ago brings Morris his third cup of coffee. "You see how many coffees I drink? Too much sugar," Morris mutters.

He shows me some newspaper clips he's brought with him about his sons, as well as two envelopes on which he has written, in an elaborate script of which he is clearly proud, his sons' names, Sheldon and Elliot.

On the back of a scrap of paper, he demonstrates signing his name. He warms up for a couple of seconds, then dashes off an illegible but esthetically appealing bold, curlicued signature. He signs his name three times, as if to prove to me that this creation is no accident. "I practice this many times," he says.

The bum from the donut shop, now wearing a white floppy hat and visibly drunk, stumbles up to Morris. He's yelling incomprehensibly, trying to get Morris's attention, but Morris ignores him.

"Hey, I hear you're a millionaire!" the drunk finally offers.

Morris stops speaking to me long enough to say, 'Right!' then continues where he left off.

The *Village Voice* drivers are back from breakfast, and Morris pays them, leaning on the stack of *Times* as he writes out a check.

Two Puerto Rican men start up a conversation with Morris in Spanish. I understand just enough of the language to gather that they are commenting on the newly swept street and sidewalk.

The drunk with the floppy hat stares briefly into the shul hallway, then walks off.

Trucks come and go at Sloan's next door.

A Black man in denim delivers crates of corn and sacks of onions.

A red-headed Dairylea delivery guy accidentally drops a crate of milk. The Royal Dairy men, also unloading their cargo of milk and butter and sour cream, crack up. As the spilled milk crawls toward the street, branching into a pale hand flattened against the sidewalk, they can't stop laughing.

Another customer asks for the *TV Guide*. "No, I don't get yet," Morris says.

There is a momentary lull in the flow of customers, and Morris sits down for the first time this morning. He scans a *New York Times* and clips out an article: A local congressman has floated the idea that, rather than cracking down on prostitution, the largely unoccupied offices of the new World Trade Center towers could double as a Red Light District at night, echoing the function the nearby docks had served in colonial times.

The Newsstand ...

This stand like mine is exceptional. Where you see on Broadway stand like this? Such stand like mine you cannot get.

First way my stand different, every newsdealer has covered newsstand, so they protect their papers from rain and from dirt and from sunburn — like mine get sunburn. I have open stand, and I cannot make a cover here because it's two buildings. But, I'm here for so many years it doesn't pay me to bother anyway. So, the way I stay, it's all right. That's one way.

And, second way is that I have more space than they do. They have only limited space, whatever they occupy. I have enough place here, what I don't sell I put in the cellar. So, I'm better off, eventually.

If it's raining too much, I usually stand under cover of the neighborhood stores, Sloan's or cleaner. Eventually. If only a short while, I cover up with plastic. If it's rain longer time, then I stay under the awnings. They let me to stay. So, that's another difference, me from other stands. They stay in one place. I have always to move.

And I must have a license. If I have a store, yes, I have a right to put newsstand outside. I have no store. I'm not veteran, either. If I would open this stand today, I wouldn't get no license. But because so many years, I continue to get.

Big stand at subway, 96th Street, they got because their father was in Spanish-American war. But not every veteran can get — there are thousands of veterans. You cannot get. His father die, his children and grandchildren get it.

Big stand or small, whatever it is, license costs $10 a year. They renew my license all the time.

Customers:

The pace picks up on Broadway and 98th Street.

Women with children in tow head off to school. Kids and messengers whiz by on bicycles. People of all sizes, colors, ages, and economic statuses run for the bus or hurry down the sidewalk toward the 96th Street subway station, pausing only momentarily to buy their papers. Men with briefcases and big ties buy the *Times*, the *News*, the *Post*. Students and professors buy the *Voice*. Old people with canes stop to kibbitz and thumb through the *Forward*, the *Jewish Press*. Others buy *El Diario*, the *National Enquirer*, the *Wall Street Journal*.

As he takes their money and hands them their change, Morris's responses are brief and efficient:

"Yeah."

"Yes, sir."

"Right."

"Fifty cents."

"Can I have change for a twenty, in singles?" a college girl asks. She has a *Voice* in one hand, a $20 bill in the other.

Morris takes the twenty, stuffs it into one pocket, and withdraws a fistful of singles from another. He counts: "Two, three — hold your hands."

She complies.

"Four, five, six, seven ... ten. Wait."

He turns to another customer to sell a copy of the *Daily News*.

"Eleven, twelve ..." Morris reaches into his pocket again. "Seventeen, eighteen, nineteen." He fetches change from an apron pocket. "Fifty cents and a *Voice*," he says, completing the transaction.

From the stack of papers behind him, Morris periodically replenishes the supply on his makeshift benches. "I sell 300 *New York Times* every day," he says.

The rabbi's wife, a woman about Morris's age, winds her way between the newsstand's benches and up the stairs to the shul. She returns a few minutes later carrying a bag of trash. Halfway down, she drops it, spattering Morris, me, and the newspapers with garbage and broken glass. "I'm sorry," she says in a strong Yiddish accent.

Morris mutters under his breath but starts to clean it up.

"Can I help?" I ask. He shrugs, motions me away, and finishes the job. He and the rabbi's wife talk with each other in Yiddish for a minute, then she heads back up to the shul.

Morris explains that they will make, on Saturday, a kiddish, and that a man will be catering the event. He shrugs again. "So she tells me. What do I have to know? *You* have to know, not *me*. He'll come, he'll bring to you, whatever."

Mothers lead their toddlers to daycare centers. Older kids stroll by in groups of two or three, unaccompanied by adults.

A man in black-framed glasses, a long black coat, and a broad-brimmed black hat comes down from the shul. He sports a full gray beard. "Moishe!" he says. "What happened? They took away the ladder?"

Morris and the man speak in Yiddish for several minutes. Afterward, Morris summarizes.

"Ladder is missing from third floor. Was a robbery recently. They came into synagogue, broke the floor, and came down with ladder from the shul. Robbers got into jewelry store and they took from there something. Now, somebody take away the ladder, so they shouldn't come down if they try to do again."

"How did they get into the shul?" I ask.

Morris shakes his head. "I don't know. I close up stand three o'clock, and somebody did during the night," he says. "Every store has key. These old stores have no toilets, so they use here. And, these stores *also* give key to strangers, customers, to use toilet, which they shouldn't. Now this happens. But, it's not my business, it's the landlord business."

While we're talking, the drunk with the floppy hat comes by and tries to walk off with a *New York Times*.

"Moishe!" the orthodox man says, pointing to the drunk.

"Go! *¡Vete!*" Morris shouts, waving him off.

Another Puerto Rican man comes up to Morris and comments on the newly swept sidewalk. "Moonies," Morris says.

The Puerto Rican man nods and makes a circular gesture beside his right ear. "*Loco*," he says.

A stout woman in a light jacket asks Morris, in a Russian accent, how the windows of the Radio Clinic on the corner got broken. I'd bought my first answering machine there a few months before, a PhoneMate with a reel-to-reel tape recorder.

"Was yesterday fight between two guys. One push the other one through the window," Morris says.

He returns to scanning the papers.

A prune-faced old man brings Morris a jam jar of homemade coffee. "He brings me it every day. He's a good neighbor." Twenty minutes later, the man retrieves the jar.

A dark-skinned man with slicked-back hair asks, "How much is the paper, a quarter?"

"It depends," Morris says. "There is paper from 5¢ to $5. Which one you want, the $5?" He laughs. The man shakes his head and buys *El Diario* for a quarter.

In a flurry of activity, four or five people come up all at once to buy papers. Like a dealer at a blackjack table, Morris takes their money and dishes out their change.

The roar and rumble of rush hour traffic on Broadway is palpable.

Someone buys a *News* and hands Morris a dollar. "Right. Eighty-five cents."

Another stream of people come to buy papers. Their descriptions sound like a verse from a Bob Dylan song:

A brown-haired girl with two dogs on leashes.
A cigar-puffing man in a green patterned shirt.
A jolly old gentleman with purple beret.
A tight-lipped young woman in an off-white summer suit.
A four-foot-tall man in a felt hat with a feather.

And from Morris, the refrain:

"Yes."

"Okay."

"One dollar."

"Eighty-five cents."

Behind Morris, an older man and woman — are they a couple? — operate a rudimentary assembly line, fetching papers for him and replenishing the stacks.

Russia ...

Where we used to live, Ukrania, I should tell you, it was the best part of all Russia. Is a big place, like whole Mexico, or maybe even bigger. It's like in Canada, good earth. They produce a lot vegetables and wheat, and the peasants there were very well off. They had two horses, they had three cows, they had a lot — they were well-to-do.

The only thing, they did not cultivate their earth properly, because they were not educated. Before 1917, ninety percent of Russian peasant population was not even know how to read. Since come the Russian Revolution, they made obligation to every child to go to school, and they made all kinds facilities for the peasants and the workers which they didn't have before the Revolution. That's why there was Revolution in Russia in 1917.

My father was a rich merchant in the big village where we used to live. If I say name in Russian, you would not understand. What's difference? It's fifteen kilometers from the big city of Dnepropetrovsk. *Dnieper*, name of river. *Petrovsk*, he was a Russian leader. Before, was Yekaterinoslav, my city, but after Revolution they changed to Dnepropetrovsk because Yekaterinoslav was named from Yekaterina, that was queen of Russia. So after, they put different name.

My father was grain dealer. We had a general store that's our own store, and besides, we had also — how do you say in America, with the color red where the farmer keep the cows? In the red ... *barn*! He had a barn where they put wheat and corn. Used to buy from the peasants all around and send away to Yekaterinoslav with horse and wagon. And from that grain they made in mill flour, to make bread to eat.

My mother had eleven children, my brothers and sisters. She manage in the store, was the saleslady, very good saleslady. And next to that store was also a building, straw-covered building. I don't know English word. My father only used to buy. He didn't do no selling except to take care of the grain.

We were very much affected by purges. In Russia, Jewish people were very restricted where they lived. In our village, used to be seventeen Jewish families. No Jewish newcomers could come to live there, because police chief would not let nobody from the Jewish people. For instance, my father was not rabbi, but he was religious. We would not eat meat that was not kosher. So, to have a kosher meat, we needed a *moil*. We have to send for him from the city, but he could not live there.

We had pogrom, 1905. I was only two years old at that time, because I'm born in 1903. They robbed us, tried to kill, but other peasants saved us. In 1912, most of the Jews from our village, the relatives, they left Russia. Then, 1912, was free, you could leave. But my mother didn't let my father to go out from Russia, because she say, 'Why should you go to America? You make good living here.'

After Revolution came, because my father was rich, and besides he was a Jew, they tried to kill him. But, gladly, luckily, he escaped. Happened he was not home that time because he went for purchase of merchandise.

I was learning in another city, Novomoskovsk, that's another fifteen kilometers. I was living with my uncle. Once, when I came home, it was a lot of shooting. Somebody tried to get into our house and probably would kill off all of us, but my mother heard, we all start to cry — my brothers, sisters. The peasants came, and finally they saved us, like in 1905.

Night after, another rich, Christian family was wiped out. Twelve in family, *all* was killed. And our store was all burglarized. Was no order no more. My mother didn't want to sleep no more there. We ran away. This was, I think, 1918, before German occupied the place.

Well, what's use to talk? They destroyed everything. The money we had in the bank, gone. We lost the store, we couldn't live in our house, we came another town about fifty kilometers away. Of course, we were suffering.

By that time was civil war in Russia, and nobody expected the communists will win the power. Nobody thought. My father bought two houses in 1918, that is, after Revolution. But then when the communists won power, all the property they took away — if you had a house, it's not yours anymore. So we lost everything. Instead to be a rich merchant, my father start to sell bread to make a living.

So, happened 1914, World War I. In 1917, Revolution. And 1922, my father died naturally. He was a big smoker.

After, we tried to get out of Russia as soon as possible. My father had relatives in Canada, and my mother had two brothers here in America.

Cutouts:

From an apron pocket, Morris pulls out a double-pointed, blue-red editing pencil and sharpens both ends with a penknife. These, along with his scissors, he keeps always at the ready.

Whenever he has a free moment, Morris scans the pages of the newspapers and magazines he sells, marking articles with the red side of the pencil. These, he clips and, sometimes, annotates in blue. After he's made Swiss cheese out of a publication, he tosses it into one of the wooden crates that support his benches and moves on to another. On the *Times* op-ed page, he spots AGNEW, ON ZIONISTS, HIS NOVEL. He skims the article and clips it. ISRAELI SETTLEMENTS: A POLICY CLUE also literally makes the cut. Lost in identifying, classifying, and marking up papers, Morris hardly notices when an occasional paying customer comes by.

Just now, he's clipping a story from the *Wall Street Journal* about the White Motors company. He circles a couple of sections of the article in blue and draws a red X through the flip side, then carefully folds the clipping and stuffs it into a business-sized manilla envelope, which he stores in a shoebox beneath his bench.

I have been watching him do this all morning. "What do you do with all those clippings?" I finally ask.

"Cutouts," Morris says. "From *Times*, from *News*, all about Israel, stock market and ... everything what's fit to read, not bullshit." He reaches beneath his bench. "I show you."

He fetches the envelope and hands it to me. On the front side, embellished with the calligraphy he has invented for his signature, is a name and an address in Washington state.

"So, you see how I wrote? Elliot Kavesh. My son."

The *E* in Elliot is about an inch and a half high, full of elaborate curlicues and twists, and the *W* in Washington is likewise embellished.

I return the envelope. "Very fancy!" I say.

"You didn't *see* fancy," Morris says. "I have at home another envelope which is *much* fancier."

He pulls clippings from the envelope: a Dear Abby column, a picture of the Titanic from *New York* magazine, which he's annotated in blue. "My son gets local papers, but not the *New York Times*, *Daily News*, etcetera."

From the crate, Morris retrieves an eviscerated *New York Times*. "For instance, I already notice article, this, about Zionists. You see about Zionists? Very interesting what they say about it. Because, I'm a Jew and my sons are Jews, of course. So, this I cut out."

Morris tosses the paper back into the crate. "I take from all the papers. *Wall Street Journal* has all about stocks. And *Christian Science Monitor*, it's very educational paper. I only get two copies — nobody buys it. Costs a quarter. But it has nice articles. I send to my sons. Wouldn't you like to read this every morning?"

Morris pulls another article from the envelope. "Here is ISRAEL: DANGEROUS COURSE. This I cut out. I'm a Jew. I'm interested. I send to them." He shrugs. "I don't read it. I have no time to read. *They* read. I only see what's fit to mail. And papers I can return, so it doesn't cost me anything."

He replaces the envelope in the shoebox. "This is my hobby. My happy hobby," he says, smiling.

Morris fetches another manilla envelope from the shoebox. This one, also adorned with his nearly unreadable calligraphy, is addressed to his son Sheldon, in New Jersey. He shows me a cutout from the *Post*, a column by Earl Wilson. With his blue pencil, he's drawn boxes around several paragraphs he wants Sheldon to see. He reads:

"*Question*: When your son finishes college, what will he be? *Answer*: About 35." Morris laughs — a deep, guttural sound. "Not 22, but 35," he says. "There are no jobs, but he'll be 35." He laughs again, harder.

"Here is more." He reaches into the envelope and unfolds a recent *Newsweek* cover. On it is a photo of two young men wearing caps and gowns. They're standing in the street, one operating a bright red jack-hammer, the other wielding a shovel. The headline reads: WHO NEEDS COLLEGE?

"You see what college boy does? I send him that."

Morris shows me an article he's outlined from today's *Daily News*. "This I will send to my sons, so they should know," he says. Yesterday, before noon, three armed men forced their way into the change booth at the IRT station two blocks away, on 96th and Broadway.

"He made woman clerk to lie on the floor and he handcuff the man." He shakes his head. "The neighborhood change a lot. Even when you go home, you have that problem. I have problems for my own safety, you know?"

Whenever he's not selling papers or kibbitzing, Morris pursues his happy hobby. "Whatever is fit to read, something that's important to know, I cut out. Afternoon is best time because it's slow," he explains, "but now is break from rush hour."

He rifles through this week's *SoHo Weekly News*, licking his index finger and thumb as he turns the pages. He finds nothing of interest there, but from the *New Britain Herald*, he clips an article on birds, then stuffs it into the envelope addressed to Sheldon. From the *Wall Street Journal*, he spots an article on Boeing and Northrup. "My son in Seattle work for Boeing, so he will read." He flips through the *Jewish Journal*, the *Jewish Press*, the *Christian Science Monitor*. "If I see something fit to mail, I cut out two of them. First I cut out for one, and then I know already what to send the other."

On a second copy of the Earl Wilson column, Morris shows me he's circled EARL'S PEARLS: DIALOGUE AT THE B'KLYN COPA. He reads:

"I'd rather have a million friends than a million dollars."

"Listen, when you have a million dollars, you *have* a million friends."

Morris points to the column. "You'll have a million friends, and they all want your money."

Education ...

When I was in school in Russia, I train to be engineer, mechanical engineer.

I couldn't get into high school because they didn't take me as a Jew, so I went to another town. Over there, they took me. I study in public school, but it's *high* public school. I finish 1918, after Revolution.

I want to go in the college. But, 1918 was a bad time in Russia. The Germans occupied Ukrania. Somebody recommended me I should apply to the technical school, belonged to the railroad of Katerynynska. In English is something like Railroad Technical School. They were taking Jews, because after Revolution, there was no difference Jewish, gentile, or anything. I was first Jew who got into that school.

I was supposed to learn four years, but I didn't finish. Fourth year, I run away. And I'm glad I run away, because even if I would be engineer in Russia, I would be probably less better there than I'm here as newsdealer.

In America, you don't have to be engineer. I'll tell you, I saw caricature in *People* magazine just two weeks ago: 'Here comes the plumber!' I showed you that? And comes with Rolls Royce with chauffeur. Only you have to be good plumber, and you'll make $15 an hour.

Not a day, $15 an hour. Plumbers, they need plenty. And he makes better than engineer. So, now, if you get married and have a son, don't make him engineer. Even truck driver, drives a big truck, he makes $500 a week. Engineer don't make that much. So you don't need to be engineer, right? Even you're good repairman or good tailor, in America you make as good as anybody else.

Besides, if I would finish as engineer, I don't know if I would be alive. You know why I say? Probably I would stay in my city. When Hitler came there, he annihilate all the Jews in Russia.

I had one of my brothers in Russia, and he didn't want to leave with me. So what happen during the Second World War?

My brother's wife is not Jewish. She's German, Russia German, born in Russia. I brought her to America. She's a doctor now in New Jersey. During war, she was in Kiev. They had a son, and when Hitler's army occupied, they came to her and said, 'The boy is Jewish,' because her husband was Jewish. So, they send her to Germany to go in hospital and work on the prisoners. Over there, she found out what happen my brother. He was taken into Red Army and he was taken prisoner by the Germans, and because he was a Jew, he was killed. The Russian *soldiers*, the Germans put to labor, to work. If he's a *Jew*, they used to kill them automatically.

Hitler.

So, we were lucky that we get out from Russia before. How do I know if I would not be killed? I'm glad I run away. I'm glad in both ways.

The Clothing Salesman:

The pace quickens. It's lunchtime.

Morris takes off his coat and stuffs it under the bench, beneath the stack of *New York Times*. "You see, now I am hungry and I can't eat."

I offer to get him a sandwich. Morris shakes his head. "I send somebody."

A woman about thirty, neat and trim, wearing a white button with SAVE OUR LIBRARIES in red text, buys a *Times*.

A moment later, a professor-type also buys a *Times*. "Nice new hat," he says to Morris. "You look like a gentleman."

Morris says, "You like it? I'll sell it."

A man in jeans and a black t-shirt comes up and asks Morris if he's seen a dog. He's carrying a bag of groceries and a leather leash.

Morris shrugs.

"Somebody must be playing a trick on me. Somebody let him loose." He leaves the groceries at the newsstand. "I'll be back in a minute," he says.

Thirty seconds later, the dog, sans owner, comes bounding out of Sloan's.

Morris shrugs again.

Several people, in quick succession, ask Morris for the *TV Guide*. "No, I don't get yet," Morris says.

"Mendel!" Morris calls to a middle-aged man who has been reading one of the Jewish papers. They exchange a few words in Yiddish, and the man sets his paper back on the stack and heads down Broadway. "I send him for coffee and an egg sandwich," Morris explains.

A Black man with close-cropped hair and a sparse mustache comes by carrying a shopping bag full of clothes, with more clothes draped over his arm. Among the latter is a blue-and-white striped suit. He sets the bag down and displays the jacket against his body. The style is JFK preppy, circa mid-sixties.

"You want it?" he says to Morris. "Ten dollars, jacket and pants."

"What I need this for?" Morris replies. "I have plenty suits at home. I don't wear them."

The salesman, down but not out, gets some assistance from a Brazilian man in his forties, Alfredo, who has been watching the transaction.

Alfredo says, "It's beautiful, Morris. You should at least try it on."

Morris repeats, "I have plenty of suits."

"Oh, but not like that, Morris," Alfredo says. Do you see the color? Beautiful! Like your hat. You wear that jacket, Morris, people will come over here to take your picture."

The salesman brightens. He hands Morris the jacket.

Morris tries it on.

"Yeah, yeah. How do you like that?" the salesman says. "Beautiful, right?" He glances at Alfredo for confirmation. Alfredo nods, but he's barely suppressing a laugh.

Morris hands the salesmen the jacket. "Jacket, I don't need. I give you $3 for the pants."

The salesman grunts unhappily. He shakes his head, picks up his bag of clothes, and heads uptown.

But in ten or fifteen minutes, he's back, with the suit still draped over his arm.

"*Eight* dollars" the salesman says.

"No, I don't need," Morris says.

"For your friend. Ask your friend," the salesman says, gesturing with the suit in my direction.

Morris turns to me. "If you want buy, you can buy," he says, and returns to selling papers.

The salesman hands me the jacket. It's slick, polyester. "What are you doing?" I ask.

"I buy and resell like this." He speaks quickly. "It's business. I would have a store, but it's too much overhead. It's like a thousand dollars, and it's not worth it. What if you don't get no sales?"

He sets his bag of clothes on the sidewalk. "I have good clothes. He buys from me."

I hand him the jacket. Sensing, shrewdly, that I'm an unlikely prospect, he tugs on Morris's sleeve. "Morris, you want to take this for your relatives?"

"I have plenty," Morris repeats.

"For your friends, maybe?" There is a hint of pleading in his voice, but his appeals fall on deaf ears.

He walks off again.

Morris shakes his head. "He graduate from City College," he says.

Two minutes later, the salesman returns, still carrying his bag of clothes. "Will you give me a dime, please?" He's breathing hard.

"Are you joking?" Morris asks.

The salesman sighs. "I'm not selling the suit. I got a meter."

Morris gives him a dime. The salesman jogs awkwardly up Broadway, hugging his shopping bag to his chest with both arms.

Morris shrugs.

Flight ...

I leave Russia 1923. My mother sold everything and we came to Moscow. But she couldn't left, because that time America did not recognize Russia.

Well, what shall I do? My father died, my mother already applied to go to America, and they would not let her out. So, in Moscow we decide, I and my mother, that I go first, illegal.

They had American consul in Latvia, in Riga, Baltic Sea. I leave two weeks before her. I didn't tell anything at my school, I didn't let nobody know. I was with seven guys, with horse and wagon, night time, because if they would catch me, they would put me into prison. Or who knows what?

I pass by the frontier, and then luckily, we saw a Russian soldier, we paid him money, and we rode over. And luckily, we came into Latvia. I run away from Russia!

In Latvia, I told I'm refugee from Russia and I want to go to America. I start to apply for American visa, but I couldn't get no visa — I didn't have passport. I had to pay $100 fine to Latvian government because I came Latvia without permission. My uncle supposed to send me $600, he only send me two-fifty. Anyway, I had to spend three months, and then, by the time I got my visa to go in America, quota was closed. Was a new law here, 1923: no free immigration.

After Latvia, I couldn't come to America. So what shall I do? I came to Mexico. From Mexico I brought my mother to Mexico, and gradually we came to America.

The Drunk:

Morris is talking with Harry, a wiry little man who could pass for a jockey if he lost three inches. He introduces himself as an indoor astronaut. "I used to be an elevator man," he explains.

Before I have a chance to find out more about him, the drunk with the floppy hat, like the Cat in the Hat, returns.

"Hey, Mac! You know my name. Why you mistreated me? Or everything I'm comin' back! Yeah! Heavy! You boo boo. He-ho. Excuse me. You know you're a verynicefella? Beh! He! Ah ha ha ha! Fuggu!"

Morris extends his right leg and bares his ankle. "Shake my hand!" he says.

The drunk replies: "Fuggu! Eee-oh-gas-a-sack! Oh-haw! Je-jonk. Yo. Yo. Ah-ee-oh. Bap!"

Morris turns to me and comments, laughing, "You think I'm bad? He's worse!"

"Hey, man, that's heavy," the drunk says.

Up close, I see that he has no front teeth, and that most of his remaining teeth are flecked with gold. The mix of alcohol and tooth-lessness slurs his speech to near incomprehensibility, but these obstacles do not impede him.

He starts to do shaky knee bends, bracing himself on the stack of *Daily News.* "Down, up, down ..." he chants, roughly in time with his body movements. He stops after a few rounds and turns to me. "Hey, hey. He got a one-track mind," he says, gesturing to Morris. "He never think of up and down. He think I won't." He resumes. "Ho! Eee-up! Down. Gook. Poderoderseemesay."

The drunk's performance spawns a secondary activity: Morris and Harry make similar noises and similarly bounce around. I feel like I've fallen into the monkey house.

"Tell me," I ask the drunk, "how do you know so much?"

"I taught myself," the drunk says. He removes his hat and takes a bow. "Ratha-nutha-babe!"

Morris stops bouncing around, but *his* hat remains firmly planted on his head. Harry grabs my shoulder. "Please! Please!" He can't stop laughing. "Don't encourage him! Oh, God, don't start!"

"Look!" the drunk exclaims, pointing down the block. "You see me by myself. Oganatocha!" He turns to Morris. "Gimme somethin' I don't know."

Morris again pulls his pants leg up and displays his ankle. "All right!" he says. "Shake my hand. Shake this!" With surprising balance for a man his age, he bounces his leg up and down in a crude approximation of a handshake.

"Hey," Harry says abruptly, interrupting the fun, "it's gonna rain!"

For a moment I figure this remark to be diversionary, but no, the sky is indeed darkening.

"Look, you have to go," Morris says to the drunk. "I must cover papers before rain comes."

"Well, somebody speak a little too loud, eh?" the drunk says, flashing a toothless grin.

"When you go to dentist?" Morris asks him.

The drunk continues to babble. Morris gathers plastic sheets from the shul hallway. "All right," Morris says, pointing at me, "you talk to him. He's my interpreter."

The drunk obliges and shifts his focus to me. He continues his babbling and mostly unintelligible monologue, punctuated with *Hoo! Wee! Wah!* "Look! You know one thing?" he says, coherence momentarily breaking through, like the sun poking through clouds, "When I come by here sometimes, I see you, and the rest of 'em. I don't think you've ever seen that."

I suspect he's not just drunk, and that he's one of the recently released mental patients who inhabit the nearby SRO (Single Room Occupancy) hotels. Then he startles me. "Because you're too loose," he continues. "If you tighten up, maybe. But you're too loose now." Too loose, indeed. But what would it mean to "tighten up"?

By now, Morris has finished covering the papers with plastic. He comes to my aid.

"Hey, what color hair have you?" Morris says to the drunk.

"I don't know," the drunk replies. "You said change it."

"What color *hair* have you?" Morris repeats.

"Well, she tell me what to make it, I don't know."

"And what color on the *head*?"

"Inside?"

"*What color hair have you?* Black? What color hair?"

"Yeah, beautiful. But it ain't no mo'."

"And on the head? On the head, what color?"

"Oh! Yeah, beautiful. Hey! Anytime you pass Teaneck, write."

Harry pulls me aside. "He comes by here all the time, talking like this."

"How do you get rid of him?" I ask.

"We just let him talk it out, and like now, we don't pay attention."

At last the drunk wanders off, like Halley's Comet briefly intersecting with the Earth's orbit and then zooming back to deep space again.

Harry and I rejoin Morris. "And your living you make from that?" Morris asks.

"I hope to," I say. "But not from talking to guys like him!"

Morris laughs. "I want to tell you something," he says. "Today is anniversary my mother open newsstand here. In two years, I'm going to make a big celebration: Fifty years on the West Side. Two years from today, if I'm alive."

"Come around in two years and he'll buy you a coffee," Harry says.

Morris ignores the jibe. "I have to go to *Times*, to *News*, so they come around here and shoot the pictures. You can come, bring copies of your book. I autograph."

"Yes, fifty years," Harry says, putting his arm around Morris's shoulders. "And I've known him for thirty-four, since I came to the neighborhood."

Mexico …

I came from Latvia to France. There I recognize some other friends from Russia. I say, 'Listen, what shall I do? I'm not going to remain in France.' There were *thousands* of immigrants! I say, 'I'm going to Africa, to Australia, to Zealand, to Alaska, to … no matter where I go! I don't care.' So a Frenchman tells me, 'Why don't you go to Mexico? After two years you'll be able to come to America.' Mexico was free immigration. So let's go to Mexico! I came to Mexico. But I was not two years, not three, five. *Seven* years, and my mother send me my wife to Mexico and I married her, and I came here.

I couldn't get no jobs in Mexico. I have to do my own business to make a living. *Todavía yo recuerda* — if you understand Spanish. I was traveling salesman. I go with Morris's Hardware and I sell all kinds of tools, cheap German tools: *cinceles, cuchillos, limas, martillos, tenazas.* I travel all over in the remote places of Mexico, to the frontier of Guatemala.

I used to work hard, make good money, and then I didn't do anything month, month and a half, having good time. Why? Because I am always thinking about to come to America. I thought if Mexico is good, in America must be *much* better. So when I come here in 1930, I was very disappointed: Depression, people selling apples on the corner, no job. And I thought to go back to Mexico, but my wife didn't let me. That's why I remain here. Otherwise, I would go.

But I'll tell you, before the war, was little immigration from Poland, Russia, Eastern Europe. People didn't go to Mexico, they went to Canada, United States, Argentina, and also Brazil. Nobody came to Mexico. When I came in 1923, it was like United States in 1890. It was a lot. All the Jews who did come to Mexico then, they are multimillion-aires now. They're very well off.

I went there about four years ago, and I saw some of my landsmen who stay in Mexico. They are all businessmen, in industry. They have beautiful homes and beautiful cars. They are not struggling for life like I struggle here seven or eight days a week.

What would happen to me if *I* remained in Mexico, I don't know. I suppose I wouldn't be any *worse*. I *suppose* so. But you don't know what way your decision will lie. You know what I mean?

English:

"Now, the Russian Jews that come to America, even they are businessman, doctor, they are here taxi drivers, or washing the floors, or selling potatoes," Morris tells me. "You know why? Because they don't know the language, and to be a doctor here, you have to pass the exam. It's a big struggle."

A stocky guy with a brush cut buys a *Post* for a quarter, and Morris doles out 75¢ change. "Hey," he says, "I gave you a ten!"

"Sorry," Morris says, and counts out nine singles. To me he says, "You make me mix up sale!" But then he continues his narrative.

"Spanish I knew right away," he says, "because I was 20 years of age when I came to Mexico. I was alone there, so I never spoke Jewish, I never spoke Russian. I took the language very quick. But when I came to America, I spoke mostly Jewish and Russian. With my mother, we spoke Russian, and with my wife Jewish, because she was Hungarian and I didn't know Hungarian. So it took me longer, but the spelling, I got that quick."

"*Diario*," another customer says, holding out his copy. Morris quickly makes change.

"I learn to spell in English by memorizing words in newspapers I sell, especially words not easy to spell because they don't follow rules. For instance, *business*, which is very common. Or *association*. Nobody spell for me. *I* do, because I have a memory." He smiles knowingly. "I bet you don't know how to spell Massachusetts!"

"Yes I do!" I say. Morris laughs as I spell out M-A-S-S-A-C-H-U-S-E-T-T-S.

"That's right!" He laughs again. "That's it!" He pauses for a moment. "Give me a pencil."

I hand him the soft black pencil I use for copy editing. He grabs the nearest piece of paper, a *Daily News* delivery slip, and flips it over.

"Here is common mistake. People write *newsstand* like that — " Using the stack of *Posts* as a standing desk, Morris writes, in large, even letters *newstand*. "But should be like this — " In the same careful hand, he writes *newsstand*. "You see, two *s*."

"Right," I say. "I had to look that one up, and I was born here."

"Or my granddaughter wrote *granfather*. She makes a mistake." He points to the *n* and *f*. "Should be *grand*," he says.

As he's writing, Jonas comes around the corner and sees me at the newsstand. He's on his way to the laundromat two doors down, a duffel bag of dirty clothes slung over his shoulder. He waves to me as he approaches.

"Morris, this is Jonas," I say. "A friend."

"*Dobriy den*," Jonas says.

Morris raises an eyebrow. "You speak Russian?"

Jonas smiles. "*Da! Priyatna paznakomitsa.*"

Morris laughs. "Nice to meet you, too," he says.

"Jonas is an International Affairs student at Columbia," I say.

"Ah! You will meet friend here, was translator at United Nations," Morris says.

Evidently pleased to have Jonas in attendance, he continues. "I want to tell you, Spanish is very easy, but English is complicated. For instance, you write *knife* K-N-I-F-E, but when you write *knives*, you write V-E-S, right? And knife, *k*, you don't even pronounce *k*. I memorize all this."

"It's not logical," Jonas says.

"I learn from reading," Morris says. "Listen, after all, I am not ignorant like you think. I go in engineering college in Russia, but I didn't finish. And I was going to technical school. I was first Jew who got into that school, after Revolution." He looks at Jonas but nods in my direction. "I tell him this already."

"Believe me," I say, "We don't think you're ignorant."

"No way!" Jonas says.

"I know lots of things, but I don't use it," Morris says. "My signature, I didn't do that overnight. I tried to perform. You know what I mean? Try out, to practice it."

Morris begins again to write. As he had done earlier in the day, he tears through three nearly identical versions of his elaborate signature, efficiently executing his fancy, bold strokes.

"This is my signature, Morris Kavesh."

"Holy smoke!" Jonas says. "That's very impressive."

Morris hands Jonas the piece of paper. "It's kind of a Russian *K*," Jonas says.

"Well, it's a Russian *K* and American *K*. It's the same *K*," Morris says. Turning to me, he adds, "Anyway, I like your pencil."

"Want it?" I ask.

"No, no, no, no," Morris says, and hands the pencil back to me.

Pointing to the piece of paper, I ask, "Do you mind if I take that?"

Morris stiffens. "What, you want my signature?"

"As an illustration. For your story."

Morris shakes his head vigorously. "No, no. My signature I don't give to nobody. That I do not do." He quickly stuffs the paper into his shoebox.

"No problem, Morris," I say, but as he turns to attend to a customer, there's a new chill in the air that has nothing to do with the rain.

America ...

My mother married in Mexico, and *I* got married in Mexico.

I brought my mother to Mexico because she couldn't come to America. She had already two brothers in New York, my uncles. There was here a man who came to America, 1905, from pogrom. He knew my mother before she married my father. When my mother came to Mexico, this man find out from my uncles that my mother is a widow, so he came to Mexico and married her. She came here as American citizen's *wife*.

After my mother became a citizen, she brought all children under 18. By American immigration law, her husband could not bring, because they were not *his* children — only my mother could bring after she become a citizen. But she could not bring right away after she married. So, she was orderly, took her a couple of years, and then all the children came except *me*. Even as citizen, she could not bring me because I was over 18. What can she do? She send my wife to me in Mexico as sweetheart, American citizen, and I married her. So, we all came here.

Luckily, my marriage was lucky. I didn't care *who* I married — I married just to become a husband of American citizen, to come to America. I came! And luckily she was a nice woman, she helped me in the business, I had two sons which was very good, and now, my sons are well and I'm well. And I'm healthy, too.

I came from Mexico on a ship *Orizaba*. It took about five days, I don't remember exactly. I came with the third class.

They send me to Ellis Island for inspection, if I am sick or not. The inspector over there told me to take off my pants, to examine me. He said something in English. What the hell I knew in English? He knew I am Jewish. So, he tell me: '*Tsuris, kippurus, machus. Farshtayt?*'

You don't understand it? *Tsuris*, that's a Jewish word, means trouble. *Kippurus*, you know, Yom Kippur and holiday. *Machus*, that's a Jewish word means also troubles. It's like Pharaohs, and history, and Passover. How do you say in English? When they came from Egypt, God gave them ten *machus*? Plague! And *farshtayt,* he ask me if I understand.

So, when the inspector told me, '*Tsuris, kippurus, machus,*' I told him in Jewish, '*tseyner, beyner, meyn kop!*' *Tseyn*, teeth. *Beyn*, bones. And *kop*, the head. He made a fun in Jewish, so I give him a fun in Jewish back, joke for joke, without thinking. I still remember this.

By the way, yesterday, 20th of May, was exactly day in 1930 I come in America from Mexico. So how much am I here? Forty-six years I'm here in America. It's a big story to tell, but in the end, is good.

The Businessman:

The sun is out again, and Morris has removed another layer. He's down from a coat and sweater to a short-sleeved shirt and, of course, his apron.

A guy comes up to him and asks for the key to the men's room in the shul hallway.

"Not for customers," Morris says, gruffly. "Just for business, and for the shul."

"C'mon, man, I really gotta go," the man complains.

They argue back and forth. Morris eventually relents.

"Thanks a lot," the man says, and pats Morris on the shoulder.

The manager at Sloan's, a heavy-set man with black curly hair, comes over to the newsstand. He kids with Morris for a couple of minutes, buys change from him, then returns to the supermarket. I recognize him as the one who brought Morris his first cup of coffee.

"I have good neighbors," Morris says, gesturing toward Sloan's. "They let me to sell. When it's rain, they let me stay under the awning. They change my money. Good neighbor."

The *Post* is finally delivered around noon, and *TV Guide* is not far behind. Morris begins to scan the new arrivals for cutout candidates. Meanwhile, I'm talking with Alfredo.

"So, Morris is a Jew, he married a Hungarian girl, she gave him two sons, two PhDs. Sixty-five thousand dollars a year, the boys make, right now. One work for the Boeing people over there, and the other one work for Allied Chemical over in New Jersey. Two PhDs and he's complaining! Forty years ago, fifty years ago, he come from Europe, he stayed in Mexico waiting for his turn, you know? He was waiting too long, so he had to get married. Right Morris? You couldn't stand five pesos for a woman? So you marry one. It was easier and cheaper, right Morris?"

Alfredo winks at me, then glances at Morris, but Morris continues to skim the articles in today's *Post*. Alfredo tries again.

"I ask him once," Alfredo says, "'Morris, what is your God?' Morris says, 'Cold cash!' His God: cold cash." Alfredo shakes his head and laughs.

Without looking up from the *Post*, Morris says, "Now tell him about yourself, don't talk about me."

"My life is an open book, Morris," Alfredo objects, "you know that. But your life is a closed book. Nobody knows about you because you never say anything about yourself."

Alfredo winks again. Nevertheless, he obliges.

"I'm going back to Brazil," he tells me. "I been here for twenty-eight years, and what I got? Nothing. I was with the State of New York my last job, on the board that supervises the OTB, the racing track and everything. Then come the big layoff and they kick you. Kick you. It's a headache."

He lights a cigarette, then offers me one. I decline; I'm trying to quit.

"I know plenty of people, but the economy over here is not so good. People out of work, and it's strained all over. I think it's better back home. I have connections over there, nice people, and they are building every day. For what I have in mind to do, it's just flourishing. I go with the peak experience, the whole know-how from over here, which is very important." Alfredo smiles. "And, of course, life goes by easily in the tropics — beaches and beautiful women. Much better than over here."

Alfredo takes a drag, taps the ash. "So, I made up my mind: I don't stay here no more. I was married before, and divorced and I have an 18-year-old. I'm gonna leave him behind — he goes to school, so it's no problem. I told him, 'Anytime you like, take a plane, come down.'"

He takes another drag and exhales smoke rings. The intoxicating smell wafts over me. "But the problem is I met a girl. Beautiful woman. She's 45, I'm 49. She has her own business, and she is a widow. Would be perfect match. Perfect! I would invite her to come down with me for the summer — I have a big family, big house — and see if she likes or not."

He tosses the cigarette to the ground and grinds the butt into the pavement. "But I come a little too late. She has a family she loves and provides for, and to get together with somebody else, has to be somebody who's gonna help her, right? Today, women are with you for security." He pulls the cigarette pack from his shirt pocket, then puts it back. "But, this girl is the perfect match for me."

Alfredo glances back at Morris, still reading the *Post*. "Morris!" he says, loudly enough to pull him away from his cutouts.

"What you want?" Morris says.

"I ask you this because I like you, Morris," Alfredo says. "You are double my age. You were married, you have two children, you are a widower. I am a divorced man — "

"You ask me what?" Morris says, an impatient edge to his voice.

"What you think I should do?"

Morris sets the paper down. "It's how you feel!" he says. "Don't ask me how to do. If you feel better to go home, fuck Brazilian, don't fuck American. Go home! And if you want to fuck American, then stay here!"

Alfredo guffaws. "Okay, Morris. That's what I want to hear, Morris!"

Morris gets up from his stool and takes a step toward Alfredo. "Listen, I want to ask you same question: What color you like better, red or green?"

"Well, Morris, makes no difference."

"How can I tell you better? Is there any choice? I like green, you like red."

"That's right, Morris. Exactly."

"You tell me two extremes."

"I'm going to invite her over, to spend a couple of months. We'll fly down together. It's a good idea?"

"I tell you what happened to me," Morris says.

While he and Alfredo are carrying on, a woman tries to buy a *Daily News*. Morris takes her money. "Just a second," he says, reaching into his apron for change. Then, "What you give me?"

"A dollar!" she says. Morris counts out her 80¢ change.

He turns back to Alfredo. "Now, I tell you what happened to me. When I was in Mexico, I want to come to America, and I couldn't come unless I'm the husband of American woman. My mother send me a woman, happened to be she's young. If she would be a hundred years old, I would marry her, too. You know why? I would become her husband, come to America, divorce her, and fuck yourself!"

"That's right, Morris!" Alfredo says.

"Right! So, I took a chance to marry a woman I don't like it, just for to sell me myself for America. Happened to be I was lucky. But now, you take that chance, too."

"No," Alfredo says. "Because with you it was different. You was waiting for to come to the United States and you met your wife."

"Right! But I had to marry her! I didn't even know her!"

"She gave you two children."

"But suppose I would not like her, suppose she would be too — "

"She gave you two PhD's! What the hell are you talking about!"

"All right! So hear my answer! So *you* marry and *you* have two children."

"Well, I got one already, Morris."

"You have one. So what?"

"But she has four, it's five altogether. I don't need any more."

"So I tell you what you do. You do the same like I, get married, you have two *more* children, and you'll be as happy."

"Exactly, Morris! But this happened a century ago, Morris!" Alfredo laughs.

With that, Morris shakes his head, walks back to his stool, and picks up the paper he was scanning.

A moment later, he sets it down again. "He asks me my advice," Morris says to me. Then, to Alfredo: "Why you ask me such questions? It's how you feel!"

"Well, Morris," Alfredo says, "I think that's the point. If I marry her — "

"Then you know the answer! Then you know what to do!"

"Morris, love don't give you $50,000. So I have to give to her — "

"So I'll tell you what to do. A sign I saw: 'Buy American, fuck American!'"

Alfredo laughs. Morris guffaws.

"That's my only joke," Morris says. "Use American prostitute!" Morris laughs till he can hardly speak. "Fuck American!"

An old man, leaning on a cane, asks me, "What the hell are they talking about?"

Morris goes back to his cutouts.

Another old man, the cleaner from next door, joins Alfredo and me. "Going back to Brazil?"

"Yeah, to Brazil. I just sold my apartment last night, tomorrow they're gonna sign the lease with the landlord and get everything taken care of. It's beautiful — the way I want it."

"Hey, you going back for good?" the cleaner says.

"Yeah, I guess so," Alfredo replies.

"No kiddin'! Soon?"

"Yeah ... Maybe the end of the month."

"Hey, who's gonna give you the good stuff out there? Here, you used to get the good stuff."

"Well, yeah, but that's okay. I'm gonna miss all my friends, really, 'cause I been in this neighborhood for the past twenty-eight years."

"You stay in stock?"

"No, I was over here in the stock exchange before."

"Yeah, that's what I mean, in stock."

"No, no. No more in that. No more. I have a degree in law over there and economics over here, but there I'm going into a different field, because over there, when you are over 40, forget it. What I'm gonna do there is be a consultant."

"I'm gonna miss you," the cleaner says. He reaches out a hand for Alfredo to shake. "In case I don't see you no more."

Alfredo takes the cleaner's hand in both of his. "No! You see me. I come over here every day until I go. Every day." He pulls a wire crate from behind the bench for the cleaner to sit on. "Let me put this over here for you."

The cleaner sits. "Thank you," he says.

Alfredo turns toward Morris. "Every day I come. If I don't come to see him, I die. Right, Morris? I have to take twice for the blessing daily, right Morris?"

"Yeah," the cleaner says. "The rabbi told me he's gonna give you the title Honorary Jew."

"Because I provide the guardianship of the synagogue every day, right Morris? I be a doorman, watching out."

Alfredo is quiet for a moment, and a wistful look comes over him. "I'm gonna miss you a lot Morris, you know?" he says.

"Yes, yes. Freedom of speech," Morris says, his eyes still on the *Post*.

"I'm telling you!" Alfredo insists.

"Yes, go on, bullshit!" Morris says.

"No parusky rusky, Morris. No parusky. No parusky, Morris," Alfredo says. "What I'm gonna do over there?"

Morris looks directly at Alfredo. In a softer voice, he says, "You'll invite me, in New York."

"Well ..."

Morris smiles. "And we'll go on Amazon River."

Adventurous ...

I don't know what's so interesting about my life. Everybody has his lifetime story. *You* have lifetime story.

Maybe you haven't got such life story as mine, because my life was more adventurous: Adventurous almost killed when bandits came to my house. Run away from Russia adventurous. Adventurous to come to Mexico without money, then come to America without anything, and have family, have nice children, grandchildren. And the way I am now, something to be thankful, and nobody else but me. Nobody helped me, nobody did me. I did myself.

Even I came America, it was a struggle here, too. There was so much unemployment. I'm the man with a good education, with every-thing, but in America I don't know English, so I had to work like a laborer. I work in the laundry, I have to press shirts with all the colored women. I work in bottle factory, my hands were swollen. Very hard work, and it was not work for a Jewish man, you know? Because I was educated man. And I had also to send my wife to work, downtown in the garment center, to make a living. I was disappointed. I felt very inferior.

I say to my wife, 'What the hell I'm going here? I have no future here.' I didn't want to stay, I want to come back to Mexico. But my wife didn't want, as I told you. And good thing I didn't decide that. After all, eventually, I have newsstand, my sons, and now they're fathers, happy fathers.

Well, we Europeans, especially Jews, have a more rich story to tell of their lifetime, right? You were born in America. You didn't have no adventures. You don't know any of this.

The Indoor Astronaut:

On the median strip across from the newsstand, a Black man in a yellow t-shirt and leather pants is playing a *djembe*. Another guy taps his Afro comb against the *djembe's* black body. Beside them, a wino sings in Spanish and taps the blade of a pocketknife against his bottle to keep time.

An older man with thinning white hair combed across a bald spot, the way my grandfather combed it, looks on from a nearby bench, and two women sitting on a Jersey barrier across from the impromptu band talk as if nothing out of the ordinary is happening — which is, in fact, the case for 98th and Broadway.

While Morris is speaking Yiddish with a heavy-set man in a green tweed suit, a guy in a blazer steps up to the newsstand.

"What do you want, *Times*?" Morris asks.

"What do you think? I'm here every day."

"I think maybe you want to give me Christmas present that you didn't give me yet." He laughs.

"I give you every Sunday," the man says, laughing along with him.

"Right, right." Morris takes a dollar from the man and hands him a *Times* and his change.

In the midst of this exchange a woman brandishes a *Forward* and says to Morris, "You owe me $5. Don't forget!"

"Yeah, I owe you. I wouldn't forget, don't worry. I didn't have time to go to bank yet." Morris points toward me. "He took me all morning."

"Don't blame me!" I say.

Morris brushes me off. But to the woman he admits, "For a moment I forget, but I wouldn't forget."

"I'll see you tomorrow," she says, and waves to him as she heads down Broadway with her paper.

Harry has been watching this exchange. He says, "Moishe. *Morris!* How much you owe *me*?"

"I owe you ... a fuck and a half!"

Harry says to me, "Put *that* in the book!"

"That he has a dirty mouth?"

Morris puffs out his chest and pounds it with his fist. "Yeah, I like to be a man! *Macho*, in Spanish." He points to Harry. "But he is harmless. He can't do anything with girls."

"Are you just gonna take that?" I ask Harry.

"Somebody, you know, that is important, I would react. But him?" Harry shrugs. "He's like a computer: garbage in, garbage out. Right, Morris?" Harry shrugs again, this time exaggerating the movement so his mouth also seems to shrug. "It's mind over matter. I haven't got a mind, so it don't matter."

Everybody laughs.

"So," I say, "this morning you said you were an indoor astronaut."

"Yeah, but I been retired two years. First I was an indoor aviator, but I changed with the times. And I went a lot farther than the moon." He flashes me the same exaggerated grin, moves a hand slowly up and then down. "You get it?"

"I got it," I say.

Harry sits on a wire crate behind one of the benches and gestures to a vacant one. I join him.

"I never got past the eighth grade," Harry says, "but I done a lot of things. I started working as an elevator man in 1927 at the Hotel Cumberland, down on Broadway and 54th. Now they call it the Bryant. They paid me $12 a week. It was prohibition, so I made a little extra running bathtub liquor for the patrons."

Hotel Cumberland

A man comes by and grabs a *Daily News*. He holds out a dollar. Harry nods toward Morris. "Ask the guy with the apron," he says.

"I was there a couple of years," Harry continues. "In 1928, '29, Dutch Shultz becomes a partner in the nightclub across the street. They call it the Chateau Madrid. They needed an elevator man to run the patrons from the lobby up to the club. It was just one floor, but they don't wanna walk. He offers me $15 a week, plus meals — steaks, everything — so I worked there until the place got raided and the cops shut it down."

Harry looks around, then leans forward. His voice drops to a whisper. "Mr. Shultz used to come in and he says, 'Kid, ditch this' and hands me a gun with a real short barrel. I'd go down to the basement where there was a lot of junk and hide it under some clothes or something. In case the place gets raided, he don't want to have a gun on him. When he was leaving, he'd tell me to get it for him."

I glance around, too, imagining Broadway fifty years ago: lavish hotels, the high-class men and women parading in their fancy dress, the sounds of street peddlers bartering and the *aoogha* of Model Ts and Model As.

"I don't expect nothing, but I show up anyway. The bodyguard says, 'You were right. He told me to give you the fifteen bucks. Here's twenty.' And he lends me his key, so I can get my uniform."

A woman comes by and picks up a *Post*. "Excuse me," she says. "Do I pay you?" This time it is I who point to Morris.

"I worked in another place after that," Harry says, "and I met a lot of movie stars. That's how I got to be an extra in *The Macedonians*. I dressed up like a Macedonian, whatever that is. From that, I got into more movies. Each one, they pay me $10."

Harry flashes his signature grin and raises his eyebrows like Groucho Marx. "After that, I got into burlesque. Six or seven years I did that. You know how there's a straight man and a clown, and the clown always gets kicked around? I was the clown."

His show biz career was cut short when Mayor La Guardia, in an attempt to control organized crime, outlawed striptease and burlesque. "So I went back to being an elevator man. I was an indoor aviator until they started shooting people into space. That's when I graduated to indoor astronaut," Harry says.

The Neighborhood ...

When I start here with my mother, was a very nice, very fine neighborhood — I should say even aristocratic. Predominantly Jewish people. West End Avenue, everyone had doorman and elevator man.

Was no self-serve elevator. You saw only white people, you didn't see no colored people here, no Puerto Rican, no Latin American. At that time, I used to sell two, three Spanish paper a day. Now, I sell fifty or sixty.

None of the stores you see today on this block not existed in that time. It was all fancy stores along here. Here was a men's hat store. Then was a cake store — not baking, just selling cakes. Next to me was Fleisher's Restaurant, very fancy restaurant, as I told you. On corner was Davega store. You know Davega store? They sell furniture, radio, sports games. Now, no more Davega stores. And what else? Came cleaning store, but cleaning store already changed hands. All these are new stores.

The neighborhood start to change after Second World War in, I should say, 1955. For the last twenty years. Start to come a lot Latin American countries' immigrants: Puerto Ricans, Santo Domingans, looking for a better living, for better jobs. Gradually, gradually, gradually they start to move into this neighborhood, the same like *our* East European Jews start to come here in 19th century and beginning of 20th century. 1923, the quota for immigration was closed for those people — I was one of them. I couldn't come, even I got my American visa before the law came out. After that, start to come the — what you call Cuba and Tahiti? The Antilles Islands. And the neighborhood start to change.

Well, I don't feel too happy about it. It don't make difference to me about white or Black or Spanish or whatever you are, but the white people used to buy more papers. They were business people. I used to have two or three magazines, like *Life*, *Look*. Now I don't have. I cannot sell them. It's too expensive, they are 75¢ a magazine. And, they steal from me — I have no place to hide them. So I don't bother.

Besides, I have problems for my safety. Used to be was so safe. I come here early in the morning with my change apron and sell papers, and never happened to me anything for all the time. Last years, I was twice mugged here.

Time is different, now.

The Neighborhood:

A blonde woman in her sixties comes up to the stand while Harry and I are talking. I've seen her around the neighborhood.

"Morris!" she says. "Will you keep my boyfriend away from me?"

"Boyfriend!" Harry says.

She laughs, pats Harry on the head. "That's right," the blonde woman says, "he's my boyfriend."

She pats Harry on the cheek. "Oh!" Harry says.

"That's good," Morris says. Then: "Don't tell me you like harmless boyfriends?"

"No, sir!" the woman says.

"He's harmless," Morris says.

"I'm harmless!" Harry agrees.

The woman walks over to Morris. In a stage whisper, she asks, "That's why he runs like a bat out of hell, right?"

"Right," Morris replies.

"Right!" Harry says. Then, to Morris: "What'd she say?"

"See ya, fellas," the woman says, and ambles down Broadway.

A few minutes later, Morris is telling Harry and me about a day last week where he had to leave at 10:00 a.m. "I run out of *Times* — somebody stole all seven bundles before I come here to work. They don't charge me for that, they give me credit, but I didn't make no money, either."

"They couldn't bring more?" Harry asks.

"I call *Times*, they tell me other dealers also complaining bundles stolen. They can only deliver three, so I had to close up early," Morris says. "I took vacation day. I went to the East Side to a Jewish deli and had a corned beef sandwich. They charge me $2, but it was good corned beef. Then I went to the zoo on Staten Island."

Morris shrugs. "Three hundred fifty *Times* is worth about $50. Maybe they take them up to the Bronx and sell them for $10, I don't know."

"The bastards," Harry says.

"Never happen before. One or two, often. But not seven. One time, I come and I find a guy loading bundles into station wagon. I said, 'What are you doing with those bundles?' He said he was delivering them to 96th Street. I said, 'Those are *my* bundles!' But, I let him go, just take back the bundles."

Harry

The conversation shifts to changes in the neighborhood.

Harry says:

When I come to the neighborhood, 1942, it was all beautiful, white neighborhood. Now, it's shitty. I'm afraid to walk the street. You're not safe. In the *daytime*, you're not safe, and as soon as it becomes five o'clock, I wouldn't come out if Columbus was here!

You're walkin' around, they come, 'Hey, bub! I wanna quarter!'

I tell 'em, 'I'm lookin' for a job!'

'Bullshit!' they say. 'Gimme the goddamn quarter!'

I say, 'If I had it, I'd give it to ya.' And they curse you and every goddamn thing, especially 95th Street and Broadway. You go to 95th from here, three or four will stop you. My advice? If anybody says anything to you, no matter what, you didn't hear nothin'. Look straight ahead. Keep walkin'. Because it's awful.

I can't do nothin' about it. I live in a rooming house, and I got cheap rent. I'm paying $50 a month and the same room above and below me now is $20 a week. All I got's my Social Security. So I stay in the jungle. My floor is all Black, and Haitian. That woman who called me her boy-friend? She lives on my floor. I'm the only white man up there.

I gotta play ball! When you're in Rome, do as the Romans do. If they say something, I'm with 'em.

There's one toilet for the floor. They go in the bathroom, they piss or something and they don't flush the toilet, I say to 'em, 'Hey! You forgot to flush the toilet.'

'What about it? So what?'

I say, "Nothin'. I'll go in and flush it for you.'

Or, they'll go in the kitchen, leave the table and the stove dirty. If I say, 'Wipe it off! Why should I wipe off yours?' they give me dirty looks. So I play ball with 'em. Whatever they say, okay, that's it. If I see that it's comin' to an argument or something, I say, 'Oh, well, maybe you're right.'

Like they say,

I never trouble trouble unless trouble troubles me.
And if trouble doesn't trouble me,
why should I trouble trouble?

In other words, the hell with it!

Alfredo

Harry points to someone approaching the newsstand. "There's another friend," he says.

True to his word, Alfredo has returned for his twice-daily "bless-ing." There are greetings all around, then he joins in the discussion.

Alfredo says:

I come over here in 1949. Most of the community was Jewish. Riverside Drive and West End Avenue was the best apartments in the city. Nice, solid construction, and everything. Everything. All the rich people, going to shows on Saturday nights. On Sundays and holidays, picnics on Riverside Drive on the grass, playing music. And such a beautiful view — it was very nice, very nice. Even over here on Broadway it was clean, you know? Clean, clean neighborhood.

Then, they start moving out. All the Jewish people are giving up their apartments over here and move out to the East Side, because they demolish the Third Avenue subway and the neighborhood got real swank. They start settling over there, and then Long Island, and Harlem start growing up and coming down this way. They still have some remains of the old timers, but very few, very few. It's dead over here now. Dead. Today, you can't even walk after dark.

The strain, it's economical, it's not social. The rents are so high, the stores that have been here ten years, twenty-five years, they have to move out because they can't afford no more. So new people come in. You see the Korean, Japanese, Chinese taking over. They don't care if they work ten hours, fifteen hours each day, as long as they make the money. The fruit store up the block? Those people are working fourteen, sixteen hours every day so they can pay the rent. It's a family, and they don't hire nobody, so they can make it. These guys who work for themselves? They have to pay double the rent. They can't stay no more. Oppenheimer, the butcher? He been here for more than thirty years. Just moved.

That change all the neighborhood. The Paris Hotel, here on 97th and West End Avenue? Fifteen years ago, used to be one of the best in New York, even better than the Waldorf Astoria. I lived there four years. Had an Olympic swimming pool was free for the guests, with hot water, a salon upstairs, sundeck. Beautiful! Most Beautiful! Ask Morris.

It start to deteriorate five, ten years ago. Deteriorate and deteriorate. Today, you're scared to step in. It's a hotel, but it's mostly a rooming house. You go over there now, one-third of the hotel is empty. And what they got in there is prostitutes, pimps, dope peddlers, and everything. You want the room, you pay the price, you got it, no questions asked.

They got a few full-timers over there, they can't move out because they pay little rent. But they suffer. You got a problem, you go over to the police station over here on 100th Street and say, 'Somebody rob me, somebody break into my room.'

The cops say, 'Where you live?'

'The Paris Hotel.'

'Oh, we don't endorse the management.'

That's all they say to you: 'We don't endorse the management.' To hell with it! Even cops.

That's the way the neighborhood has gone.

The Theater

Spanning the block between 96th and 97th Street is the half-demolished Riviera and Riverside Theaters building.

Demolition of the structure, once home to a magnificent 1,700-seat live theater, began last year, but it halted when the developer ran out of money, leaving the façade and the wall facing 96th Street still standing, unsupported by the rest of the block-sized structure. A few weeks later, the south wall collapsed in the middle of the night, crushing the line of cars parked alongside it and injuring two people hit by flying bricks.

Harry

Back to Harry:

A couple weeks ago, I seen this guy walking, and there's blood coming out on his head like he had a spigot on. He said he came out of an empty store, next to the theater. But I saw the window was broken, the bottom half was gone. So as he came out, he hit his head against the glass, made a gash.

He was Spanish. I come up to some Spanish people on the corner. I say, 'Tell him to sit down.' Somebody went to the telephone, dialed 9-1-1 for the police, emergency. An ambulance came about twenty, thirty minutes later. Police, no.

They all start saying that a rock fell down from the theater. I say, 'What are you talking about? He came out of the window.'

'Nah, nah, nah. We saw the rock.'

I took a few of them to the window. I say, 'Look, the blood is on the *other* side of the window, where he cut himself.'

And they say, 'Oh. Yeah, yeah.' But hundreds of people, they're all Spanish, are saying 'The rock, the rock. A rock fell and hit him on the head.' They all start saying, 'Sue them! You get thousands of dollars!'

'Sue 'em for what?' I say. 'No rock hit him. He did it to himself. He cut his head open with the glass there.'

'No, no, no, no!'

And I think to myself, 'Oh, boy. Maybe I'll get myself in trouble here.' So then I say, 'Yeah, I guess maybe you're right. Yeah, yeah, I think a rock did fall down.' I hadda say something, otherwise I get a knife in my back. I say, 'Yeah, yeah. A rock did fall down. Yeah.' And I'm thinking, 'All right. Where's the rock?'

Every day, there's something going on like that. This is the 24th Precinct. All the papers say this is the worst precinct in the whole city. There's more trouble here than Harlem.

Safety ...

Situation now is not safe here, as used to be. Every year it becomes more dangerous. You have a problem when you even sleep in your apartment. They got into my apartment twice, but they were disappointed because they were looking for money and I don't keep there. Only they cut my mattress.

I don't worry about sickness. I never was sick in my life. Never! I don't afraid, because I *believe* and hope I never will be sick up to the end of my life. I'm only afraid somebody shouldn't hurt me.

I'll tell you what happened. Last summer, it was Sunday, beautiful day. About two o'clock in the afternoon comes a colored fellow and leaves me a bike, here. Big bike. And he goes in supermarket. I was busy. He tells me, 'Can I leave my bike? I'll be right back.' Without asking my permission — I didn't tell him yes, okay. When he came back in about ten, fifteen minutes, the bicycle was gone. Somebody stole it.

So, his wife is with him. She got mad. I say, 'Listen, I didn't tell that you should leave the bike. I'm busy, I cannot watch your bike.' She beat me on the head with her bag and throw all my papers on the ground. And after she beat me, she took away my glasses and walked away. I couldn't fight her, her husband was standing there. All the people are looking didn't do a damn thing.

So, now I didn't have no glasses. It cost me more for new glasses than colored fellow's bike. So anybody wants to leave packages with me, I say 'I'm sorry.'

Hear what happen to me about six years ago: I came Sunday morning. Every day I come, here is milkman, you know, people go to work. Just when I open the door, somebody comes from the side. A guy was in a car, sitting, with a big knife. He came to me right away, held the knife to my head. 'Reach in your pocket. Give me your money.'

And *luckily*, I had $10 in my pocket. He took.

He put me, 'Lay down!' I lay down. 'Have you more?'

'No!'

'Turn around! Lie down here on the floor and turn around. Don't get up!'

When I got up, I didn't see him no more. But blood was coming from here, under ear. I go right away to the telephone booth, I call up the police, but in moment was police car. I told him, 'Listen what happened.' So they took me to Saint Luke's Hospital, they give me some kind of injection, for, you know, the point of the knife.

Luckily, I had $10. Suppose I wouldn't have? Suppose I come from home, I don't carry money? And even that, he was not satisfied.

And I tell you something between you and I: Later I saw him. It was Sunday morning, and he lived next to me — Hotel Yale, that is small, cheap hotel. I recognize. He had big eyes, and glasses. I didn't want to accuse, because how could I prove that was the same one? He said, 'Maybe I can help you?' I say, 'No, I don't need help.' I don't want him near. He probably would come and tell me, 'Give it to me," and then ... Well, I don't want to tell it.

I struggled enough for my livelihood. Now, you see I'm retired. I have no worries of anybody except that nobody should give me a knife, like those bums you see around here. You know what I mean? I come early in the morning, anything would happen, right? Or late at night on Saturday night. I'm not worrying, but in case should happen again, I would not resist. Right? Because you're never sure what could happen to you. Even I give him money, maybe he thinks I have more, who knows?

That's why I like when somebody's sitting with me. I have a Puerto Rican man who sits with me Saturday night, bodyguard. But even that is not good protection. Can come two guys. Right?

Besides, I have arguments with him. He borrows money from me. Eventually, he pays me, but he wants too much: 'Give me $10! Give me $8! Give me $5!' He's not working. He told me he gets about $550 a month — pension, Social Security, home relief, I don't know. But he is gambler, with racing. Sometimes he shows me bunch of money — fifteen hundred, thousand dollars — and other day, he's broke. And he is a big thief, too. He sits here, anybody pays him money, if I don't see it, he puts in the pocket.

Ah, what's the use to talk about it?

You have to be careful, right? These days, especially. I just look with my four eyes, that's all. When I am coming home, I look on both sides, to see if anybody's following. You have to watch.

Every dealer has this problem of safety. Every dealer, every building. I just try to be careful.

I live like in jungle.

Hats and Girls:

It hasn't rained since before noon, but the old man who comes down from the shul wears a raincoat over his black suit. "Can you lend me your hat?" he asks Morris. "I got a wedding next week."

"Everybody talks about my hat," Morris says.

"This is the third comment on the hat today," I tell the man in the raincoat.

"I bet all three were by men," he says. "You wait till the women come." He nods to Morris, then walks on.

"What time have you?" Morris asks. "Maybe I go check for mail."

I show him my watch.

"I'm a funny man," Morris muses. "I never carry handkerchief, I never wear a ring, I never wear a watch. When the people say, "What time is it?' I go like this." He pulls his pants leg up and his argyle sock down. "I say, 'I forgot my watch.'"

"Excuse me," says a petite young woman with a cute button nose, a $5 bill in her hand.

"Yes!" Morris says.

"*Times*, please."

Morris hands her a newspaper and change. "Five dollars."

"Comes an elderly woman," Morris says, "and I was busy besides that, and she gives me thirty pennies for two papers, and insisted I should count. I say, 'Lady, why should I count? I know you wouldn't give me more.'"

The drunk with the floppy hat stops by again, this time carrying a bottle in a paper bag. He emphatically utters his incomprehensible syllables, tips his hat again, and stumbles down the street, weaving from side-to-side with metronomic precision.

Morris tells me, "Comes to me a man, and he says, 'Morris, what's wrong with you?' I say, 'Forget that. Better ask what's *right* with me.'"

A woman with soft white hair hands Morris a subway token and he gives her an *Enquirer* and a *Daily News*.

She curtseys. "Thank you," she says in a voice as soft as her hair. Then her eyes dart between Morris and me and she adds, "You shouldn't copy one another."

Morris smiles. "*Adios*," he says.

She curtseys again and continues on her way. Morris circles his right ear with his index finger. "Cuckoo," he says. "But is good customer."

"Comes to me a Spanish fellow," Morris says. "He tells me, 'You have as much money as Rockefeller.' I say, 'No, Rockefeller has *less*.'" Morris laughs at his joke. I do my best to join him.

A red-haired woman in a green dress and silk scarf stops by. She hands Morris a cup of coffee. His smile lingers. As she and Morris speak Russian together, I see his hard edge fade. Morris hands her a *Post*. "I'll see you later," Morris says in English. She walks to the corner and waits for a break in traffic.

Morris returns to his stool and picks up a *Forward* he's been scanning for cutouts. I sit on the crate next to him and raise an eyebrow as I nod my head in the redhead's direction.

"That's my girlfriend," Morris says.

The surprise registers on my face. Morris shakes his head. "No. Not girlfriend. Good friend, good woman. She likes me, I like her. She brings me coffee sometimes and she takes care of the newsstand while

I am gone. I say, 'Take care. I'm going home for a minute' and she will do. So I give her papers once in a while."

"I see," I say.

"She's not *girlfriend*," Morris repeats. "She's too high class of a woman. If I would go out with her, I would have to spend $50. And for her you must have a car. I don't need that."

"I see," I say again.

"My girlfriend doesn't live here," Morris says. "She's on East Side. I know her twelve years. She is from Yemen. She's Jewish, she's nice. And she's not expensive. With her I don't have to spend a lot of money — $6, $7 on her, $5. Usually, we go to Jewish shows, movie, and to cafeteria to eat." He leans back and smiles. "Naturally, after, I go to her house and I do my sex job, too."

"Really? At 73?"

Morris nods. "At 73."

"Congratulations!" I say.

Morris smiles again. "I am still potent," he says.

The Newsstand Today ...

My wife died twelve years ago and my mother died six years ago. When my mother died she was 90 and was still working, and I'm still working.

I work every day. And I enjoy my work, because you see, fresh air makes me healthy. I never get sick, I never missed a day. And I never have a day off. Well, I take a month vacation, but that's only for the last thirteen, fifteen years.

The people ask me, 'Why don't you take a day off?' I tell them, 'I only believe in hard labor.' Well, I'm just joking. I don't believe in hard work too much. Some days I have to work, not hard, but longer hours, but I know I don't have to support my wife and children no more, right?

I get up like a soldier. I know I have to do, and I get up. I work early in the morning till afternoon — two, three o'clock. I'm here all day. When my mother was here, she used to change with me every three hours. Now, I am alone. So, I drink coffee. That's my food. You know what I mean?

Weather, I don't give a care. In the rain, I go under awning from Sloan's, awning from cleaners. I'm here a long time, the neighbors very good to me. As a matter of fact, the other day when it was a big rain, they let me to stay inside, in the entrance. Wintertime, I don't feel cold, I'll tell you why: I put here electric heater to warm my hands. I don't need no gloves. Body — uhh! — I'm protected. So I don't give a care.

To have a newsstand don't mean that you can make a living at it. You need customers to buy papers. But I'm here for so many years, they come to me.

Every morning I go to subway, buy tokens. Most of the time, I give to my customers for change. It's a good idea. They give me a dollar, I give them a quarter with a token, that's 75¢. Instant change, and they have a token. Tokens *better* than quarters. It's quicker, and I don't have to go in the bank for quarters, and customers don't have to stand in line in the token booth. They are good, and I'm good.

Everybody likes me in this neighborhood. First of all, a very long time they know me as a hard worker. They know I never fail and I'm honest. And I always try to serve them cheerfully. They always find me in a good mood, and I make all kinds of jokes. Like, somebody comes to me, I say, 'Good morning, and welcome to my 15¢.' Or, a man comes to me, wintertime, was very cold, and he tells me: 'Keep cool.' And besides that, I show them my writings. They're proud, of course, that I'm a good father, because they know all about my sons.

Used to be another newsstand next block. At that time I sell less. But he's not there for about four years, so all the customers come here. The people go by here on way to subway, they need to buy papers. *Times* every day I used to sell 150, now I sell 300. *News*, I sell about 150. Spanish paper, I sell about fifty, as I told you. The others, I sell only two, three. I make about twenty percent.

People ask me, 'Why do I sell the *Daily World*, which is communist paper?' I say, 'You tell me not to sell the *Daily World*, the other tell me not to sell the capitalist paper. If I listen everybody, I go out of business!' I don't care what they buy. Let them buy shit, what I care, as long as I make profit, right?

Only thing is, I don't sell nothing sexual. Some of them have it, but not on display. Downtown, they have on display. But I cannot sell and

I don't want to sell this paper, because, you see, I'm a community dealer. If I had on display that, children come, and they might look, I lose my reputation as honest dealer. Anyway, to me is important to sell *Times* and *News*, to make my living. I don't want to work here extra couple hours to make 5¢ on those magazines.

Here I work every day, I *just* make a living. If I would be an elevator man who works five days, I would make more. But I'm happy. I don't want to be elevator man. I want to stay here.

I don't have to work anymore. After all, I don't need much money to live. My rent is cheap — I live there a long time — my food is not expensive, my clothes I have plenty. So why should I work? I'm not going to live to 120, right? I could go without work.

But I feel joy in working. I'm my own boss. I see people. I do cutouts. And, I make a live dollar. Do you know what I mean, a live dollar? That means dollar is always active — a dollar that I spend today I make tomorrow another one, because I'm working. If I don't work, I only can depend on what I have, right?

Besides, the one day that I *don't* work I cannot sleep longer anyway — I'm accustomed to get up early in the morning. So: Ehh! Uhh! And then I get up, and then I'm lazy and I feel already not in my right. You know only days I don't work? Jewish holidays. Yom Kippur. Because it's a shul. It will be disgrace if I should work those days — they throw me out.

So those days, I don't work. And I don't know what to do with myself. I get lost.

The Teacher:

On the crate next to me, behind stacks of newspapers, sits a man in his middle thirties, his face oval, hair longish and red-brown, his glasses gold with wire rims, much like mine. At the moment he's reading the *Financial Times*.

"Do you come here often?" I ask, as if I were trying to pick him up at a bar.

"Yes," he says.

"How come?"

"How come I come? You see that I read all the papers? Don't you see that?" He shows me the paper he's reading. He speaks with an Eastern European accent I can't yet place. His tone is sharp.

"It's my library. I read all the newspapers here." He waves a hand across the sea of periodicals surrounding him. "I can take a quick look at the *Wall Street Journal*, at Jewish papers, at all the range of papers, free."

He sets the *Financial Times* down. "And I'm not the only one. There are maybe fifteen guys every day coming. We are all friends. You come, especially the weekend, you'll see how many." He points behind him to the shul vestibule. "Sometimes they are sitting on the steps like a reading room."

I nod. I've noticed. "Also, Morris talks to us, he is not lonely. And, it gives him a certain safety. He doesn't want to be alone here. So, he has his considerations for that, too." He pauses for a moment, tips his head first one way and then the other. "I think I gave you a fair answer, from all sides."

"How long have you known Morris?"

"Two years, since I am in the neighborhood. First, I just was buying papers, and gradually I got to know him. I'm very good friends with him."

Out of the corner of my eye, I notice someone buying a *Times*. "Twenty cents," I hear Morris say.

"For me it's very convenient, coming here," the teacher says. "I'm teaching in a Jewish parochial school, a high school on Bank Street, if you know the neighborhood. My work is afternoons and evenings, so soon I am going home and having lunch and then I'll go there."

Another customer buys the *Voice*. He hands Morris a dollar. "You want token?" Morris asks.

"It's an opportunity to read all those papers," the teacher explains. "I mean, without paying money! You see, I also borrow some papers. When I came here — I don't know if you saw — I gave him a paper that I had home. I borrowed from him and returned. I'm not the only one, by the way; it's a whole Chinese business, a cycle."

I hear Morris talking with another customer. "No more *News*?" the customer asks. His voice has an unexpected twang that reminds me of Burl Ives.

"No more," Morris says.

Morris takes off his apron and stuffs it in the crate where he stores his shoebox and cutouts. To the teacher, he says, "I go home for mail for a few minutes. You take care?"

"If you go home, yes," the teacher says.

"Nothing else."

"All right."

"Okay, I'll be right back." He gives the teacher a handful of nickels, dimes, and quarters. "That's all," he says. "I have no more change. Don't give nobody without paper. Okay?" The teacher nods, firmly.

"I hope the mail is there," Morris says.

As he is about to leave, a woman taps him on the shoulder. "Would you give me change for a quarter?"

"Not yet, not yet," Morris tells her.

To me, he says, "I'll show to you articles about my sons." He glances at the teacher. "I'll be home. I'll be back."

Morris readjusts his pants, then shuffles down Broadway.

"Usually he gives change to everybody," the teacher says. "Anybody that passes by here, they all know that he gives them change. Many people also cash checks."

A customer asks, "No *News*?"

"No, sorry, all sold," the teacher says. "We have the *Post*."

"I'll try 96th Street," the customer says.

"Morris is not in a good mood today, so he hollers a little," the teacher says. "He's a little bothered with all the small change and such. After all, he's not a young man, so he has his ups and downs. There are days when he's in a very jovial mood."

Another customer approaches, bearing a copy of the *Post*.

"Yes, sir," the teacher says. The customer hands him 20¢, which the teacher stuffs under a newspaper with the rest of the change.

He points to my steno pad. "For whom are you writing?"

"For myself," I say. "I'm writing a book."

The teacher nods. "Oh, you'll find a lot, here," he says. "But also go with him home. You'll see many things. You'll see how he lives, first of all. Then he'll show you all kinds of pictures, tracing back to his history. He speaks several languages, as you know: Russian, Spanish, English, and Yiddish. I don't know if you had an opportunity to see him exchanging with conversations with customers in Spanish, Russian, one after the other."

"Yes, it's interesting," I say. "It's also interesting that he likes what he does, and that he does it even though he doesn't have to."

"He works here voluntarily," the teacher agrees. "He is 73 years old."

"*Diario*?" a Puerto Rican man asks hopefully.

The teacher glances around. "Ah, sorry, No *Diario* left." He thinks for a moment. "*No más.*"

"*Gracias*," the customer says.

The teacher turns back to me. He tips his head toward the entrance to the shul. "Morris never goes to the synagogue, he's not religious at all, but yet he will feel embarrassed because he is not. It is a part of him that's what we call mixed feelings."

"How do you mean?" I ask.

"What I tell you here is very accurate, in my opinion. You talk to him, ask him, he'll tell you the same thing." Nevertheless, he lowers his voice. "He was really brainwashed that religion is opium, like Lenin said. The man was molded in his very young age, in his teens, in Russia, when the Revolution took place —if you want to call it Revolution, or the seizure of power by the Bolsheviks. I was born also in what is the Soviet Union, now, but it's really Lithuania.

"His upbringing, maybe until the age of 10, was in a Jewish *heder*, a religious school. But later, of course, after 1917, the Jewish community was completely shattered by the communists: All the institutions were abolished, closed down forcibly. And being a young man, enthusiastic, he was influenced by certain of those ideas. Nevertheless, he left the country, I don't know when, in '21 or '22. I think his brother was killed in the civil war there, or his father died young — he'll tell you the details of it. He'll show you the pictures, too, when you visit him at home.

"So, he's not practicing religion, he's not going to synagogue. However, he has strong sentiments about his Jewish origins. He's — what you call it — he's a very fervid Jewish ethnic and nationalist. His strong support for Israel, his contributions: He gives a lot of money to various schools and charities in the Jewish community. So you see, this is a much more encompassing thing than just strictly religion, as far as Jews are concerned. It's a much wider phenomenon, and he's very much about it."

The teacher leans back and folds his arms across his chest. "I would say that's the explanation."

Later, I ask Morris if I can visit him at home, away from the noise and hustle and bustle of the corner. He declines. "Since my mother died six years ago," he tells me, "I don't let nobody come into my house."

I feel the distinction between myself and Morris's newsstand friends.

Home ...

I have six-room apartment, and right around the corner. My apartment is rent-controlled and I live there forty years, so I don't pay no more rent than you pay for one room. It's very handsome, because I don't have to go on subway, and in two minutes I am here.

But my house is dirty. I don't even take care of it. I hate to do home work except the very little bit for my food, which I must have.

I'm very neglectable. You know what I mean? Very neglectable. Since my children left, my wife died, mother died, I live in only three rooms. My shirts, I don't give to the laundry once in three months. My shoes, my clothes, all over the room. I cannot stay too much home. I have nobody to talk to. That's why I don't take care of my apartment, because I feel loneliness to do that. So I neglect.

I have telephone home. I only had a call from friend once. My family — my sister, my brother — I don't talk. I never use, except that my son every once in a while calls me up, or my girlfriend I speak every night. That's all.

I never had a car and I don't want to have a car because I don't *need* a car. It's a headache. I don't go no place. Not to friends, where they live, and not to nobody. Just, right here. I have a lot relatives here, but nobody invites me, nobody tells me, and I don't care about it. I have no time. Well, with my woman friend I do go out once in a while, but like Sunday, she went to her relatives, so I went to Ninth Avenue by myself. We used to go out Friday night, now I go out with her once in three weeks, to eat, movie, something like that.

As young man, I had my family. I didn't need no friends, because my mother, my wife were there. I come home for three hours, I sleep, my wife makes me dinner. Now, I am alone, except my friends here helping me.

I'm lonely, but I have no time for lonely. I stay here all day. In afternoon, I am busy to go buy food. I come home, I eat, right away I lie in bed. I feel my age — I get tired very, very easy. Then, I return here and I am busy to make my returns. That's work, too. I have to sort them, then I have to make a list, so I should know if they gave me right credit for the papers.

Comes nighttime, I watch television for one hour. Mostly I like to see all about wild animals. Eight o'clock tonight will be something about bears. Yesterday, was all about eagles, because they're on brink of extinction. Did you watch that?

And then I go to sleep. That's every day.

I don't read books. I have no hobbies. Only hobby I have is the cutouts.

And then ... also I have hobby to look at nice magazine writing, nice wording, like you saw the envelopes I write. I try to memorize how to write that. And a hobby I like is to see window shopping: go on Times Square. And I have a hobby to see museums, zoos, and to see on television all about animal world, which is my best hobby. And, of course, if I can see musical or something, it's all right. And then I have a hobby to walk. Before, I used to walk twenty, thirty, forty blocks in New York. When you travel by bus and subway, you don't see. I like to walk and see slowly all that. That's another hobby. And then I go to Seattle, Staten Island, New Jersey.

That's my hobbies. And I haven't got much time for hobbies, either.

Lonesome, yeah, I am sometimes lonesome. But that's why I like newsstand, because I spend my time, and I make couple dollars, too. I enjoy it, even in wintertime, doesn't bother me. If some time I don't be able to work longer, I would work only couple hours in the morning and go home. Still I make my living, right? How much I need? I don't spend much.

So, I fill my time, and I have no time to be lonely, and I'm not lonely. I'm happy.

The Translator:

A thin, older woman, her gray hair mostly covered by a blue and silver scarf, approaches the newsstand. "I see you have a new hat today," she says.

"Yes, that's right," Morris says.

She smiles. "Every day you have something new."

They exchange a few words in Russian. Morris moves the milk crate he has been sitting on to a space behind the stacks of papers. "You sit there," Morris says.

She takes a moment to catch her breath. "Thank you," she says.

Chivalrous, I think. But then Morris adds, "I go to bank, and I'll be right back. Okay?"

She assents. He hands her some change, which she pours into a depression she's made in her lap.

After Morris leaves, I sit beside her and introduce myself. She tells me she is Mrs. Jacobson.

"You're one of Morris's friends who reads the papers and helps him out?"

She shrugs. "We have known each other for a long time," she says. "I do it often for him."

"*Voice*," a student-type says, tapping his foot, offering a dollar bill. She takes it and hands him 50¢.

"Thanks!" he says, and hurries off.

"My friends see me here, they look at me strangely, but I don't care. I like to sell papers," she says.

Between customers, she tells me about her life.

"I grew up in St. Petersburg. We were allowed to move there even though we were Jews because my father was highly trained construction engineer. When I was young, he built a sugar factory in Odessa. He took the whole family there to see it.

"I went to school in St. Petersburg. I graduated from Bestuzhev. At the time, was the only women's college in all of Russia. Very well known. Books were written about that school.

"I speak French and German both. My family was wealthy and we had a German maid and a French maid, so I had a chance to speak these languages at home. My mother also encouraged me to learn English because you never know what will happen to you. For me, German and French were enough. It happened she was right, but I wanted to play the piano and to dance! I didn't learn English until I came to America." She sighs. "That was in 1945, after the war. I didn't want to leave, but we had no choice. I don't like to think about those times."

An old man with a copy of the *Forward* in hand smiles and greets her. They speak briefly in Yiddish.

"We came first to Philadelphia," she continues. "My husband was a Russian lawyer, and I passed the foreign service examination. He made translations for the State Department and I got a job as translator for United Nations. That is how I came to New York."

She pauses to catch her breath. "I was for twenty years with United Nations. I was translating from French to Russian and from Russian into French. Many, many Russians were there, Soviet people. Very nice people, very enjoyable, *cultured* people. But still, I hate the government." Another pause, longer. She continues, more quietly. "I was sent twice to Paris. I was very happy. That was the best time of my life. And then, I lost my husband, my two sisters, my brother ..."

Tears come. "I have my son and his wife, and two college boys in Philadelphia, my grandsons." She pulls a handkerchief from her purse and wipes her eyes. "My son wants me to live with them, but I don't want to be a burden — they have their lives." She sighs again. "We didn't go out when I worked for U.N. We never went to restaurants, always ate at home. We didn't have time. We were always working so *hard*. Now he is gone."

A couple of teenage boys drift by, one of them carrying a boom box on his shoulder. He's playing funk, loud, while the other boy dances alongside him.

"Forgive me for saying, but American young people are coarse and uncultured, not like at home," Mrs. Jacobson observes. "At home, even the *children* know literature and poetry."

I don't know how to respond. To tell her that I, a young American, love literature and poetry, too, would seem defensive — although it is true.

More customers arrive. I watch as she attends to them. Unlike Morris, Mrs. Jacobson is slow and deliberate, her hand trembling as she takes their money and makes change.

A few minutes later, Jonas swings by on his return trip from the laundromat. He sets down his duffle bag and I introduce Mrs. Jacobson. Jonas, intuiting her origin, introduces himself in Russian.

"*Pazvol'tye predstavitsa,*" he says, then adds, offering her his hand, "Jonas."

Soon, they are engaged in what appears to be half conversation, half recitation, with first Jonas, and then eventually Mrs. Jacobson, speaking in verse. She comes alive, performing in what seems to be a call and response.

Customers, momentarily as enthralled as I am, stand and watch. Perhaps because they notice the small audience they have gathered, Jonas and Mrs. Jacobson end their impromptu recitation. While Mrs. Jacobson busies herself with selling papers, I take the opportunity to find out what I have just witnessed.

"We were reciting Pushkin," Jonas says. "She told me she likes Russian poetry."

"You know Pushkin by heart?"

"Oh, just a few poems," Jonas says. I'm impressed and tell him so. Although I spent my last three years in college studying and writing poetry, there is little I could recite in English, much less in another language.

Jonas shrugs off the compliment. "One was an elegy, just called 'An Elegy'," he explains. "It talks about a man who is moving into middle age and reminisces about his youth, the drunken orgies they used to have and how wonderful it all was. Then he looks on to death and says, 'Well, it was nice. Maybe there will be good times in the future, too.' Another was a Byronic-sounding poem about Georgia, in the south of Russia. Pushkin lived there for a while. He talks about having visions of a girl he once knew, and how the songs someone is singing remind him of that girl, and how painful it is to remember this other life he had. And another poem is famous even here because it's from a Scottish ballad. You've probably heard it," Jonas says. He sings:

> As I was walking all alane,
> I heard two corbies makin' a mane.
> The one unto the other did say,
> Where shall we go and dine today?
> Where shall we go and dine today?

"It's about two ravens discussing where they'll get their next meal. One tells the other there's a dead knight lying under a tree in the field. It's a mystery poem, because it leads you to believe that the knight's wife knows why he was killed, and who killed him, and it seems like the one who killed him is going to be coming to stay with her that night. But the poem's not explicit about it."

Jonas stoops to pick up his duffle bag and slings it over his shoulder. "The last one she knows much better than I do. I know just the first few lines. It's called 'The Bronze Horseman.' It's about the statue of Peter the Great riding down on a poor, unfortunate citizen of St. Petersburg who dared to criticize Peter for the way he reigned."

Jonas, who in this moment reminds me of the compassionate, gentle Prince Myshkin of Dostoyevsky's novel *The Idiot*, takes his laundry and his leave. Watching after him, Mrs. Jacobson observes, "Very nice. You feel intelligence from him. Education."

With Jonas's departure (and Pushkin's), Mrs. Jacobson wilts again. She points toward a woman slowly walking toward the newsstand, hunched over, leaning on a tall red cane. "She is all alone, and very sick. And every day she walks. This, you have to look forward to?" Mrs. Jacobson says.

She's still short of breath from her recitation. "Are you okay? I ask.

"Do you really want to know?"

"Yes, of course."

"I am not well," she says. "Illness started after my husband died. I was on vacation, and my brother-in-law came. I couldn't breathe. Doctor says it's *nervous*. Sometimes, it's more quiet, but today I can't breathe."

She rummages in her purse.

"I live on West 98th and West End Avenue. I used to walk fifty blocks when there was the strike and I was at United Nations. Fifty numbered blocks and six avenue blocks! The doctor says maybe I will be able to walk better again, but I don't think so. Now I cannot walk even two blocks to drugstore."

At last she finds what she's been looking for and produces an envelope. "They gave me this, but I didn't pick it up." She hands the envelope to me. Inside it is a prescription.

"I can go," I say. "What's your pharmacy?"

She tells me. "But you will have to wait there fifteen minutes at least," she says.

"It's not a problem," I say.

"Young man, I don't know how to thank you."

"Jonas really liked reciting Pushkin with you. And I like helping you," I say.

She hands me a $5 bill. "After today, I can tell my friends that there are some nice young American people. Because not all of them are."

Now it's my turn to shrug off a compliment. "If Morris comes back before I do," I say, "can you tell him where I went, and that I'll be back soon?"

Health ...

Happen to be that I am physically well developed. I mean, strong. I never get sick. And if I do have cold, I don't pay attention. I never get sick in my life, except accidents. Or that time when the blood was coming up. That was after my mother died, four or five years ago.

In winter I have electric heater to keep warm my hands. When it was very cold day, I used also to put my mouth to heater to warm me up. So, the hot air in my lungs, from the heater, mixing up with the cold air, irritate my lung. All of a sudden, sometime later, I come home, uhh! And a spoon of blood come out. Blood!

I felt chest. God damn, I feel perfectly. So what the hell the blood comes out? What for? And then another day, came out less blood. I got scared — I don't know what the hell to do. I thought maybe I'll die all of a suddenly.

I went to hospital. I say, 'Listen what happened to me: Blood came out from my mouth. Must be something wrong.' They check out my blood, my skin. They say, 'Nothing wrong.' Nothing wrong! I say, 'But the blood came out! Where is that from?' They tell me, 'We'll have to take you for observation.'

They took me for observation. They keep me for two weeks, and then the doctors told me, 'You have irritation the upper part of the lungs.' I told the doctor, 'I know where that comes from! That comes from my heater.' He says he doesn't think. He thinks it comes from my feet, because I have varicose veins. He gave me rubber socks and everything, but I still say that comes from the heater.

Now, when I use the heater, I never put my mouth. I put up to warm my neck, but not my mouth. Every morning, I cough, and it comes out like from the nose, and that's from the irritation. But I feel all right. There must be some kind of a little hole in my lungs.

Pictures:

When I return from the pharmacy, Mrs. Jacobson's medication in hand, I see that Morris has also returned. He isn't empty-handed, either.

Gathered around him are Mrs. Jacobson and the cleaner from next door. Morris is showing them color snapshots. He peels pictures from a small stack, passes them to Mrs. Jacobson or the cleaner, and then, afterwards, sets them on a space he's cleared on the bench. He invites me to join them. I'm reminded of being a captive audience for my father's slide shows and embarrassing home movies, but of course I comply.

Harry joins us a minute after I do. "Hi!" he says to Morris. He gives me his characteristic smile.

"Hello," Morris says, barely taking his eyes off the photos he's displaying.

The first several pictures are of Morris and his family at his grandson's Bar Mitzvah celebration last summer. "This is at the table, there, at the Bar Mitzvah," Morris is saying. "This is my grandson, and this is my in-laws. This is me, and this is my other son in Jersey."

The next photo shows a large group wearing suits and yarmulkas, posing outside a suburban temple. The Bar Mitzvah boy is front and center. "This is the best picture," the cleaner says. "This here is the best."

"Who are all these people?" I ask.

"All my cousins," Morris says.

A customer picks up a *Post* and holds out a dollar. Morris takes the bill and stuffs it in his apron, then retrieves a handful of pictures from a plastic bag. "This was when I went to Lake ... Lake ... I forget. Lake Chelan."

"Can you *please* give me 75¢?" the customer says.

Harry takes Morris by the shoulder and nudges him in the customer's direction. "You're so busy, you don't want to make the change?" he asks.

"I'll make right away," Morris says.

After this brief interruption, we return to our usual programming.

132

Some of the same characters reappear in the next batch of pictures, but the scene is colored in deep greens, luminescent blues, and blinding whites. "You see Indian, that?" Morris asks. He points to what looks like a totem pole. "Next to this is my grandson, standing."

Morris peels another picture from the pile. "This is, I'm *in* Lake Chelan, on the back of boat, and there is mountains. It was very sunny day."

"I have more," Morris says as he dips his hand into the plastic bag. He places a photo on the bench and we are in the suburbs again. "This is, I'm in my son's yard, former home — he bought another home. In the front of the house, I was standing." He turns to me. "How do I look?"

Surprised by the question, I lean in for a closer view. From the past, Morris looks back at me with a slightly strained smile. I say, "You look younger."

"Well, that was about seven years ago," he says.

We return to the mountains: A rustic inn, brown statues, gleaming water, brilliant sky. "Also at Lake Chelan. Mountains in the background. You see mountains?"

We all ooh and ahh appropriately. Morris continues: "This is the boat we were riding in the Lake Chelan. Lake is very deep and very long, in the state of Washington among the wilderness, among the mountains. Here are all the mountains." He passes the photo to me, and I hand it to Mrs. Jacobson, who hands it to Harry, and then to the cleaner, who hands it back to Morris, who lays it on the bench.

"This is, I was on Mount Rainier, on the very top, there is no more road, and this is Sunnyside Inn, something like that. I was standing on the mountain. And this is the Inn, Paradise Inn. And there was a mountain of snow in the front of it big as a house. You go Mount Rainier, and then you zig-zag, and then that is where you get your rest. Paradise Inn, on Mount Rainier. My son took the pictures."

Morris glances around. "Customers waiting," he says. He gathers the photos back into a pile, stuffs the pile into the plastic bag, and stows the bag under the bench.

"Okay, enough," he says.

He takes a $5 bill from another customer and turns to me again. As if this detour to the Pacific Northwest were only for my benefit, he adds, "You know what? I need money, too. What do you think, I millionaire?"

Food ...

The only thing I'm unhappy is that I haven't got nobody to take care with my food. It's the most problem that I have: Food. I don't eat good.

I nosh. I stay here all day, I don't know what the hell to eat. I know people, I say bring me a sandwich. I send a lady to get me tea. I send for hamburgers. I get an apple, a pear, cream cheese.

You see how many coffees I drink? Everybody brings me coffee. But that's not the point. The point is not the coffee or the money that I spend. The matter is the sugar that I eat. Too much sugar! I cannot enjoy coffee if it's not sweet — I cannot drink. I take three spoon of sugar in every coffee, so that's eighteen spoon of sugar a day, which is too much. At my age, they say I may get diabetes. Who knows? But so far, I do all right.

Now, they tell me to get another sugar, Sweet and Low. I'm afraid to take it, because that must be a chemical. I would drink at least two, three of them, every coffee. I'm afraid that if I would drink ten, twelve a day of those Sweet and Low, maybe it makes to my body more damage than the sugar, because sugar is natural and that is a chemical. So I use sugar. To hell with it.

When I come home, I don't know how to cook. What do I do? I haven't got nobody. I buy strawberry with sour cream, or I buy lox or herring, or whitefish with onions and tomato soup. I eat. Of course, after, I'm not *hungry*, but it's not the same food I eat when my wife was alive. I like good food, good homemade food.

Like, yesterday, I went Ninth Avenue. There was a big fair, so I went over there. There is a lot of food, but, *none* of them I could eat, because all junky food — Chinese and Italian shit junk food. It's not a food like a man should eat. Then, after it was over, I was hungry, I want to go downtown to eat Jewish food, but I am tired. I went to 42nd Street and I had steak that costs you two-fifty, which I don't care to eat it either, but it's better than to eat that junk food they were selling on Ninth Avenue.

If I have time, I go downtown to eat. You can go any place with subways, with buses. Transportation for the senior citizen is reasonable — I pay 25¢, only — and good dinner costs me three and a half, four dollars. That's a little expensive, but I hate to eat whatever I buy from groceries because it's not cooked.

I knew better about food than you do. My mother never cooked, but my wife cooked good dinner for me. Now I haven't got those dinners. But, you can't have everything, right? That, I got compromise. It's not so terrible for a person alone.

My Partner Is All the People Whom I Know:

The weather has turned again. It's raining heavily, and it feels like the temperature has dropped twenty degrees in the past hour. "I wish they stole papers today, and do me favor," Morris says. "I could go home!"

I'm standing with him in the vestibule of the shul, where he's set up a makeshift newsstand. When customers come, he grabs a paper from one of the stacks and quickly completes each exchange. "Friend from the cleaners offer I move my papers under the awning, but I said no, I stay here," Morris says. He rubs his rain-spattered arms briskly. "*Times* said it right this morning: 'Unseasonable cold.' I didn't prepare."

Harry, wearing a black raincoat and a hat, soon joins us in the vestibule. He unsnaps the raincoat and removes a loosely folded *Forward* from his jacket pocket and hands it to Morris, who sets it on the stack of *New York Post*.

"Good idea," Morris says, tugging lightly on Harry's raincoat. "I have in cellar." He holds up two fingers. "Two minutes," he says.

Morris hands Harry his apron. Harry puts it on and takes a step forward. Morris hurries down the stairs.

"Do you mind watching the newsstand for Morris?" I ask Harry.

"Nah," he says. "One hand washes the other. Nobody reads the papers for nothing. We all do different favors for him. You saw that guy bringing coffee? He brings coffee, he picks up a paper, or he picks it up before and brings it back, like I did. Or now, he goes downstairs, customers come, I'll take care of 'em. Or he says, 'I gotta go home for ten minutes.' Ten minutes. Shit! It takes him half an hour. And ... that's it. Like I said, one hand washes the other."

Morris returns with a khaki poncho slung over one arm. Harry hands him the apron. "Thank you," Morris says. He dons the apron and poncho and returns to his place in the doorway.

It's still raining cats and dogs, and there's not a customer to be seen. "Your friends have been telling me about the relationships you have, how you do favors for each other," I say.

"What kind of favors?" Morris says, with unexpected harshness. He gives Harry a sharp look. Harry shrugs and displays his clown smile. "I have no favors," Morris says. "People do me favors because I go away — I go home, I go for my mail, I have to eat breakfast — they watch my stand. I am alone, right? That's the favor."

Harry steps forward to defend his friend. "And the people — like me, I read the papers. When I'm finished, I put it back."

"So, that's friends using me too, right? Morris says. "You see they take my paper free, which no other newsstand would let them. I have to let them, because they watch me, and I have to give them something." Gesturing toward the basement stairs, Morris says, "Today, I went down there, he watches my papers for two minutes. I have to trust my friends, somebody I know, right? That's the way. And I work every day."

Harry and Morris momentarily transform into a chorus of old men. Together, they shout: "One hand washes the other!"

Harry sings, *That's the sto-ry!* and I can imagine him, under different circumstances, doing a little soft-shoe.

"That's all!" Morris says. "That's what is the relation of the people. I have no people to help me. I am alone, right? So I need a friend."

In a softer voice he elaborates. "Now it rains. Luckily, I am dry, I go downstairs for raincoat. Sometimes I am all wet, I have to rush home to change my clothes. I can't leave strange people here to watch my stand ten minutes. I need somebody whom I *know*, and who is honest, too, right? Because when I'm not here, he might take all the money and give me *bupkis*. Five dollars business, he'll give me only $1."

"Right! Or $2!" Harry says.

"So it would be too expensive. So .... that's kind of relationship."

A young Black man steps out of a cab and dashes up to the doorway, covering his head with a briefcase. "You got a *News*?"

"Sold out," Harry says. "Want a *Post*?"

The man nods. Harry hands him a *New York Post* and takes a quarter.

"How many people do you have this kind of relationship with?" I ask Morris.

"Everybody I can see trust," Morris says. "Him most frequently. Comes to me in the morning and the afternoon. If I go home for mail, because I want to send my son whatever I got that is important for me to put in letter to him. Or to bank, to deposit some money. Or I go to eat. Or — excuse me — or I go in bathroom, too. You must have friends, right?" Morris claps a hand on Harry's shoulder. Harry shrugs again, but his smile is warm and not the least bit comical.

"So," Morris says, "I have no wife, no children to help me, right? Everybody has a wife, or children, or partner. I haven't got. My partner is all the people whom I know."

Ambition ...

Here on Broadway, you see prostitute, drug addict, people sleeping on bench. I think what every good citizen think about it: They're just nonsense, to the good people who live in this neighborhood. Maybe they do like that because they have no ambition, I'm not that smart to know. All I know about is *my* people. To be a Jew, that's all.

Where did you see a Jewish people like that? You don't find no Jewish people to be like that because Jewish people is *ambitious* people. We Jews are ambitious to make better our living, to give our children better living. And teach them to be Jewish, like a Jew should be.

If you have no ambition, even you have a light work, it's hard to you. But if you have hard work and you have a lot ambition, then it's not hard, right? Take example from me: Wintertime I stay here, work, cold, and I'm not desperate. Why? Because I have ambition.

You know what makes the Eastern European Jews? The father may be a shoemaker, but he wants his son to be a doctor or engineer. You know that? Every Jew. Used to be all businesses here on Broadway owned by Jewish. Because Jews have improved their living, right? They are not like other nationalities. So, every Jew, he may be a carpenter, he may be a shoemaker, but his children are doctor, engineers, and so on.

I know my people. Always Jewish people, we struggle for life. In Europe, when we came to America, we all struggle for better livelihood, you understand? Every doorman has a car, right? A car costs money, and they don't need no car. Well, let's me say, if I send my son to college, it's because I ate less. I didn't have no luxuries. I didn't have no car.

Sons:

When the rain stops, Morris quickly reassembles his newsstand, this time allowing me (and Harry) to help with the crates and bundles. Harry soon takes his leave, and for the moment, it's just me and Morris at the stand.

The last item to come out of temporary storage is Morris's shoebox with its collection of today's cutouts, the plastic bag of photos and, as he promised, magazine stories about his sons.

"Here is my son, Elliot Kavesh," he says, handing me a photocopied clipping. "You see *Boeing News*, March 18, 1971? I have also more, different ones."

I read the short article:

Winning cost-savings awards is not a new experience for Elliot Kavesh, SRAM engineer. In 1970, he was selected as the SRAM cost-improvement program Man of the Month on two occasions. He recently was named Aerospace Group Suggestion System Man of the Month, an award seldom received by engineering employees. Kavesh suggested reducing the cost of accommodations at certain hotels and motels for employees on travel assignments by making the reservations direct, rather than through a central reservation service. He received an award of $1369 for his idea.

Morris rummages in the shoebox and retrieves more photocopies, each folded into thirds, as if they arrived in a business-sized envelope.

He carefully unfolds them. "Now, this is two magazines, 1973, *Business Week* and *Chemical Engineering News*," he says.

These articles are much longer. One is headlined, ALLIED DEVELOPS NEW AMORPHOUS ALLOYS.

"This is article about my son Sheldon," Morris says. He skims the article, skipping from place to place, pointing out Sheldon' name each time he is mentioned. "Here is Sheldon Kavesh, my son. Here is all about that." Morris hands me the page, which describes his son as the inventor of an alloy used to create metal filaments wound into spools of wire.

The drunk with the floppy hat, now sans hat, intrudes. "Baap! Woop!" he says. Morris shoos him away. "C'mon, c'mon! *¡Venga! ¡Despues!*" Morris cries.

Unrattled by this intrusion, Morris shows me the *Chemical Engineering News* article on the new alloy. "Okay. About my son, mentions again. Twice mention." He runs his finger over the text, scanning for the description of Sheldon's contribution to the invention. When he lands on his son's name, he says again, "That's my son, Sheldon Kavesh."

While Morris and I are focused on the articles, an elderly woman has been waiting with a copy of the *Times* in her hand. In a nasal voice, she says, "My husband was an inventor. Who is your son that invented something?"

Morris looks up from the article. "Sheldon Kavesh," he says.

"What did he invent?" she asks.

"A new material for Allied Chemical," Morris says.

"What?" she asks.

"Don't you understand?" Morris replies.

"Of course I understand!" she fires back. "My husband was in that business, so I know."

Morris shows her the *Chemical Engineering News* article. "Here is that mentions, 'And engineer Sheldon Kavesh invented a way to form a wire.' Someplace there is whole story about that."

Morris carefully re-folds the articles and tucks these treasures back into the shoebox.

With the sunlight comes a stream of customers.

Someone asks for the *News*. Morris says, "No more *News*."

For a few minutes he's preoccupied with selling papers. When the customer stream abates, he says, "I show you something else."

From the shoebox Morris withdraws an envelope. He removes a piece of paper and hands it to me. It's a letter from Elliot in which he talks about a $4.5 million missile contract at Boeing he'll be working on. The letter ends: "P.S. Thanks for the cutouts — I really appreciate receiving them every day."

Morris is smiling when I look up from the letter. "You see there," Morris says, proudly pointing to the P.S.

"I don't see my children too often," he tells me. "My son in New Jersey, I see every couple weeks, but my other son, I only see him once a year, because he's far away, right? If they were living in New York, or Brooklyn, I could come to Brooklyn, stay for a couple of hours every day, come back." Morris returns Elliot's letter to the shoebox and stores the shoebox in the crate. "Of course, I write once in three weeks, once in four weeks. But there's nothing much to say — my life very ordinary. I'm in the same place, same time. And I'm still alone."

He smiles again. "But another pleasure gives me, is when I send the cutouts. When they get this mail from me, cutouts, it is just like I correspond to them. I believe I'm talking to them. By mail."

Religion ...

I don't belong to shul here. I don't belong to any temple. But I'm a Jew. I'm hundred percent for Israel, but not religious.

I got Jewish education. I was learned by rabbis, in Russia. I was going *heder* — that means Hebrew school. I mean, I don't go in synagogue, I don't pray, but I read Jewish very good.

People think if you are not religious, you are not a good Jew. They tell me, 'Why don't you go upstairs?' They say, 'You are Jewish.' Of course I'm a Jew. But not religious. I say to them, 'I believe in two things, cash and girls. That's what I believe in.' (I'm only telling joke.) I'm not going for God, but I am for Israel, to have Israel nation.

You don't have to be religious to be a Jew. You don't have to wear a beard, you don't have to wear yarmulka, you don't have to pray. You know who is a good Jew? A soldier, who stays with carbine, protecting

Israel. That's what is a Jew. I just gave donation for Israeli children, $75 for Passover, through my girlfriend. But I wouldn't give nothing for the synagogue. I wouldn't give none of these bums a penny. Let them support themselves. But for Israel, yes, because I am a Jew.

My life belong to me, and I do the way I want to live, not my children or anybody else. That's why I don't care. When the people tell me go in synagogue, I say, 'Listen, you believe that? Great! It's freedom of religion.' But it's a freedom of no religion, too, right?

I believe in science, not religion. Although I respect them. Sure, I respect every religion. I want to tell you something between you and me: I was brought up in Russia, and I got Russian education, too. And they teach me that religion is the opiate of the people. I believe that then and I still believe it, even I hate Russia now. I'm just talking to you about my private opinion, you know?

Here is one thing I'm very unhappy. My son in New Jersey is kosher, his wife is kosher. But my other son, in Seattle — he eats everything, because his wife cooks it. She's Jewish, she's Sephardic, but they are Jews who come in gentiles. I don't care, but still, I respect more my son in New Jersey, because he keeps to the Jewish tradition more than the other one.

I don't eat kosher, but I hate to see my children eat pork. I don't know why, but I feel it. Eat, I don't care. I can eat shit — excuse me. I eat kosher and not kosher: ham, bacon, salami, pastrami. I eat all this. Even my wife was alive, she was kosher, but I had special dishes. And I eat bread on Passover — my children don't know. But I would hate to see my children eat bread on Passover. Even, I'm not religious, but I want my children to be Jewish.

I don't know for your religion, whether you're a Jew or Spanish. You know, I look if you are a nice person, you are my friend. But still, but still ... I wouldn't want my children to get married to the gentile woman. No! This is because I believe a Jewish boy should have a Jewish girl.

My son and his wife, I never tell them what to do or how to do. But one thing I would hate: if my children would marry a gentile woman. I would quit my children. And I'm not religious. Because they would lose Jewish race. You know what I mean? The child only not be Jewish and not gentile. I don't care about religion, but I care about

Jewish race. Jewish race should be Jewish, pure Jewish. You know what I mean? I would hate to see that. I always was afraid they shouldn't marry gentile. Even I gave them Jewish education. But, you never know.

I am very Jewish-minded, except that I'm not religious. But one thing I give the Jewish credit: Religion, Jewish religion, made them survive all these thousands of years. Because Jewish religion made those people get married with only Jewish, not gentile, and they survived. The religion.

Alaska:

Morris has brought something else to show me. "I don't got much time," he says, "but you want I should read you the letters I wrote in Washington?"

"Sure," I say.

From his ubiquitous shoebox, Morris retrieves two photocopied pages. It's a busy part of the day and customers are trying to buy newspapers as he reads, but Morris fends them off, dishing out "Just one minute" to every comer until he finishes each letter.

"This I wrote from my son's house in Seattle before leaving on trip to Alaska," he says. He reads:

Wednesday, April 9, 1975

I thought of greatness of this world we live and felt like I am newly born at 71. Indeed, it's quite big difference more than 50 years ago when at age of 20 I arrived with some kind of fear to Mexico. At that time I had my youth, strong pep, and courage and was ready for struggle and hardships. But now I'm depending only on my ready cash, traveler's checks, and my son's hospitality.

A well-dressed Spanish-speaking man, who has been quite insistent, finally gets change for a $10 bill. A college kid buys the *SoHo Weekly News*.

Morris hands me the first letter and moves on to the second. "This I did on boat ride home from Alaska," he says. He reads:

Wednesday, April 23, 1975.

On board ferry liner "Malaspina."

Am riding back already from my all-Alaskan FUNtastic trip talked about, dreamed about, and now my own seen-about.

I am riding through greatest valleys and forested inlets on the water of Pacific of the world's famous Inside Passage of Alaska — of most spectacular beauty and wonder scenic settings and photographer paradise delight. Unbelievable spectacles of all the way of solid wall of the vertical snow-covered highest mammoth mountains and abundant wildlife.

Incredible vast plush wilderness steady occupies my admirable mind and far beyond of my imagination of my daily hustle and bustle in New York.

I saw three bald eagles majestically gliding in air above island we pass. Also most beautiful mirror reflections of mountains in some very calm waters from bright sunshine rays. In all, it was great of Greatness to see — the Greatest Land on Earth — Alaska!

"I write these at night, and during the day I was out," Morris explains. "I mail this to everybody — friend, family, and of course my sweetheart. Before I send, I do a lot of correcting. I make photostat copies over there. Otherwise, takes for me too much time to copy by hand."

"You have *By-Lines*?" a customer asks.

"*By-Lines*," Morris says, handing him the paper and completing the transaction.

A construction worker in khaki work clothes picks up a *Post* and asks Morris, "Are you still alive?" He says to me, "He's gonna live to 95."

"Your letters really made me feel like I was on that trip with you," I tell Morris.

He nods. "I give them to Seattle papers, but they never publish them."

"I don't know why not," I say. And although I believe I *do* know, I also see how, in the right light, Morris's letters are pure poetry.

The guy in the floppy hat, hat restored, circles back. He screams in gibberish at no one and everyone, then staggers off. Morris ignores him.

"I had such wonderful time that you cannot imagine. It was eight days in the water. We came to Alaska, and came back. Usually I go to Seattle in July. But last year I went in April because my grandson was Bar Mitzvah. Weather was exceptional good, when I took trip to Alaska. Not even one cloud."

Another customer, another transaction. Morris goes on. "I made a friend on the boat and he invite me to where he live in Anchorage. Would be very interesting to me. But I didn't go because I already bought my return ticket. It would cost me extra money to fly from Anchorage to Seattle. My son would send money from Seattle if I need, but I thought, why should I miss the boat ride back, because it's paid already both ways?"

Between customers, Morris elaborates on his other adventures in the Pacific Northwest.

"I read in *Atlantic* magazine about a month ago, 'God's country.' Headline on the wrapper and on the magazine: PACIFIC NORTHWEST, IT'S GOD'S COUNTRY. Oregon, Washington, British Columbia. I send to my son. Over there, people come very little from the East. Here they all go Florida, California, South, but nobody goes Northwest, and it's really beautiful country part of United States — except the weather: usually cloudy, rainy."

A woman buys a paper and leaves without her change. Morris shouts after her: "Lady, I didn't give you enough! Lady!"

Morris goes on without skipping a beat. "One trip I went by boat from Portland to the highest mountain in Oregon — I forgot name, there's a lot of mountains there. Eleven hours trip. I was riding along Columbia River. To the right side, Columbia River — wide, quiet, blue water. To the left side, right to the prow of the boat, highest mountains. When you see this nature, you feel it, how nice is this world."

Morris muses for a moment. "What else he took me?" A customer comes and goes. "I cannot forget, about eight, nine years ago, my son took me around Olympic Peninsula. From Seattle, we went by car 500 miles in one day, round trip. Olympic Peninsula is the one part in United States which is still in the same situation since Christopher Columbus discovered America. All rain forests, not penetrated.

"We ride on coast of the Pacific, going into rain forests. Wood is green, trees covered with green moss more than one foot thick. You just push your hand through! You go there and you get lost. And you are afraid of snakes, but there is no snakes because snakes don't live in that kind of weather. He took me to Lake Chelan — beautiful! I showed you pictures. We see deer, little squirrels, small squirrels. We go to farms, to Crystal Mountains. I was on the top of the world!"

Morris meets my eyes, his aglow with uncharacteristic intensity. "That's why I wrote in the letter, 'Not anybody can see in New York.' If I wouldn't have my business, I probably would live there. I would not live in New York, despite I like New York. I would have a car, and with car, I would see that by myself, see those places, go traveling there in the Northwest."

He glances around him, taking in his stand, his corner of *this* world. "Now, it's time to travel while I'm able to — how long can a man work? I'm 73. But unfortunately, I don't think I ever live there because I never would give up my business. This is a business unique. I don't want to give up just for that."

Israel ...

My sons, everybody, tells me to go to Israel. I am a hundred percent Jewish, and I love Israel, but I don't see anything interesting for me in Israel. What can I imagine to see? So I see wall. Ehhh, I bought once a painting of wall. And besides, I'm not religious. Some people go for religious matter, but I'm not.

My two sons have gone to Israel. One of my sons was there last year, and my son from Seattle was two years ago. They went by boat. The son from New Jersey went with his family, with his two children. The other one went him and his wife only. I didn't go, and I don't know. If I go to Israel, I have to spend at least $1,000. Maybe there is possibility I'll go next January, because the fare is less. Because now is season, costs more. Maybe I'll go then.

I have not my choice to go to Israel because I'll tell you why, and that's the most important thing: If I would have somebody to work here, maybe I would go now to Israel, but I don't want to leave my stand alone too long without work. One month is enough for me not to have to work.

And I like to see America first. In America there is more to see than anywhere else in the world. I like especially nature, and nature I see mostly in Northwest. I would want go all over America to travel, but traveling is the most expensive. You have to pay in hotel $20, $30 for a night to sleep. It's ridiculous! When I go to Northwest, I spend *nothing*, except carfare, and I see a lot. Why? Because I have my son there, house, transportation, we go there $10 a day.

But I love Israel, I love Israel like my own mother, because I am a Jew. There is a lot of things to change the world, especially we are Jews. Right now they have trouble in our country — I mean Israel, which belongs to the Jews. I read that every day in papers. I would be very happy that could be changed.

They should let us to live like *every* nationality, live in peace, and cultivate, and to have the culture flourishing, and so on. If I could change, there should be safety in this world to live in. We shouldn't have no wars. No war, no crime, no robbery. They should treat us like everybody else. Should all nationality live in peace. Then everybody would be happy, everybody would be all right. Right?

Parents:

"I ask Morris if he had a will," Harry is saying. "Morris says, 'What do I need a will for?' I explain to him there's complications if he don't have one. Morris tells me, 'They want $35 for a will!' So I tell him even if it cost $100, it's still worth getting it. You never know."

Harry's comment seems to turn Morris in a more reflective direction. Out of the blue, despite the cacophony of a busy afternoon on the corner, Morris asks Harry to hold the fort and signals me to sit with him near the entrance to the shul. We drag two milk crates there, and Morris confides in me in a way I've not yet experienced.

"For the elderly now it's not so good in New York," Morris says. "I believe that. Because elderly man, they can't walk at night, is dangerous. And also, is very expensive wherever you go."

Morris pauses. He lets out a deep sigh.

"The children here in America don't take care of their parents the same as the children in Russia used to make before," he says. "I don't know about the gentile people, but the Jewish people, when they had

146

an elderly father, he used to live with the children, and they took care. Now in America, the father gets old, they send to nursing home. Or, if he lives alone, they don't care. They have a good time, the children. They don't take care of the elderly parents the way it used to be."

A brief pause. An unfamiliar look in his eyes. "I never was sick, but if it happens, probably my sons would come to visit me, and that's it." His jaw tightens. An edge creeps into his voice. "I already felt ingratitude on my son in Seattle on last visit to him. Didn't I tell you? I'm old father. I'm working, independent. And I give a lot to my son. But he disappointed me. After that, I don't want to come no more there."

"What happened?"

"He invites me every summer for a visit. Usually, I come during July, when they have lot of sunshine. Last year I had to come in April because his son, my grandson, was Bar Mitzvah. I don't like to leave here in April, but I came. I arrived there April 1st, and a week later, April 8th, was Bar Mitzvah in the temple there. It was a lot of guests, Jewish and gentile, which my son invited. And my son from New Jersey came also for two days, to be in that celebration. Also my cousins from Vancouver. You saw pictures."

I nod. "I did."

"My grandson made beautiful speech. In synagogue. In English, of course. Long speech, and in that speech, he openly declared gratitude of my visit all the way from New York, his grandpa, Morris. After that ceremony was, of course, a special room in synagogue where guests have cold drinks, sandwiches, all kinds of delicacies."

An ambulance's siren serenades us. Morris ignores it. Around us the flow of people rushes by. Bits of discussion in Spanish and English waft over us, but he is 3,000 miles away.

"After everybody left and everything finished with," he says, "I step in my son's car to go home from the temple. In other car was riding my other son and his wife, and I was with my grandson. And my son told me, 'You use my home as hotel.' He said when I come to Seattle, I should not stay a month, I should stay only two weeks, because to take care of me a whole month was too much for him and his wife."

Morris's face animates, his voice rising in volume almost to a shout. "What kind of care they give to me? Nothing! I used to sleep there at night. In the morning, I *right away* take a bus, go to Seattle for $2, and I stay all day. At night I come and they serve me supper. I don't need that supper! That supper I could eat in Seattle for $2, two and a half."

He shrugs. "But I thought, why should I spend money there? I come to my son's home, I eat there, right? But I notice that the supper they didn't give me very pleasantly. Ehhhhhh ... something like I'm unwelcome, you know what I mean? She watches television, my son working. So I was something like a boarder for them. When I get there, I gave them nice presents, *more* than what hotel would cost me if I stay in the best hotel. But they didn't like because I stay one month there and they want me to stay two weeks."

Morris's eyes harden. "That's *insult*, when he told me stay in hotel. Did he not invite me to his Bar Mitzvah? Where he *expect* me to stay? In hotel? Happened to be that my cousin from Vancouver came, they put him in a motel to sleep, with his wife. Why did you not put hotel to *me*? And if you want me to your *home*, why the hell you tell me to use *hotel*?"

He clenches his fists. "I give him presents, nice presents and everything else, and on premises of the synagogue, an hour after I saw my grandson thank me for coming to them, he tells me I use his home as hotel. Isn't that insult?"

I nod my agreement.

"It's terrible feeling." Morris's voice rises in volume again. "*If* next day wouldn't be another celebration, in a big hall, with dances and music, and *if* my son wouldn't be there from New Jersey, and *if* I wouldn't be invited, and *if* I wouldn't make already agreement to go to Alaska, I would right away be packing, and I would leave his house and go in hotel or I would go back to New York. Right away. But I couldn't make, because I would upset my other son. If I would leave, would not come, next day, people who ask, 'Where is your father?' And make him very feeling bad? And then, I want eventually to go to Alaska, because cost me $200 for eight-day trip and I was very excited. So I couldn't cancel."

Morris's voice trembles as he says, "Otherwise, I would *right away* pack my valises and would go to hotel or YMCA, that costs $5, $6 a room, stay another few days, and I would go home. That's why I never would come to him no more, and if I *ever* come to Seattle, I won't stay with him. I will stay in hotel."

Morris stares out at the traffic streaming by on Broadway, but he's seeing another world. "I used to buy savings bonds for his children and send him. No more! I used to send to my grandchildren stamps with the numbers, for collection. Plate blocks. I stopped to send. *If* they didn't take care of me, why should I take care of their children?"

"But you still send the cutouts," I say.

"Cutouts, I send. Doesn't cost me anything. I send cutouts, but I wouldn't send him not a penny present, not his birthday present, not his children present. I wouldn't send him nothing. No more."

Morris shakes his head. "Next morning, I get up early, and his wife told me that I should eat breakfast. I say, 'I'm not hungry.' I left. I run away. I take the bus to Seattle. Came at night, my son says, 'You were mad?' I say I was mad. I didn't want to say to him no more because that time my other son was still there. I didn't want to make upset everything, you know what I mean? After that, he came here for Bar Mitzvah of my other grandson, from New Jersey. We went to eat — they came for couple days for celebration — and I say, 'Elliot, I want to talk with you.' He didn't want to talk with me. I say, 'Okay, don't talk to me.' He wouldn't talk to me about this matter."

Morris shakes his head again, then turns to me. "Well, that's how the children do now," he says. He points to my notepad. "You can write. He knows how I feel."

Morris crosses his arms. "I'm only happy that I know my son sooner than later, what happened in Seattle. Suppose I needed to take care, if I have no way to make my livelihood? Suppose I have no stand? Suppose I have no money to live? Who would take care of me? He would not take it. I see that. If he didn't want to take care of me for two weeks as a *guest*, he look to me like a *pest*, because that's what it was. First week I was there a *guest*, second week I was there a *pest*."

"What about your other son?" I ask.

"I can't say anything to you about my son in New Jersey. I never experienced. I know they give me children very good to me, my grandchildren. Of course, I stay there for four hours and go home. Maybe if I would stay there more ..." Morris laughs. "Maybe they would not appreciate. I cannot say yet. I don't want to think about it."

Morris stands, and I stand, too. We remain near the shul entrance. He takes a slow breath.

"I want to thank God I don't have to depend on my children's support. I don't say they're bad. I suppose every children is the same. What happened to my brother and sister when my *mother* was sick? Were they better? They didn't took care of her. My *wife* took care of her. And if my wife would not take care of my mother, I would take my wife and I don't care what would happen. I would take her from the ass and I would throw her out from the house. *Even* she's my wife. Because I love my mother."

Morris puts his hand on my arm and grasps it lightly. "I have one brother, he lives in Brooklyn. I don't talk to him. I'll tell you why.

"My mother lived with me thirty years. My wife took care. When my wife died, my mother, six years later, she became sick, and I ask my brother his wife should come to my house and cook dinner for her, because she was so sick. I am here at newsstand, I have nobody, my mother is old woman. So my brother says, 'My wife wouldn't come.' I say, 'You son of a bitch!'"

Shouting, now, Morris says, "I told to my brother, 'My wife took care of *your mother* for thirty years, and your *wife* cannot come around to take her to cafeteria to feed her?' So my mother died after that, and I don't want to talk to him anymore."

Morris pauses, drops his voice. "I told him, that when used to be Mother's Day, he used to send *big cards*, Mother's Day cards. But when my mother was sick — *his* mother, too — he didn't lift the first finger. He used to bring her dinners, from Brooklyn: chicken dinners, chicken soup. Once in two weeks. I say, 'You want your mother to eat that soup for two weeks old?' I say, 'Why can't your wife come and *cook* for her at least every other day?' He lives in Brooklyn, it's not so far. I don't talk to him."

Morris's voice chokes, and tears come to his eyes. "What do you think I don't talk to him? Because that time I was very *upset* ... His wife ... she didn't want to take care of his mother when she was sick. And I still continue ..."

Harry, ever watchful, joins us, customers be damned. "Sit down!" he tells Morris.

Harry takes Morris by the shoulder and tries to nudge him back to his stool. Morris ignores him. He says to me, "I told my brother that, you son of a — "

"Don't use that word!" Harry admonishes. "He'll put it down on the record. Don't say bad things. Don't say nothin'. They might read the book." He turns to me. "Of course, you can scratch it out."

Morris says, "I would let them to read that, so they would know. My brother *and* my son." Unexpectedly, he laughs. "Anyhow, who will read that book?"

"Who?" Harry asks. "You'd be surprised! It might be one of the best sellers. Yeah! *The Life in New York City*. Might be on television and everything. Then they might come and say, 'Gee, look what he said about me in this book. He has no business saying that!' You gave him permission, but that don't matter to the lawyers. Uh-uh."

Morris, his equanimity restored by Harry's intervention, just shrugs. He replaces his crate behind the bench, and I follow his lead. "Ah, I don't give a care," he says. "Why do I care about? I'm happy they are well, and that's all."

Harry says, "You're *happy*?"

Morris nods. He waves his hand over the newsstand. "*This* give me my joy in life. Why should I give a care? Despite of everything, I want my son be well, be healthy, even he didn't treat me like supposed to treat. I don't give a care. I don't go to him no more, that's all. Right? And if I want to see, to go to Pacific Northwest, to Alaska, I paid my airfare anyway before. If before I didn't pay hotels and food, so now I don't have to give presents, I have that money for food and hotels."

"Yeah, well ... don't go no more," Harry says.

"I don't," Morris says. "I will take vacation someplace else this summer. Or I will stay New York and see tall ships."

Harry nods. "Don't open the window," he says, and guides Morris back to his stool.

Morris sits. A customer arrives. "*Times*?" Morris says.

America ...

The Americans don't know anything. They never had war in their country, right? Except for Revolution and Civil War. But we, in Europe, and especially in Russia, we have many wars: First War, Second War, Nazis. You know what happened to the Jews when the Nazi occupy? Hardships, no freedom of religion. I don't care of religion, but no freedom of to live in Russia.

I know what means to be persecuted. When I had to go in high school, I couldn't get in because they took only five percent Jews. Jews was not allowed to live wherever they want to. They couldn't live in Moscow, only in certain parts, ghettos. And, I know what everybody in Russia say: You are damn Jewish. So you Americans don't know what we had. And I had only part of it. By Second War, I wasn't there. I already run away from Russia.

In America, any place in the world, you can go — they let you out. Go ahead, who needs you! You want to go away to Germany? America let you go ahead! Nobody keeps you here! If you want to go to Russia, go ahead! But if you live in Russia, they can't get out — the Russian Jews, they won't let them out.

Over there, they don't need Jews. Why they don't let out? Because, if they let the Jews to go out, everybody else would leave this country. I tell you joke about the Russian refugees, the Jews who came from Russia. Kosygin told this joke: 'If we let out all the Jews from Russia, then everybody will try to get out of Russia! In the end, will be remain both of us.' So he says, 'Why both of us? You alone.'

You see, in Russia, many people don't agree with communist regime. It's not a freedom, it's dictatorship. The rule of the gun, not election. The rule of the gun. You can't talk. Here, you can say, 'Fuck you, Johnson! Fuck you, Ford! Fuck you, Nixon! I'm not afraid of you or of anybody policeman.' But in Russia if you say, 'Fuck you, Stalin, fuck you, Breshnev,' you know what you get? Siberia.

Now, I'm in America. I'm happy because there is freedom, freedom of religion and freedom of no religion, whatever it is. Nobody tells me what to do and nobody tells me what I can. You know what I mean?

I'm not big politician. I don't want it. But I know as a matter of fact there is some discrimination here in America. I read in Jewish paper the banks do not employ Jewish help. They discriminate. And before, if Jewish engineer used to apply for a job, he couldn't get no job. There was discrimination. Now, they take everybody, because technology become big, they need computer engineer, they need chemical engineer, they need all engineer. Now they take them, because they need talented people. Before, they didn't take them. But that's all covered up, you know what I mean?

But personally, I don't find no discrimination here whatsoever. I'm glad to be here, as I told you that. I know I have a freedom of living here. Nobody tell me, 'You damn Jew!' If I want to send my sons in school or I want to go, I go. Really. That's why I love America.

Because, when I was student in Russia, everybody told me '*djid*, *djid*, *djid*, *djid*, *djid*' — that's Russian, that means 'damn Jew.' It's a bad word. Even when I was in Mexico, they call Americans *gringo* — it's also not so nice word. When I was traveling, they ask me, 'Are you *gringo*?' I say, '*Yo no soy gringo*' — you know, I'm no gringo — '*Yo soy Alemana*' — I'm German. I didn't want to tell them that I am Russian, and besides that I'm Jewish. Because Jews they call *Judeo*, in Spanish. That's a bad word. They could say *Israelito* or *Hebreo* or whatever it is, but they call *Judeo*. *Judeo*, it's not religion literature word.

We Jews in Russia and from Eastern Europe — we Jews, *especially* Jews — we suffered a lot, which you Americans didn't have it. If I think what happened before, I'm ... I'm ... I'm crying because what I experience. I'm crying. You don't know ...

Well, it's came to my emotions.

Money:

It seems everybody in the neighborhood is talking about Morris and his money.

When I told Stanley, my downstairs neighbor, that I was going to be spending the day at the newsstand, we had what was probably our longest conversation (outside of his frequent complaints about how us walking on the wooden floor drives him and his aging mother crazy). "Ah, Morris. Did you know he owns all kinds of stocks, and that he makes $25,000 a year from that newsstand?" Stanley said.

These figures are loosely corroborated by Morris's newsstand friends. Harry mentions that Morris owns $150,000 in stocks, has bank accounts throughout the city, and that he bankrolled one of his sons $3,000 trips to Israel. The trip story is repeated by the Jewish parochial school teacher, only the figure he gives is $4,000. Both of them tell me Morris donates to charities and gives gifts of up to $200 to his sons and grandchildren, even though his sons earn somewhere between $50,000 and $65,000 a year — depending on who's providing the estimate.

Ace reporter that I imagine myself to be, as I sit on a milk crate, observing the ebb and flow of customers and dollars, I commit to discerning truth from fabrication. In a quiet moment, I say to Morris, "I know you're reluctant to talk about finances, but I'm wondering — "

I get no further. "You don't talk to me about finances," Morris says brusquely. "It's foolish *anybody* to talk to you about finances. Nobody will give it to you. Such things you cannot ask."

Morris's body stiffens. "I don't have to tell you my financial problems or my financial success!" Morris shouts. "*Nobody* tell you personal that, whether he's poor, he's rich, he's millionaire — multimillionaire or multi-*pobre*. You don't ask such financial questions. Nobody tell you what he has, what he doesn't have — why should I tell you?"

"I was just wondering," I say.

"And, you tell me something also question. You tried to get information about me somewhere else?"

"A guy in my building talked to me about you, and it made me think. There seem to be a lot of stories people tell about you."

"People talk, people talk, people talk a lot. People have all kinds stories. People think I'm very rich here. They see money on table. 'Oh, you have a lot of money.' But I'm not rich at all. They don't know I make less than elevator man. Elevator man makes now $200 a week. What I make here? Fifteen dollars a day? What the hell is that? If I would be rich man, I wouldn't sell papers. Wouldn't work that hard. And if I do work, it's my business. Why you ask such questions?"

A passing truck enforces a moment of virtual silence.

"But, for me it's good," Morris says. "Because I make playfully, right? Because besides I get my $300 Social Security."

A customer asks, "Do you have the *News*?"

"I haven't got no more *News*," Morris says. "*Post*, yes."

She buys a *New York Post*.

Morris's body language flashes *Discussion Closed*. The journalist in me persists anyway. I've heard, from Alfredo, that Morris put his son through MIT, no mean feat for a man who runs a makeshift news-stand in a rough part of town. "Well, you must have made more earlier, when you were here with your mother," I say, "because you were able to put your sons through college and grad school."

"What the hell?" Morris snaps back. "So what? I save my money, no? *Everybody* saves his dollars, right? We were open till twelve o'clock — that time was no radio, no television. Sure, one son cost a lot. My other son doesn't cost me a penny — he went to City College, was free."

Undeterred, I press on. "Earlier, you mentioned White Motor stock. Do you own that?"

"Don't ask such questions what I have, what I don't have! No! White Motor stock, I have it — how you know about White Motor?"

"*You* told me. When you were talking about the cutouts."

"As a matter of fact, I'm financially broken, because I lost money in stocks. I have White Motor, I pay $31, now it's worth $5. And that's finished."

Morris taps his hand on the short stack of *Financial Times*. "You don't ask whether I have White Motor or I have Blue Motor. That's question of personally, and it don't mean a thing. In America you don't have to be rich to buy even stock. You could buy with $500 stock. For $100 you can buy five shares, many companies. So you don't have to be rich. And in five years from today, what you paid $100, you'll get $10 for it! I would be two and a half, three thousand dollars richer today if I *didn't* buy. So, that's it."

A customer interrupts. "Please, I've gotta get going," she says, and holds out a hand for her change.

"Every Jew, every man, saves," Morris says. "You cannot live day by day, that. You *have* to save your money. My family was not wealthy. We used to save every penny we could, right?"

"Did the whole family live in that same apartment you live in now?"

He nods sullenly. "Yeah."

I imagine them — a man, his wife, his mother, and his two young children — living, here, in a six-room, rent-controlled apartment, and I remember the six in my family living in our tiny brick house in a blue-collar neighborhood in Buffalo. Not so different.

"I'm like everybody else," Morris says. "If you get salary, you don't spend all your salary, right? You'll save a dollar. Because if you don't save that, the day that you *don't* work, you'll starve. So everybody has to think about saving. And I do as everybody else."

Momentum still carries me forward, damn the torpedoes. "People walk by here on the street and it looks like you're a poor man — "

"I'm not rich man either," Morris says. "Even I'm poor man, so what? If I'm poor man, somebody will give it to me more for the paper than it is? And, I wouldn't ask them for a dime, right? Right. So, what is difference, how *I* am or how are *you* or how *he* is. I don't care. I'm not interested about anybody else, I'm only interested about myself, for my own safety, for my own wellbeing, and that's all. And, of course, I have to do my best, to survive."

Morris fishes around in the pile of cutout scraps. "Like, I saw a picture yesterday on television, at one o'clock in the morning. 'Survival.' Did you not watch it? It's very interesting. I think I see in paper about it. Two hours. They're comparing man and animals, about survival."

Morris pauses. "You have to think about your survival, you have to save it, your money, right?" he says. "*Everybody* has to save in America. The poorest man saves. That's why is savings banks, right?"

"The poorest man probably *doesn't* save, because he has nothing left over to save," I say, though as I make this objection, I remember, from earliest childhood, my family's insistence on saving, my succession of piggybanks.

"Don't tell *me*!" Morris says, "Everybody, *everybody*, saves. The poorest man saves in America. What is he doing if he doesn't save? Suppose he's not working tomorrow?"

"He ends up collecting welfare."

"Welfare. But welfare will take him three weeks or a month to get. Meanwhile, he'll starve. Don't tell me that! He has to *live* tomorrow! If he doesn't save everything for tomorrow, what he *eats* tomorrow? *Till* he gets welfare."

"They end up in the streets, hungry." I pan around Broadway. "You see them out here."

Morris shakes his head firmly. "Why you go in the bank so many people there? And never before that — I'm here forty-eight years.

When I used to go in the bank, no line. Now, you come, hundred people in line."

A roly-poly man with glasses and a brown mustache asks Morris, "Can you give me the new *By-Line*?"

"Tomorrow a new *By-Line*," Morris says.

Morris goes on, "Hundred people in line. What they stay in the bank for?"

"To withdraw their money," I say.

"That means they *save* money," Morris says. "So why you ask such question? Even the poorest man — I see all poor people in the bank, right? And they all save money, seems like."

"They saved money while they were working, probably," I attempt, weakly, to counter. "Now they're withdrawing it."

"Okay! So everybody saves," Morris exclaims triumphantly. "You don't save? I'm very pity on you."

"I do," I admit. "But I haven't got much to save."

"Well, I haven't got much either."

"Look, I'm sorry," I say. "I didn't mean to upset you. It seemed to me that you've struggled, and I wanted to show how you'd finally succeeded. For the book."

"Succeeded in what?"

"Financially."

"What do you mean financially? I'm not financially succeeded."

"Well, you're not a failure, either."

"With good will power, and sacrifice, and so on? With ambition. If you have no ambition, you don't get nowhere."

Morris continues to rummage among the cut-up papers and then flips through today's *Times*, still looking. "They probably took out. The show about animals and man and survival," he says, abandoning the quest.

A customer asks, "*El Diario*?"

"No, all gone," Morris replies.

"Have they got it anywhere around here?"

"Maybe next stand, 96th Street, across the street," Morris says. "I don't know."

To me, he says, "If I'm poor, I'm poor for *me*, not for *you*, right? Because you wouldn't give it to me anything, you wouldn't get anything. And I'll tell you: If you want to be rich, I'll tell you what you do. Sell papers. You'll be multimillionaire!" He throws his hands up. "Right?"

In a voice louder than I intend, I say, "I don't think you're rich! I don't care!"

Morris laughs, more good-naturedly than I expect. "I don't care if you think or if you don't think!"

I sigh. "I was just trying to check with you about stories people tell about you," I say.

The nut with the floppy hat eyeballs the stand, his chin in his hand, his head tilting from side to side.

Morris says, "What you want?"

The floppy hat man hands Morris two dimes and wanders off. Morris and I, equally puzzled, both shrug.

"People tell you about me," Morris says. "But *I'll* tell you: I live the worse than the worst, poorest people in the world. What do I have of my life? Do I go somewhere? Yesterday was beautiful day, but I finished two o'clock, I was all exhausted. Instead to go downtown to eat *good* meal, I came home. I want to eat, but I thought, I'm not dressed yet, I'm not washed, by the time I go I'll be twice as hungry, and then I'll be tired. I couldn't even go. I bought in supermarket something, I ate — without appetite, but I ate. I don't eat a good dinner. I eat shit, excuse me."

A woman offers Morris a dollar. "Here, Morris," she says.

"Yeah, thank you very much," he replies, returning a *Times* and change.

"And when you go to my apartment," Morris says, "it's a jungle. My apartment is dirty which you won't find in nowhere else. I sleep on one bedspread that I don't put even for two years already. I sleep on a dirty sheet and my head on a dirty pillow. If I would show you, you would be surprised. But I don't give a care as long as I have my own, you know what I mean?"

A young woman with close-cropped blonde hair and a punk outfit smiles as she saunters past the newsstand. "Congratulations!" she says.

"For what?" Morris asks.

"You have a new hat!"

Morris throws up his hands again. "Everybody talks to me about my hat!"

New York ...

I never live anywhere in America except New York, but I know it is not like rest of United States because when you go in New Jersey, go in Pacific Northwest, you see beauty.

I like New York because if you buy merchandise, you can get a lot bargains, if you know how to shop. If you watch the advertisements or you go shopping downtown, go from store to store, you get your good price. That's what I do. Another thing in New York, it's diversification. You can go a lot of movies that charge a dollar, dollar fifty — a lot of movies, a lot of selection.

In the other cities, no. Take Seattle. I like Seattle very much, but the business section is very limited part of the city. The rest, it's like you go on West End Avenue. You don't see nothing unless you have a car and you go from there places.

There's a lot of things wrong in New York, but there's a lot good in New York, too. The only thing that I don't like New York, especially, is safety. You have no safety here, as used to be.

I come at six o'clock, I have to lock the door behind me, because you never know what could happen. New York is not safe. Here is less safety than other places. Even, I read once in the paper, the safest city in America is Seattle. That I read about a year ago.

I'm glad my children living not in New York, because they have more privacy, their own home, and not to be in the streets of the city. Because New York, I figure out, is not a good place to live them now, because of safety and of all that jungle going on here. I'm very happy that.

Sex After Death:

The afternoon wears on. A couple of guys are sitting at the stand reading papers. Morris is straightening out the thinning stacks and consolidating them so they fit onto one bench.

"Is there anything you want me to put in the book that you haven't told me?" I ask him.

He smiles. "Yes," he says. "I will tell you inside." He carries one of the milk crates into the vestibule. I do the same. When we're seated, he says, "I'm in the movie *Sex After Death*."

"Are you serious?"

He laughs. "Is playing Second Avenue, right now. I was twice interviewed. You go and see, *Sex After Death*, cost you dollar till 5 p.m. — 12th Street Cinema, Second Avenue and 12th Street."

As we sit together on our crates, he tells me the tale:

"About six years ago, came to me a people, the photographer and so on, and they tell me, 'We want to take your interview.' Well, they want to take interview, go ahead. That was wintertime. And he talk to me. He's a doctor of sexology, I don't know. Anyway, in the morning, they took interview. He asked me about sex. So, I told him whatever I had, my own experience. And at the end, he gave me $5. Okay, then I forgot. I thought probably he will write medical science or something.

"About two and a half years later, somebody tell me, 'Listen, we saw you in a movie.' I say, 'What are you talking about?' 'We saw you in a movie.' I say, '*You wrong.*' 'No, we saw you in a movie. Even the sign was in the movie.'"

Morris points to the shul's sign and laughs. He goes on:

"Anyway, I went to look at, on 57th Street, and I saw it was me interviewed in movie *Sex After Death*. That picture was going all over United States. I was in Seattle, I saw picture was there. You can see now, 12th Street Cinema. Two days ago, I happened to go to Jewish show on 14th Street, and I saw advertised there, *Taxi Driver* and *Sex After Death*."

"What did you tell them?"

"Well, he ask me about... Well, you'll see. But, it's ridiculous movie." His voice drops to a whisper. "Naked woman, naked men and everything. Dirty movie."

"You could probably sue them, you know, if you wanted to."

"Well, I don't want. They gave me $5. So, I pay for the movie already $5!" Morris laughs. "I saw twice." He laughs harder. "Go see it. Should be still there. In today's paper, you can see, 12th Street Cinema. I would like to go again."

160

"In case I miss it, would you mind telling me what you said?"

Morris shakes his head. "I don't want to tell that, because I cannot tell my girlfriend. She knows about movie. She want me to say to her what I said, but I didn't want she knows about because I was talking about previous girlfriend. Anyway, I tell her that was before I met her."

Harry, ever curious (and protective), pops his head in the entranceway. "I'm telling him I was in movie *Sex After Death*," Morris says.

Harry nods. "A long time ago."

"About six years ago," Morris says.

"I'll go back out," Harry says. "I don't wanna interrupt your life story."

"No, that's all right," Morris says. "You don't bother me."

Sons …

Tomorrow afternoon, after I close here, I'm going my eldest son, Sheldon, in New Jersey.

He went to MIT. He had scholarship from New York State, but I lost it because he went out of state. I paid for him to go to MIT. And he was working summertime. That was in 1951.

He went to high school in Bronx, something around 180th Street. He was supposed to go in common school *here*, but he didn't want to go because there is not smart kids go there. So, I had an uncle in Bronx, and we make that he lives there, and he went to that school. I forgot the name.

Sheldon was interesting in chemistry since he was a kid. High school, he got gold medal in science, and he won Westinghouse competition. I have, home, paper which he got from the school and I have cutout from the newspaper: WESTSIDE YOUTH WINS NATIONAL HONOR, about my son, about me. Didn't I show it you? He became famous, and MIT invite him to that school. As a matter of fact, they invite him also in military school and other school in Minneapolis. There was a lot written. I have all that home.

My other son, in Seattle, went in City College.

Seattle, I go once a year. But lately, for the last four years, I go to my son in New Jersey every two, three weeks, but only for four, five hours. I close up the stand two o'clock Friday. I take the bus quarter after four and I arrive at six o'clock. At eleven o'clock, I take the bus back to New York, get home twelve, because Saturday morning I have to be open. For whole day, I stay only on Jewish holiday.

I'm very proud of my children, because they have a good job, they're educated boys, they have a nice living, their wives are working — one has a store, and other is a teacher. And they give me my four grandchildren, two from each son: One is girl, one is boy, and they're all good in school. My granddaughter, 17, she won already competition from West Point, she got gold medal. Boys are very, very smart, and they are good in music. My grandson plays two instruments. Very good.

All my friends, mostly, were never married. They are what you call bachelors. So they have no children, no grandchildren, you know? They don't got nobody. I'm a man different.

My son who lives in such wonderful place like Seattle, it's very satisfaction. And that Friday afternoon that I go to my son in New Jersey, I feel like a king for a day. You know why? Because I have nice ride, I come to my son's beautiful home, I see beautiful grounds, I see nice grandchildren. I spend four hours like he would be my own. And I am happy.

I bring to my grandchildren in New Jersey sometimes gifts, and when I go Seattle I always bring. Small, that's all. They don't need it. But, of course, I can afford to give them. Which grandfather wouldn't give it? You know, there is English word: 'The greatest part in the art of living is having the gracious heart of giving.'

That, I saw on a card. I memorize that. Also I remember this, what I used to send on cards every New Year:

*It's nice to start the New Year
with the happy thought of you.
It's nice to send good wishes
and hope they all come through.
Thinking just how very much
your friendship means to me
and wishing you a New Year
that's just as happy as can be.*

I memorize how to write English, good words. I memorize everything.

Sister:

I leave the newsstand for half an hour to get some lunch and skim through my notes. When I return, a light drizzle begins. Morris's newspapers begin to spot with water, but he seems oblivious to it. He's stooped over, searching haphazardly through the day's trash, discarded scraps of papers he's cut up, and piles of papers he's not yet transferred to the returns in the shul alcove.

"You take it from me!" he says, his face red, eyes furious. "What you put it?"

Startled, I say, "Took what?"

He glares at me. "My signature! *Daily News* delivery slip with my signature I show you," he says.

"I don't know what you're talking about," I say. "I didn't take anything."

"Should be *here*," Morris says, waving a bulging manilla envelope. "Only slip missing from today is that." He stands, glares at me. "*Always* I put it here. What you do with my signature?"

Spreading my arms in exasperation, I repeat, "I didn't take *anything*."

"I give my signature to nobody!" Morris says.

"Morris, I didn't take it. You told me you didn't want me to have it, so I let it go." My eyes grow moist, my voice cracks. "I would never steal from you," I say.

Morris sits down. He busies himself with fetching the plastic sheets he's stored under the bench and covers the stacks of papers. "Okay, okay, I believe you," he says, when he's finished the task. "Is a small thing. Doesn't matter." Not until that that night do I remember Morris stashing the slip in the shoebox, and by then it's no longer important.

A few moments later, a customer asks, "*El Diario*?"

"*No tengo más*," Morris tells her sternly. She wrinkles her brow in surprise. A black dog, tied to a parking meter, barks incessantly. "*¡Basta!*" Morris shouts at it.

I remember what the parochial school teacher told me about Morris's moods.

A stooped old man in a black suit has been reading the papers, apparently unmindful of our encounter. Morris summons him. "Here," he says, handing him some change. Morris points to a nearby coffeeshop. "I don't know what they charge for container coffee from there. Give me three spoon of sugar, mixed up. See that they mix up. I give you 30¢, but I think it costs less."

The old man pockets the change and shuffles down the block. Belatedly, Morris calls after him, "Thank you."

Customers come. Customers go.

"Have the *Post* and the *Times*?" a young man says.

"No *Post*. Here is *Times*," Morris replies gruffly.

A woman asks, "Can you change a five for me? I need it for the bus." Morris complies, his movements mechanical.

Morris and I are alone at the stand now, but he's not saying much. The cleaner from next door comes up to him. They speak quietly in Yiddish. Morris turns to me and says, "Can you mind stand? I need to make phone call. I come back in five minutes."

Given our confrontation a few minutes ago, I'm startled. "Okay," I say.

He reaches into his apron and pulls out a handful of change. "Five minutes," he says.

Morris and the cleaner go into the cleaner's shop. I sit alone at the newsstand, taking in Broadway from Morris's vantage point, remembering the times when, as a boy, my father had me mind his store.

In under five minutes, he returns. I ask, "Morris, are you okay?"

His face showing evident strain, Morris says, "I apologize to you. I'm not in good mood. My sister sick — she had a hemorrhage. After I close, I have to go to *Times*, eat, visit her in hospital."

His outburst — and his odd show of trust — now make sense to me. "I'm really sorry to hear that," I say. "Is it serious?"

"I don't know. I speak to her daughter now," Morris says. "I am not close with her, because she wouldn't take care when my mother was sick, but now, when *she* is sick ... I go. She is older than I am, she is

78. Second time this year she has been in hospital. Maybe this time she pass away, I don't know."

The Girlfriend ...

My woman friend, whom I know, she cheers me up. She calls me, I see her. She doesn't let me to spend a lot of money with her. We don't go in restaurants, expensive places — we go in cheap places to eat, buy donuts, and so on. She doesn't even ask me, she's just glad to be with me. That's why I appreciate. Because the other women, before I knew her, they took advantage of me. 'Take me to the show, take me to the bar,' which I don't even drink. I hate. In bar I never drink anything except soda.

Somebody gave me her telephone, a woman used to buy from me papers after my wife died. That woman lives here, 97th and West End Avenue, and she told me, 'Your wife died? You're not married yet?' I say no, and I jokingly told her I have no girlfriends. She say, 'I have for you a woman, good woman.'

Anyway, she gave me the telephone number, but I didn't call her. Because at that time I had another girl. So, she comes in two weeks, that woman, and she told me: 'You didn't call her!' I say no. 'Why not?' Then, I call her up.

That was when it was World's Fair in New York. What year was that? About 1964, '65. She lived in the Bronx, so I call her up and I told her, 'This is Morris Kavesh, and if I tell you Martha, then you'll know what's all about, that Martha recommended.' So she say, 'Oh, yes! Martha told me about you.'

Well, so I make an appointment in Bronx, over there where's Yankee Stadium, Concourse Hotel. There are some telephone booths, she'll have yellow parka. And we went to World's Fair.

Since then, I go out with her. Twelve years.

She's very stingy. She proposed me to get married after a year and a half. I told her, 'Listen, Ella, I want to tell you something. I'm not engineer, and I'm not doctor. I'm a hustler. I'm working hard at my newsstand, and still working, hustling, by the newsstand.' She ask me, 'What you make?' And I told her, but she says it's not enough. I say, 'Yeah, but what's the matter with *your* income?' So she say to me,

'What do you care about *my* income? *My* husband make *my* money. Look at somebody else who wants to get married to you! I don't want to marry you, because your money and my money, whatever I have, will be *our* money, not yours and not mine.'

After I didn't come for two weeks, she phones to me. I don't answer. She comes to me at the newsstand. 'Morris, I cannot live without you! I want to be with you.' I say, 'Yes! I'll go out with you, but I want to have a paper made by a witness.' What do you call them? Notary Public. I say, "That paper says we will continue the friendship without any obligation for support or for marriage.' And I tell her she should sign and notarize.

And that's what. Right?

You Feed Me Tomorrows:

The sky darkens. People passing now wear light coats. Drizzle turns to steady rain.

Morris transfers his piles of unsold newspapers to the shul hallway. He doesn't bother to cover them. "Who the hell cares about?" he says. "When they get wet, I return them. Wet or dry, whatever, I close up at this time anyway. They are no good no more for tomorrow. Right? This is not shirts that I sell."

Next to go into the hallway are the weights Morris uses to hold the papers down. He lifts a crate onto the remaining bench and starts loading them into it.

"Now problem is to feed myself," he says.

"Why is that a problem?"

"I have to buy something to eat."

"So you go to the store ..."

"That's the problem."

He drops each weight into the crate.

"Going into the store?"

"And buy, and to cook it."

The last weight makes a loud clang. "Well, that's it," Morris says.

He insists on hauling the heavy crate into the hallway. "You don't know where to put," he says. "Every day I do this. Why today should be different?"

In a reversed performance of his morning assembly process, Morris layers the planks, crates, and his stool into the hallway. He removes his apron, rolls it up, tosses it into a milk crate, and locks the shul door. Tonight, after his visit with his sister, he'll come back to tabulate his returns. "You see, my work is not over yet," he says.

Under Morris's arm is the shoebox. He fishes out the envelopes of cutouts for Elliot and Sheldon. "I wanted to mail something else to my sons. I like to use my 13¢ stamps. But there is nothing worth to send," he laments.

We walk together to the corner, where he mails the envelopes as is. "I'll see you soon," I say. "I hope your sister is okay."

"Yes," Morris says.

We shake hands. I look up at the miserable sky. "Weather didn't get much better," I say, "but it's supposed to be nice tomorrow."

"You feed me tomorrows," Morris says. "I'm worrying about today!" He laughs. "I'm only kidding," he adds.

"Do you ever get tired of it?" I ask.

Morris shrugs. "What would I do if I don't sell papers — sit all day on a bench? For me is better to sell papers than to sit all day on a bench."

Just as we turn to go our separate ways, a heavy-set man with slicked-back, grey-streaked hair stops and joins us. He's wearing a white sport coat, and over it a gray trench coat. "Morris!" he says. "I can see you three blocks away with your hat!"

Morris gives him a half-smile and tips his hat. "I become famous with my hat," he says.

Retirement ...

You say about retirement? I never expect to retire.

I would be very lonesome if I wouldn't work. You read articles in the press every day about lonely. Here, today in *Post*, is story, LONELY IN AMERICA. Very interesting. Did you read it? Is every day, all about loneliness. Why are they lonely? Because they have nothing else to do, they live alone. Some people die from it. They don't find no joy in life. Right? I don't read it, because I have no patience, but I know it is.

As a matter of fact, I know many people who retired, they die soon. They get bad circulation. I read in the paper, and they were facts, about people who worked all their lives in a factory, they stopped working. Because they're working for a boss, they work inside, so when they retire they are happy because they see sunshine, fresh air. But then they have not much circulation, and in another few years they die, from loneliness. You know what I mean? I know I would be same. I don't know if I die, but I know if I don't work, I wouldn't be happy.

I'm more happy here. Newsstand is not working in factory. *Already* I am in fresh air that makes me healthy, and good appetite. *Already* I see sunshine. While I'm here at the stand, I see people, I talk to you. If I wouldn't work, I wouldn't be able to talk to you.

I don't work in a store that I have to tell that this is a good apple, or bad apple, or it's a good pencil, bad pencil. When you buy merchandise, you have to sell it, otherwise, tomorrow it goes out of style. You see my merchandise? After I set up the papers, I don't have to advertise. My merchandise advertise for *itself*. And everybody needs a paper, *and* everybody has money to buy that. Right? You don't need $5, like to buy a pair of pants. With 15¢ you can buy a paper, and you have to buy *every* day. Pants, you buy only once a year. My merchandise always goes out of style, and I don't have to pay for what's out of style because I return them.

It's good business. I have no headaches. I have no worry whatsoever. No kind. If I sell papers, don't sell papers, who cares for that? If the papers don't sell, I return, and *basta*. I still will eat my herring, still eat my two eggs. Of course, I have headaches watching that nobody steals from me, or if it's a bad day, windy and cold, and I have to be frozen, I have some kind of extra work. But that's all minor problems.

If I would have $100,000, would I sit on the bench? Would I say, 'Well, I have $100,000. I don't have to work'? No. That wouldn't make me satisfaction, to be idle, because I wouldn't be happy. I would feel *scientifically* well, but not *practically*. So, I still would sell papers. Even *million* dollars, I still would sell.

You see, I'm accustomed to work. I enjoy. If I had to stop my life, the way I work, I would not like it. This is my joy of living. What else can I have, huh? I don't want to get married again, because if you're married, you may have problems. Why should I have problems? If you want to have a woman, you can always get, right? Cheaper than to be a husband! (I'm joking.) Besides, I haven't got much time for that because there is always work here.

I don't talk about retirement. I don't want to retire. That's all. I don't want to retire. I sit here and sell papers. People buy, and I look at the paper, take a glance, then I know what to cut out and I cut out, put in my envelopes, and send to my sons. Then I go home, two o'clock, one o'clock, and I have the whole day in front of me, right? I'm retired *while* I'm working. So why should I?

I have no more any obligations. When my children, and my wife, and my mother was alive, I had to get through, to support my family, right? Now, I don't have to support nobody. I don't have to worry about myself. I have enough to eat. I have enough to live for the rest of my life. So what's the difference, if I made it today $5 or $10 or I didn't make it? What do you think I'm working here? I could retire. But I don't want to retire.

Besides, here I see a live dollar. I go downtown, I spend $5 or $10, I don't have to give a care because I know tomorrow I'll make another five. That gives me joy, joy of carefree. When you are retired, you care because you live on certain income — that's all, you get no more. If I *don't* work, those $5, $10 count.

If today I would start working the way I do now, I never would start, but it's in my blood already. If it's cold, if it's rain out, I take it for me for granted. So why shouldn't I work? Of course, gradually I feel that I'm not youngster no more. When I work a lot, I get tired. But I still like woman, and I still like to live, go good eat, and go somewhere else. I'm old in my age, but I'm not old in my spirit.

For me, most important in my life is my newsstand. It give me joy of life in my old age, because it brings me profit, and brings me joy of talking to people, and not too much worrying about my business. I read all the papers and I get nice information, I send to my sons cut-outs, I make couple dollars, I go downtown, I spend it, I don't give a care. I don't have to retire. If I want to retire, I can work every morning to eleven o'clock, because that's the time I make my money, and go home, and take a day off, too. This is my life *semi*-retired: I'm retired, and not retired.

My children will tell me, 'Never give up this stand, because if you'll give up this stand, you'll be very lost. So, if you don't want to work every day, work three days a week, work four days, cut your hours, but work.' And I know that.

I don't want to give up my newsstand, because this is my heart. So, I sacrifice everything for being here.

Buying the Sunday Times:

The next time I see Morris it's Saturday night. I'm with Ruth. We're on our way back to my apartment from a movie and I stop off at Morris's to buy the Sunday *Times*.

Newsprint is scattered everywhere and Morris is disheveled and flustered. "Not complete. I don't have the first two sections, they don't deliver," he says quickly. "Labor trouble. If you want buy, you can come and pick up rest of paper in the morning."

"Okay," I say. I give him a dollar. "How's your sister?"

"Better than I thought," Morris says, handing me the incomplete *Times* and my change. He shows me the loose skin and protruding veins on the back of his hand. "She had a face like that," he says. "Just skin. I never saw her like that, but she was sitting in a chair, was talking. I thought she's lying in a bed, like my wife, with all kinds of bottles with medicine. But she was not like that. Well, she's not a youngster. So, I hope she'll be all right. I hope so. I'm glad I saw her."

He quickly reaches for another dollar from another customer. He explains, "Papers came tonight late. I have to rush."

The next morning, I go out to fetch donuts, coffee, and the rest of my *Times*. Harry, Alfredo, the teacher, and a couple of other regulars are arranged around the stand, relaxing, reading, kibbitzing. Morris still looks harried.

The stocky guy with thinning brown hair in front of me asks, "Any more *Times*?"

"No more. You save money." He looks surprised. Morris explains, "Not complete."

When it's my turn, Morris elaborates, "Six o'clock, I call up the *Times*, I order 200. They say they will deliver, they don't deliver. And I'm crying all morning: I could be selling them." He hands me my sections. "I must stay open because people come by like you, pick up missing sections from last night. Now, too late, even they deliver. Maybe I sell fifty."

I know Ruth is probably up by now, but I decide to hang around a little longer and absorb the buzz.

A grumpy, heavy-set woman in her forties complains that her husband bought a *Post* an hour ago, thinking she was buying Sunday's paper. "He's a tall man with a white mustache — "

"Yeah, yeah, yeah, yeah," Morris says. "He bought from me Sunday paper."

"When he gets home," she says, "I see it's *Saturday's* paper." She shows him the first section.

"What you want?" Morris says. "That's Sunday *Post*."

Before the woman has a chance to object, Harry intervenes. "Saturday and Sunday's the *same thing*," he says. "It's marked *Saturday*, but it's one paper for *both* days. It's called the *weekend* paper."

"Weekend *Post* comes Saturday," Morris confirms.

The woman, flustered, apologizes. "I didn't know," she says.

A young guy in a blazer asks for the *Times* and Morris repeats, "Not complete."

"Why don't you just say you don't have the *Times*, if you don't have the *Times*?" the customer says. "What is this 'not complete'?"

"Some are coming for the sections from last night, so I have to tell them," Morris says. He tips his head toward me. I show him my two *Times* sections.

"What? *You* have to tell them?" the guy says. "If they want the two sections, they'll tell *you*: 'I bought the paper last night. Do you have the other sections?'"

I say, "He's been here forty years, and you're trying to tell him how to run his business?"

"Right," the guy says.

Morris chuckles. He says, to me, "The egg learns the chicken. I am the chicken, and he is the egg, and now the egg learns."

"Teaches?" I offer.

"Right," Morris says "The egg teaches the chicken what to do."

Happiness ...

All my past, I'm happy, because if I wouldn't run away from Russia, I would remain Russia, my mother would remain Russia, and whole family would be killed by Hitler, 1942. I wouldn't be here alive today. This way, I came to Mexico, I brought my family here, all come here. It's like you have a choice of two things, you don't know which is what. Who knows? You don't know your future. Good thing I took right choice.

Even when I was in Mexico, I married my wife, I took a chance. I say, 'I have to marry a woman I don't like it? Who forces me?' I was 26 years of age. But I *took* that choice, and I married my wife, and happened to be I got a good choice. You know, happened to be. Otherwise I would be still in Mexico.

Every Jew who comes from Europe, they have their own life story. I have *good* story, because I came before this whole trouble started, and I was lucky. So, I have Thanksgiving Day today and every day.

And besides, I make a living here in America, and besides I have everything to be thankful for, and I know that, and I am happy. Thanksgiving Day, holiday, it's *really* holiday to me. I'm just thanking *everything* that happen to me and my family. I mean, of course I lost my wife, and I lost my mother, you know what I mean? But ... we all have to go, sooner or later.

I have a good spirit. You know why? I have everything to be happy. When the people tell me, 'Morris, but you work every day! In cold weather!' I say, 'No matter is that.' I'm still the most happy man in the world. It's not what you have, it's what you *feeling.*

I'm happy because I reach all my age, 73, and hope to live much longer. Happy because I have a young heart — I'm 73 years *young*! You'll be 73, too. Happy because I'm healthy, never sick. I don't know about doctors, I don't know about hospitals.

Happy I have my family — I have good children, my two sons got good education and they're very well off. I have nice grandchildren, they're good students.

Why shouldn't I be happy? Why *shouldn't* I be happy?

Happy because I'm not a roomer, I got my own apartment. And, of course, because it's my rent control, too. Happy because I'm my own boss, and not work hard, and I see people and enjoy, and besides I make a live dollar. Happy because I have my newsstand right one block from where I live and I don't have to travel in subway. Happy because I don't have to ask for a dime in the street — I don't depend on nobody, not my children, either.

So what else you want? What you want me, to have a golden egg to eat?

Happy I'm in America, too, in a country that I don't have to be like in Russia. You know what I mean? That they say you're a damn Jew, they didn't let me to go in schooling. In America, I am a freedom. I am a free man, right?

So far, I was fortunate in every way: fortunate I left Russia; fortunate I married my wife, I came to America; fortunate I had my two nice boys; and *fortunate* I had my children before I was too old, because it's nice to have children when the parents are young. Right? You don't want to have a child when you are 70 years old.

I say why should I *not* be happy? Happy in every way. What else do you want me to be, to live on Fifth Avenue and have a Rolls Royce? Of course, I could go higher and go to the moon, too! Why not? Why *not*!

How many days do I work in a week? I work eight days, because Saturday I work during the day and I come back at night. But even seven days. Who works seven days? Not too many. Do I have a day off? Do you see my stand close here? No. And despite of everything, I'm the happiest man in the world. I don't envy you that you work five days. I work eight days or seven days, and I'm happy. Because I don't know any better. That's how it is, and you can't take away that happiness from me. I hope that will continue until the end of my life.

Now, I'm hungry, and I got good appetite, and I'm going to eat my sandwich without any worry, whether the rain got wet my papers or not. To hell with the papers! I make my day working, and I don't care about. Right?

You know why I am happy? I look on my life different way. I'm happy the way I am because I know that other people are *worse* than I, and some people are *better* than I, but I don't look who's better from me. I look at those people who are worse than me. It could be better, but it could be worse. It's easier to get worse than better. So in spite of everything, I'm the most happy man. Right?

I am like the worm that got into radish. I mean apple. The worm come into apple sleeps there, eats there, he doesn't mind. I'm the worm. This is my apple, here on Broadway.

The Famous Dancer:

The next month, I move a mile uptown to Claremont Avenue, just west of Harlem. After I settle in, I stop by 98th Street and Broadway to visit Morris.

As I approach the newsstand, I see Morris standing with an older man who has a beret on his head and white stubble on his chin. They seem to be discussing a letter the man is showing Morris. The parochial school teacher is also there, ensconced in his reading room.

Morris is still wearing his baby blue fedora, no longer quite so new. He spots me. I smile and wave. He points to me and says, to his friend, "Here comes the young man." They all seem happy to see me.

"How is it going, Morris?" I ask.

He shrugs. "The same."

"So, what is happening with your book?" the teacher asks me.

"I have an agent," I tell him. "He sent a proposal to two publishers, but so far, nothing."

Morris shakes his head. "I'm not a kind of man worthy to write about," he says.

I ask the teacher, "What do you think?"

The teacher says, "Of course. There are thousands of immigrants like him."

"My story is not so interesting," Morris insists.

"It is, Morris," I say. "Really." After a moment, I ask him, "What *is* an interesting story, then?"

"Interesting is story of peoples who escape the death camps during the war, like rabbi here." He nods toward the shul. "He hide in basement for ten months. He still writes to the man who hide him. That is story fit for a book. You want story, you talk to him."

"But *you* escaped from Russia," I say.

"For me, this was not so difficult," Morris says. "I tell them I was not Jewish so I can get out, and they believe me because of how I look and because I speak Russian without accent. But one of the friends with me could not get out."

We're quiet for a moment, then the old man with the beret says, "You are lucky they didn't look at your *shmuck*." We all laugh.

"Yes," the teacher says. "He was also lucky they did not ask him to make the sign of the cross." As if I were a student he is querying about the Talmud, the teacher asks me, "You know what means *shmuck*?"

"I do," I say.

While we talk, a slender young man in pale blue slacks and a white silk shirt comes to the stand to buy a *Times*. Morris grabs him by the shoulder and nudges him closer, until they are standing side-by-side.

"He is famous dancer with American Ballet Theater," Morris says. "He lives here on 98th Street. His parents are Cuban. He is very famous. He has Cadillac, he was just in Turkey. And he is only 21!"

The young man smiles, embarrassment and affection evident on his smooth, brown face.

"He give me ticket, one time," Morris says. "Audience make him standing ovation." He looks at the young man, his smile proud and avuncular. "I introduce you to everybody who comes here!"

The young man smiles again, eases out of Morris's grip, takes his *Times*, and continues down Broadway. The teacher also takes his leave. "I will return later," he tells Morris.

Before I go, I assure Morris that when I find a publisher, I'll let him know. "I'll make you famous, too!" I say, only half joking. Morris just smiles indulgently. He and the man in the beret resume reading the letter, and I go on to the train.

Later, sitting on the IRT, it occurs to me that Morris is already famous in his own realm, and that he needs no help from me.

Finding Morris ...

I had been buying my newspapers from Morris Kavesh since I moved around the corner from his newsstand nearly two years before. I saw him just about every day.

For much of the first year, I worked in sales in midtown Manhattan, a poor match for my personality and skills. I bought the *New York Times* from Morris on my way to the subway. He and his stand were visually interesting to me: a self-contained whirl of activity on crazy Broadway, a pinwheel spun by its own wind. Because Morris's stand, unlike all the other news vendors I'd seen, was not in an enclosed kiosk, when it rained, the top few papers got wet. When it was sunny, they yellowed, and at busy times, they were often frayed. Every day, I would sift through the stack of *Times* for one which was not too damaged.

In the evenings and afternoons, Morris sat behind his improvised benches, but in the morning, he stood. In the welter of multiple hands holding out cash and the chorus of voices beckoning "*Times, News, Diario*," he sometimes seemed a little dazed, but he reliably took my change and told me 'Right!' in a voice made raspy, I supposed, by decades of hollering to customers over the roar of Broadway's traffic and their own insistent demands.

I liked having the *Times* to read on the train, and I especially liked buying it from Morris. His "Right!" was a reassuring touchstone in an otherwise dismal day. I nearly always bought my papers from him, and if I happened to buy one elsewhere and returned home with it, I'd cross the street so he wouldn't see me, even though I knew he was unlikely to notice and, even if he did, to care.

After I was rid of the job and it of me, I would amble out to the newsstand later in the morning. It was less busy then, but still, a minute or two often passed between my arrival there and my departure with that day's news. In the interval, I observed the newsstand more closely.

Sometimes Morris sat on a stool or wire milk crate, black-rimmed glasses perched on his nose, intently scanning one of the many periodicals he carried, marking articles with a blue and red pencil or clipping them with shears. Often, he was slicing his hands and fists through the air and spraying the immediate vicinity with fine mist as he argued, in what sounded like multiple languages, with customers and others who visited the stand.

I would wait until an appropriate break presented itself and meekly say, "*Times*." Morris's round, lined face would crack into a smile. He'd take my dollar, hand me my change, then return to his scanning or arguing as though the interruption hadn't occurred. I never minded the delay. I had no special place to be.

As the seasons changed, I was increasingly struck by the characteristic which Morris himself later noted made his stand a "business unique" — that he had no kiosk — and by the consequences of this arrangement not only for the papers, but also for Morris.

At that time, my notions about Morris were simplistic. I felt sorry that a man his age had to endure bad weather without protection. In the rain, I would see him hurriedly hauling the heavy stacks of papers beneath the awning of the cleaners next to his stand, or into the entranceway of Sloan's, the rain soaking through the layers one by one. In the winter, he kept an electric heater the size of a loaf of bread beside him and with it he would warm his gloveless hands. When it was windy, his papers blew here and there; I had more than once seen him and the others at his stand scurrying to retrieve them. I assumed, based on his worn sneakers, greasy work pants, and the makeshift nature of his newsstand, that he was barely scraping by. I saw him as immigrant poor, hard-working, a little desperate. A stereotype.

If the open character of his newsstand subjected Morris to the vicissitudes of weather, it also, I came to see, opened him to the helter-skelter life of the neighborhood. I noticed that there were frequently several people gathered there, and that over time, many of them reappeared. They were not merely buying papers, or skimming them to decide whether or not to make a purchase, or just shooting the breeze for a moment or two. They were regulars, hanging out sometimes for hours, and more than occasionally it was not Morris but one of them from whom I bought my *Times*.

Morris's discourse with me was still limited, but now I saw that with others it was far more diverse. He spoke fluent Spanish with a round, bald man who often stood beside him. I'd overheard him speaking Yiddish many times, and also a Slavic language I surmised was Russian. That he spoke at least four languages, while I had mastered only English, intrigued me. As the months passed, the newsstand began to seem like a "business unique" to me, too, and eventually, it occurred to me that there must be more to Morris than met my eyes.

A turning point occurred when I took his picture.

I'd just started using my roommate Henry's darkroom and was avidly photographing the street scene on the Upper West Side. I caught a shot of Morris at his post, reading, while an old man and woman sitting at one end of the stand argued. A few days later, I showed the photo to Morris and asked if I could take more pictures of him.

"Pictures? Why you want pictures?" he asked. "You work for newspaper?"

"I just like taking pictures," I said, "and your newsstand is very interesting to me. In all New York, I've never seen another quite like it."

While he thought over my request, Morris sold a few papers. I waited. "All right," he said. "Where you want me?"

In one photograph, Morris is standing in front of stacks of Sunday *Times* that reach to the middle of his chest. His hands are in his pockets, and he's wearing a red *TV Guide* apron. On his feet are tattered red sneakers, on his face a half-smile, and beneath it the weight of a lifetime of hardships overcome.

Morris asked me to make copies, and I brought him a few that Sunday. He proudly showed them to his newsstand friends. "How much you want for these?" he asked, reaching into his apron.

I told him I didn't want anything, but he insisted I accept a Sunday *Times*. I asked him a few questions. He began to talk at length about his newsstand and his past, unmindful of waiting customers. The wiry little man I would come to know as Harry, the indoor astronaut, redirected him. "Okay! Change of a dollar for a *Post*. She's waiting!" But then Morris went right on talking.

From that day forward, whenever I bought a paper, I would ask Morris how he was, and he would reply with some variation of "Better to ask what's *right* with me" and break out laughing his deep, guttural laugh. Saturday nights, when Morris — accompanied by a burly Puerto Rican man I would later learn was his bodyguard — was out selling the early edition of the Sunday *Times*, I'd stop by with Jonas, Henry, or Ruth, and he would joke with us. But it wasn't until I was about to leave the neighborhood that I proposed doing a story on him and his newsstand.

Morris wasn't especially taken aback, which surprised me. "Other people write about me already. I show you," he said.

He retrieved his cardboard shoebox from beneath one of the improvised benches and withdrew a wrinkled photocopy of an article from *(MORE)* magazine and a short piece from *The New Yorker*. Both prominently featured his newsstand.

"I'm impressed," I told him.

I think Morris would have been happy to talk to me all that afternoon, but I wanted to experience a panoramic view of him and his newsstand. I asked if I could come by another day and spend more time.

"Come tomorrow, 6:30," he said. "Not a minute later."

That night, I prepared a list of questions for Morris and typed them onto index cards. Among other topics, they covered the newsstand's operations, its history, his own, the neighborhood and its decline, Morris's family and relationships, his thoughts about New York City and America — about fifty cards altogether. I may have been relatively new to reporting, but nobody could say I wasn't thorough.

Our last encounter was not the first time Morris let me know my many questions were an issue for him. With each new round, he reiterated his skepticism.

"It becomes a nonsense, you coming with questions, questions," Morris said at one point. "With all your questions, you will know more about me than even *I* do!"

"I'll know more about you," I told him, "than I do about myself!"

"I want you to tell me who's buying this book and how many pages it will be," Morris said. "You go in a bookstore, you see a *million* of books. Who buys them, who sees them, who knows them? People don't even see them. Who cares about me?"

"Lots of people would. You'd be surprised," I said.

Morris shook his head. "Mostly people are selfish," he said. "Here in America, especially. In Europe, you live like one family. Here, you never even know who is your neighbor." He got to the point. "I don't think I am a man who is fit to be written in a book."

"What kind of man is?" I countered.

"A man accomplished, famous: doctor, scientist."

"Those are the kinds of people everybody writes about," I said. "People like you are, in a way, more important."

He smiled. "Well, what I say to everybody: You are right, too. Right?" Then he laughed. "Okay, now what do you want to ask me?"

And the conversation continued.

Each time we had this interchange, I wondered if I truly believed what I had said. Was I that naïve? But thinking about it now, I stand behind it, still.

A Night on the Town

The air was thick with summer heat, the streets were quiet, the sidewalks nearly empty.

On the corner of 10th Avenue and 46th Street, just ahead, I saw a girl, and I lingered for a moment, watching.

Silver stars on her jacket and studs on her belt caught the sun as she turned, beckoning to the few cars that passed. She shrugged, then called to a man on the stoop of a tenement across the street. I felt a tingling in my loins and tried to ignore it. I moved on.

An hour or so later, heading back that way, I saw her slumped in the doorway of an abandoned warehouse, savoring the shade and listlessly dragging on a Marlboro, the red and white pack jammed between her belt and abdomen. Standing beside her was another girl, tall and big-boned, and off to her left sat the scrawny, Afro-haired young man I had seen her calling to before. I lit a cigarette. They're just kids, I said to myself.

"Kinda early to be out working, isn't it?" I asked the girl. She looked at me with glassy eyes and jerked her head in the young man's direction. Her hair was like straw, and there were still traces of adolescent acne on her face. "*Some*body works me too hard," she said.

"Him?" I asked.

"Yeah, me," the young man said. "I work her seven days a week, twenty-four hours a day."

I could feel his eyes studying me from behind dark glasses. The two girls exchanged glances. I dropped my cigarette and ground the butt into the pavement. Just kids, I thought again.

"My name's David," I told him, squatting low so my eyes were even with his. "What's yours?"

"Clayton," he said, more readily than I would have imagined. "But they call me Clay." Waving his hand toward the girl with the stars on her jacket, he added, "and she's my old lady, Kathy." The other girl introduced herself as Betty.

"Nice to meet you all," I said, and sat down.

Debut

On a Friday night almost three weeks later I was on my way to the corner, and everything was jumping: Drag queens chatted on street corners, boys glided by on bicycles and skateboards, men gathered in groups, laughing and talking and sucking beer from splits, while well-dressed couples made their way to fancy restaurants and Broadway shows, apparently oblivious to it all. I walked across town on 46th Street, taking in their faces, looking for Clay and Kathy, but none of these faces were theirs.

But another girl, pretty in a homey sort of way, was standing on the corner when I got there. She had freckles, a turned-up nose, and shoulder-length, auburn hair. The tops of well-formed breasts, cream-colored under the nearly full moon, protruded from her green and orange bikini top, and faded blue jeans gripped her thighs and hips. I watched her for a few moments, hoping she would see me. When she didn't, I took a couple of steps forward, then asked, "Do you happen to know a guy named Clay or a couple of girls named Kathy and Betty? I met them here a couple weeks ago, and they said they'd be around."

She started. "Well," she drawled, her green eyes darting between me and the cars streaming up 10th Avenue, her face brightening and darkening with the shifting headlights, "I don't know the people you're talkin' about, but you see that car on the other side of the street?" She pointed toward a beat-up sedan. "There's a guy sittin' there who's watchin' for me, and he knows *all* the girls around here. Talk to him. His name's Frankie. Tell him Cookie sent you over."

A heavy-set man in a faded, plaid shirt, his hair long and graying, sat hunched over on the stoop where I'd met Clay and Kathy. His large, rough hands dangled between his legs. He gazed in my direction, but seemed not to see me. I took another deep breath, then asked him about Kathy and Clay.

He sighed. "They burn you?"

"Burn me? Uh, no, I'm a writer, and I wanted to talk with them — "

"Because you wanna write about prostitution, right?" he said, grinning. "I haven't seen 'em around," Frankie said, "but they might be out later. Clay's woman's name, by the way," he confided, "is really Ginger. But don't tell her I told you, if you see her."

Growing less nervous, I asked him if I could sit there while I waited for Kathy/Ginger and Clay. "I'd just as soon talk with you," I said.

He shrugged. "Why not?" I got nothin' else to do while I'm waitin' for her. But please," he said, when I took out my notepad, "do me a favor? Don't use no name, no description of the car, no license plate number? I'm a happily married man, believe it or not. I got a wife and three kids, I got a good job, I just bought a house ... my wife'd kill me if she knew I was out here tonight."

He wiped his forehead with the back of his hand. "I'm not usually out here doin' this, you know," he went on. "I'm just doin' a favor for a friend of mine who couldn't make it, watchin' his chick for him, that's all. I just happen to know about this because I grew up with it."

Frankie's friend, he told me, was in debt to loan sharks for a couple of grand, and they were threatening to get rough if he didn't start paying them off soon. I asked Frankie to tell me about these loan sharks, but he said he didn't really know much about them. "I never borrowed from them," he said. "I do it ... legal. The hard way, sometimes, but that's the way it goes, right?" He nodded toward Cookie. "She's out here tryin' to raise a hundred for her old man's first payment. And I just wish she'd hurry up — 'cause I wanna get home and be with my family."

We watched the street together. Cars turned the corner every few seconds, pausing just long enough for the men inside them to check out the girls. Frankie grew increasingly impatient. "See how she's missin' 'em as they go by?" he said. I nodded. Even I had already noticed something odd about her behavior. She was nowhere near as smooth as the girls I had seen on the Upper West Side.

A white van pulled over a few yards from Cookie. "C'mon, c'mon!" Frankie muttered, tapping his foot and kneading his hands. "He's waitin' for you!" The driver, a bearded man in his twenties or early thirties, backed up. Cookie leaned into the open window on the passenger side. They talked. "She's takin' too long," Frankie observed after a minute or so. As if on cue, Cookie slammed the door. No deal.

Cookie started to walk back to the corner, but changed her mind halfway. She cut across the street, toward us. Frankie rose slowly and met her at the curb. "I was gettin' worried, with him sittin' there all this time," Cookie said to him, tipping her head in my direction.

"It's cool," Frankie told her. "Don't worry. He's a writer."

"Oh!" Cookie said. Turning to me, she added, "I'm sorry, I thought you might be a cop." I shook my head 'no' and smiled.

"C'mon, Cookie," Frankie said, gripping her arm and directing her toward her corner. "It's gettin' late. I wanna be home by twelve."

He sat back down on the stoop. "What's with her?" I said when she was out of ear shot. "She new at it?"

"Uh-huh," Frankie said. "She just got into New York. This is her first time out."

"Her first time out?" I repeated.

"Uh-huh," Frankie said.

Her Unfortunate Break

A dented brown Mustang pulled up next to one of the cars parked across the street. Its driver, shrouded in shadow, honked his horn, and Cookie sidled over to him.

"Okay," Frankie said, "if he wants to make it with her, I'm gonna follow them. You wanna go for a ride?"

"Sure," I said.

Cookie climbed into the Mustang and they took off. "Let's go!" Frankie hollered.

He was behind the wheel and I was beside him in seconds, but we waited until the john's car was halfway down the block before we started after them. Frankie continued to fill me in on Cookie. "I'm sorry to say, I introduced this guy to the loan shark," he confessed, "and I don't wanna see him end up in the dump." We pulled away from the curb. "He met this girl three weeks ago," he went on. "She's from Chattanooga, Tennessee ..." He glanced around him, sensing something wrong. "... she claims her stepfather had relations with her at a very early age ..." With the road? "... and she's been on the run since she was 13 years old ..." Or the car? "... so she says." The tires!

Thumpabump! Thumpabump! Thumpabump! "And I got a fuckin' flat tire!" Frankie slammed his palm against the steering wheel. "God dog!" The john's car was pulling away fast. "I can't chase her on the flat. I wish she'd stop and let me get her at the corner!" The brown Mustang disappeared onto Ninth Avenue. "I can't believe I got a fuckin' flat tire. I gotta get her outta that car — she don't know where to go or what to do!"

We picked up speed — ThumpaBUMP! ThumpaBUMP! — and jerked around the corner after them. "I'm gonna ruin that fuckin' tire," Frankie whined. "Damn friends! Don't make any friends, Dave, I'm tellin' ya. It don't pay."

"This is one bad fuckin' night," I observed.

We pulled alongside the john's car, stopped at a light. "Open the window, would ya, Dave?" Frankie asked. He leaned across the front seat and hollered to the john, "I'm sorry to say this, but I know the girl." The john took his arm from around Cookie and rolled down his window. Frankie repeated himself, then explained, "I gotta get somethin' for her later, okay? Could you please bring her back later?"

"Sure, man," the john said. He smiled and waved us off.

"Thanks a lot, my friend," Frankie said.

Cookie appeared in the window over the john's shoulder. Whether she was puzzled or annoyed was hard to discern. "I have to see you later," Frankie said. "I got a flat tire. I'll meet you back there, okay?"

The light turned green. Cars honked at us from behind. As the Mustang pulled away, Frankie shouted, "I gotta give her some weed!"

—

"Look at the cops," Frankie said. "And I got a fuckin' flat tire. I'm gonna pull over, Dave."

We limped around the corner and into a parking space. The tire was shot, and changing it turned out to be no easy job. First, Frankie couldn't find the jack handle and had to substitute a long screwdriver, which kept slipping out of the jack's socket, skinning Frankie's knuckles. When at last he did raise the rear end of the car enough to pull off the bad tire, he found that, because the car was parked on an incline, it was still too low to replace the flat with the spare.

Breathing hard and sweating, Frankie kicked and shoved the unyielding tire, swearing under his breath as he tried to force it into place. "Fuckin' tire!" Frankie groaned.

"I hate to ask you," he said, "but could you do me a favor, Dave?" I nodded, oddly eager to be of use. "I don't know if I can get this fixed in time to meet her. You know what she looks like, right? Can you go to the corner, tell her what happened?"

"Sure," I said.

"Tell her to wait for me. Tell her I'll be right there," Frankie said. "I don't want her to be alone when she gets back." As I was about to leave, he added, "I only know her for a few hours, and would you believe it? I'm worried about her."

—

I sat on the stoop where Frankie and I had met earlier in the evening, waiting for Cookie and watching the other girls on the corner. People passed in and out of the building, stepping around me, many of them trailing dogs of assorted breeds and sizes. I noticed above my head a small metal sign, painted green with white lettering. It read:

NO LOITERING OR LITTERING
BY ORDER OF POLICE DEPARTMENT

I decided to take my chances.

Still riding the flat, Frankie returned about ten minutes later. He parked in front of the stoop and walked over to me. "She's not back yet, huh?" he said.

I shook my head.

Frankie shrugged, then took his jack and the long screwdriver from the back seat of the car and again set about changing his tire.

When he removed the flat, this time he examined it. He pried out a piece of glass about an inch and a half long, a remnant of a Coke bottle. "Wow," Frankie said, "when I pick up glass, I pick up *glass*."

I watched him work. His movements were clumsy and mechanical, as if his mind were elsewhere. "He's takin' advantage of her," Frankie said after a few minutes. He was soaked with sweat, his breathing labored. "She should never be out that long." He wiped his greasy hands on his pants. "With one of these guys, there's girls out here that'll tell you after a couple of minutes, 'C'mon, you're takin' too long.' She don't know any better."

Job done, Frankie tightened the lug nuts and shoved the flat, the jack, and his tools onto the back seat. We returned to the stoop.

"Where do you think he took her?" I asked.

"Probably down by the water some place."

"They'll do it in the car, then?"

"Yeah. Most of the men out here can't go for the money to get a girl in a decent surrounding."

Frankie gazed blankly at the two girls who had taken over Cookie's post. "I couldn't tell you what she's gonna do or not do," he said. "For all I know, she's talkin' to the guy and she's thinkin' about runnin' away with him, right? Which I wouldn't blame her for doin'. Would you wanna be out here doin' it for some bum?"

"Why do you think she is?"

Frankie shrugged. "I don't know. I guess she's in love with the jerk who's makin' her do it, right? Or somethin' to that effect." He paused, then turned and looked me in the eye. "Which isn't me, in case that's what you're thinkin'," he said. "The money she makes she's gonna turn over to her old man, or whatever you wanna call him, which he's gonna turn over to the people he owes money to." He spat on the sidewalk. "She's out here sellin' her body for that shit."

"This guy you're calling a jerk — he's a friend of yours?"

"Yeah. It sounds terrible, but, you know ..."

A patrol car pulled over near a fire hydrant someone had opened across 10th Avenue. One of the cops got out to shut it off. The girls on the corner strolled down the block and, after the cops left, strolled back again. Frankie and I watched, as if we were old friends catching a game together.

"You say you're gonna write a book? What, on city life?" Frankie asked me. I nodded, and told him about some of the other people I'd met. As we talked, we saw, almost directly across the street from us, a man in a white T-shirt, walking with a tall, stacked blond, throw a wine bottle onto the street. Shards of glass skittered across the pavement. "You see that?" Frankie said. "They do that to slow the cars down, right?" The man and the blond stopped by the side of a car parked near the corner. They talked. "Now, he's gonna put his woman to work," Frankie said.

We waited. "I wish she'd get back, so I could quit my worryin'. I'll tell you what happened: If this guy don't come back with her, he probably took her some place. Even, he got friends that were layin' for her. Either she's gonna get the shit kicked outta her by him and his friends, or he's gonna take her some place and Lord *knows* what the hell he's gonna do. Drop her, take her into Brooklyn, keep her, maybe, over the weekend. And use her. 'Cause she's not" — he fumbled for the word — "streetwise, or whatever you wanna call it. She's dumb, for this. She don't know what she's doin'. It was her unfortunate break I got a flat tire."

Frankie scanned the area. "If she does come back," he said, "she's gonna get scolded. I can't take this shit."

Frankie stood. He checked his watch. "Look," he said, "I'm gonna go to where she was supposed to take the guy, then I gotta make a call. I gotta check in. I'll be back in about ten minutes. If she does happen to come back, tell her not to move, just to *sit here* with you. I don't care if the world's comin' to an end — let her wait here, okay?"

A Change of Scene

The john dropped Cookie at the corner just as Frankie returned from his call. They met a little ways up the block. I hung back a while to give them a chance to talk, then walked toward them.

Frankie was all smiles, but Cookie seemed edgy and distracted. She pulled a bill from her bikini top and handed it to Frankie, who stuffed it in his shirt pocket.

Business transacted, the mood grew more cordial. As I drew near, I overheard Frankie asking questions, and Cookie, louder and giggly, answering him with phrases like 'negatory' and 'ten-four.' "She's from the Midwest," Frankie explained when I joined them.

They continued to talk. I noticed Frankie calling Cookie 'Marna.' I asked her if her name was 'Marna/Cookie,' trying awkwardly to make a joke. She laughed indulgently. "I'm Marna Jane," she explained, "but everybody calls me Cookie."

"She's really Cookie," Frankie said, his voice a little stiff.

Suddenly a wave of exhaustion swept over Cookie's face. "If I'm gonna bust this town," she said stonily, "I gotta get somethin' to drink."

The three of us moseyed up the block to a grocery store, where Frankie bought Cookie and himself each a Coke, and treated me to a beer. "We were afraid something had happened to you," I told Cookie as we left the store.

"Nooooo," she said, smiling seductively.

Frankie was worrying about the cops hassling us if we stood around, so we all got into the front seat of his car and headed up 10th

Avenue. Cookie turned on the radio, but Frankie shut it off right away. "Please," he said, "talk to me while we drive. Where the heck did you go?"

Cookie sunk into the seat. "Same place," she said.

"Down by the river?"

"Uh-huh."

"I gotta be blind."

"We were behind the buildings. I got brains. I ain't dumb. You know why?" Cookie jerked her thumb at a scooter cop parked by the curb. "They busted three chicks down there tonight, and now they're gonna look for another one. I just seen that cop five minutes ago."

Frankie's knuckles whitened as he gripped the wheel hard. "Damn!" he said. "You wanna write this down, Dave?" he asked. "They're *bustin'* the girls when they shouldn't be. There's too much fuckin' *crime* goin' around for these hard-ons to be out here bustin' girls who aren't really hurtin' too many people. Let me tell ya — you can put this down — they had one cop here, I don't know his name, but he actually *hits* the girls with his nightstick."

"Let one of 'em hit *me*," Cookie snarled, "he's gonna get a knife" — she lined up her words like dominoes — "right ... between ... the legs. I'll put him in the hospital deader 'n' a doornail." She turned to me. "I'm mean," she explained, giggling, "when it comes to fightin'. But I'm sweet as a kitten, otherwise."

Seconds later her bravado faded, and she slumped deeper into her seat. "Frankie," she whimpered, "I wanna get outta here."

Frankie sucked in his breath. "Look, how about if I take you some place farther down, if that'll put your mind at ease. We'll just stay out another hour, okay?" he asked.

"My behind," Cookie said.

"What?"

"I said, 'my behind.'"

"You don't wanna stay out that long, huh?"

"Shiiit. I'm gettin' fed up."

"You're puttin' me on the spot, Marna," Frankie said.

We drove on.

—

"This is your first night out?" I asked Cookie.

"First night in New York, yeah," she said. "But I used to do it in Texas. I never thought I'd see the day I'd become a prostitute, but I've been doing it since I was about 19."

"And you're how old now?"

"Twenty-one. In a month or so."

I pressed her for information about her past, and with a little prodding, she told me more about herself.

"I left home when I was young, went out, worked, had my own apartment. I used to be very heavy into drugs, and I've got scars all over my arms, all over my body, just from fights — knife fights. When I was growin' up, me and my parents didn't hit it off together, and I used to want to kill myself and want to get away from them. So, that's the only way I knew how to do it — run away from home. And I started very young, at 13 … Like, that's when I first started screwin' guys, to put it in plain English."

While Frankie moved slowly up one block and down another, seeking a better location, Cookie went on with her story. "This was in the state of West Virginia," she said. "But, like, in different states I'd run away. I'd go to Minnesota, Texas, Tennessee, California, Oklahoma … Baltimore, Maryland. You know, just different places. New York, for instance. Like, I've only been here, what, four weeks?" She looked to Frankie for confirmation. He nodded. "Yeah," she went on. "I mean, it's really just … I don't know … Well, I can't say I'm proud of myself, but it's one way of makin' a living, I guess. I can say that."

"It's the oldest profession in the world," Frankie observed. "So they claim, right?"

We drove on.

—

"What did you charge the john who picked you up?" I asked Cookie.

She was slow to answer. "Well," she said, clearing her throat. "Well, like, it's … ten for a head, and it's twenty for … the other." She drew a deep breath, added quickly, "and, like, all he got was a head, so that was ten." She twisted her body toward Frankie, suddenly self-conscious. "He's askin' me all these questions and he's writin' it down!" She turned back to me. "Don't you dare put that in the paper!"

Her reaction surprised me, and for a moment I didn't know what to say. "It's okay," I told her. "I won't use your real name. I'll just call you Cookie," I said, hoping to assuage her fear. "I've met other girls who call themselves Cookie."

"Yeah," Cookie sighed. "I guess there's too many 'Cookies' in New York."

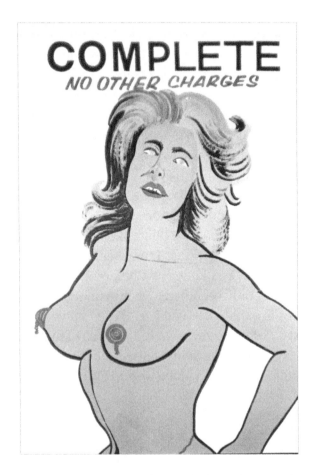

We stopped at a light. She changed the subject. "Since you're a writer," she said, "maybe you'd like to hear some of my poems and songs?" She pronounced the word *poms*. "I've been writing a lot of 'em, lately."

"Sure," I said.

Before she could tell me about her poems and songs, we saw a dark-skinned woman in her late twenties or early thirties about to cross the street with two small boys. The younger boy — chubby, with curly black hair and big eyes — balked, and the woman dragged him by the hand into the street. When he resisted, she bent over and slapped him on the side of his head three or four times, scolding him savagely in Spanish. He cried. Infuriated, the young woman slapped him again. The older boy drew back and watched. He did not look surprised.

Cookie could hardly contain herself. "Oh, you whore, you!" she screamed, scrambling across Frankie to the driver's side window. The child stumbled to the curb. The woman dragged him to his feet and, holding him by one arm, slapped him repeatedly with her free hand. "Frankie, lemme outta here!" Cookie cried. "Oh, you bitch!" she shouted.

"Relax!" Frankie told her.

"I *hate* to see a mother like that!"

"So do I, but be cool. It's gonna help him, you getting out?"

"But *look* at that, Frankie," Cookie pleaded.

The light changed, and Frankie made the turn. "She don't deserve a kid," he said. "She don't."

"Oh, Frankie," Cookie said, still watching, still trembling, "that's not right. I swear," she went on, "I would love to see somebody come up the street and just smack the holy *shit* outta her."

"She don't deserve a kid," Frankie repeated.

—

We continued our quest for a new location, cruising, some streets throbbing with light and motion, others dark and deserted, hunting for that Goldilocks mix of just enough traffic and the absence of police. "I'm gonna die," Cookie groaned suddenly. "I've had it." She began to whimper. She turned to Frankie for support. "And if he doesn't like it, that's tough shit, right?" she asked.

"Well," Frankie said, "for now it is, but — "

"Plus," Cookie said miserably, "plus, the baby is moving. The baby's just movin' too much, that's all," she said.

"The baby?" I asked. My eyes moved to her exposed belly pressing against her jeans. "You're pregnant?"

"Yup. Naturally," she said. Her tone became matter-of-fact. "Two to four months. My second."

"Your *second*?"

"Yup," she said. "My first is nine-and-a-half months old. His name is Prometheus." At this she brightened, flashed a smile. "He's in Des Moines, Iowa, with my sister-in-law." The father of both children, she said, was the same man, a Puerto Rican.

If it could, my head would literally have spun 'round at these revelations. It was not until much later that I wondered whether a woman two to four months pregnant could actually feel her baby moving.

—

Frankie stopped the car near a factory that had shut down for the night. "I gotta talk to her, private, for a coupla minutes, okay Dave?" he asked. They sat together on a concrete ledge a few feet away. I didn't hear their actual conversation, but I surmised he was telling her she was going to have to stay out a little longer. I don't know for sure what else they talked about, but when they returned to the car, they were both chatting and seemed more relaxed.

Cookie wanted to know how big the piece of glass in Frankie's tire was. "Put it this way," Frankie told her, smiling, "I guess I'll be going to Bambergers tomorrow to get a new tire."

She rested her head on his shoulder and stroked his chest. "Aww, you poor babe," she cooed.

"I'm not poor," Frankie declared. "This could be a lot worse."

Cookie continued to fondle Frankie, her hands moving from chest to thighs, then lightly caressing his crotch. I pretended not to notice, as I felt my own prick swell. Frankie moaned softly. He tried to slip his hand around Cookie's waist and down her pants, but she pushed him off. "No," she told him. She replaced his hand on the wheel.

"He's gonna get it," she said to me, winking.

"You promise?" Frankie asked. "If I didn't know Bobby, I wish I could."

"What he don't know won't hurt him," Cookie said.

Encouraged, Frankie tried again to put his hand down her pants but was again rebuffed, this time with verse. Cookie recited:

Expectations are mine alone
What can I say?
Vows are known.

—

As if her dalliance with Frankie had never happened, Cookie turned toward me and asked, "What about you, Dave? Do you write poems, too?"

I told her I wrote prose now, but that in college I thought of myself as a poet. Frankie interrupted. "Excuse me, Dave, for a minute. I'm sorry," he said. He jerked his thumb over his shoulder. "Right, we just come off 11th Avenue, okay?" he said to Cookie.

"Ten-four," she replied.

"That's a big ten-four, forty, roger, and all that good stuff," Frankie said. "Okay," he went on, "now, I'll show you."

We pulled into an underground parking lot. "Very, very quiet," Frankie said.

"No security guards?" Cookie asked.

"No security guards, no nothin'," Frankie said. "You could go right behind that truck over there in the corner. And, matter of fact, you're gonna have two body guards tonight, looks like, insteada one."

"Well, that's cool," Cookie said. "I mean, if Dave doesn't mind hangin' out with you. And," she continued, turning to me again, "and, if Dave doesn't mind me, the way I act."

"I don't mind anything," I assured her.

Frankie asked her if she knew how to get to the lot. "Negatory," she said, giggling. Gauging Frankie's mood, she quickly forced herself to become more serious. She added, "But it won't take me long to learn."

Frankie rubbed her thigh. "You're beautiful," he told her.

As we drove to the corner Cookie would be working from, Frankie carefully went over the route from there to the parking lot. He had to repeat the directions several times before Cookie understood, but at last she seemed to get it. When we got to the spot, though, there was a police scooter parked on the sidewalk.

"You're not goin' out over here, sweetheart," Frankie said. "They just closed off the street."

We headed further uptown, but found cops there, too. They seemed to be everywhere. "Jesus, what am I gonna do?" Cookie wailed.

Frankie thought it over. "I'll take you over to the East Side," he said. "Twenty-somethin' street. It probably won't be so hot there. That's where the Black dudes with the El Dorados and five or six girls in their stables hang out. The cops are probably gettin' paid."

Cookie wanted to pick up some weed first. "My head ... I ... I ... With these cops, I'm freakin' out, you know?" she said. "I'm gettin' very paranoid, I hate to say."

"Relax," Frankie told her. "We'll stay out just a little longer, and then I'll bring you over to Brooklyn, to Bobby."

Frankie thought that Clay — of Clay and Ginger fame — might have some stuff, so we drove around the neighborhood, looking them, but they weren't at any of their usual spots. "Ah, come on Ginger," Frankie said, beating his palm against the steering wheel. "Clay's not out, Ginger's not out — "

"Well," Cookie said, "why don't you ask somebody if they seen 'em?"

"You think they're gonna tell me? Most of these people, when they see me, they think one thing: cop."

"Why's that?" I asked.

"I don't know," he said. "I don't think I look like one."

"Well," I said, "you do look a little like Al Pacino in that movie."

"Ho, ho ..." Frankie said, "well, thank you. I wish I was makin' his kinda money."

—

It was looking like we wouldn't find Clay or Ginger. "Ah, fuck this shit," Frankie said, "excuse my French. My language ain't the best in the world. We're goin' crosstown." Weed foray abandoned, he gripped the steering wheel with renewed determination.

As we crossed over to the East Side, Cookie still seemed uptight. Frankie tried to cheer her up by making fun of the drag queens hanging out on the street corners. "Did you ever see a woman with legs like that?" he asked. "God help the girl who has legs like that."

He squeezed Cookie's leg. She smiled. "Oh, I think mine are very firm," she said.

Cookie started to relax into the ride. We again began talking. "Can you see doing this years from now?" I asked her.

"Hell, no," she said. "After this kid, I'm goin' back to topless dancing, and I'm not having any more kids. Two's the limit, for me."

The next day, in fact, she was supposed to start a new job setting wigs, something she said she'd done in California. "If she has any problems," Frankie chimed in, "I'll teach her, 'cause I'm an ex-beautician."

"Did you want these kids," I asked Cookie.

"Naturally," she said. "I mean, abortions and adoptions, those are two things I don't go for. But I'm not exactly against contraception. Like, it depends on how much hot water *I'm* in, and, if I got a dude like I do now, how much hot water *he's* in."

I asked her about this "dude." "I'm not really that involved with him, you know? But I really like him a lot. So I'm helpin' him out."

"How long have you been together?"

"Frankie?"

"Three weeks," Frankie quickly said.

"You mean you just met him when you came to New York?" I wanted to add, 'and you're selling your body for him?'

"Put it this way," Frankie said. "He's one of the few guys who had a kind word to say for a little while, treated her decent for a while. He just borrowed the money — well, not too long ago. So you can say fate, or whatever — it could just be fate that she came along at the wrong moment. Maybe it woulda been a hell of a lot better if he didn't borrow the money and she came along, right? Maybe she wouldn't be out here now."

"To be honest with you," Cookie said, "I've never really met anybody like him. I mean, I've met worse, *really* worse, but he's kinda hard to figure out and kinda hard to understand. He doesn't explain things. He just says 'do this' or 'do that.' I don't know. Maybe he just doesn't think. Or maybe he doesn't realize the things he's comin' out with."

I asked Cookie if it bothered her that he didn't explain. She thought about it for a few seconds, glanced again at Frankie, and then admitted that it did, kinda.

—

By then we were heading downtown, toward the Gramercy Park area. I remembered a story about a 15-year-old runaway who was strangled to death by a trick in a hotel near there a year or so before. "Do you ever worry about getting hurt?" I asked Cookie.

She took a moment to answer. "Yeah," she drawled, "because, see, this last guy had what you call a deadly weapon in the car."

"*That* guy?" Frankie asked.

"Yeah," Cookie said. "We were just sittin' there, and I really got scared. He was pointin' it at me and wavin' it around and I didn't know if I should scream or get out of the car, or what. It kinda freaked me out," she admitted. "That was another reason why I didn't get back so soon."

We drove toward the river. Frankie surveyed the area. "Here, it isn't too hot," he explained, turning toward her. "The cops very rarely bother the girls. Over here, they work right on the street, park in between cars and make it. Mostly, it's no screwin', just a little head." He paused for a response. None came. "Or would you rather go to Third Avenue, where there's a lot more girls and a lot less vehicle traffic, but where you have less of a chance of gettin', you know, into trouble?"

"When we get to Third Avenue, I'll decide," Cookie said.

"You better hurry up and decide," Frankie said, "'cause I wanna go *home*."

"I know it. I don't want Victoria to lose her — "

"I ain't gettin' nothin' tonight, sweetheart. I know she's mad at me."

"Just tell her to scratch her left boobie and get glad. Or tell her to shove it up between her toes. Tell her *something*" — her voice edged toward panic — "I don't care what you tell her. Tell her you had to work late, that's all."

—

We crossed over to Third Avenue. "I hope there's no spooks in this territory," Cookie said.

"You don't talk to them," Frankie told her. "They come over to you, you just don't bother. Don't even walk over to the car, okay?" He stroked her stomach and added, with some tenderness, "And no more hassling this thing with money with these people, okay babe? You tell 'em the price, they wanna hassle with you, forget it." He continued to rub her belly. Cookie's eyes began to tear. "I'm glad you're doin' that," she said softly. "My stomach's cold."

We pulled over at 14th Street and Third Avenue.

Frankie told Cookie to have the trick take her all the way out 14th Street to the Con Edison building. "It's gonna be dead around there," he explained. "You go between two cars, or you park in front of a car and work from there." Again he went over the directions several times, until he was certain she understood. "I'll be followin' you through," he concluded. "Let's get outta this damn shit in a little while, okay? Let's get home."

"Frankie?" Cookie said, her eyes taking in the dingy tenements, the massage parlors, the winos walking the street.

"Yeah, sweetheart?"

"Why you had to pick this territory, I'll never know."

—

We dropped Cookie off a few blocks further downtown. As I opened the door to let her out, I asked how long she thought she'd have to keep doing this. She sighed. "To be honest with you, I don't have the slightest idea. But I hope this is the last. In Texas, I'm used to it, but in New York, I'm not." She gave Frankie one final, imploring glance, then moved toward the corner.

"She's pretty nervous, isn't she," I said.

"I would be, too," he said.

"Why did you bring her down here?"

He shrugged. "It's on the way home."

Cookie had taken no more than a dozen tentative steps when she was intercepted by a Black wino, who grabbed her arm and started to paw her. Frankie leaped out of the car as quickly as his bulk would permit, slamming the door behind him. He ran toward Cookie and the wino, hollering: "Marna! Marna!"

"Get lost!" he yelled at the drunk, pushing him away. "Go! Go! Quit your woe shit!"

Cookie was close to tears. Frankie put his arm around her shoulders. "Was he messin' with you already?" he asked.

"Yes!" Cookie sobbed.

Frankie gripped her shoulders. "Okay," he told her, "protection's workin'. He ain't gonna bother you no more." Still trembling, but angry now, Cookie responded: "I know he ain't. Because if he does," she looked menacingly after the drunk, by then staggering up the block, "he's gonna get it right in the *balls*."

"Okay," Frankie said. "You gonna stay on this corner?"

"I dread the thought of it," Cookie told him, glancing around her again, "but all right."

"Look," Frankie said, giving Cookie's shoulders a final squeeze, "when somebody starts botherin' you like that, just come back to us."

"Okay," Cookie said.

—

Frankie and I waited in his car. A couple of potential johns stopped for Cookie, but she didn't get in. "She's too much," Frankie said. "I'm not gonna come out with her no more. One favor's enough. That's the second guy she turned down, in the Lincoln."

A few minutes later, a maroon station wagon pulled over. The driver beeped for Cookie. She looked back at us. "Go ahead, stupid, go!" Frankie said in a stage whisper. "These guys ain't gonna stand around for her when there's girls up the block willin' to *jump* on the car."

Cookie made her way slowly to the car. "I don't believe she did it in Texas," Frankie told me. "My personal opinion is, she's new."

Cookie got into the station wagon. We could see them through the car's rear window, two moving shadows.

"I tell ya," Frankie went on, "the guy she's goin' with is supposed to give me a hundred to bring in tonight, but I'm not stayin' out here much longer, so whatever she makes, I'm gonna bring in, and fuck the rest."

"She just made ten bucks before?"

"Twenty. See, when she first got outta the car, she was picked up within a minute. The last time took like ten minutes — she was out there maybe five minutes, before you came over to me. So it wasn't long. She could turn a trick every fifteen, twenty minutes, but she's not ..." He sighed. "She's doin' this, I hope, not outta love, 'cause if she's in love with this guy, she's a jerk. A bigger jerk than I thought she was."

I asked Frankie how she met this guy Bobby. "I'm to blame for every goddamn thing," he confessed. He sighed again. "I was workin' on a job, and this guy Bobby's brother was workin' with me, and I met her at a pizza place, and she didn't have no place to go. I'm certainly not gonna bring her home to Momma's house or to my house, but I know Bobby was divorced from his wife, so I said, 'Hey, you wanna stay with my friend? Far as I know he's a decent dude and he'll treat you good.' So, she said yeah. That was the first night she came into New York. She had nothin' but really a buncha rags she was wearin'.

He bought her some nice clothes, but naturally one pair a clothes ain't gonna last three weeks. They were lookin' kinda bad, so I bought her what she's wearin' right now."

"Did your friend put her up to this, or was it her idea?"

"He put her up to it," Frankie said. "I work with these guys for eight, ten, twelve hours a day, but what they do in their private life, I really don't know. Except," he added, grinning a little, "except, now I learned one thing."

The wagon still hadn't moved. "He's hesitating," Frankie observed. "She's probably tellin' him where to go. Let's hope he don't mind ..."

A moment later, the john's car glided slowly into traffic. When it was nearly a block ahead, we pulled out after it. "Here we go again," Frankie said. "This time, we'll watch her."

Gadding About Town

The john took a right at the next corner. "Oh, shit!" Frankie cried out. "How many times I gotta tell her? I told her 14th Street, right? What's this to you?"

"Twelfth Street," I said.

We followed them east almost to the river, then through a maze of side streets, always trailing by a block or two, running red lights so as not to get too far behind. "Why don't they pull over?" Frankie asked. "What's she waitin' for? It's dead, it's dead. What is she *doin'* to me?" he moaned. "Oh, man," he said, "is this guy takin' her for a *ride*?"

On a particularly desolate street, the john stopped. We stopped a couple of blocks behind him and waited. There were no cars between us. "This looks stupid, you know?" Frankie said.

"Maybe he's trying to see if you're following him," I suggested.

"He's doin' a good job of it," Frankie said.

The john soon took off again. Frankie waited until a car passed us and then resumed the chase. The john headed further downtown, leading us through neighborhoods bathed in bright, pink-tinted light. Groups of men stripped to undershirts drank beer around the stoops of crumbling tenements. A handful of kids screwed open a fire hydrant and sprayed passing cars, laughing demoniacally and gesturing lewdly with their hands. I closed the window to avoid getting drenched. "He don't know where he's goin'. He's gettin' himself really into some hot water now," Frankie said. "He's goin' to a pretty bad part of New York."

The john turned uptown and meandered through a half-dozen side streets until he was nearly back to where he picked Cookie up. He stopped again. We stopped, too, and again we waited. It was so dark that all we could see clearly were the taillights of his car.

After about a minute, the john flicked on his left blinker and started to move up the street. He turned at the next corner. "He's takin' her back," Frankie said. "He's not gonna take her out no more. To hell with this shit. I'm gonna get her now. This is too much, in one night, for my head."

We came to the spot where the john had stopped. Frankie was about to swing over to Third Avenue to pick up Cookie when I spotted her leaning against a plywood fence covered with posters. "She's right there!" I cried, pointing.

Frankie stomped on the brakes. "He kicked her outta the car, huh?" he said. Then he saw her himself. She was wobbling, holding her neck, and her face was twisted with pain. "He hit her?" Frankie said. He beeped his horn, leaning out the window, shouting, "Hey, Cookie, hurry up if he hit you!" He shouted still louder, "*Cookie, get in the caaaar!*" When she looked our way, he added, "We're gonna get him. C'mon, Cookie!"

Cookie staggered to the car, still holding the back of her neck. She was sobbing. I got out of the car and let her in, then sat down again beside her. "What happened?" Frankie asked her.

She said nothing. We waited.

"He seen us followin' him, right?" Frankie guessed.

"Right," Cookie said, choking through her tears.

"And he hit you."

Cookie nodded, rubbing her neck and muttering "Oh, fuck!" in a hoarse whisper.

"What happened, insteada cursin'?" Frankie asked. "He gave you a crack in the neck?"

Cookie nodded again, then emitted a sharp laugh. "He was a god-damn fuckin' *Chinese*!" she spat out. Her breath came in gasps. "I told him to turn down 14th Street ... and he turns down 12th ..." She rotated her head and grimaced. "I know one thing," she said. "I'm gonna have a bruise and a half tomorrow!"

"What did he tell you, that there's people followin' you and he didn't like the idea, or — "

"He didn't like the idea of the *price*, either," she snapped. Her voice was growing stronger. "I told him before I got in, and he said it was okay. Then when I told him to turn down 14th Street, he got even madder."

"I'd like to see his station wagon *now*," Frankie threatened.

"He says, 'No, we're goin' down to my apartment.' 'Oh no we ain't,' I tell him."

"What was all that riding around about?" I asked her.

"A game," she said. "I started to get out two or three times, at the red lights, but he seen me grab the door handle. Plus," she added hurriedly, "he was askin' me a bunch a questions, and I think he's a cop."

"He's not a cop, or he'd of busted you," Frankie observed. "He seen the car followin' him?"

Cookie nodded. "Yeah. I says, 'There ain't nobody followin' us. You're dreamin'.' And he goes like this —" she swept the tip of her finger across her neck, under her chin, as if she were slitting her throat from ear to ear. She began to whimper. Hopefully, she asked, "Did you get the license plate number?"

Frankie shook his head. I explained, "It was too dark. We were too far away."

The car started to move.

"Was it like this in Texas, you raising money for some guy?" I asked Cookie.

"It was me, myself, and I," she replied. "And I carried a switchblade. I used it more than once. And let me tell you, those guys never forgot it."

"There must be an easier way for you to make a living," I said.

"She's gonna try, tomorrow," Frankie said.

"I can hardly swallow," Cookie said. "Shit! I just wanna see his car, that's all I ask. Just let me see that car."

"Okay," Frankie said. "I'll swing over to Ninth."

We drove in silence for a while. I wondered what would happen if by coincidence or miracle we managed to find the maroon station wagon.

"All I can say is, I'm sorry," Cookie said.

"What are you sorry about?" Frankie asked. "You didn't do nothin' wrong."

"Are you sure?"

"Huh?"

"Are you sure?"

"Sure," Frankie said. "What'd you do wrong? You tried for him."

"Huh?"

"You tried," Frankie repeated, rubbing her leg.

—

We were sitting at a red light when I saw the john's car about a hundred yards away. It looked like he was picking up another girl. I visualized a showdown:

We are tearing across the intersection, trying to cut the john off. He spots us and pulls away before we reach him, and we give chase.

We jolt through crowded, twisting streets, weaving from curb to curb, slamming into parked cars. He nearly loses us when he throws his wagon into a slide and spins completely around, but we manage to stay on him until, at last, he turns into a dead end. We have him.

Frankie whips open his door, hikes up his pants, and slowly, menacingly, swaggers over to the station wagon. Hesitantly, I get out the other side. I see the john climb out the passenger side of his car, his hand behind his back. Is he concealing something? Frankie is almost upon him. From where I'm standing I can see the sparkle of metal reflecting the street lights, and I can also see that Frankie, the avenger, suspects nothing.

For a moment or two I am frozen, but I shake my voice loose, and, nearly certain my warning will come too late, I finally call out: "Frankie! Look out! He's got a — "

I blinked the scene away and pointed toward the station wagon. "That's him, isn't it?" I said.

"Yup," Cookie said.

"Where?" Frankie asked.

"By that light," I told him.

"That's him?" he asked Cookie.

"Damn straight," she said.

The john had his left blinker on. "He's gonna make a U-turn. Ohhhhh! Isn't that so pret-ty?" Frankie said. "Oh, c'mon, make a U-turn, mister ..."

The john's car did not turn around. His light changed before ours, and we watched as he disappeared around a corner a block farther down.

"I tell you," Cookie said, "if that chick he picked up has any sense, man, she'll get that sonofabitch."

We remained at our light, waiting for it to change to green. Frankie asked me, as we waited, if I happened to read about a Chinese guy who'd picked up a Black girl down at the Bowery. "He took her over to a place and about twenty guys gang-banged her."

Cookie nodded. "I think that's why he wanted to go to his apartment."

Our light finally changed. Frankie asked me if I was going to hang out in the area. I told him no, I was going home. He offered to take me to the subway. "I hate to drop you off around, you know, the streets," he explained. "You could probably handle yourself, but it's no use bein' in a neighborhood that isn't necessary. 'Cause I'm gonna be splittin' into Brooklyn to bring her back to Bobby."

I accepted the offer. Frankie drove to the Bowery and Delancy Street stop, near the entrance to the Williamsburg Bridge. The three of us talked for a few minutes before we split up.

I asked Cookie about her plans. She said she was thinking about getting her own apartment. The women's wig business, she figured, paid pretty good. I told her she might find a cheap place, maybe with a roommate, on the bulletin boards in the stores near the universities, but as the words left my mouth, I imagined her rooming with NYU students, turning an occasional trick on the side, and knew before I'd finished that it would never happen. Frankie told me that what she was really looking for was a guy that'd keep her, "that isn't gonna pimp her or any of that shit."

"Who knows, Frankie?" Cookie said. "After your divorce goes through, I might just say, 'Hey, c'mon, move in.'"

"Divorce?" I said. "I thought you said you were a happily married man, Frankie."

He faltered for a moment. "Happily married?" he said, "there's no such thing. We lived happily for about five years, and then it started going bad 'cause she came from a rich family, and I lived in a project most of my life. She was a fashion designer, she was makin' good money — but now I'm makin' decent money — and she couldn't take the strain of havin' three kids and not havin' a big payroll."

Frankie slumped in his seat. "My in-laws just gave my wife the down payment for a house, and the judge said give it another six months. Her parents think the house will pacify both of us."

I heard myself saying, "Well, I hope it does."

"Whatever, right?" Frankie said. "My children are more important than her. I hate to say it, but that's how I feel."

I hunted for the right thing to say. "Let me split, okay Dave?" Frankie said. "'Cause I wanna be home before twelve. Maybe we'll see you again. I might be down in that area next week."

"You think you're gonna do this again?" I asked.

"I got to," Frankie said. "I gotta start payin' these people off, or that man's gonna get hurt."

"Yup, that's it," Cookie agreed.

"But next time," Frankie added, "I'm gonna make sure she has a room to work out of, insteada off the streets. That's what she'll be doin' next week: out of a room."

He glanced at his watch. "Dave, I'll see ya, okay? Let me get goin'."

He reached across Cookie and offered me his hand. "Okay," I said. We shook hands warmly. "Maybe I'll see you. Thanks for the ride to the train."

I got out of the car. "Bye, Dave," Cookie said. She smiled. "It was nice to meet you."

"Likewise," I told her, returning the smile.

I got out of the car and waved goodbye. As I watched the taillights of Frankie's car merge with the traffic headed over the bridge, I remembered a woman I encountered three weeks earlier, just after I left Clay and the straw-haired girl he called Kathy.

She was overweight and looked well into her late thirties. Her hair was a brittle, bleached-blond, and she wore too much pink eye shadow and a pink pants suit that didn't fit her right. She stood in front of the Circle-in-the-Square Theater on 50th Street and smiled as she asked, in a voice like syrup, "Do you wanna go out?"

"It's kinda early, isn't it?" I replied. It was not yet noon.

"Nooooo!" she cooed. "There's a lotta early birds out. You oughta try it."

"Maybe," I said, "but not today."

I lost sight of Frankie's car. Disoriented, as if I'd walked out of a movie in which I'd played a minor role, I descended into the subway and began the long trip home.

Manhattan Notebook

I'd been working all morning and needed a break.

Out my window, I looked down on the great spider structure of the elevated tracks, and just beyond them the edge of Harlem.

I climbed onto the fire escape. The sun was high, the sky clear and brilliant. Pigeons swirled overhead in great interlocking arcs, an occasional straggler breaking from the group and arcing out on its own. They circled low, close to the rooftops, in ever-tightening loops, their wings emitting a collective whisper as they screwed down toward the coop two buildings over, and home. *This* was my home, now.

I tapped my shirt pocket, but the cigarette pack was flat, so I headed down to SafeTees, the local market, for more. My new roommate had told me the man who ran it was "a very special person," and I wondered, briefly, if there was something going on between them, but it was none of my business. I just wanted a pack of smokes.

I lived on the fifth floor. The elevator stopped for me, but before I could press "B," it continued on to the sixth, heedless of my desires. A small old man wearing a grey hat entered. I noticed a tattoo on his wrist — from the concentration camp, I assumed. We'd never spoken, and we said nothing to each other as we rode down to the basement.

Younger and quicker, I made it out of the building several seconds ahead of him. Near the iron gate that opened onto the street, a young man, pale and all bones and angles, lay sprawled on the pavement. I knelt down beside him. His face was covered with rough, red scales. His eyes were open.

The old man joined me. I held the young man's wrist, checking for a pulse. The arm felt limp, a dead thing, but his heart beat steadily.

"I know him," the man from the sixth floor said. His accent was Jewish. "He is drunk. He lives in the building. I know his family for years."

"Can we help you?" the old man said to the young drunk. We tugged him to a sitting position. He mouthed a word that could have been "drunk," but he made no sound.

"He is drunk," the old man repeated. He motioned to me. "Come on." We each grabbed an armpit and pulled the young drunk to his feet. When the old man and I let go, he remained standing. He clutched his keys in one hand and attempted to balance with the other.

"Can you make it?" the old man asked.

The drunk man took a few steps forward, staggered, then caught himself on the fence. "All right?" the old man asked.

The young drunk shook the old man's hand and kissed him on the cheek. He turned and did the same with me, then wobbled toward the basement door. "Are you sure you can make it?" the old man asked again.

The drunk man turned and made the "okay" sign. He waved to us shakily. "God bless you," he said.

The old man and I headed toward the corner, where we would soon part ways. On the way, he told me, "This one is always drunk. He was in the army, and since then, always drunk. His father died a few months ago."

"Why does he drink?" I asked.

"Irish," the old man said. "They are always drinking, you know."

Laundry

It was Sunday morning. The faces drifting by were not the ones I saw on Monday, the weary faces moving impassively through the streets.

It was too early for the transvestites and the junkies to hang out on the corner, smoking cigarettes and gossiping, and it was too hot for the winos to stretch their scrawny bodies out on the benches in the middle of Broadway.

I squatted outside the laundromat on the hot ground in the hot sun, tingling and sweating as the warmth of the sheet metal storefront soaked into my back. Cigarette butts, squashed plastic cups, matchbooks, clods of dust and hair, and broken glass surrounded me. The heat from the pavement burned into my feet.

A 50-year-old bag lady, gaunt and worn, rummaged through her coat. I'm certain I was the only one who noticed. She muttered, "You saved them with a million dollars. When they came back from the victorious war, they took over the country, they made it the way they wanted it. The savages don't fight the same way the civilized soldiers do."

She lit a cigarette. Her mouth was toothless, or nearly so. She continued: "Retreating back into the past, the dim dark past ages, that's where America goes, the dim, dark savagery." She took a drag and blew out a cloud of smoke. "We've got more savages in this country than we've got in the whole jungle," she said.

Cigarette ash drifted over me.

I saw her again a few days later, standing under the marquee of the burnt-out Riviera Theater, eating an apple down to the core, wholly absorbed in the process.

Ruth said she figured bag ladies slept on the subways and fed themselves by ordering coffee in restaurants and clearing the leftover food from the plates of the people around them. "I bet you could eat quite well that way," she said.

"I've never seen a bag lady in a restaurant," I said.

"Maybe you haven't gone to the right places," she said.

Marian, the King

Outside Sloan's supermarket, Marian gazed into the doorway of the shoe repair shop. As I passed, she muttered, "I've never been in that store before. Do they sell shoes there?"

I shrugged. "I don't know. I've never gone in there either."

Marian was the most strikingly dressed of the neighborhood bag ladies. Her outfit that day: a striped blouse, ruffled skirt, plaid socks, and a white hat. Adorning her attire were sunglasses, two buttons that read *I AM The King,* assorted trinkets around her neck, several brace-lets, and two metal belts, from which hung a whistle, a small radio, and a tin cup. A plastic pen dangled from each ear.

"You're looking good today, Marian," I said. "Can I take your picture?"

She smiled. "No thank you, dear," she said.

I shrugged again and smiled back. "Okay, no problem."

Apropos of nothing, Marian offered, "I'm from Pennsylvania." She tapped the transistor radio that hung from her neck. "It's second-hand. It's broken, so I don't know what's going on." She paused for a moment, glancing skyward. "Is Rockefeller still Vice President?"

"Yes," I said, "he's still Vice President."

"I like Rocky," she said, "but I wish he'd send me some money."

She laughed. I laughed. "Me, too," I said.

"You know Rocky had two wives, Mary and Happy? And Mary, she's from Pennsylvania, just like I am." She sighed. "Now I go wher-ever the welfare puts me." With a wave of her jewelry-laden hand, Marian gestured down Broadway. "I live over on 94th Street. I got a room there."

"Would you like me to visit you?" I asked.

She shook her head violently. "No, no, no, dear. Nobody comes there. It ain't safe. My landlord's been plotting and scheming and try-ing to *get* me. He's taking my weight off, making me lose my hair." She reached up and stretched her thin, curly hair. "See that?"

I nodded. "I see."

"He's trying to learn all my secrets, and then he's gonna take over my identity, put *my* name on somebody else and somebody *else's* name on me," she said. "He won't let me buy anything, not even a pair of shoes." Her voice dropped to an indignant whisper. "They wanna lock me away somewhere. They got no right to do that."

Her hands trembling with momentary rage, Marian said, "They locked me up too many times *already*. They kept me locked up in Pennsylvania for six years. Here in New York, *fifteen*." She scowled. "They had no *right* to do that to me. There's nothin' wrong with me! It's just the opposite, it's them insteada me."

She tilted her head and moved it back and forth, bird-like. "You see them women in stores, the white women, who talk about me?"

I nodded. "Uh-huh?"

"It's none of their business what I do. It ain't none of their damn *business*. They oughta put some of them, and a few of the models, on welfare, so's they'll know what it's like."

"Of course you do," I said.

As if summoned, just then two older white women walked by. They stopped a dozen feet past us, out of earshot, and talked with each other.

"The old battleaxes," Marian said bitterly. "I worked for rich people like them before. I know about 'em. They want everything they can *get* from a man, if his pocketbook can afford it." As if she were posing for an ad in a women's magazine, she held out her arm and displayed a ragged sleeve. "There *they* are in their fine clothes, some of 'em walking around 100 years old. I came outta the hospital with nothing 'cept what I had when I was locked up, and I get my clothes from rummage sales. I don't even have a decent pair of shoes."

She swayed back and forth, her trinkets emitting faint, almost melodic clicks. "I don't want no twenty-two-room house," she said, "but a person's got the right to buy herself a pair of *shoes*."

Marian picked up one of her shopping bags. "I gotta carry all this around because of two reasons: One is that I don't want to be thought of as a call girl. The other is that I don't want 'em stealing from me."

"Someone steals from you?"

"You didn't know? They *run* through there in the welfare hotels. I can't even open my door to go to the kitchen without I might be missing something when I get back to my room." She scowled again and gave out a faint growl. "My welfare check is $65 a month. That's down from $80 every two weeks. I been on welfare eight times, and each time it's a different office. This one's the worst."

She picked up her other bags. "All these problems is because of the wars, and the filthy rich. And the government." She took a step down Broadway, then turned toward me again. "They want something and they *take* it," she said.

She gave me a half-smile and a little wave. "Okay, dear," she said. "You have a nice day, now."

"You, too, Marian. See you later," I said.

You might be the devil

Just outside the 96th Street subway entrance, a bag lady stood, begging. She stuck out her hand and asked of every passerby, "Dollar? Dollar?"

As I approached, she smiled, one lone tooth showing. I said, "I'll trade you — I'll give you a dollar if you let me take your picture." I showed her my camera.

"Oh, no," she said. "No pictures."

"Okay. No pictures, no dollar. But why not?"

"How do I know who you are? You might be the devil!"

"If I were the devil, why would I be walking around here?" I gestured toward the stairway to the platform, littered with trash and cigarette butts. "I'm not the devil," I said.

"That's what he does. He walks around the graveyard like that. I read in the Christian books that you have to watch out. When somebody knocks on your grave, you better make sure it's God because it could be the devil, and then he'll get into your body." She tipped her head to one side and back again. "He's two-faced, you know."

"But you're not dead yet, so you don't have anything to worry about," I said.

"No, not yet. But I'm watching out. And you better watch out, too — I'm serious."

The Grapes of Wrath

I sat on the pavement of the uptown IRT platform at Times Square, leaning against a scaly blue support post. I was re-reading Steinbeck's *The Grapes of Wrath*. Grandpa had just died in Mr. Wilson's tent.

Pa said, "We're thankful to you folks."

"We're proud to help," said Wilson.

"We're beholden to you," said Pa.

"There's no beholden in a time of dying," said Wilson, and Sairy echoed him, "Never no beholden."

Al said, "I'll fix your car — me an' Tom will." And Al looked proud that he could return the family's obligation.

"We could use some help." Wilson admitted the retiring of the obligation.

I thought of what an elderly friend who had lived through the Depression on a small farm in western Oklahoma had told me. "All the time I was growing up there," she recalled, "if the neighbors hadn't come in and done the chores, milked the cows, when we had that severe attack of the flu, I don't know what we would've done, what would've happened. But there was always a neighbor. Then when *they* all got the flu, my father was over there doin' chores for them. There was always this exchange going on. Otherwise, if they hadn't all helped each other, it would have been very difficult for all these families to have survived."

I was jerked back to the present by a soft, pleading voice. "Excuse me, sir," it said. "Can you spare some change so I can get somethin' to eat?"

I looked up from my book, startled and annoyed.

He was tall and Black, his hair close-cropped. He wore checked pants and a worn beige jacket too thin for the weather. He continued, softly, "I'm sorry to bother you. I don't like to do this. But I haven't had anything to eat in two days, and I'm hungry. Anything you can spare ..."

I stood up. As I reached into my pocket, I explained, "I'm out of work," but it didn't make me feel any better. I had about 40¢ in change. I separated out a 1907 Indian head penny I'd been carrying for some time and handed him what remained.

"Thanks," he said. He counted the change, then shuffled over to the other side of the platform on bent, crippled feet. He approached a well-dressed business-type, who rebuffed him, then continued to limp down the platform.

He looked immeasurably tired.

Ratso Rizzo

I was hurrying toward the tunnel that connected the BMT to the Flushing and Broadway lines when I spied a rumpled, unshaven little man. He reminded me of Ratso Rizzo, the character Dustin Hoffman played in *Midnight Cowboy*. He was transferring bunches of rags from several plastic shopping bags to a coin locker near the tunnel.

After a minute or so, he turned to me and, in a voice full of furor and indignation, asked, "You want somethin'?" In a rage, he cried, "You got nothin' better to do? Get out of here! Get *out* of here!"

I've been trying for weeks...

I stepped out of the uptown RR at 42nd Street. I was heading home from the Bleecker Street Cinema, where I'd seen a double feature: *The Godfather* and *Godfather II*, an all-day solo extravaganza for $2.50.

As I walked toward the ramp to the IRT train, I saw an old woman lying on her side on one of the blue benches. She was trying, without success, to raise herself to a sitting position. I hesitated as I passed. She caught my eye and stared at me with what felt like terror.

She wore an old tweed raincoat, torn on the left side from the armpit to somewhat below the bottoms of her breasts — or where her breasts should be, though several layers of clothing concealed her basic anatomy. Her hair was grey and ragged, tied in a rough ponytail. Now I could see that she was younger than I'd thought, maybe 55 or 60, though that, too was difficult to determine precisely.

As I took a couple of steps closer, I recoiled, involuntarily, at the smell, a terrible stink that lingered in my nostrils long after I left the station. (Even now, I can recall it.) By then she had raised herself half-way to a sitting position; it seemed she could go no further. Her eyes were grey and full of fear, but not crazed like so many others I'd seen who lived on the streets and subways.

"Do you need help?" I asked.

She nodded. "Yes! Yes!" she said. "I've been trying for *weeks* to get somebody to help me." She spat as she spoke. Like so many, she had no teeth.

"Look at my hands," she said. She held them out to me, palms down, fingers splayed. They trembled and were nearly black with grime. "And my legs." She pulled back the hem of her coat. She wore torn black tights and her legs, beneath them, were thick and mis-shapen, inflexible. They bulged at the tops of her low-heeled shoes. "I need some place to sleep," she said.

"I'll try to find someone to help you," I told her.

"No, don't!" she said. Fear shone brightly in her eyes. "I just need some place to *sleep*," she repeated.

"I'll be right back," I said softly.

I walked toward the ramp and spotted a portly conductor arguing with a drunk. After the conductor maneuvered the drunk toward the ramp, I went up to him and described the plight of the woman on the bench. "I think she's sick," I said. "She can't move her legs."

"I'll take care of it," he said.

Instinctively I knew, too late, that he would not help her, and, too late, I understood her fear. I waited, and I watched from a distance.

The conductor found a transit cop, and both of them walked to-gether for a few yards, apparently discussing the situation I'd brought to their attention. Soon, the conductor returned. "He'll take care of her," he said, tipping his head toward the transit cop. I nodded. He ambled down the platform.

The woman on the bench had, at last, gotten herself upright. I watched as the cop spoke with her. I couldn't hear what they were saying, so I moved a few steps closer.

The cop tapped the back of the bench with his nightstick. It made a sharp *crack* that echoed through the platform. "Move along," he said, in a tone you might use with a stubborn pet.

The woman glared at him. She raised her frail voice. "I'm not hurt-ing anybody. I never hurt *any*body," she said.

The cop tapped the back of the bench, harder this time.

Miraculously, the woman rose to a standing position. She did not leave. "I have my rights!" she shouted.

The cop sighed. He raised the nightstick from the bench and held it against his chest like a bandolier. The gesture was not *explicitly* menacing. "You gave *up* your rights!" he shouted back. "Now *move on!*"

Miraculously, she did.

On the Train

A skinny young man in a black leather jacket passed out worn leaflets claiming that he was deaf and that he sold these leaflets, which contained the hand signs for the letters of the alphabet, to make a living. He walked through the car, leaving a leaflet on each empty seat. I picked one up from the seat beside me and looked it over, considered spending a quarter on it, and set it back down. I wondered whether he had tried to find an easier way to make money.

A few moments later, I heard from the back of the train a plaintive voice. "Excuse me, will somebody on this train help out me and my wife? We're trying to get enough money to get back home." The voice belonged to a middle-aged man in dirty green pants and a polo shirt. "The conductor will not bill us because we do not have proper I.D. Please. We'll mail the money back. We'll do the same for somebody else, some time. Please help us. It could happen to you, some time."

He moved through the car in the opposite direction the deaf man had traversed. In front of each passenger, he paused, repeated his request, waited a few seconds, and then went on to the next. No one acknowledged him. When he came to me, I hesitated. Should I help him out? Should I believe him? While I deliberated, he took a step further down the car and reiterated his plea to the next passenger.

When he reached the door between cars, he passed through it, on to the next one.

Matches

Ruth and I were riding uptown on the Broadway local. As we reached Times Square, I finished a story I'd been telling her since we'd boarded the train in Chinatown.

I was working on a piece on rent control for the *Westsider*. That morning, I'd gone down to the Housing Authority to pick up a pamphlet their information person promised would answer "all the questions I don't have time for." Actually, she had answered none of my questions. "I have other calls," she'd told me. So I made the trip. The pamphlet hadn't answered any of my questions, either.

But that's just the background to the story I was telling Ruth.

On my way to the Housing Authority, I'd seen a bag lady sitting on one of the blue fiberglass chairs on the BMT platform at Times Square. She was swaddled in blankets and wore, on one foot, a battered shoe. The other foot, swollen to the size and shape of a large summer squash, was covered only by a torn, flesh-colored stocking. She clutched a white plastic shopping bag between her legs.

My impulse was to take her picture, but just then my train pulled into the station, so I moved on.

—

In the back of my mind was something my friend Jonas had said not long before. We were sitting in the kitchen of my apartment, dull light seeping in from the airshaft like smoke. "You know, you're one of the few people in New York who actively exploits bag ladies," he said.

"I'm not exploiting them," I responded. "I don't make any money from it."

Jonas cracked a smile. "I didn't mean that as a criticism. It's just another way of looking at it," he said.

"I'm trying to get people to *notice* them," I said. "They have terrible lives and nobody cares."

Jonas laughed. "You're lucky," he said. "If the world were perfect, you'd be up the creek."

I cracked a smile, too. "I'd find something to do."

Jonas shook his head. "You'd commit suicide."

We had a good laugh at my expense. But I hadn't told Jonas the whole story.

When I was a boy, my father bought a radio that picked up police and fire calls. He'd gotten it to stay on top of crime in his store's neighborhood — he'd been robbed several times, once at gunpoint, and carried a thirty-eight under his vest for protection. But the fire calls soon became an obsession.

On days off, my father would drop whatever he was doing and rush out to the scene of any nearby fire. Often, especially if it was a four- or five-alarmer, he took my brother Mike and me with him. In mute, terrified fascination, we'd watch the dance of burning buildings and fire hoses that accompanied the crackling of property incinerating — along with, sometimes, its unfortunate occupants.

If I'd had a camera then, I would have taken pictures of it all. *That* was how I was drawn to bag ladies. The camera was my shield.

—

After my fool's errand to the Housing Authority, I headed home. Reversing my downtown trip, I stopped again at Times Square to change from the BMT to the Broadway line.

A couple of hours had passed. As I stepped out of the train, I saw the same bag lady, still huddled on the same chair, still staring absently at the empty rails. I crept up to her, camera ready, and was about to press the shutter when she turned to me.

"Got a match?" she croaked.

I quickly dropped the camera to my side and let it hang from its strap. I rummaged through my pockets, found a book of matches, and handed them to her. "Keep them," I said.

She turned her attention back to the rails, pulled a cigarette from some hidden pocket, lit it, and inhaled. I took pictures. Unexpectedly, as she exhaled, she turned to me again, and through the viewfinder, I saw her briefly regard me.

I walked away, shaken by an expression that registered as muffled anguish, though it could as easily have been indifference. After I'd taken a few steps, I stopped. I fetched a dollar from my pocket and rehearsed the line, "Here, buy yourself some lunch" before I delivered both the dollar and the sentence as casually as I could.

She fondled the wrinkled bill with her grubby hands for a second or two. "Thank you," she said. She didn't seem to remember that it was I who had just given her the light and I who had taken her picture.

I told Ruth this story. "That's what upsets me most about New York: the bag ladies, the fact that they exist and that they're completely ignored. I've never seen people living like that."

The car jerked. "If they upset you, why do you take pictures of them?" she asked.

"Because I can't *not* see them," I said. "Through the camera, they become subjects, not real human beings. But this time was different."

—

The motorman's voice over the loudspeaker said, "Times Square. Change here for the Seventh Avenue lines, the shuttle to Grand Central, and the BMT. Step lively, now, and watch the closing doors."

One set of passengers traded places with another, a round of musical chairs. As the train jerked to a start and resumed its uptown course, I noticed a short Black man with a crooked smile shuffling his feet and dancing near the doors. He swayed from side to side and chanted:

Ah neeeeeeed a quarter.
Don't know how Ah'm gonna git it,
But Ah know Ah'm gonna git it.
Ah neeeeeeed a quarter.

He meandered unsteadily past us, reached the end of the car, and reversed direction. In front of each passenger, he danced, looping one arm through a handle or wrapping it around a pole while he extended the empty palm of his free hand. His feet never stopped moving. Soon it was our turn.

"'Scuse me, ma'am," he said to Ruth. To me, he said, "Sorry for interruptin' you, but Ah *neeeeeeed* a quarter."

Spraying us with a mist of saliva and alcohol, he went on, "I'm gonna be honest wi' you. I need a quarter to buy me some *wine*. I wanna get Cold Duck, but I'm gonna get me some wine, cause that's the cheapest thing. How 'bout it? I'm bein' honest wi' you."

"Well," I said, "I'm gonna be honest with you, too. I don't want to pay for you to get drunk."

"C'mon, man! I'm bein' *honest* wi' you!" he exclaimed.

"Honesty's not always the best policy," I said. "I'm not gonna give you a quarter to go out and buy wine."

Ruth whispered in my ear, "You should join the WCTU, David." Chagrined, I added, "Look, I don't care if you drink. I just don't want to pay for it."

He stood there, stymied, mutely shaking his head as the train rattled and clanked along. When we arrived at 72nd Street, Ruth got up — she was meeting her roommate for a movie. "I'll call you," she said, amusement evident in her eyes.

My new acquaintance sat down in the space Ruth had vacated. He seemed lost in some mix of muddle and thought, wrinkling his brow, muttering softly and, with the din of the moving car, inaudibly. I glanced around for another seat, but the car was packed. I read Miss Subway's virtues for the 45th time that month.

At last, he spoke. "Yeah," he said with authority, "you gotta *chungachooch*."

"What was that? I didn't quite get that."

"You didn't *git* it?" He laughed. "I'll 'splain it to ya." He mumbled incomprehensibly but with great vigor for about a minute, gesticulating with both hands the whole time, and concluded, "...so you gotta *chung* a *chooch*. Ya see?"

I didn't see. "Would you mind going over that one more time?"

He chuckled slyly and raised an eyebrow. "You give me a quarter," he said, "I'll 'splain you all *kinda* stuff."

Quick, but not quick enough. "You already told me what you'd do if I gave you a quarter."

Crestfallen, he said nothing more for the next few stops.

"Listen," I said, as I rose from my seat and grabbed a strap. "I gotta get off. Good luck."

"Yeah," he sneered.

As I stepped toward the open doors, he added, doggedly persistent to the end, "You know, you give me a quarter, someday I might help *you* out."

Will you take me home?

The platform was crowded and at first I didn't notice the spare, hollow-faced little woman.

She was talking to a blond woman I took to be in her early thirties. With her conservative-but-tasteful attire, not-quite-plump face, and respectable eyeglasses, she might have been a marketing analyst for, say, Colgate Palmolive. She was doing her best to ignore the entreaties of the bedraggled woman who, I noticed, was barefoot despite the cold.

I walked slowly toward them. The frail figure, sensing my attention, turned to me, her bright, round eyes hopeful as she asked, sweetly, "Will you take me home? I don't have anywhere to sleep. Will you take me home with you?"

Unconscious

At the foot of the stairs in front of the immense statue of Washington on horseback in Union Square Park, a man lay on the pavement.

A young woman sat at the top of the stairway, perhaps ten feet from him. Her attention seemed wholly taken up by the rush-hour traffic on 14th Street. Three men hung out off to the side, drinking beer. They, too, appeared to be completely unaffected by the sight of an unconscious man sprawled on the pavement. Passers-by scurried up and down the stairs without pausing.

I thought at first he was drunk, but he bore little resemblance to the bums I usually saw in Union Square Park. He wore a bright red, embroidered shirt and rumpled bell bottoms. His hair was long and curly, he was clean shaven, and his black mustache was neatly trimmed. He looked about my age, 25.

He lay on his side, moaning, legs crossed, head tilted awkwardly. With each breath, he nodded toward his chest and then moved his head back again to the pavement. His eyes were half-open, his eyeballs rolled toward the top of his head, revealing only their whites and twin slivers of irises.

I gently shook his shoulder to try to rouse him. No response. "What's wrong with him?" I asked the girl at the top of the stairway, startling her out of her traffic meditation.

Regaining her poise, she replied, "He's resting. He was only a little tired. He's just resting."

I looked around for a cop, but instead I ran into an off-duty security guard. I told him what I'd seen. "That's not my job," he said. "Go find a cop or something."

"Where can I find a cop around here?"

"A cop? I don't know where you can find a cop. They're all on strike, aren't they?"

I scrambled across 14th Street to a phone booth and dialed 9-1-1. Heading back to the young man by the statue, I hoped the cop on the other end of the line would, as he had reluctantly promised, "send somebody to check it out."

It was only after I started taking pictures of the still-unconscious figure that anyone took notice.

An elderly Jewish woman came up to me and, shaking her walking stick, exclaimed, "Why doesn't anybody help him? Somebody should help him!"

"I already called the cops. I'm waiting with him until they come," I said.

She smiled and patted me on the cheek. "I wish there were more people like you," she said. She rambled on for several minutes about her husband and his cataracts. "He was one of the finest photo retouchers in New York in his day," she assured me. She looked me in the eyes. "You know, you don't look too good yourself," she said, and walked away.

I took a few more photographs. A Black man, one of the three men I'd noticed off to the side drinking beer, set down his bottle and hollered, "Hey, man, whaddaya doin'? You oughta be helpin' him, 'steada takin' pictures."

I yelled back, "I'm doing a book on New York. This is part of New York. And I just called the police."

"Oh, that's a different story, man," he said, "that's a different story altogether." He walked over to me and the unconscious man. "But you shouldn't of called the cops. They ain't gonna do nothin'. You shoulda called a *amblance.*"

Others joined us. Soon we were a group of about ten gathered around the insensible young man, who had not altered his position or the rhythm of his nods and moans. We discussed what might be the matter with him.

"He's drunk," one bystander offered.

"Look at his eyes," I said. They were still rolled toward the back of his head. "I think he's having some kind of fit."

Another bystander ruled out epilepsy because he wasn't foaming at the mouth. Others conjectured about the kinds of pills he might have taken. "Musta been those brown ones," the man who had first joined me in my vigil concluded, "those Seconols."

Several minutes passed, and the buzz of speculation from the still-growing crowd mounted, though no cops had shown up. Abruptly, a new member of our gathering, a Black man in his late forties or fifties, matter-of-factly said, "You want to wake him up? I'll show you how to wake him up."

He bent down, lifted the young man's head with one hand and grabbed him at the back of the neck with the other, then did ... something, and the guy on the ground immediately sat up, like a sleeper startled from a dream. He glanced around, his eyes bloodshot. "Where're my friends?" he asked. "Where'd they go?"

While another guy helped him to a bench, I turned to the miracle worker. "How'd you know to do whatever you did?" I asked.

"When you been around as much as I have," he said, "you know, man."

The Wino and the Prostitute

Dusk was settling in, and I decided to stop in a liquor store on 14th Street for cigarettes. Outside the store, a wino — thin, grizzled beard, perhaps fifty — was drinking from a paper bag. As I left the building, he abruptly crumpled to the ground. I heard the bottle smash beneath him, saw its dark contents spread out onto the sidewalk, shimmering in the glow of a streetlight.

The wino, bewildered and disappointed, struggled to his feet. Blood spurted from his wrist in a thin geyser that erupted to the rhythm of his heartbeat. The wino stared mutely and uncomprehendingly at his arm, now slathered in fresh blood. His crotch darkened as he peed himself.

"You're bleeding!" I told him. I had never seen an injury like that, but I knew what it meant. "You cut an artery." I helped him to the ground, leaned him against the side of the building, and wrapped my handkerchief around his wrist. Underneath his shirt, caked with dirt, he was all bones.

I knotted the handkerchief as tightly as I could, but blood still oozed through the cloth. The sour stench of wine, sweat, and piss overpowered its metallic odor, but this balance was already shifting. "Keep your hand there," I said, maneuvering it around the makeshift bandage. "I'll get help. Don't move," I said.

I'd noticed a payphone near the door, opposite the checkout counter. There, a heavily made-up streetwalker in a tight miniskirt and platform shoes leaned against the wall, talking. I tapped on the phone's metal enclosure. "I need the phone," I said, "it's an emergency."

Startled, she scowled and waved me away.

"There's a guy bleeding to death outside. *Get off the phone!*" I insisted.

With one hand, she lodged the handset between her breasts, mouthpiece down. With the other, she shoved my chest. "*Get lost!*" she hissed.

I stuck my head out the door and looked up and down the block in the waning light. I saw no likely locations for another phone. The wino still sat in a pool of blood, piss, and wine.

I stalked up to the clerk, who had silently witnessed the exchange with the prostitute. Leaning toward him, both hands on the counter, I jerked my head toward her and said, "I need to use that phone or somebody will die."

The clerk held both hands in front of him as if he were warding off an attack. "Okay, okay!" he said, his accent Indian or Pakistani. "I will get the manager." Only later did I realize he must have thought I was threatening him.

A minute later, a balding, chunky guy with a thick mustache emerged. "What's the problem?" he asked.

"There's a man outside bleeding to death," I said. "I need to call 9-1-1."

The manager frowned. He glanced at the prostitute and then turned back to me. "There's another store about a block down. They probably got a phone," he said.

"There's a guy bleeding to death outside *your* store," I said, with as much force as I could muster. "You have to get her off *that* phone!"

"Huh?" he said.

"C'mon."

I took him by the arm and led him outside, where the wino now lay flat on the pavement, his bandaged wrist on top of his belly.

"He fell on his bottle and cut an artery," I said. I lifted my right hand a foot and a half above my left wrist. "Blood was spurting out to here. He's still bleeding."

"Okay," the manager said. "Okay."

Inside, he stepped up to the prostitute, tapped her on the shoulder, and nodded his head in the direction of the door. "Out!" he said. She huffed. He glared and repeated his head movement. "*Now!*" he said.

The prostitute sighed. Into the mouthpiece, she said, "Honey, I gotta go. Talk to you later." She scowled at me again, handed the manager the receiver, and waggled her ass out the door.

I dialed 9-1-1. The dispatcher sounded bored. This was no longer surprising. "Where are you again?" I repeated the location. "Okay, I'll send someone to check it out."

"He needs an *ambulance*," I said, recalling the advice of the miracle worker in the park.

"We'll get someone to check it out. They'll be there soon. Thanks for your concern," he said flatly.

Outside, I waited with the wino. He moaned and shifted, but blood no longer dripped from his wrist. He was still breathing when two cops arrived, scraped him off the pavement, and shoved him into the back of their patrol car.

Kelleher

A couple of weeks later, I was in the park again, panning my camera to see what I could see, pausing briefly to frame potential shots. The grubby gent on the park bench across from me called out, "Why not do it now?" Waving, a newspaper clenched in one hand and a half-finished beer in the other, he repeated, "Why not do it *now*?"

I pointed to my chest and gave him a quizzical look.

"Take my picture," he said. So I obliged.

That's how we got to talking, David Kelleher and I, but not until he'd sung me a half-dozen Irish folk songs, twisted to suit his fancy. His small eyes grinned as he sang, and though he had no teeth, he had some voice, I'll tell you. And his songs! Not the stuff I'd want my mother to hear. He said he'd been offered money for singing only once, and that was $25 to stop. "But I kept right on singin', hopin' they'd up the offer, till I was bodily escorted out the door."

He invited me to share his bench, and as I said, we got to talking.

Kelleher took a swig of his beer and wiped his mouth with the back of his hand. "I just walked off a job washing dishes at the Neighborly Hotel," he said. "Left me paycheck uncollected and walked out. I come in a few minutes late this morning and the steward at the place was pissed. Asked me, 'How do you feel this morning?' in that snide way some people have of asking questions and scolding you, all at once."

He set down his beer for emphasis and explained, "I looked him straight in the eyes, just the way I'm lookin' at you, and I said, 'I feel like chargin' Hell with a bucket of water.'" He smiled confidentially. "Now, that steward was a mealy fellow, and besides he was an orthodox Jew. He didn't much like me language. It wasn't nice. 'Even the cook don't talk to me like that!' he said."

Kelleher took another swig. "I coulda choked him right then, treatin' me like that, when I done him three men's work the day before. But I stopped him verbally instead, though sittin' here now I nearly wish I'd gone at him with me fists. Nothin' would've satisfied him. That's the way they are."

He set the empty bottle down. "I've got only a few dollars in me pocket, but I'll find work. A man can always find work," he said. He leaned back and linked his hands behind his head. "You've got to distinguish between a *man* and a *stiff*," Kelleher said. "A stiff, whether he's rich or poor, gets by, doing as little as he has to, right? A man, he works as hard as he can at whatever he does because he's proud to do so."

Kelleher told me he could tackle anything he set his mind to, and I believed him. "I left Ireland when I was 20 and I'm 43 now. I come to work and to learn, and not to lose me brogue, either," he said. "There's not a machine I can't take apart and put back together. But I'm not braggin'. I didn't come here to impress nobody. I call a spade a spade and not a diggin' implement."

He went on talking, perhaps to me, or maybe just to hear his own voice. "I'll confess, I come from a broken home. I finished school when I was 13, and I went to work for a dollar a day, seven days a week, to help bring me family out of poverty, and I worked another shift at home."

He spoke of working twelve days and twelve nights without sleep, and of shoveling concrete for eighteen hours a day and walking away singing. "I loved it," he said, smiling, "but the other stiffs there didn't much like me for it."

And he told me about a girl he'd loved once, whose family insisted she marry another man. They thought he wasn't good enough for her. They thought he was after her property — she owned a little house in the Bronx. "So she married the other guy on the rebound. I knew it couldn't last, the marriage, and it didn't. I don't blame 'em, her or him either. I didn't have nothin' to offer her except m'self."

When we parted ways, we shook hands for a solid minute, each of our hands turning white with the strain. His handshake was the firmest I'd ever felt.

BROOKLYN

My Interviews with God

Q: What do you get if you cross an insomniac, an agnostic, and a dyslexic?

A: Someone who stays up all night wondering if there is a dog.

– Groucho Marx

If a man who thinks he is a king is mad, a king who thinks he is a king is no less so.

– Jacques Lacan[1]

If Jesus showed up today and had a press conference in Santa Monica, and he walked on water, half the press accounts would write, "This guy is supposed to be the Son of God, and he can't even swim?"

– Arnold Schwarzenegger

PRELUDE

It was early spring, 1977. The crusts of snow had mostly melted, the crocuses were out, and the rains had not yet arrived in force. The faint stench of ailanthus (the misnamed Tree of Heaven)[2] wafted through the open window.

I sat at an improvised desk in an attic bedroom, diligently pecking away at my first contracted book, a history of American folk music. Though not the "big break" that had so far eluded me, this contract was a significant opportunity, if also a distraction from what I believed to be more significant work.

I had retreated from Manhattan a few months before and now lived in a three-story building in Brooklyn's Fort Greene neighborhood, adjacent to Bedford-Stuyvesant. The house, sheathed in pock-marked yellow stucco, had been homesteaded by a 64-year-old pediatrician who called herself "Doc." She'd bought the previously abandoned property with the intention of populating it with young people who would, in exchange for room and board, do the work needed to transform the building from ramshackle house into home. By the time I arrived on the scene, she was two years into it and maybe forty percent there.

Housemates came and went. Most were architecture students from nearby Pratt Institute. One was an art librarian at the Frick Museum, another a puppet maker who worked for Sesame Street's chief puppet master, Kermit Love. (Her most recent creation: Big Bird.)

And then there was me.

I spent half the work week renovating the interior. My current project was repairing and refinishing the spiral staircase that wound through the building like strands of its DNA. The remainder of the week, including weekends, I wrote.

I'd arrived at this place, in this role, because I was six months past my book contract deadline, my unemployment insurance had run out, and I'd long since spent my advance. In my near future was getting some kind of job, and I was afraid the consequent delay in fulfilling my contract would put me at risk of forfeiting it — a potentially fatal career move.

Luckily, my girlfriend, Ruth, was an art librarian at the Met. Aware of my plight, she suggested I call her friend at the Frick, who had recently told her about a vacancy in the Brooklyn house. One of the Pratt students was leaving for six months to work on a housing project in West Virginia.

The prospect of free room and board appealed to my sense of financial and young-writer-trying-to-make-it urgency, but there was more to moving to Brooklyn than that. After three long years, I was fed up with my hand-to-mouth existence on the Upper West Side. Manhattan was a cornucopia of quirky, intriguing people, potential adventures, and so many artistic and cultural opportunities that no matter how many I sampled, I always felt I was missing out on something. What it lacked, however, unless you inhabited the stratospheric realm of the rich, I deeply craved: quiet.

When I rounded the corner onto a tree-lined street of brownstones and brick houses to meet with Doc, my impetus for venturing out to Brooklyn was still the Promised Land of living rent-free. But it was another promise, of escaping the maelstrom of Manhattan, that sealed the deal.

—

Now, let me tell you about the man who lived on my block who believed he was Jesus come a second time to bring down destruction on the Earth.[3]

GENESIS

My work is from the days of old, from ancient times. I don't have to be a dream.

In the Beginning

It was mid-afternoon and I was settled into working on a chapter about the roots of gospel music and the blues. After a productive morning, I'd rushed through lunch, anticipating an equally fruitful afternoon. Within twenty minutes, I was back at my desk, reviewing what I'd just written, pencil poised to make whatever corrections craftsmanship required. This book may not have been my passion, but

I knew that regularly handing in quality work would keep the contract going. After an hour or so of faltering progress, however, I realized I'd re-read the same four paragraphs several times.

Focus wasn't usually my issue. Transforming bad sentences into good ones, finding *le mot juste*, was my favorite part of the writing process. I loved the *snap!* when everything came together. But now, I was irritable and distracted, my concentration shot.

My first thought was that there was something wrong with me. I went through the list of suspects — health, money, Ruth, money, work, money — and nothing seemed more than usually problematic. Maybe I was just tired. I went downstairs to the kitchen, fixed myself another cup of coffee, and returned to editing.

Within minutes, I felt a faint nagging sensation, like an incipient headache. I tried to push through it, but found myself still staring at the same page, reading its contents repeatedly without comprehension. Determined to salvage the afternoon, I pivoted from editing to the less demanding task of retyping corrected pages, but this also proved futile. My mind wandered, and where it went my fingers followed, spoiling the page. In a frenzy of aggravation, I tangled the typewriter ribbon, spilled correction fluid on re-typed pages, and tumbled the stack of finished pages to the floor.

I pushed my chair back from the desk, exasperated. And I sat. Just sat.

In the stillness, I became aware of an odd sound, something between a barking dog and a babbling brook, its volume and pitch rising and falling at irregular intervals. It seemed to come from a considerable distance, yet it carried well, like a shout across a lake. I went to the window and, listening intently, determined that there actually *was* someone shouting, and that it was this sound that had derailed me.

I've always been highly sensitive to noise and, consequently, somewhat obsessed with the quest for silence. My move to Brooklyn had only partially satisfied this need.

A house with other occupants is never really quiet, so I wrote when it was empty — my landlady was seeing patients and my housemates were in class or at their respective jobs. Most of the time, the three stories of atmosphere were sufficient insulation from the neighborhood's ambient noises which, compared to the din of the Upper West Side, were already, admittedly, minimal. I'd mostly become enured to the faint, sporadic emanations from the street below of radios, cars, and conversations. This new sound, however, had an insidious quality that, once detected, could not be ignored.

My housemates would be home soon, and I didn't want to squander the remaining time I had to myself. "This, too, shall pass," I said out loud. But it wasn't passing quickly enough. I shut the window. The noise still penetrated. I tried masking it with music, but the insistent rhythm overwhelmed whatever I played — even Blind Gary Davis couldn't drown it out.

I'd had it.

"Who the hell *is* that?" I asked myself, running my fingers through my hair. "And why won't he just *shut the fuck up*?"

I grabbed a jacket and raced down the staircase and out onto the street. By the time I got there, however, the sound had stopped. Glancing up and down the block, I saw nothing unusual. I waited a minute, then trudged back to my room. As I reached the second-floor landing, the shouting resumed. Bristling with irritation, I did a quick about-face and flew down the stairs. Before I got out the door, however, the sound had stopped again.

"Enough!" I shouted. I returned to my room, cranked up the record player all the way, plugged my ears with bits of toilet paper, and forced myself to work through the afternoon, determined to end that loathsome racket should it dare again to disturb my peace.

—

The next day, there it was. But now I was ready.

I've always been a night owl, and it usually took until mid-morning before I was fully awake. But that day, I'd been aroused several times by a disturbing dream. I could no longer recall its contents, but each time I awoke, I had to reassure myself that everything was all right. And then the dream continued. By the fourth or fifth installment, I abandoned all hope of sleep and decided to take advantage of the morning.

After a shower and a cup of coffee I felt remarkably invigorated, as if I were electrically charged, my senses augmented by some internal amplifier. So the instant my unseen nemesis (as I now thought of him) began to speak, I hurtled out onto the street.

Like a hound seeking its prey, I perked my ears and quickly determined the sound's general direction. Teeth clenched, mentally armed for argument, I stalked off down the block.

The day itself was perfectly ordinary. (But aren't they always? How many of us, looking back on those moments when our lives take a turn, can honestly claim a genuine premonition?) Images, none of them remarkable, still hang in the gallery of my mind: Neighbors arrayed like miniatures on a toy cityscape, coming and going, strolling down the tree-lined sidewalk or sitting and talking in their small, fenced-in yards. Three houses down, two men struggling to transfer a heavy sofa from a U-Haul into an apartment, the billowing cushions jamming the doorway. Next door, a small boy sliding down the railing of his front porch, shouting "Look at me!"

As I approached Fulton Street, the babbling brook, louder now, called to me like a fog horn in the mist. Just ahead, two dogs barked and wrestled, blocking my path. I side-stepped them, unfazed by the impediment, unstoppable.

Across the street, in the front yard of a brownstone near the corner, I saw him. A large, dignified-looking, barrel-chested Black man, perhaps fifty years old, stood behind a cement birdbath, leaning on it with both arms as if it were a lectern, declaiming to no one. He wore a dark gray suit and black shoes. His white shirt was open at the collar and he had no tie. I paused directly across from his building and watched, half-hidden behind a tree.

The small, slate-covered yard was strewn with sheets of paper held down by round, flat stones. On each sheet I could barely make out writing and symbols in blue ink. Toward the fence, but still within reach of the birdbath/lectern, were several large books, more stones holding them open to particular pages. The man spoke in a loud, variably pitched tone, his accent so sharp I was unsure that the language was English. Even at close range, his voice sounded more like water pouring from a jug than it did ordinary human speech.[4] I strained to hear what he was saying, but from my vantage point I could make out only an occasional word. "Everlasting" came through with particular clarity.

I was still irritated, but the fire had gone out of my belly. In an effort to avoid attracting attention, I tapped my foot and checked my watch, as if I were waiting to meet someone. I felt exposed and a little ridiculous. Had he noticed me? Had the neighbors? I longed for the comfort of a cigarette, a habit I'd kicked a few months before.

I glanced up and down the block. Reassured that nobody was paying attention to either of us, I decided to confront him.

Before I stepped off the curb, however, the man I would come to think of as "the Speaker" began a ritual. He stopped talking, dropped his arms to his side, and turned to face the small window in his front door. Standing in silence, he rocked gently back and forth, swayed by winds only he could feel. I saw his face mirrored in the glass, a pained expression distorting his mouth and brow. If he saw mine reflected there, too, he gave no sign.

For a few minutes, the Speaker stood there, still except for his hypnotic rocking and the continuous modulation of his facial expression. Then, abruptly, he did an about-face, walked back to the birdbath, and stooped to pick up one of the thick books from the nearby pavement. He examined it for a moment before setting it on the makeshift pedestal.

Next, he raised his eyes to the early afternoon sun. Squinting, arms crossed at the wrists, face twitching, he stepped slowly backwards toward the house, stretching his crossed arms skyward as he moved. He halted after two or three paces, and for half a minute twitched his nose, blinked his eyes, and slowly crossed and uncrossed his arms. Then he rotated ninety degrees and repeated this procedure. Another minute passed. He turned his body toward the sun once more and again stepped backward, palms outstretched, until he came to a stop with his heels about a foot from his stoop.

By this time, an audience of three children had gathered — two young girls and a smaller boy. I'd noticed them at the house with the U-Haul. They leaned on the far side of the Speaker's fence and observed him, the girls with mild, intermittent interest, the boy more intently, as if he were absorbed in a favorite television show. The Speaker turned twice more in ninety-degree increments, each time repeating his twitching, blinking, arms-crossing routine, until he faced his front door again. He stood in silence for a minute, then rotated his body 180 degrees toward the street.

He stared straight ahead. For a moment I thought he'd noticed me, but I was mistaken. Still entranced, he stepped into the middle of his yard, moistened first his left and then his right index fingers, and wet the bridge of his nose three times with each. Finally, he marched past the birdbath to the iron fence, gripped the tops of two adjacent posts, and leaned forward, his eyes open but transfixed.

Watching this bizarre display, I felt somewhat transfixed myself. For those few minutes, I had almost forgotten my self-appointed mission, but when the Speaker ended his ritual, I awoke from my spellbound state. I emerged from semi-concealment and strode across the street.

As I approached the curb opposite his building, the Speaker started to talk again, this time in a voice considerably more shrill than what I'd heard so far — a harsh sound somewhere between the screech of rusty brakes and chalk squeaking on a blackboard. I stood only a few feet from him, but he still seemed unaware of my presence.

"You see it? See there? Over your head? You see it?" he shouted. "Three suns he has made! Three suns!" He lifted his head and arms, turning his palms up, embracing the sky. "I have to show you how to pick one!" His voice cracked with each exclamation. "That's to show you I'm *different* than you! That's to show you I'm different than any*body*." His face twitched again as he leaned on the fence, addressing his invisible audience. In deeper, more resonant tones, he said, "My work is *hon*orable. My work is from the days of old, from ancient *times*. From *everlasting*, I was sent up."

The rumble of the U-Haul pulling away masked his words for a moment, but his tone remained forceful, his gaze intense. He dropped his arms and, turning his head from side to side, declared: "That is how I am! That is how I *am*! I could stay inside my house and you see the light shinin' through my *skin*! I could stand right up at night and show the *light* in my body! And in the glass in the mirror! And the *window*!" He raised his palms to the sky in triumph. "I am perfect! I am light!"[5,6] he shouted. "I don't *have* to be a dream!" He lowered his arms, closed his eyes, and resumed his rhythmic rocking forward and back, forward and back.

I reconsidered. I was not up to crazy, just then.

For the next several days I strove to continue my work above the intermittent, cacophonic burble of this strange man. I tried an assortment of ear plugs and headphones, and I sampled many varieties of background music, from classical to hard rock. I settled, finally, on a selection of blues recordings, their rhythms matching his and their messages my mood. But nothing really worked.

Occasionally, when at wit's end, I went down the block to observe him, always from a distance. Sometimes I caught his actual words, but more often, all I could make out was energetic squawking and vigorous gesticulations, interspersed with his bizarre rituals.

I noticed that the Speaker was ignored by passers-by, neighbors, and even by other residents of his building. In a flash of what seemed like brilliance at the time, it occurred to me that if someone were to actually *listen* to him, he might stop talking.

Irritation yielded to intrigue, and intrigue spawned a plan: I would try to be that person. But days passed and I heard nothing, nor did I see him when I walked by his building on the way to the A train. The Speaker had vanished.

As those days turned to weeks, I wondered idly what had become of him. Then I grew absorbed in my work and ceased to care.

INTERLUDE ONE

For most of my childhood, I was mesmerized by the planets, the solar system, the galaxies, the makeup of the universe itself. Posters of early Soviet and American space missions plastered the walls of the bedroom I shared with my younger brother. I was six years old when the Russians launched Sputnik into space, and like many other kids, I decided that it was my duty to help America win the space race. From that moment forward, I focused my energies almost exclusively on math and the sciences. My goal was literally to become a rocket scientist.

I entered college in 1969 as a freshman engineer. That was the year we beat the Russians to the moon, and I hoped to be part of the effort that would take us to Mars, Venus, or wherever the next leg of the space race led.

Long before I set foot in Brooklyn, I'd abandoned my ambition to be a NASA engineer. But my curiosity had not diminished, only changed its orientation.

THE FIRST DAY: Reading is Knowing

I am Jesus Christ! I am Emmanuel! Reading is knowing.

Night and Day

It was on a Sunday morning, a month later, that I next saw the Speaker.

Church had just let out, and the streets rang with the yelps of children free for the remainder of the day. I was in the kitchen, working on the *Times* crossword puzzle and a second cup of coffee, when I

254

heard that faint, familiar burbling. Although still in my slippers, I left the house at once and sprinted down the block.

I approached the Speaker from my side of the street and stopped just opposite his brownstone. He stood inside the slate yard, a foot or two behind the black wrought-iron fence that separated yard from sidewalk. He wore a striped, short-sleeved shirt, bright green pants, and black patent leather shoes. Although his shirttails were out, he was otherwise immaculate. He spoke in the same half-singing, half-barking fashion I'd heard before.

This time, I waited until he was quiet, then strode across the street, determined to take decisive action. But as before, I paused at the curb, strangely reluctant to step fully into his space.

I Am Jesus Christ! I Am Emmanuel!

It was unseasonably warm that day, and humid. The Speaker was motionless, his eyes tightly closed, a film of sweat coating his cheeks and forehead. A thin breeze blew, and in the dappled light that filtered through the trees, his face glistened. I briefly assessed the risks of what I was about to do.

The hope of restoring tranquility renewed my resolve — as did, I admit, my curiosity. I stepped over the curb and onto the sidewalk and said, tentatively, "Hello?"

The Speaker opened his eyes and gazed at me, unsurprised. This subtle movement was startling. Perhaps absurdly, I was reminded of a dramatically oversized child's doll, the kind whose eyes opened and shut depending on how you held it.

"Hello," he said.

I dismissed the image of the doll. "My name is David," I said. I gestured up the block. "I live over there, in the house on the corner."

The Speaker nodded, his gaze still fixed. "Yes," he said.

Anxiety momentarily fogged my mind. Involuntarily, I shook my head to clear it and forced what I hoped was a congenial, interested smile. In the exaggeratedly patient voice I usually reserved for hushing talkative people in movie theaters, I said, "I've heard you speaking out here. You're a preacher, I assume?" Without waiting for his reply, I continued, "I wonder, could you tell me what you've been preaching about?"

His eyes sparked to life. "I don't preach," he said, his voice now deeper, more resonant. "I am God."

I drew a quick breath. In my travels through the streets of New York, I'd heard many an unusual claim, but never this one. I stammered, "You are *God*?"

"Yes!" he shouted. He glared at me indignantly. "I am Jesus Christ! I am Emmanuel!" He stepped forward and grasped a fence post tightly in each hand. "Emmanuel is *God*," he said fiercely. "That is his *name*."

A cold flush washed over me. Reminding myself of my purpose (and grateful for the fence that separated him from me), I stood my ground. "I don't understand," I said cautiously.

"The Son have many names," the Speaker explained in a quieter tone. "That word Emmanuel mean 'God with us.'[7] That is in the book of St. *Matthew*. Whenever God come and say, *Emmanuel*, that mean the *Son*. Every time God call *Israel*, that's the Son. Every time He say, *Trus, Son of Man prophesized*, that's the Son *again*."

I was no more enlightened by this explanation.

He blinked his eyes rapidly for several seconds, as if he were signaling by semaphore, and then spoke slowly, deliberately, like he was talking to a child. "*Every* one of them names, *every* one of them words in the Bible, is a *dream*,"[8] he said. He gazed at me directly. "You see?"

Of course I didn't see. How could I, then?

Before I had a chance to respond, the Speaker, sensing my confusion, fetched a thick, black book from a metal table and balanced it on the railing. It was one of several such books he had placed around the yard, all Bibles, as far as I could tell from my current vantage point. He motioned me to draw closer. "God spoke them words here so you must know who is *who*.[9] I show you," he said.

Reading Is Knowing

He opened the heavy volume, licked the tip of his index finger, and flipped through the thin, dense pages. Only a few seconds passed before he found his place, marked with one of numerous scraps of paper inserted between them. "The Bible was made to go from Genesis to Revelation," he said. "See here? This is Genesis, the first chapter."

The Speaker read aloud, moving his finger along the text. His voice dropped into a Paul Robeson baritone, but in an unfamiliar dialect. Much like the poets I'd heard recite their works in the many readings I'd attended, his tone was musical, the accents arranged according to a pattern of his own devising.

> In the beginning God create Heaven and <u>Eart'</u>,
> and the Eart' was without <u>form</u> and <u>woid</u>
> and darkness was <u>up</u>on the face of the deep
> and the spirit of God <u>moved</u> upon the face of the <u>water</u>.
> And God said, <u>Let</u> there be <u>light</u>, and there was <u>light</u>,
> and God <u>saw</u> the light that it was <u>good</u>.
> And God <u>diwide</u> the light from the darkness,
> and God <u>called</u> the light day and the <u>darkness</u> he called <u>night</u>,
> and the evening and the morning were the <u>first</u> day.

He looked up from the Bible. "See there?" he said, tilting the book toward me, his finger still on *the first day*.

I read the familiar words. "Yes," I said, still bewildered.

He grunted softly, his eyes shining.[10] Tapping the page, he explained, "That is a *dream*."

"A dream?"

He closed the book and held it before him in one massive hand. "Readin' is knowin',"[11] he stated. He waved the book before me as if he were presenting evidence at a trial. "You see, when God come in a dream, sometimes only one word he say. *One word!*"

"One word?"

"One word!" the Speaker repeated. "For the Bible tell you that, too, When a dreamer have a dream, and it come to pass, and the dreamer speak a word and it come to pass, then you know that God truly send him. But when it do not come to pass, it is not the words of God. So, you must know a *prophet* from a *false* prophet."[12]

He looked at me, expectation in his eyes. "I'm sorry," I confessed. "I still don't understand."

Almost imperceptibly, he shook his head. "That's why you got to be able to *read*," he said. "God don't send a man who can't *read* to be a prophet.[13] Because if ever a dream *hit*, you got to know whether you could do the works of that prophet or *not*."

I strained to follow his narrative. Each time I felt close to connecting the dots, the whole thing spun apart. A diagnosis, however, was already forming in my mind. I knew tangential thinking and ideas of reference. As a psychiatric hospital volunteer, I had witnessed both often, and I had likewise observed these signs in the bag ladies I'd encountered on the Upper West Side.

Undaunted by my evident obtuseness, the Speaker returned to the book still open before him. He stabbed at the open pages. "My Bible supposed to be read right *down*, right *down*, right *down*, right *down*. You're supposed to skip *nothin'* in the Bible, for if you read *there*, and skip *here* and go over *here*, then you don't know what's down *here*. You didn't read it! You don't know God's word at *all*."

He glanced up at me and touched my shoulder, then drew me closer, a surprisingly intimate gesture. I allowed it; there was still the sturdy fence between us.

Again, his voice dropped an octave. "From Genesis to Revelation mention every way how the Son of Man comin', and you got to be able to trace your *dream* from this. You got to *prove* it by the Bible, else you cannot say your word is accepted. You see what I mean?"

He released my shoulder. "I think so," I said. I struggled to catch the gist of what he was trying to convey. Whose dreams? What did they prove? And to whom? I *had* read the Bible, cover to cover, but nothing I remembered from its thousands of verses shed light on the Speaker's words. Yet I was also cognizant of a shift in the energy that passed between us. With the Speaker's touch on my shoulder, like the spark of life between God and man in Michelangelo's *Creazione di Adamo*, something *had* been transmitted: I'd felt, for just a moment, the intensity of his desire to be understood. I, too, knew that yearning.

I had the eerie sense that a collaboration was commencing. Any lingering fear for my safety dispersed. I would, at least for now, continue to let him make his case.

The Speaker smiled. Had he sensed this change of heart?

Just as I was about to request that he clarify his thoughts about the Bible, dreams, prophecy, and his claim to divinity, a thin, bald-headed man, apparently also a resident of the building, shuffled through the front gate. He tapped the Speaker on the shoulder and cocked his head toward the book still propped up on the fence. "Is that your Bible?" he asked.

Without looking up, the Speaker answered, dismissively, "Yeah. You see I got my Bible."

The bald man winked at me.

The Speaker resumed reading, his voice rising and falling like the surf.

> And God said, <u>let</u> there be light in the forment of the Heaven to de<u>wide</u> the day from the night,
> and <u>let</u> them be for signs and for seasons and for <u>days</u> and <u>years</u>,
> and <u>let</u> them be for <u>lights</u> in the forment of Heaven to give light upon the <u>Eart</u>,
> and it was <u>so</u>.

"So you see," the Speaker said, catching my eye again, "you got the light of day."

The bald man chuckled, shook his head, and continued on into the building, but his interruption brought me to an awareness of the pull of two opposing forces: curiosity and impatience.

Should I go or should I stay?

I had no interest in taking Bible lessons from a schizophrenic, my tentative diagnosis. And yet, as I listened to the Speaker recite these so-familiar words in his idiosyncratic tongue, I had been struck, with startling clarity, by their eloquence. Those few short lines from the Book of Genesis answered the greatest questions posed by mankind.

Let there be time.

Let there be space.

Let there be light.

Let there be stars and sun in the sky.

Though no stranger to the Old Testament, until that moment I had never appreciated its intrinsic wisdom, poetry, and power.

"I use the Bible," the Speaker continued. "I got many." He swept his hand over the books scattered about his small yard. "But I could remember the whole Bible out of my head," he claimed, "and I could sit right down and write the Lord's words to *complete* it."

He returned the heavy volume to the birdbath, rested his hands on the fence, and stared directly ahead. What he saw I could not imagine.

A couple of teenage girls walked by, one talking and gesticulating while the other listened. The Speaker paid them no mind, but their presence made me acutely aware of the absurdity of being out on the street in my slippers, discussing the Bible with a man who believed he was its subject. I wondered, in a moment of self-consciousness, if these girls were imitating the Speaker and myself, but they moseyed on down the block, oblivious of us, just as they seemed to be unseen by the Speaker.

The conversation had taken an unanticipated turn. I'd started out that morning with the singular intention of discouraging this unusual man from speaking, but now he intrigued more than annoyed me. Though still lost in the whirlpool of his reasoning, floating in that vortex I also glimpsed bits of meaning.

As an English major, I'd prided myself on my ability to trace subtle motifs in complex works of literature and, as a reporter, to ferret out the heart of a story. Here was a living, breathing mystery beckoning to me to solve it. I'd caught the Speaker *in media res*. But I knew that embedded in any narrative, at any point in its telling, is also its beginning and an intimation of its end. Already, I could see that his was not a simple tale, and I was up for a challenge. I would see where this took me.

I glanced at my watch and this simple action grounded me in reality. I remembered that Ruth had expected me to call. What could I tell her? 'Sorry I'm late, honey. I was talking to God and time just flew by. You know how that is.'

"Well," I told the Speaker, "I appreciate you explaining all this to me. I have to be going now. Maybe we can talk again?"

"Okay," he said amiably. He smiled and added, "Thanks for listenin'."

"No problem," I said. "My pleasure."

After I'd gone only a few feet, I turned to wave goodbye. But the Speaker had already resumed his oration. As I headed up the block, the harsh babble followed me, its volume scarcely diminished by the increasing distance.

INTERLUDE TWO

Although as a boy I nearly failed Hebrew school and immediately after my Bar Mitzvah stopped practicing Judaism, I have long been fascinated by spiritual matters.

Initially, I was attracted to Eastern religions, but a "Bible as Literature" course in my junior year of college shifted that focus. The course was taught by a new professor and former nun fortuitously named Diane Christian. Not long out of the convent, she was pursuing secular life with gusto. Mine was her first class at the university, and that gusto included assigning us the entire Bible, front to back, from Genesis to Revelation.

Much of the Old Testament was already familiar to me, but the New Testament was my first encounter with Jesus since the Christmas carols we sang in elementary school: *pa rum pum pum pum.* After my meeting with the Speaker, I found myself harkening back to those years, when I had delved more deeply into the teachings and history of the Christian God than I had ever looked into the God of my forefathers.

I didn't stop with the sanctioned versions in the New Testament. I avidly read the Gnostic gospels as they became available, pored over Bible concordances, and endeavored to see, through the eyes of Christian scholars, their proofs that the ancient Hebrew prophesies foretold the coming of Jesus as the Messiah. I was particularly drawn to his mentorship of Judas. Though their relationship went terribly wrong, it was also the impetus for 2,000 years of Christian history. Not bad for a rogue preacher from a one-camel town.

—

Coinciding with my interest in the spirit was an equally intense fascination with the inner workings of the mind. As an undergraduate, I took every psychology class I could fit into my schedule and dabbled in both individual and group psychotherapy. I knew, instinctively, that for me, these realms offered more richness and depth than the math and science which had preoccupied my kid-scientist world.

These activities led me to volunteer at Buffalo State Mental Hospital, where I mingled with some of the schizophrenics on the ward. On my weekly visits, they always seemed happy to see me and would launch into energetic monologues on their intricate relationships with the voices that informed them, rapidly and seamlessly switching between the worlds of their overheated imaginations and mundane, day-to-day life on the ward. I left each visit feeling like I'd been tripping on LSD.

During this time, I read *The Three Christs of Ypsilanti*, the true account of a Michigan psychologist who brought together three men, all of whom believed they were Jesus Christ, in the same hospital ward, hoping to effect a cure. (Alas, that experiment failed, and each dismissed the others as false prophets.) With the Speaker, I realized, I had an opportunity to interact with someone under the same spell — though I would not, of course, treat him like a lab rat.

Reflecting on all this after our first conversation, I remembered a passage from Carl Jung, who wrote that if he had a patient who said he lived on the moon, the first thing he, Jung, must do is fly there. Although I was not a psychologist and the Speaker was not my patient, but I felt a similar resolve. My task, however, was easier than Jung's. A quick walk down Grand Avenue was far less demanding than embarking on a voyage to the moon.

—

In our first meeting, my interviewing skills, honed by three years of newspaper reporting, were slightly hampered by the Speaker's unique syntax and pronunciation of English. Later that day, I found a trick to overcome this obstacle.

Though I've never been good with languages, I was adept at accents. French, German, Spanish, Russian, Indian, and even Japanese variants of English came easily to me, and I slipped into dialects so readily that when I traveled in Great Britain or the South, people accepted me as a native. I practiced the Speaker's tongue, echoing his speech rhythms and playing with his pronunciations out loud to myself, with my housemates, and on the phone with Ruth. I was confident that this imitative act would serve me well in future conver-sations, should they occur.

I was, however, less sure about the Speaker's unusual reading of biblical texts. I was struck by his use of *Trus*, a word he appeared to have coined. Fortunately, I enjoyed linguistic puzzles. In college, I'd carried a dictionary of English etymology in my bookbag, and I'd used it often to decipher Joyce's *Ulysses* and the esoteric poems of T. S. Eliot, Ezra Pound, and Charles Olson. Cracking the Speaker's code should be child's play, by comparison.

—

As I lay in bed that night, I thought about the Speaker. What could I surmise from our brief encounters? That he believed himself to be God, Jesus, a prophet, or a combination of all three; that the Bible somehow proved his assertions of divinity; and that said proof was related to dreams — his own, those of the biblical prophets, or perhaps both.

What I did not know was what had driven him to this delusional state. Nor did I know anything about his existence outside his front yard. Here was a person who had once been a boy, had a home, lived a life before Brooklyn. From where had he come? What brought him to Fort Greene? How had he arrived at the belief that he was divine? What did he want to tell us, his neighbors?

A related question, answered incompletely, was why I cared, but I was willing to let that one slide for now.

THE SECOND DAY: The Spiritual Work

Has to be a God in Heaven. The Father's master workman. Works of miracle. The spiritual work. The sentence for the dream. Striking down power come now.

Sky and Sea

The following morning, I again woke early and found it impossible to return to sleep. Unable to concentrate on my work, I decided to give myself the day off.

I was curious about the Speaker's biblical references. I dug out my copy of the King James Bible and leafed through it, scanning for phrases he'd cited, exploring their context. Like so many others, I believed that in these pages lay clues to the mysteries that preoccupied me — in my case, not of faith, fate, or the universe, but of the Speaker himself.

Some of them, anyway. The rest, I knew, could come only from their source.

I fetched a stack of index cards from my desk. As I'd often done for other interviews, I wrote out my questions, one per card, as much to cement them in my mind as to prompt me, should I find myself at a loss for words. These were, of course, somewhat different from my usual queries. But then, this was a somewhat different interviewee.

I awaited the Speaker's return.

Has to Be a God in Heaven

Shortly before noon, my preparedness was rewarded. At the first whisper of the Speaker's oratory, I was jogging down the block, on my way to enlightenment, excited by the prospect. Since my move to Brooklyn, life had been static. It was thrilling to make another foray into the unknown, and also to revisit the psychological, spiritual, and investigative pursuits that that had so engaged me in previous phases of my life.

A few doors from the Speaker's house, I slowed to a walk, trying my best to be inconspicuous. The air was cooler than it had been the day before, and the sky was hazy, with dark clouds scudding across the distant sky. I was sweating slightly from my brief run, and I felt a chill as the wind picked up.

Today, he wore a black suit and pale pink shirt. Once again, he seemed unaware of my presence. Again, he crossed his arms, turned in all four directions, manipulated his facial expression, blinked and closed his eyes. The pattern wasn't identical to what I'd witnessed on our first encounter — he didn't moisten his nose, but instead touched his palms to the sides of his face and held them there for several seconds — but the overall effect was similarly bizarre.

"*Has* to be a God in Heaven, you *hear?*" the Speaker abruptly exclaimed.

My practice with his accent served me well. Previously, from that distance, I could make out little of what he said. Now, his words came through loud and clear, as if in high fidelity.

"You gotta be *cleansed* from all un*righteous*ness, all sin, to be able to be like that Son in the Heaven," he proclaimed. "You don't get it *easy*. You gotta be clean and pure to be a God in the Heaven, you hear?"

His face twitched, then he leaned forward on his fence, extending his upper body over the sidewalk. "When you reach a God in Heaven, you could do anything you want! *Any thing* you want in Heaven, you could do when you reach a God," he said. His voice rose in pitch, cracking at the ends of sentences. "They say I have a split personality. Say I am unhappy! I explain they never reach a *God*! You gotta be a God and you gotta be a Son to be a God. You gotta be the sun, of sunlight, to be the Lord."

After this brief ejaculation, the Speaker stood silent, face turned skyward. Emboldened by yesterday's meeting, I crossed the street and walked right up to him.

"Hi," I said.

He tilted his head toward me. His eyes appeared to clear. "I do my work," he said calmly.

"I know," I said. "I was watching you from across the street. I didn't want to interrupt." I smiled. "I'm interested in what you're doing. Do you mind if I stay?"

He wrinkled his brow for a moment, then shrugged. "No, you don't bodder me," he replied. "I home today. I ain't going out no place." He stroked his chin. "I know that you is not with me at all times, so you will only see a part when you is here."

"Thank you," I said. "I don't want to get in your way. Just let me know when you need me to leave."

"Okay," he said.

"Good," I said, completing the negotiation. "Would it be all right if I asked a few questions?"

Instead of the simple "yay" or "nay" I had expected, the Speaker responded by unlatching his gate and gesturing to me to join him in his yard. "Sit," he said hospitably, pointing to a stone bench.

I complied, though with some apprehension. He shut the gate behind me with a firm clang and dragged a metal chair over, its legs scraping the slate. He sat across from me, arms folded over his chest. I noticed for the first time a gold band on his ring finger. Though I felt no fear, it registered that he was powerfully built, there was no fence between us, and he was between me and the gate.

The Father's Master Workman

"So," I began, settling into this new, more vulnerable configuration, and also into my role as interviewer, "when we talked yesterday, you said you were God, but you also said you were Jesus Christ. I'm a little confused."

The Speaker nodded knowingly. "I explain that," he said.

While I waited for his reply, I took in this closer view of his yard: the peeling brown paint on his door, a second wire chair, the small metal table, the stone birdbath. I confirmed that the books were Bibles of varying dimensions, and the scraps of paper were indeed covered with blue writing in a loopy, uneven script. The steady rumble of traffic on Fulton Street was like white noise.

He leaned back in his chair. "The Bible tell you God create all things through Jesus Christ," he said.

I nodded slightly. "Okay," I said.

He set his hands on his knees and leaned toward me. "That's because God is *in* Jesus Christ. So, just like the *Father* can create all things, the *Son* can create all things."

That seems logical, I thought, automatically leaning in, my hands also moving to my knees.

"And if all things was made by the Son," the Speaker said, "the Son was just as good as his father. To make all things, he *have* to be able to do the works of God himself. Right?"

"Okay, I follow that," I said, though I couldn't yet see how this answered my straightforward *this* or *that* question.

"The Son is the Father's master workman," he said. "You find that in the Book of John. *All things was made by Him and without Him was not anything made that was made.*"[14] The Speaker studied my face for a moment, as if to gauge whether to go on. "The work that the Father put the Son to do is work that only *God himself* can do. No other human can get that work done except the *Son*,"[15] he explained.

"But which one are *you*," I repeated. "God or the Son?"

He sighed the sigh of the patient mentor addressing the dull-witted mentee. "Jesus Christ is God, *too*," he said.

In that moment, the gears in my mind ratcheted forward. "So, when you were reading from Genesis about day and night, dividing the waters, creating the light of day … that was the Son?"

He threw open his arms and laughed, a full-throated, hearty laugh accompanied by a gold-flecked smile.

I laughed with him. But as the Brits say, I was gobsmacked.

I knew about the Holy Trinity. I had read John and the Corinthians. But until that moment I still thought of Jesus as a fellow Jew, born in Bethlehem some two millennia ago. Because of my secular orientation, I had missed what I realized was likely the most crucial concept of Christian thought: that Jesus was not only the baby in the manger, and not only the Son of God, but also the creator of the universe, and that although the baby in the manger was born billions of years after the Creation, he was also there before the Beginning.

I'd read the words, but I hadn't understood them. Now, they confounded my linear sense of time. But that's not what gobsmacked me.

What blew my mind — to use a more American phrase — was this: The Speaker, therefore, must also see himself as having existed not only from the moment of *his* birth, but for all eternity.

Maybe this shouldn't have shaken me. I was a lifelong science fiction fan and an aficionado, especially, of time travel and temporal paradox stories from Philip K. Dick to *Dr. Who*. In a story, I would take in stride a tale of a man who sat in a small slate yard and proclaimed himself to be the progenitor of space and time. But the Speaker was not a character in some science fiction story. He was my neighbor.

Works of Miracle

This, I would need time — linear time — to process.

Meanwhile, I made my best effort to maintain a neutral expression. A garbage truck lumbering down the block provided a welcome distraction. As the truck moved on, I retreated to the comfortable role of interviewer and mentally scanned the index cards in my shirt pocket for a new question.

"I've been wondering about something else," I said.

The Speaker tilted his head to the left. "Hmm?" he said.

"What were you doing a few minutes ago, when you crossed your hands and closed your eyes?" I imitated the motions I had seen him make.

"Oh, that's a miracle," the Speaker said, tossing this off as if it went without saying. "That's a way you do miracle. God lay the foundation of the Eart' by stretchin' out his arms. He prove miracle by his hands. *With outstretchin' arms God create Heaven and Eart'.*"[16]

"And that's what you were doing today?"

"The Bible tell you that nothing is impossible to God."

I persisted. "I understand, but since the Earth has already been created, what were you doing just now?" I raised and crossed my arms again.

"Well, I am still doing my works," he explained. "That is my work! Works of all miracle. *All* types of miracle. *All* works of miracle."

"Crossing your hands like that?"

"Any *how*," he said emphatically. "Miracle don't do just one way." He shook his head firmly. "No, not at all. The Spirit has warious ways. His *word* is a miracle, and his works of *hand* is a miracle, too, when he come to perform it. God work miracle with the hand, he work miracle with the foot, he work miracle with the mouth."[17]

He licked his lips. "Don't *mind* exactly what you see I'm doing. As long as it pertaining to my work, that's my work: miracles in Heaven and Eart' and seas and all deep places. That is my privilege and my power. To do miracles."

Was this, I wondered silently, how Jesus had fed the 5,000, turned water to wine, raised the dead? "These are all different miracles?" I asked.

He grunted. "You have to *prove* that the Son was sent," he said. "People know that if a man is sent from God he gotta be able to perform miracles. If no miracle is done, he ain't gonna be *believed*. So therefore, you got to be able to perform miracles in order to be the Son of God."[18]

"So, you do the miracles to prove — "

"If you're the Son, you got to be able to speak and it *happen*. Because Jesus Christ was the Son of God, and Jesus Christ was speakin' miracles and it happen in the same *hour*.[19] What you say must come to pass. And if it come to pass, then you can't deny."

"So, you said miracles would come to pass, and they came to pass?"

"Yes. It *happen*. And I see it with my eyes. Bear witness of me. And that's all anybody got to know." He sat back, satisfied, arms folded once more.

Part of my mind slipped easily into the Speaker's train of thought while another struggled to stay grounded in reality. He seemed to be saying:

1. Jesus was the Son of God.
2. Jesus performed miracles.
3. His miracles were seen by others.
4. If you perform miracles, and they are seen, you are the Son of God.

This logic seemed elegantly simple, but also somehow circular. It was also familiar, though at the time I couldn't quite place where from. "I think I understand," I said. "But, what *specific* miracle were you performing today?"

Dismissing my inquiry with a wave of his hand, the Speaker said, "No, I don't tell that. That's my personal business, my personal work." He glowered at me. His voice tightened. "The secret things belong to *God*.[20] I don't expose my secret except I have to."

"Okay," I said, appeasingly. "Fair enough."

I had respected a boundary, and the Speaker seemed to sense this. Immediately, his expression softened and, like the passing of a cloud that had blocked the sun, the tension between us blew over.

The Spiritual Work

On my previous visits, I'd noticed the Speaker's movements among the dozen or so Bibles scattered about his small yard. He went from one to another, picking up a book, leafing through its pages, returning it to the ground, table, birdbath, or bench, then picking up another moments later.

"Can I ask you something else?" I said. "I've been wondering about this since I first saw you out here."

He nodded.

I pointed to a large, triangular sheet of paper near the center of the yard. "What is this writing on the ground?"

"That's the spiritual work," the Speaker explained. "These is anodder way I do my works. Whatever you see me put there, it register in the Heavens."

"In the Heavens?" I asked.

He nodded again. "You see, we got a daily secret."

I hesitated. "I'm not sure what you mean."

The Speaker sighed, his forbearance, perhaps, wearing a little thin.

"The Heaven got a drawin' of the Eart'," he said, "and the pen of a ready writer — that's a spiritual pen — take down everything that happen: every moments, every move, every nation, every territory. Whatever happen on this Eart', it show in Heaven. Nothin' can be hide from the Heaven, whether they be night or day."

He smiled knowingly and added, "You find *the pen of a ready writer* in the Book of Passelim, what you call the Psalms.[21] And you find the daily secret in the Book of Daniel, the prophesies."[22]

An image of his writings simultaneously transcribed in the sky by a cosmic teletype machine came to my mind. "So," I asked, "whatever you write here they see in Heaven?"

"Yes," he said. "You see, my authority is on Eart' *and* Heaven. Just as I am a prophet here on Eart', I am a prophet in Heaven. Whenever I *dream* something, I supposed to report it to the Heaven, because I'm not just workin' for the Earthly kingdom, I am also workin' for the Heaven. That's why I do it."

Of course, I thought. He would need his left hand to know what his right hand was doing.

The Sentence for the Dream

"And what about these other writings?" I asked, gesturing to the smaller piles of notes he'd placed around the yard. "Are they also messages to the Heavens?"

He swept his hand over his yard. "What I written there is what I *dream*, and the *sentence* for the dream. You see, whenever you dream a *word*, it have a sentence for that dream in the Bible. Whatever power or privilege or right you get, you get it by that dream — you come *under* that sentence. So you got to report it back to the Heaven to let 'em know that you are the same man as you find in the sentence."

The incoherent was starting to cohere. Again, I ran through his logic in my mind. "So you dream something," I conjectured, "and if you find what you dreamed in the Bible, then you report it back to the Heavens by writing it here?"

He nodded and smiled again, obviously pleased at my improving comprehension. "Yes, that's what you're supposed to do," he said. He chuckled. "You got to find that word you dream in the Bible, to know if it is God's word."

I *was* catching on. He moved from Bible to Bible, seeking the words — the *sentences* — that matched his dreams, and he recorded both his dreams and the matching biblical text on his scraps of paper. But their full significance still escaped me.

The Speaker seemed to anticipate my next question. He reached over to the birdbath and retrieved a white Bible. He set the book on his lap.

"And the next thing," he said. "If you is a prophet and you have a dream in the Book of Isaiah, you could do the *works* of Isaiah, the prophet." He tapped the Bible. "If you have a dream in the Book of Isaiah and *annoder* dream in the Book of Jeremiah, you could do what them *two* prophets prophesize, because the works of Jeremiah is different than the works of Isaiah." He tapped the book twice. "Then, if He gave you a dream in the *next* book, that's three books, so that's *three* prophets you come in to." The Speaker tapped three times, once for each prophet. "You see?"

I felt the adrenalin rush of puzzle pieces clicking into place. "In other words," I said, "each time you have a dream, and you find the same dream in the Bible, you get the powers of the prophet who had that dream?"

"Yes!" He smiled his broadest smile yet. "But," he cautioned, "you cannot go in *anodder* prophet's prophesy, except if you get the dream in that prophet's book."

I felt, again, that trippy, LSD-like sensation I'd experienced on the psych ward, as if I were being transported from this world into the Speaker's and back again. Did he dream, as Isaiah prophesied, of vanquishing his enemies? Were his dreams, like the prophesies of Jeremiah, of the massacre of innocents?

"You get the prophet's powers one by one, dream by dream, in a certain order?" I asked.

"Yes," he affirmed. "You got to prophesize where you is — this is your line. You cannot skip."

Strikin' Down Power Come Now!

Despite my short sleep the night before, I felt lighter, more exhilarated than I had in months. There were so many questions still to ask. I tapped the index cards in my pocket, debating whether to rely on them for the next query or to follow this new thread. But before I'd decided, I heard the leaves of a nearby ailanthus rustling. A cold wetness struck my hand. Dark spots formed on the slate tiles in the yard. I looked up. The sky, which had been merely hazy when I'd first come out, was deeply overcast.

In a flash, the Speaker was walking around his yard, methodically stooping to collect his Bibles and writings. As he picked up each stack of papers, he folded down a corner of the topmost sheet, carefully preserving their order.

I stood. "Can I help?" I asked.

He waved me off. "This is my work," he said. He bent to retrieve the last, and largest, piece of paper from the center of the yard.

I realized that my audience was coming to an end. "Thank you for talking with me," I said. "I'll be going now. But before I leave, can I ask one more question?"

"You see I doin' my *work*," he said gruffly. "I only talkin' to you because you comin' and you intercede, and you interest yourself."

Intercede?

"I understand," I said. "Just one?"

He hugged the stack of books and papers to his chest with one arm. He turned to face me. "Okay," he said.

"Thank you. Could you tell me what's actually *in* your writings?"

"What do you mean by *what*?" he asked, suddenly irritated. "Ain't I tellin' you? I *continue* tellin' you!"

"I'm sorry," I said. I pointed to the sheets of paper in his hands. "I meant, can you read me the words that you've written down here?"

He paused for a moment then shrugged, as if to say, Why not? He set the stack of books and papers by the doorway, protected by an overhang, and read from the topmost sheet. His manner was halting, quite unlike the way he read from his Bibles.

"And every *widgin* go into effect at once. Trus[23] is in trouble, in strong *trouble*. Jesus Christ final widgin on the nations. The battle now in the United States, battling against the *world*. Every action in Heaven and on the Eart' be turned loose in great *waters*, at *once*. Trus call for his mystery out of the great waters and seas and rivers, turn every mystery in Heaven and on Eart'."[24]

Lightning flashed in the distance, followed seconds later by a peal of thunder. As the storm approached, the Speaker raised his voice, his tone now clear, his delivery forceful and assured. "That's the final widgin," he said. His eyes narrowed. "*Let* them trouble me!" He paused for several seconds before adding, fury emanating from his body and wrath in his eyes, "Strikin' down power come now. Strikin' down power come *now*!"

The Speaker clutched the paper to his chest, and as quickly as it had come, the fierceness left his eyes. He placed this final sheet on top of the stack beside the door. Shifting to what I now thought of as his mentoring voice, he explained, "You have a strikin' down power in the Book of Passelim."[25]

Our eyes met, and I thought I detected a hint of sorrow in his. He placed a hand on my shoulder once more. "You have to have that dream," he said.

And once more, he released me.

INTERLUDE THREE

As a would-be engineer, novice literary scholar, and then a reporter, I'd taken pride in my ability to hold the apparently disparate pieces of a complex pattern in my mind, moving them about, adjusting the fit of one to another, until everything eventually snapped into place. The process involved an ongoing assessment of what fit, what didn't, and what was missing, the paradigm shifting as new data or fresh insights altered my sense of the emerging whole.

Although exactly how was unclear to me, I could already see that the Speaker's take on the Bible diverged from anything I'd encountered, even setting aside his belief that he was its subject. I wondered whether, in these divergences, there might lie the kernel of his insanity — or possibly, the key to an occult wisdom.

I reflected on what I'd sussed out about him so far.

1. His unusual movements were not rituals but were his "work": miracles of hand, mouth, and, presumably, also foot, though I hadn't witnessed the latter.

2. He used the Bible as a validation tool. This he did in at least two ways: a) When the Bible said that the Son of Man must act in a certain way, such as perform miracles, the Speaker would perform miracles and then point to them as proof of his divine nature. b) When he found one or more words in the Bible that matched images from his dreams, he regarded those matches as proof that his dreams were sent from God.

3. His dreams were also the means through which he inherited the "powers" of each of the biblical prophets, one by one.

4. He served as the communications link between Heaven and Earth, telegraphing what went on in this world to the Heavens. He was a prophet in both realms.

5. He was also, concurrently, the always-existent Christ, creator of the universe.

6. He was not *only* God, Jesus, or a single prophet, but, somehow, God, Jesus, and all of the prophets whose words he dreamed. Like Walt Whitman, he contained multitudes.

This much of the code I had more-or-less cracked. What was yet to be determined:

1. The finer details of the Speaker's theogony.

2. The significance to him of certain words, especially *thus* — for which, when I consulted the relevant Bible passages he had quoted, he consistently substituted *Trus*.

3. The Speaker's history and daily life outside the time he spent in his yard. I still knew only that he was not a U.S. native speaker, that he dressed well and therefore must have some form of income, and that he wore a gold band on his ring finger. Everything else, past and present, was a blank page waiting to be inscribed.

4. The impetus for his rage against mankind, intimated in the note he'd read to me during the final minutes of our latest encounter.

The armchair psychologist in me saw the Speaker's epistemological constructs as obsessive and delusional, but I had to admit that I was unable to quantify what percentage was madness and what *could* be genius. What I did know of the Speaker's messianic tale, so far, was already so complex that to dismiss him as simply "crazy" was no longer possible.

There was, I saw, a method to his madness. Though the odds were vanishingly small that there was substance to the Speaker's claims of divinity, I could not say with absolute certainty that they were zero. Even Jesus himself had not developed such intricate proofs of his divinity.

The amateur mythologist in me wondered how the Speaker would have fared in an earlier time. In the Gospels, Jesus turned water to wine, fed multitudes, calmed a storm, healed the sick, raised the dead. How could I be sure that the unexplained healings, weather changes, and other transformations that happened daily in *our* world, today, were unrelated to the Speaker's gesticulations, facial manipulations, and other ritualized actions? Might the Speaker, had he appeared in

Galilee two millennia ago, likewise have gathered disciples around him, and from them spawned a following that grew to billions? Again, the odds were vanishingly small, but still they were non-zero.

As I pondered all this, I found myself momentarily questioning my most basic assumptions, as if in an acid flashback, beginning with the Beginning.

I saw three possible explanations for Creation:

1. The universe is a mixture of nonsentient matter and energy, operating under a set of forces we only dimly understand and might never fully grasp.

2. The universe is itself a sentient entity, still growing from the seed of a conscious singularity whose origin we cannot comprehend.[26]

3. There is a sentient being (or beings) beyond our comprehension that had set the universe in motion, preceded its existence, and still governs it today.

Number one I have believed since I was able to conceptualize time and space and origins — about 10 years old. Number two, Buddhism has led me to consider. Number three I'd never seriously entertained. Now, however, all three seemed equally probable — and equally unknowable. Each is an act of faith, a postulate upon which the theorems of science, philosophy, and religion have been built, but which can never be proven.

If this most fundamental question could only be answered through an act of faith, how could I be truly sure of anything else?

As a budding NASA engineer, I had always looked to facts as the arbiters of reality and seen knowledge as progressive: Old paradigms yielded ineluctably to newer, more encompassing ones. I believed that on the shoulders of past geniuses, succeeding generations would achieve ever-greater certainties, successively discerning and discovering ever more durable truths. I had extended this point of view not only to science, but to all ways of apprehending the world. But as I reflected on my encounters with the Speaker, I questioned this framework.

Today, people like the Speaker were characterized as mad, burdens on society, their proclamations viewed, at best, as irrelevant and more commonly as pathological, but in the days of the ancient Greeks and of my own Old Testament Jews, they were the oracles and prophets, their wisdom and guidance sought after, their dreams and visions revered. Who was I — who is *any* of us — to judge whether a madman is God or God a madman, and on what basis do we make those evaluations?

As I pondered this question, I recalled a Sufi tale about a man who lost his mind, then found it again.

A messenger reveals that on a certain day, all the water in the world will be replaced with different water, and this new water will drive men mad. Only one person heeded this warning. He set aside enough water to last him for a long time and secluded himself. On the appointed day, as had been foretold, all the water in the world indeed stopped flowing and was replaced by the new water.

When the man who had drunk only the original water ventured forth from his concealment, he found that everyone he encountered now thought and acted in a way that made no sense at all. Greatly dismayed, but also reassured that his decision had been wise, he returned to his private store to quench his thirst. But as weeks turned to months, he found he could no longer bear the loneliness of being so separated from his kind.

He drank the water they had drunk.

Immediately, his fellow countrymen were relieved to see that he, the madman, had been restored to sanity.

Could any of us truly know who has drunk the water and who has abstained?

THE THIRD DAY: Trus is God

Dreams and visions from Genesis to Revelation. The Son got to be able to read. The teacher from God. The Light from his eyes. The Spirit of God coming in the shape of a dove. God never exposes his Son in an island. The 'fatherless' in the Bible. The Lord is the last name they make in Heaven. Trus is God. A shame and a disgrace. The kingdom is doomed. The prophesy will go bad.

Earth and Plants

After my second interview with the Speaker, I felt a subtle change come over me. Most immediately, I noticed that he was no longer an irritant. I worked contentedly, and I welcomed the faint babble of his orations. My original mission of getting him to *just shut the fuck up* wafted away in the gentle spring breeze that blew through my attic window.

My work and his could now peacefully co-exist, and I took some satisfaction in that. However, it came at a cost. What began as an attempt to remove distraction had evolved into obsession, though I didn't see it that way at the time.

Now I was digging into the Good Book whenever I wasn't occupied with house renovations or my music book. The more extensively I read, the more plausible the Speaker's biblical interpretations seemed. If nothing else, he knew his material well, possibly better, even, than my ex-nun professor.

I soon blew past the Old and New Testaments and the Apocrypha, branching out into both popular and esoteric texts on mythology, mysticism, and religion. I delved into specific concepts the Speaker had talked about, including the idea that dreams were a means of inheriting prophetic and other spiritual powers. I was surprised to find that this belief was common to both ancient and modern cultures.

In my investigations, I was looking for clues to fully delineate the Speaker's pattern of beliefs. Though I still regarded him as suffering from some kind of psychosis, I could appreciate that he had a consistent methodology for justifying his claims and defining his role in the world order. I couldn't help noticing that his was more refined than my own.

As the Speaker's theological system unfolded in my mind, my cynicism diminished. Now, if I mentioned the Speaker to friends (which, as time passed, happened more frequently), I no longer spoke with analytical detachment. Instead, I playfully entertained the notion that his claims of divinity were literally true: that he was the Second Coming of Christ, and that life as we knew it might soon come to an end. One night, I joked that I was building an Ark in the basement, and asked my friends if they would be willing to help in its construction in exchange for a berth. The response was uncomfortable looks all around. "I'm just kidding," I said. And I was. Yet I was also drawn to the man and his tale.

Despite the Speaker's delusions, or perhaps because of them, I felt oddly comfortable talking with him. I noticed he had also changed. Now, when I passed by his house, he would interrupt his oratory and wave a hand or greet me, much as a professor might welcome a favorite student stopping by to say hello. My interest in his story undoubtedly played a part; even the Old Testament God needed Adam to talk to.

In a small way, I had indeed become a part of his world, and he a part of mine.

The more I pursued my interest in the Speaker, the less rigorous I became about my own work. Though my landlady never complained, I knew I wasn't holding up my end of our house renovation deal. I still plugged away at the book, but that, too, began to lag. When my editor called to ask about the final draft, I made up a story about trouble scheduling interviews with some of the better-known musicians; I'd actually completed them months before. As soon as I hung up the phone, a weight lifted from my shoulders and I plowed back into the Speaker's world.

All of this I was okay with. My only real burden was the increased friction with Ruth, who didn't share my newfound enthusiasm. She begrudged the time I spent on my researches and repeatedly warned me of the dangers of dealing with a maniac. I acknowledged my preoccupation. But couldn't she see that this new "hobby," as she called it, had re-invigorated me? I begged her to bear with me. Reluctantly, she agreed to wait and see.

Precisely four weeks and a day passed between my second and third interviews with the Speaker.

I was on my way back from the Palestinian market on Fulton Street when I saw him at his usual station, performing his now-familiar works of hands and mouth. Carrying a small bag of groceries, I stopped directly in front of him and waited until he noticed me.

It took only a moment this time — he seemed to immediately sense my presence. He opened his eyes and smiled gently. To my surprise, without any preamble, he invited me to join him. Now there were two chairs at the metal table, as if he were expecting me.

I took one and he the other. The Speaker set his arms on the table and stared at me openly, awaiting my next question, like no time had elapsed between the present moment and our previous interview. Perhaps for him, none had.

I was ready, too.

With other interviewees, by this time I'd be asking about back story: Where were you born? How did you grow up? What can you tell me about your family? Your friends? Your career? But on the way to meeting the Speaker, I remembered Jung and his lunar voyage.

The Speaker was a dreamer, so I must go to his dreams.

Dreams and Visions from Genesis to Revelation

Stepping again into my interviewer role, I asked the Speaker, "How did God first come to you?"

Not unexpectedly, he said quietly, "As a dream." He sat erect and his voice deepened. "The Son of God is known by a dream."[27]

"Sometimes you talk about dreams, and sometimes about visions," I continued. "What's the difference between them?"

He nodded thoughtfully. "A widgin is a dream and a dream is a widgin," he said. "Both ways, your eyes gotta be closed, you gotta be gone from this world, before you could see."[28]

"I'm not quite sure I understand." (This had, by now, become a refrain.)

"A spiritual person's eyes could be closed, and yet he *see*. That's why odder people, they can't understand him. They didn't see it! And yet it was true."[29]

I gestured for him to say more.

"When your eyes is closed from this world and there's something appearin' in front of you in your sleep that you see before you wake, that's a *dream*," he said. "Yet that's a widgin. Even like a trance, when you're noddin', and your eyes close, and you catch yourself, and your eyes open? Well, that is a widgin, too. So that's why I say a dream is a widgin and a widgin is a dream.[30] All them ways, the Spirit talk to you."

Assessing me with his dark, unblinking eyes, he elaborated. "The Spirit is *God*, you know.[31] And the Spirit could appear *and* disappear. In a dream. God could stand up in front of you and talk in your sleep and He tell you what you have to say when He done and you're awake.[32] In English."

The Speaker had already told me about finding "the sentence for the dream" and writing it to the Heavens on his scraps of paper, but now I saw that for him, dreams — and "widgins" — had at least one more function: Through them, he could directly receive the words of the Spirit.

He amended my thought with a caveat. "Every one of them words in the Bible could be said by the Spirit in a dream. But you got to *find* that word in the Bible, to know if it is God's *word*." He spread his hands. "You can't know if you're sent from God *except* if you find the word what you dreamin'," he said. "You *have* to be able to translate it from the Bible, to prove that you *is*."

Another detail filled in: Like the images he saw in his dreams and visions, the words of the Spirit also must be validated by the text.

"How many dreams and visions have you had?" I asked.

"I had from Genesis to Revelation," he said.

"The whole Bible?"

"Yes."

"All at once, or little by little?"

"Little by little," he said. "It take *years*." He leaned back and repeated, "It take years."

His claim to know the Bible by heart no longer seemed an exaggeration. How many times had he pored over the text, word by word, seeking confirmation that what he had received in his dreams was a true message from God?

The Son Got to Be Able to Read

"How old were you when you had your first vision?" I asked.

"Ain't no special time for God's Son to have widgins," the Speaker said. "Because the Bible must be like how it is."

He smiled regretfully. "Sometimes," he confided, "I have dreams that I never told a man until I start to prophesize. I had them for *years* before comin' to this country, but I didn't pay them no mind." A shadow passed across his face. "The Son of God see them things in his sleep and he ain't got nobody to tell him. He got to find his way for himself."

Like Jesus before him, the Speaker's seemed a solitary path. A Gospel hymn came to mind:

When Jesus walked that lonesome valley.
He had to walk it by himself.
Nobody else could walk it for him —
He had to walk it by himself.

"You had nobody to guide you," I offered.

The Speaker hesitated for a moment. "I'll tell you the truth. I had my Bible, but I wasn't *readin'* it constantly," he admitted. "I didn't know what it *mean*."

His eyes grew moist. I had an impulse to console him, but, mindful of both my role and Ruth's warnings, I contained it. "What made you start to read the Bible, finally?" I asked instead.

"What made me start readin' my Bible? My Bible is a guide for to keep people from *sin*. That's the *world* guide. And if you feel like you wantin' to be doin' the wrong thing and you got your Bible, you're supposed to *read* it. You see?"

"So, you read the Bible to keep yourself from sin?"

He set his hands on his knees and leaned forward, toward me, as he spoke, nodding solemnly. "The Son got to be able to read all that his Father put before him, and to understand." He explained, "You see, there is words that the Bible give the Son to use. Now, unless you is a person who know what them things mean, you wouldn't pay 'em no mind, and you wouldn't know what to do. But a prophet, who is accustomed to do that kind of work, *he* would know exactly what it mean."

The Teacher from God

The Speaker glanced up at the sky, visible in patches through the trees that shaded his yard. A plane flew overhead, its jet trail dividing a splash of blue like the lands divide the sea.

I noticed he had side-stepped my question about sin. I let it go. What he had revealed instead — that the words of the Bible were intended, first, for the Son — seemed equally as significant. Like so many spiritual seekers, through the Bible the Speaker had likely found his way to the path of righteousness. But these words had also led him, somehow, to his divinity.

"I see you have a lot of Bibles," I said, gesturing to the collection he had assembled around his yard.

Returning his gaze to me, the Speaker said, "Jesus Christ got to increase in learnin', because he got to be the teacher from *God*. He's supposed to be able to teach the full knowledge of God from the beginnin' of the *world*. But, all things is not in one book. He got to continue changing from one book to one book. He got to continue climbing, continue passin' books, passin' books."

A verse from another spiritual played in my mind:

We are climbing Jacob's ladder,
We are climbing Jacob's ladder,
We are climbing Jacob's ladder,
Soldiers of the cross.

The Speaker leaned back, his hands cradling his head, his voice dropping into what I had come to think of as his God voice. "The Bible is the greatest book has ever been written," he said. "The Bible is true. And anything that is true is the greatest. A million years could pass, and yet the words of God still come back and repeat. Word of God always. Was and always."

Though my views, of course, differed from his, I nodded in agreement. "Reading the Bible helped you understand what was happening to you?" I asked, redirecting him to more personal matters.

"It start in the Book of Genesis, when I had this dream," the Speaker said. He sat erect and dropped again into his God voice: *Here is one to become like us. Put forth thy hands and eat of the Tree of Life and live forever and ever.*[33] "That's Adam dream," he said. "When I have that dream, they know that I was Adam."

"They knew in Heaven?"

He nodded, then laid his hand on a Bible that rested on the metal table. "And in the Book of Ruth is where you find that Adam is the *Lord*. That's anodder dream I had: *You have heard a rumor from the Lord Adam an ambassador is sent unto the nation. Let us raise in battle against her.*"[34]

The interplay between the Bible and his dreams and visions was now clearer to me. They were interdependent, the Bible and the dreams each enhancing the other in a virtuous cycle. From my recent research, I knew that, like the Speaker, Hopi Indians, various African cultures, and my own Hebrew ancestors all regarded dreams and visions in a manner quite unlike my own biological explanations.

Which, I wondered, was the more empowering idea, that dreams are part of the brain's housekeeping, or that they are divine instructions for entering a higher realm?

The Light from His Eyes

"Which dreams convinced you that you were the Son?" I asked.

"I have the *image* dream," the Speaker said. "That's the image of *God* in the Book of Daniel. That image show you that the Kingdom will be yours. *"The image stood before me, whose hair is of fine gold, his legs of silver and brass.*[35] And I have anodder dream, *eyes like flames of fire.* I classify that in a minute for you."

He lifted the Bible from the table and flipped to the end, then scanned rapidly and with great concentration as he ran his finger first down one column and then the next, like someone practicing speed reading. "See over here?" he said. "Now we go ahead to Revelation. This is the *Son.*"

> *And unto the Angel in the church write: These things say the Son of God, who has eyes like unto a flame of fire and his feet are like fine brass.*[36]

"That's a sign," he said. "You got to be able to give that sign to *prove* that you're the Son of God. If you are not the Son of God, you cannot give the light from your eyes. That's a sure miracle to prove that you are the Son."

I nodded. "I remember you telling me about light shining from your body," I said, attempting to join him in his world — to take the Jung Express to the moon. "You can also make the light come from your eyes?"

"Yes!" He seemed to regard my question as a challenge. "*You* can't do these things, see?"

I shook my head. "No, I can't," I admitted. "I'm just a man."

"See there?" he exclaimed. He pointed to the passage he had just read, his finger underlining the phrase *has eyes like unto a flame of fire*, as if the words themselves testified to his ability. "That's why the Bible tell you, *Trus have win his battle under the light.* Only *Thee* or *Trus.*"

I noted, again, the importance he gave to these words, though their implication still eluded me. "*Thee* and *Trus*?" I finally asked.

"Yes! Only them two names, because them names is when God come in the Son and give Him the Kingdom." He pointed again to the passage.[37] "See there? You see what God put in front of you and you didn't study it?" Before I had a chance to respond, he added, almost smugly, "Well, these are what you're supposed to look out for."

This explanation shed no further light, pun intended, but the effect of our interchange on the Speaker was profound — and alarming. He pointed to another Bible in the rear part of his yard, illuminated by the sunlight that shone through the sparse branches above it. "See I put it there? As long as you see that light come there, everyone that hate me, we gonna *kill* 'em right there."

The hairs on my arms stood at attention. "*Kill* them?" I exclaimed.

He half-raised himself from his chair, setting one hand on the table while he gestured with the other toward the splash of sunlight. He shouted, "That's fire! That ain't just light! That's burning, *invisible* fire. Burn you up!" He waved toward the fence. "Burn up this iron!"

My heart pounded in my chest at this outburst, but I forced myself to trust in our connection. Although the Speaker still sat between me and the gate, I had observed his moods rise and fall before, and no harm had come to me.

He sat down and lowered his voice, then looked at me with stern, penetrating eyes. "*Invisible* burnin' pass right through the house and *kill* you inside of it." He slapped a hand, hard, on the small table, rattling it against the slate. I flinched. "Invisible fire from the Heavens come right *down* and flash inside the house and *burn you up* right there in your *bed*."[38]

The Bible sat open on the table. He half-closed it, his fingers keeping his place. His rage left as quickly as it had come, and he smiled. Gesturing again to the bright spot in his yard, he repeated, "That's a sure miracle God give to *prove* that he's the Son. If he's *not* the Son of God he cannot give the light from his eyes."

The Spirit of God Comin' in the Shape of a Dove

The Speaker's outburst shook me out of my interviewer role. I felt as if he and I were players on a stage, acting out our drama to an empty theater. To re-center, I looked around at our surroundings for the first time in what seemed like hours, though I knew it had been only minutes. Across the street, a young woman wheeled a baby carriage toward Fulton Street, where I heard a car horn honk three times. Down the block, two teenage boys argued. A typical morning on Grand Avenue.

"Now I'll show you annoder dream, here," the Speaker said, calling me back to the stage. He turned to a place in his Bible marked with a feather. "God could come in the shape of a bowed," he said. "For the Book of John tell you, when John bear witness of Jesus Christ:

I saw the Heaven open and the Spirit of God descendin' and descendin' in the shape of a dow and it lighted upon him.[39]

"That's a dream. The Son have that dream, and when he wake up, he know who he is. Because only Jesus Christ could have the dream of the Spirit of God comin' to him in the shape of a dow."

My self-training in the Speaker's accent failed me; I had no idea what he was talking about. "Are you saying a *boat*?"

"Hmm?"

"A *boat*?"

"A *bowed*," he repeated. "A dow is a *bowed*. B-I-R-D."

"Oh, a *bird*! And a *dove*!"

He nodded. "You see, a dow in the Bible is a bowed, just like a pigeon." He scanned the sky, as if searching for a specimen. "You mightn't have them here, but we have them where we come from. We call them 'ground dow.' We have both pigeon: white pigeon, and these pigeon what you have here." He resumed his exegesis. "You see, it is a dream. And that word is there so that whenever Jesus Christ come to the Eart', and he gonna be known by the Father, he got to have that dream."

There, again, was that interplay between dreams and text. The words of the Father conveyed a message to the Son, whose dream conveyed a reciprocal message to the Father. For the Speaker, I realized, the words of the Bible were like signposts whose true messages only the ascending Son was equipped to receive. "And you had that dream, too?" I asked.

He nodded vigorously. "You see, I was lead by the Spirit.[40] For when the Spirit appear in my sleep, he say, 'I am a Spirit, I am a Spirit, I am a Spirit, that is what I am.' He put his mouth to mine, and a spoon come invisible in my sleep, and I feed him, and after I take away the spoon, the two of us walk in the Spirit together."[41]

The intimacy of this scene surprised me. "Wow" was all I managed to say.

"That is how it is," the Speaker said. "The Son gotta have them widgins, just like how it is stated. That's a spiritual work. That's the invisible works of God."

God Never Expose His Son in an Island

Despite my attempts at imitating it, I was still unable to place the Speaker's dialect. My best guess was Haitian, but I knew that wasn't quite right. My confusion over the ground doves reminded me I'd never simply asked.

"You mentioned that you had pigeons and doves where you come from. Where were you born?"

"I came from the Virgin Islands."

Born of a virgin, at least metaphorically. "How long have you been here?"

"Oh, many. I been here nearly twenty-five years."

"Did you know you were the Son of God when you lived in the Virgin Islands?"

The Speaker chuckled. "Oh, no. That's one thing God don't do. God never expose his Son in an island. Even he born there, he don't let it *happen* there." He raised an eyebrow. As if this were common knowledge, he asked, "You didn't know that?"

"No," I admitted.

"God only bring his Son in a *big* country. That's in the Book of Isaiah, the prophesy. *Trus, the Lord will turn Thee and bounce Thee like a ball until he get Trus in a larger country.*[42] He don't expose his Son in them small countries. God don't do it."

There, again, were the words *Thee* and *Trus*: A riddle wrapped in a mystery inside an enigma. But now was not the time to pursue it. Patience is a virtue, I told myself, and continued the current line of inquiry. "Is that why you came to the United States?" I asked.

He leaned forward. "God, *God* is who bring his Son here," the Speaker said.

289

The 'Fatherless' in the Bible

"The first time Jesus came to Earth," I said, "he had a human mother. Did you?"

The Speaker pressed his lips together and nodded. "I was create inside my modder's womb," he said. "The Book of Ezekiel tell you that: *from the days that Trus was create.*[43] That word *Trus* is a man that was create inside his modder's womb. You find that in the Book of Luke: *And behold Trus shall conceive in thy womb and bring forth the Son and shall call his name Jesus.*[44] That's the *real* Son of God. That's the Son of Man."

Trus, yet again. What did it mean to him? But I stayed the course. "Do your mother and your father know that you're God?" I asked.

He shook his head. "My modder and father die. That is the *fatherless* in the Bible."[45] Again his voice shifted, louder and deeper. "You read in the New Testament: *We are orphans and fatherless, our mothers are as widows.*[46] That's anodder sign of the Son of God coming. That's a dream, too."

We sat in silence for a few moments, and I took the opportunity to pivot toward the question the linguist in me had been aching to ask, one I saw as crucial to understanding the Speaker's unusual reading of the Bible and, therefore, also his claim to divinity. "Did you grow up speaking English," I said, "or did you speak another language before you came here?"

"Well, no, I grew up speakin' English," the Speaker said.

"So you could *always* read English?"

"Yeah, I could always read English."

So *Trus* was not a simple misreading or mispronunciation. I leaned toward him, resting a hand on the table. "I wondered if that was why you — "

"Speak so loud?"

"No. Well ..." But I had wondered about that, too. "Why *do* you speak so loud?" I asked.

"That's my way. You see, as long as you speakin' about the Spirit, there's *power* in you."

"Power?"

He raised a hand to the sky. "The Spirit of God is the power of Heaven and Eart'! If the Spirit could be abolished, you wouldn't have no Heaven and Eart' and you wouldn't have nobody neither on Eart' nor in Heaven."

He lowered his hand to the table and smiled. "So, whenever you come to a spiritual person, speakin' a little louder — and most especially when you speakin' about the works of God — you don't be offended. His spirit is different than yours. That's the Holy Spirit that cannot *fail*."

I found this instruction oddly relieving. The shifts in his expression and tone that I had experienced as bursts of anger might be nothing more than the Spirit of God flowing through his veins.

The Lord is the Last Name They Make in Heaven

We sat quietly for a minute, then the Speaker glanced over his shoulder. "Now this is something else I got to show you," he said. He rose and fetched a Bible from the stone bench, which he had moved near the door. He read:

> Then said I, Ah, <u>Lord</u> God! Behold I cannot speak, for I am a child. But the Lord said unto me, Say not that I am a child, for <u>Trus</u> shall go to all that I shall send Thee, and whatsoever I command Thee Trus shalt speak. Be not afeared of their faces: for I am with Thee to deliver Thee, said the Lord.[47]

"Now, you know who the Lord is?" he asked — rhetorically, I supposed, and so I just nodded. "The Lord is *God*. You see, that's anodder dream. When*ever* you see that word in the Bible, *Lord*, that mean a God. You cannot be a Lord except you is a God."[48]

He looked up from the book and waited for me to signal my understanding. "I see," I said simply.

"The Lord is the *last* name they make in Heaven," the Speaker explained. "You be called a God *long* before you be called a King and you be called a God *long* before you make a Lord." His eyes narrowed. "After you made that name *the Lord*," he said, "you cannot be carried down again."

Trus is God

I tried to grasp how prophets, kings, gods, and lords were, as the Speaker seemed to believe, rankings in some divine hierarchy. Again, I had the sensation of puzzle pieces snapping into place — and then

291

coming apart, their boundaries disintegrating like the walls of a sand castle lapped by ocean waves.

"How do you mean?" I asked.

"We go according to how it is written," the Speaker said, a slight edge to his tone. "We don't go just by hearsay. God let you know the Son is made by the *words* of God."

"I'm not quite following you," I said.

He tapped the Bible. "All them books — *every* book in the world, from Genesis to Revelation — tell of the Son of God coming. In the Book of Genesis, He said, *Trus, the Heaven was furnished and the Eart' was furnished.*[49] That's the real Son coming."

"Sorry, I'm still not getting it," I said.

I sensed his impatience, but he contained it. "In the book of St. Luke it start out, *Trus, Son of Man, Trus, Son of God, Trus, Jesus Christ*. And when he come in the Book of St. *Matthew*, he's Emmanuel, and he's Emmanuel in the Book of *Isaiah*, in the prophesies," the Speaker said.

Then the penny dropped, and like a figure emerging from the fog, another facet of the Speaker's reality came into view. The biblical personages he matched to his dreams, from Adam forward — all somehow marked by the ubiquitous word *Trus* — were not merely people who existed in their respective times and places. To the Speaker, they were each an incarnation of God, existing simultaneously across time and space, waiting to be found by the next Son of Man. With each dream, each vision, the Speaker had advanced toward his Second Coming.

Ev'ry round goes higher, higher
Soldiers of the cross.

This much I intuited. Still, I wondered, how did the word *Trus* figure in this theogony?

As if he had read my mind again, the Speaker returned his attention to the Bible he still held in his hands and said, "Here, I show you." He read from Daniel:

At the beginning of the supplication the commandment came forth, and I am come to show Thee.[50]

"Now, that word *Thee* mean the Son of God," he said. He continued reading, his finger tracking the text:

But Trus —

"See here?" He stabbed at the word *Thou.* "That is anodder name God call his *Son*; they call it *Thou* but it is *Trus.*" He continued:

But Trus are greatly beloved. Therefore, understand the matter and consider the widgins —

I could contain my curiosity no longer. I blurted out, "Why do you keep saying *Trus?*"

Startled by the intensity of my interruption, it took the Speaker a moment to respond.

"That's a *adjective* word!" he said. He looked at me expectantly, but confusion must have shown on my face. He explained, "T-H-U-S is *Trus*! T-H-O-U is *Trus*! T-R-U-S is *Trus*!"

He turned the Bible sideways so I could see where he was pointing and ran his finger down the page, stopping at the word *Thus.* "Look. You see?"

Obediently, I peered at the page. "Sorry, no," I said.

He sighed. "Okay, I show you something. You have a piece of paper?"

I found a hardware store receipt in my wallet. "Here," I said, sliding it to him.

He pulled a gold-tipped fountain pen from his shirt pocket. "Now, this is *Edward*. See? Let me spell it." He printed E-D-W-A-R-D on the back of the receipt.

"Who's Edward?" I asked.

He pointed to his chest. "That's Edward. All right. Now I show you something else." He wrote the word *Edward* again, this time in script. "There," he said, showing me the two versions of his name.

EDWARD *Edward*

"What happen?" he said.

"That's also *Edward*," I said, bewildered.

"That's what fool people!" He laughed. "Sure, it fool people." He chuckled to himself again. "Let me show you something else."

He wrote another word below the two versions of *Edward*, sounding out each letter. "T-R-U-S," he said.

He had written the word *Thus.* "It's *Trus*, see? Like when you trus' in somebody."

"But that says *Thus*," I protested.

"No, that's not *Thus*," he said. "That's *Trus*."

My confusion was still evident.

He sighed. "All right," he said patiently. "Now, you see where the *r* come there, under the *h*?" He drew an *r* over the *h* in *Thus*. "All right. See here? See what a man do?"

Thus

"I think so," I said. He'd superimposed an *r* on the *h*, as if the *r* were hidden within it. "So you're saying they're the same word?"

"It's a adjective word," he said, nodding in agreement. "It's a *adjective*."

"But it's the *same* word?"

He nodded again and smiled. "It's the same word."

"Okay. Well, I didn't want to interrupt what you were saying — "

"No. No, I just want to show you something. That's why some people cannot read the Bible. They see the word here *one* way, and they see only *one* letter, *h*. A letter split the difference, but it's the same word. You see how I show you that?"

He wrote again *Thus*. Beneath it he wrote *Trus*. "Now, you see? See how a man write that?"

"I see, but — "

"In the Bible, every one of them letters is the *same*. T-H-U-S. T-R-U-S. It's the same word!"

"Okay, *now* I see." And I did! Literally. *Trus*, in the Speaker's reading, was the hidden descriptor for God.

In my mind's eye, I envisioned the hundreds, perhaps thousands, of instances of *Thus* in the pages of the Bible, each *Thus* highlighted with its overlaid *r*, each *Trus* preceding a name. "Thus, Adam" became "*Trus* Adam," synonymous with "God Adam." "Thus, Ezekiel" became "*Trus* Ezekiel," another name for God. And on and on, each biblical personage revealed to be a divine man by this previously hidden title, this "adjective word." The generalizing power of this small change in a single letter wowed me.

"If you don't know how the adjectives work, you find a *different* word. But it's the *same* word," the Speaker said.

"Now, I see," I reiterated. "I *have* always thought it was a different word." I smiled conspiratorially. "Until now, that is."

"Adjective letters is a way of changing," the Speaker explained. "That's why the dictionary give two, three ways to pronounce one word. You pronounce E-D-W-A-R-D like E-D-W-O-R-D. It is a *change*, and yet it is the *same word*. For instance, you know how you spell *time*? T-I-M-E is *time*. But T-H-Y-M-E is *time*, too."

A truck rumbled by. While we waited for it to pass, I reflected on the Speaker's hierarchy of the Heavens. A wave of pity swept over me as I regarded this man, whose identity hinged on a misreading of a single letter. But moments later, I also felt a counterbalancing wave of admiration. His methodology was brilliant in its simplicity, in this context as revolutionary as $E=mc^2$.

"Now," the Speaker was saying, "try to understand these things, because God speak a word and people misinterpret it. They don't realize. You see what I mean now?"

"Yes, I do," I said.

He nodded firmly. "That's how it is." He elaborated: "You got to understand that the wisdom of God is a mystery to the people. If you don't understand the words of God, you cannot see God do his work. But God do his *work*! You can't understand because it look impossible. Yet it is the truth." He glanced skyward. "All things is possible with God," he said.

I followed his gaze. The rustling of a small brown bird building its nest in the nearby ailanthus drew my attention, and unbidden, a science fiction story I'd read as a boy came to mind.[51]

In a Tibetan monastery, for centuries monks had been listing all the possible names of God. They believed that this was the purpose of Creation, and that once all nine billion names were enumerated, God would end the universe. At the monks' current rate, this task would take tens of thousands of years.

To accelerate the process, they obtained a computer and hired two Americans to program it. In two days, the programmers completed their job. They collected their fee and left the monastery before the computer finished its task, arriving at the airport just as their program was scheduled to end its run.

While they waited for their flight back to the U.S., they joked about how disappointed the monks must be. As they chuckled, one of them glanced up at the sky, where one by one, the stars winked out.

The Speaker, too, had enumerated all the names of God in his many trips through the Bible, both waking and dreaming. With a sudden chill, I wondered: Was the end of everything — of this table, this chair, this little bird, this universe — also the endpoint of the Speaker's reckoning?

A Shame and a Disgrace

With this question in mind, I circled back to the beginning, to what had literally brought me to this place, this conversation. "You've explained to me about your miracles and dreams and visions, and many other things, and I really appreciate that," I said. "But I'm still wondering about one thing."

The Speaker raised an eyebrow. "Yes?" he said.

"You're out here speaking, sometimes every day. Why do you do it?" I asked.

The Speaker stiffened. Then, his chest expanding, his voice booming, he said, "Because it is my *privilege* to tell it."

"Your privilege?"

He glared at me. "It is my privilege to tell it," he repeated coldly. "I want them to see their loss and their gain. What they *lose*: kill the whole population, the majority of the world, man*kind*. Bring down on the world destruction, hell*fire*."

Again I was gobsmacked. Speechless. "You want to *kill* us all?" I stammered at last.

He leaned forward. "It is a *shame* and a *disgrace* to know that God made man, and man wouldn't *study* Him," the Speaker said. "Even when God send somebody who tell them to do better, and they read of that, they *still* wouldn' listen." His voice fell almost to a whisper. "The kingdom is doomed. The Eart' is doomed."

The Kingdom Is Doomed

The depths of the Speaker's anger stunned me. A passing motorcycle interrupted his rebuke and gave me a welcome moment to collect my thoughts. "Let me make sure I understand," I said. "You want to *kill* everyone, to destroy the *world*, because we didn't read the *Bible*?" I asked, my cadence unconsciously mimicking his.

He smiled indulgently. "No, not *only* that." With a mixture of disdain and pity, he added, "They brought hell*fire* forever, instead of doing God's law. It is a shame and a dis*grace*."

"God's law?"

"God give his Son the universe in order to make the law! When*ever* the Son come, he got to make the law to keep the people righteous, to keep them from *sinning*, so the work will go on *long*er. If they don't do the law, then God destroy the *world*."[52]

"So, we weren't righteous, and now God will destroy us?"

"Sure, because it's high time He destroy the world."

"High time?"

"*High time!*[53] You see, that's why now you have so much hardship, you don't see food, all them things that happen since I prophesize it: floods, the sun into blood, the morning to blood, the stars refuse to shine. All them kinda things is the sign of the end of the *world*."[54]

The Prophesy Will Go Bad

He dropped his hands to his sides. "You see, as long as the people don't do the law, the prophesy will go bad." With a sneer, he added, "When man become disobedient, you gotta have *fast action*, be able to *kill him* as fast as he come. God don't *play* with man after his time is up. He destroy the world in small time."

Caught up in the Speaker's vision, I found myself feeling real alarm, as one might in a movie theater when the vampire's hand rises from the grave. "Is there nothing we can do?"

"After you sin and God call you to *repent* and turn from that sin, and you *don't* turn, there's nothin' else for God to do but destroy. He ain't gonna *leave* you here. As long as God decide you gotta go, you gotta go."

The Speaker pounded a fist into his open palm. "All these things God do because man fightin' for the world, fightin' for the Eart'. He try to say the Eart' is *his*." He shook his head. "No! This Eart' is *mine*. And the people don't sin against me no more."

An image came to me: the Speaker, Godzilla-sized, swatting with his enormous paws at insectile Man as we scurried futilely for our lives. I asked, in scarcely more than a whisper and against my own agnosticism, "What about prayer?"

The Speaker shook his head. "It don't matter whether you pray or you *don't* pray," he said. "Don't make no difference to God."[55]

He assumed a milder tone. "You see, if a man is in charge of you, you got to do what he tellin' you to do. If a boss tell you, 'Well, you got to scrub the floor,' and you say, 'Well, boss, I ain't scrubbin' the floor,' he gonna tell you, 'Well, pack up your things and get out.' Right?"

I nodded. "Of course," I said.

"Well, that's how things is with God. If *man* can do that with *man*," he said, his voice rising in volume, "don't you think God got the same *privilege*?" He almost screamed that final word.

"Of course," I said, appeasing, pulling back. "Of course God does."

INTERLUDE FOUR

In an earlier interview, the Speaker had read from Genesis: "*And the Lord God call unto Adam and said unto him, Where are Trus?*"[56] He'd laughed knowingly as he pointed to the word *Thou* and said, "Now, you see *Trus* is the first man made? You see what I show you? If you never *read*, you never find out what this book *say*."

At the time, I took his unusual pronunciation of *Thou* to be a misreading of English or an artifact of his dialect. Only now did I understand that it was actually the key to his entire system of using and interpreting the Bible, essential to the conclusions he had reached.

The most puzzling piece of the Speaker's methodology was also the most innovative: that concealed within the letter *h* was an occult *r*. The letter *r*, an "adjective letter," converted *Thus* to its true form, *Trus*, an "adjective word," the ubiquitous signifier for God. *Thou* and *Thee*, when you understood them as the Speaker did, were somehow also variations of *Trus*. And all three words deified any name they referenced.

This linguistic trick was an essential element of the Speaker's logic, and it gave him remarkable flexibility in wresting new meaning from the ancient text. *Trus* imbued virtually every name in the Bible, beginning in the Beginning, with the Holy Spirit. Not only the traditionally defined prophets, but all other figures so blessed (literally) by *Thus*, *Thee*, or *Thou*, were incarnations of God who lived in their respective historical eras, and were also — because the Spirit transcended time — eternal. *Trus* applied to Adam made Adam not only the first man, but also the first in a succession of divine incarnations.

The Speaker's powerful interpretive device vastly expanded the range of biblical passages he could draw on to authenticate his dreams and visions. In addition to the visions of the major and minor prophets, fragments from the histories, the laws, the psalms, and all the books of the New Testament were valid candidates, as long as they contained the "adjective word" *Trus* or its equivalents.

I saw, now, why the Speaker insisted that the Bible must be read from cover to cover. This order was essential to his own ascension. From its first to its last word, the Bible was, for him, a single story culminating not only in the First Coming of Christ, Jesus of Nazareth, but also in the Second Coming, Edward of the Virgin Islands.

For ordinary mortals, the Bible was still the "world guide" for proper behavior it had always been. But for the Speaker, it was also an instruction manual. It was as if, concealed within it, was this message, in a code only he could decipher: "If you are the true Son of God, follow these steps to attain your full divinity." By correlating his dreams with the sentences and words of each *Trus* figure, he could incorporate into his being their fraction of God, until at last he dreamed the dream of the Holy Spirit coming in the form of a dove. This was the conclusion of his long apprenticeship and the start of his reign as King of Kings and Lord of Lords.

The Speaker's saga was akin to a superhero origin story. From ancient times, his destiny had been foretold, his path defined. Unlike the heroes of the comic books I'd read as a boy, he had come by his powers not through a twist of fate, but through hard work stretching over decades of painstaking validation in the many versions of the Bible he had acquired, sometimes finding only a *single word* to guide him as he progressed through the stages of his ascension.

You're thinking, "That's quite a stretch." And it is. But no more so than the assumptions and methods employed by Kabbalists, numerologists, or Talmudic scholars. And hadn't the authors of the *Pentateuch* itself interwoven oral histories, folktales, and myths into a narrative that served *their* purposes?[57] Who was I — and who are *you* — to say that the Speaker's interpretations were any less authentic?

I was pleased with my analysis. Like a detective pinning up photos and clippings onto an evidence board, I had created a framework into which I could fit the remaining clues.

Now I wondered in earnest about the Speaker's life before Brooklyn. There was the gold band. Had he married? Fathered children? He hadn't said. I could imagine him as a young man — handsome, strong, multi-skilled, a hard worker. And then the calling, and the falling away of all of that. But this was just conjecture. Time, I hoped, would reveal more, though it was not lost on me that these same questions were still being asked about Jesus himself nearly two millennia after his death.[58]

Chief among my questions now was what specific crimes mankind had committed to warrant our extinction. Already, I had my suspicions. Already, having assembled this much of the puzzle, I saw there was truth in the Speaker's words, at least metaphorically.

One statement from our recent encounter especially haunted me: "After you sin and God call you to *repent* and turn from that sin, and you *don't* turn, there's nothin' else for God to do but destroy. He ain't gonna *leave* you here." Was this merely the threat of an unhinged unfortunate whose genetics, life experience, or both had pushed him beyond the bounds of sanity? Or was it possible that he, like the biblical figures he emulated, was an oracle through which the truths of our times were revealed? Did labeling the Speaker a madman make his dreams and visions any less prophetic?

With our self-centeredness and our greed, hadn't we single-handedly ravaged our world? Hadn't we sinned, if not against God, then against our own species, against the creatures with whom we shared this planet, and against the Earth itself? Hadn't our hubris already brought the wrath of God upon us, embodied in the pestilence, mass extinctions, conflagrations, famines, wars, rising oceans, and all the other self-created cataclysms of our age? Hadn't our actions already led us, perhaps ineluctably, toward our demise? And wasn't it, perhaps, already too late to repent? Time would tell.

These were the notions I pondered as I thought about my next encounter with the Speaker.

THE FOURTH DAY: The Law of God

The nation was to stop sinning and do the law. As long as you sin you are not innocent. Failing to observe the Sabbath day. The Son don't sin. God put good and evil before you.

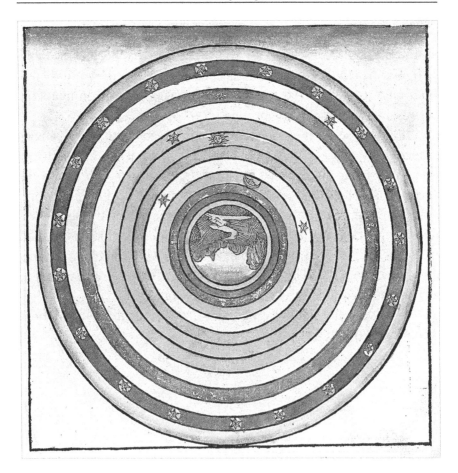

Sun, Moon, Stars

When I talked with my friends about the Speaker, their responses continued to be either dismissive — "He's just a lunatic!" — or indifferent — "I'm not interested in crazy people."

But I believed that nobody was *just* a lunatic. And I have been interested in "crazy" people since boyhood, when, as my first therapist pointed out, I became a child psychologist, tending to my mother's suicidal rages and protecting myself from a jealous father. So despite my own reservations, I found myself defending the Speaker — sometimes only in my mind, sometimes with my friends, and, more often than I liked, with Ruth, who had become increasingly apprehensive about my associating with a man she thought was not only "insane," but also dangerous.

Ruth had worried about me when I was hanging out with the bums, bag ladies, pimps, and prostitutes I'd written about in my street people stories. When I moved to Brooklyn, she'd hoped those concerns would be behind her. Meeting the Speaker — Edward — changed all that. And it changed us.

"What are you doing?" she would ask me. "What if he's like Son of Sam?"

"He's not like Son of Sam," I would say. "He may be delusional — "

"*May* be delusional?"

" — but he's not violent."

"You don't know that! Just leave him alone."

—

Ruth was at ease sitting behind me on the back of my motorcycle, and we'd gone on many rides through the rolling hills of Central New York, but she was not a risk-taker when it came to emotionally volatile people, and she freaked out whenever I ventured into potentially hazardous terrain.

An example: A few weeks before I met the Speaker, we were walking to a restaurant on my old turf, the Upper West Side, when I saw a young man standing just outside the entrance to a bar, holding a 2x4 over his shoulder like a batter waiting for the next pitch.

I stopped.

"What are you doing?" Ruth said.

I gestured toward the bar. "That guy's trying to clobber somebody."

She tugged at my sleeve. "Come *on*," she whispered. "It's none of our business."

"We can't just *go*," I whispered back. "He could kill somebody." I nudged her toward the curb. "Stay here."

"What are you *doing*?" she repeated, her voice tight.

"Just stay here," I said.

I took a few steps toward the bar. I was still a dozen paces from the entrance when he noticed me. He hesitated for a moment, then turned in my direction.

"Hey," he said, his eyes glassy, his stance menacing as he set the 2x4 on his shoulder.

I stopped. "Hey," I said.

He sneered and took a step closer. "You got a *starin'* problem, buddy?"

I could hear my heart pounding in my ears, but I stood my ground. "I'm just standing here," I said. I was bearing witness. Through my intervention, the outcome for whoever was still in the bar had already shifted.

By then a couple of passersby had also stopped, and soon a small crowd of onlookers gathered. A muscular guy straight out of *Saturday Night Fever* stepped out of the crowd. He pulled off his shoe — a wooden clog — and waved it at the 2x4 guy.

"You want to fight somebody?" he said. "Bring it on!"

Situations like these spooked Ruth. I couldn't blame her. I didn't welcome them, either — I'd never been much of a fighter. But I wasn't threatened by the Speaker, and what had begun as an attempt to quiet him down had evolved from an investigation into another kind of bearing witness. Through my intervention, perhaps his outcome, too, would favorably shift.

But I'd be lying if I said bearing witness was the only factor in my interest in the Speaker.

Curiosity and the thrill of the chase are what really hooked me. The Speaker's thought processes, his history, and his passionate devotion to his mission were what intrigued me. I wasn't looking for wisdom or insight — that he was probably insane was beside the point. Now, each time the rise and fall of his voice shivered the silence of my room, it increasingly compelled me to resolve the mystery of how he had come to his unlikely conclusions. What could drive a man to such grandiosity? And inspire such rage?

As for the thrill, whether someone was a television talk show host, a prison rights advocate, a politician, a transvestite prostitute, one of the folk musician legends of my youth, or a man who believed himself to be the Second Coming of Christ, the appeal was the same. Each person I got to know was an entire universe, and exploring it was as captivating a trip as a voyage to some exotic land.

Like many things about me, however, none of this made sense to Ruth. I knew she was only looking out for my safety, and I admit, I could be reckless sometimes. But I was a big boy, and I chafed at her admonitions.

—

Ruth and I met in our last year in college, first at an English Department party, then in a modern dance class, and again in a poetics seminar the following semester. The third time was the charm.

She was petite, cute, and her dark Mediterranean eyes drew me to her, but it was soon apparent that we could only get so close. When I was distant, she was open. When I responded, she pulled away. I called it "splitting ambivalence."

Though our relationship was turbulent from the start, we persisted through that final college year, a difficult summer apart, and then a miserable winter living together in an uninsulated attic apartment in Buffalo, each of us working dead-end jobs. That spring, she left. Whether she had given up only on Buffalo, or also on us, she wouldn't say.

To clear my head, I spent a few months riding my motorcycle though the Northeast and Midwest, then I followed her to New York. I thought we'd resolve things, one way or the other, within six months. Three years later, we were still alternating weekends at her place and mine, still hovering between breaking up and tying the knot.

—

Despite our difficulties, there was an aura of mystery to Ruth I found irresistible. On our first real date, a bicycle ride to a nearby amusement park, under the flashing lights of the Ferris wheel, she made a prediction. "I know I'm not the kind of woman you usually go out with," she said, "but the more you get to know me, the more you'll like what you find."

I smiled and took her hand. "Really?" I said, in the warmest ironic tone I could muster.

She nodded. "Yes. And you'll discover things you never knew you needed until you find them."

On the whole, her prophesy was spot on.

One of those "things" was her poetry. A few weeks into our relationship, a mutual friend asked me if I'd read her chapbook. That was the first I'd heard of it. In a tiny bookstore on Main Street, I found a copy, a thin volume with a photo on the cover that could have been the sea, clouds, or windblown desert sands — another mystery. That night, I read it all, first silently, then out loud, and then silently again, letting each nuance of image, feeling, and insight sink into my soul. If all *this* was in her, I thought, I would stick around forever.

Unfortunately, much of the passion I'd felt in her poetry she reserved for the written word. Or maybe that wasn't so unfortunate. I'd never dated another writer, and although we didn't read each other love poems deep into the night, we did write passionate love letters. Using the written word to unveil the secrets in our hearts was, as she had predicted, something I didn't know I needed until I'd found it with her.

Another unexpected pleasure was Ruth's connection with the earth. A couple of years after she returned to New York, she moved to Queens, where she and her housemate, Leslie, transformed their front yard into a vegetable garden, an Edenic oasis amid the barren lawns of their suburban neighborhood. From its bounty, Ruth made vegetarian dishes in the tradition of her Middle Eastern heritage, a refreshing change from the meager meals I prepared for myself in Brooklyn.

Visiting Ruth and her housemate in their Queens apartment was a welcome respite from the intensity of my Fort Greene neighborhood. A bonus was Leslie's boyfriend, Paul, a forensic psychologist with a quick wit who often joined us, and whose verbal volleying I greatly enjoyed. Ironically, given Ruth's fears around the Speaker, Paul would become the lead psychologist on the team that evaluated Son of Sam after he was apprehended later that summer.

—

The latest stressor in our relationship, as I mentioned earlier, was the Speaker. Short of abandoning my interview project, the only way to take him out of our equation, I believed, was for Ruth to see for herself why he so intrigued me. At first she resisted this suggestion, but eventually she agreed to meet him the next time we heard him speaking from his yard.

We were just waking up on a lazy Sunday morning the weekend following my third interview with the Speaker when the familiar rhythm of his orations percolated through the morning air.

"Do you hear something?" she said, sitting up in bed.

I sat up, too. "I do," I said. "It's him. The Speaker — Edward. We need to get going."

She sighed, lay back down, and tried to pull me under the covers.

I resisted. "C'mon, you said you'd do it."

"We haven't even had *breakfast*."

"We can do that later."

"I need to take a shower."

"We can do that later, too."

She threw her pillow at me.

"C'mon, it'll be fun."

"*Fun?*"

"Okay, maybe not fun. But it's important to me."

She made a mock-sad face. "Just for a little while, okay? I don't want to spend the whole day talking to a crazy guy."

I wanted to challenge "crazy," but thought better of it. "Sure," I said, and kissed her.

My timing was, in one sense, perfect, but in another it could not have been worse.

Ruth and I walked hand-in-hand down the street, and as we approached the Speaker, I could feel her tensing. We stopped directly across from his house.

He stood in the middle of his small yard, still orating. He wore a pale yellow, short-sleeved shirt, and dark blue pants with sharp creases. "God made man upright," he was saying. "If you go from that righteousness where God be, you become *sinful*. You cannot teach righteousness. Your eyes are *blind*."

"What is he *doing*" Ruth whispered.

"He's warning us," I whispered back.

"Us?"

"Everybody. He's warning everybody."

"About what?"

"The end of the world," I said.

"He probably have the same trouble again with you," the Speaker said. "And He don't want a second trouble."

"What?" Ruth said.

"He's letting us know we've been sinners," I said. "I haven't figured it all out yet, but I think he wants me to be part of his mission."

"He *what?*""

"I'll tell you about it later." I gave her arm a gentle tug. "Let's go."

We crossed the street. As soon as the Speaker saw us, he stopped talking and smiled quizzically.

"Hi," I said.

"Hello," he said.

"We just wanted to stop by and say hello. This is my friend Ruth."

"Pleased to meet you," Ruth said.

The Speaker shrugged. "That's one of the things," he said to me, for the moment ignoring Ruth. "People see those things in the Bible, they misinterpret."

"What things?" I asked, slipping automatically into interviewer mode.

"You see, *man was not made for woman. Woman was made for man.* You find that in ... ah ..."

"Genesis?" I said.

"No, in Corinthians,"[59] he said. "So, a man could compel a woman, but a woman cannot compel a man. And in Ephesians, the Lord say, *Wives, submit to your own husbands, as to the Lord.*"[60]

He turned, now, to Ruth. "You didn't know that?"

"I — I'm sorry," Ruth said. "I don't understand." She gave me a quick, sidelong glance that should have told me to get her out of there.

"God never gonna let a woman rule a man. The Book of Timothy say, *Let a woman learn in silence with all submissiveness. I permit no woman to teach or have authority over a man.*"[61]

This was *really* getting off on the wrong foot, but I still hoped the Speaker would say or do something — *anything* — to demonstrate to Ruth why I was drawn to him.

"Ruth is new to all this," I said lamely.

"Okay," the Speaker said. He switched to mentoring mode. Turning to Ruth, he explained, "I tellin' you this to show that God made man to rule the world, for a man is stronger than a woman." The Speaker looked to me, then back to Ruth. He paused a moment, waiting for a response that never came. "So," he continued, "whenever the *punishment* come, he who is supposed to rule gonna get the first punishment."

Ruth grabbed my arm and tugged.

"Now, I got it right here." He reached for a nearby Bible. "I show you."

"Just a minute," I said to the Speaker. Ruth led me a few feet down the block.

"I don't understand what he's talking about," Ruth whispered, her voice strained, "but whatever it is, I don't like it."

"I know," I said. "This is the first time I've heard him talk about women like that. I didn't expect it. Sometimes he rambles."

"*Sometimes?*"

"Okay, most of the time."

"I'm not going to stick around while he goes on and on about men compelling women," she said. "He's a sexist pig. A *crazy* sexist pig."

"He's not a sexist pig," I said. "All that stuff's in the Bible."

"I don't care."

"I can get him to talk about something else. Just wait a few more minutes, okay?"

"I don't want to stay here. You can talk to him if you want to, but I'm going home."

"Look, I just wanted you to see what I'm trying to do. Please?"

"I saw *enough*."

I took a deep, slow breath and sighed. "Okay, let's go," I said. "Just a sec."

I walked back to the Speaker, who was still paging through the Bible. "Ruth has to go home now," I said. "I'm going to walk her to the train. But I'll be back in a few minutes, okay?"

The Speaker glanced at Ruth, her arms tightly folded across her chest. "Now, I don't wanna detain you no longer," he said. He set the book on the table.

"No, that's okay. I'd like to talk with you. I'll be back soon," I said.

The Speaker nodded and returned to his Bible.

Ruth and I walked in silence down Fulton Street. Halfway to the A train, I reached out tentatively for her hand. To my surprise, she reached back and gave a little squeeze. When we arrived at the station, I said, "I don't have to talk with him today. Don't go."

"It's fine. I have to get ready for tomorrow anyway."

"You're sure you won't stay?"

She nodded. "Yes. Really, it's fine. Go talk to him if you want to."

Her body language was impossible to read. "Okay," I said.

We held each other for a minute, and I felt her softening. Still holding my hand, she took half a step away and turned toward the stairs. "Just don't *ever* make me do anything like that again," she said, and she descended into the station.

I was still shaken by the time I returned to the Speaker. He was sitting at his table, two Bibles open, one black and one white. His hand moved between them, his finger tracing passages first in one and then the other.

"I'm back," I said. "If you're busy now, I can go home."

"No, no," he said. He motioned to the gate and invited me in.

We assumed our customary positions: I in the chair furthest from the gate, he in the one near the birdbath he used as a lectern, the small metal table between us. He awaited my next question. I shifted into interviewer mode, and my troubles with Ruth receded into the background.

The Nation Was to Stop Sinning and Do the Law

I began with the question most on my mind. "Last time we met, you told me that mankind had been disobedient, and that it was time for you to destroy us."

The Speaker nodded. "It's *high time* mankind be destroyed."

"That's what you said. But why *now*?"

The Speaker glared at me, his face a mask of indignation. "You say *why*?" He slammed one of the Bibles shut. "The nation was to stop sinnin' and do the *law*. The law of *God*! That is in the *Bible*!"

I was momentarily startled, again, by his sudden fierceness, but undaunted. "I understand that," I said. "What I mean is, what's different about *now* than ten years ago, twenty years ago, even a hundred years ago?"

The Speaker shifted gears into his mentoring mode. Gazing at me more benevolently, he explained, "As long as you doin' God law, you stop the Son from comin' to the Eart'. But whenever the people stop doin' the law, you break the *cowament*."

I hesitated, but only for a few seconds. "The covenant? Like the rainbow sign with Noah?"

"No, no, not only the rainbow. The rainbow is a special sign. But they have other cowaments for the people, too. The Sabbath *day* is a cowament. And the *law* is a cowament that, as long as you're doing the law, you entitled to your rights."[62]

This took me just a moment to digest. "So, we were okay as long as we kept following the law?" The Speaker nodded. Like the earnest student who hoped to please his teacher, I offered, "And then we broke the covenant?"

A slight nod. "That is when God send down his Son, made by a woman, to say to them to do the law."

"And what happened?"

He slapped the table, jiggling the Bibles. "They continue sinning! So they gotta go."

"Okay, so God sent Jesus to tell us to obey the laws, and we kept sinning. I get that," I said. "So why are we still here?"

He paused for a moment then smiled. "You see, God is merciful.[63] God don't mind if man do God wrong — he give you annoder chance, and he keep talkin' to you until the final time that he gave you to stop doin' the wrong is up.[64] Not because you *pushin'* against God — you cannot push hard enough against God to push down *God* — but because that's how God work with man. But when the Son come and He *teach* you how to do the law, and you *still* don't do it, God ain't got to favor you no more. You let your time *run out*. So now, this is *God's* time. He don't have to show you no more mercy at *all*. That's when man cause the world to be lost."[65]

He gave me time to let that sink in. "If you do the law, you receive the good," he said, "and if you *don't* do it, you receive the bad. That's it. God don't gotta be patient with you no more."

As Long as You Sin You Are Not Innocent

So now, for reasons I still did not understand, our time was up. I felt a prick of irrational fear. *Had* we all sinned? Were we *all* deserving of punishment? Was I? "But, what about all the innocent people?" I objected. "Why must *they* die?"

The Speaker stood up abruptly. He looked down on me, his eyes hard and piercing. "*What* innocent? *You* are innocent?" he shouted, his body trembling. "As long as you have *sinned*, you are not innocent! That's why the law extend to everybody. It is because *everybody* sin! You sin by deed, and thoughts, and action."

He steadied himself and sat down, quickly falling back into his mentoring role. "The law of God extend to every human being that comes into the world, right? Because that is what the Bible say: *I add and I take away.*"[66]

"Okay ..."

"They got people who might not steal anything from odder people, I would admit that," the Speaker acknowledged. "But still, they do odder sins they have to repent for. You tell lie on people, and the next thing you're workin' on the Sabbath day, etcetera. Just like the government got its law here, if you do something wrong from the law of God, that's *sin*. You see?"

I took another moment to settle myself. Though the Speaker's sudden mood shifts were no longer frightening, they still drained me. "I think so," I said. "If you don't steal, maybe you lie. If you don't lie or steal, maybe you commit adultery. If you don't lie, steal, or commit adultery, maybe you work on the Sabbath. Is that what you mean?"

"Yes! And it is still *sin*. So in these categories, you are not innocent."

"I understand," I said. Involuntarily, I tallied up my sins. By his reckoning, their total was not insignificant.

"And the next thing, you're supposed to judge *every* man *equally*. No *un*justice. Unjustice is *mis*judging. God's law is truth and righteousness, and justice, justice for *all*, not only for one, but for the whole *world*. In the Bible, unjustice is *sin*. As long as a man take your right and give it to the next man, he sin."

The Speaker squatted down on the slate floor of his yard and picked up a pebble. "If right is supposed to be in *this* line," he said,

312

placing the pebble on one slate tile, "and you take right and put it *here*" he added, moving the pebble to an adjacent tile, "you *sin!*" He moved the pebble again. "You put it there, *sin!*"

He returned to his chair. "Right is right, and wrong is wrong! As long as you're doin' *wrong*, you *sin!* That's it. That's as far as it go. And sin is wickedness. Wrongdoing is wickedness."

His reasoning was, again, hard to refute. "I see your point," I said.

"If the people don't be doing what God want you to do, they gotta be punished." He opened the Bible and flipped to a marked passage. "See, this is John." He read:

> *If we say that we have fellowship with Him, and walk in <u>darkness</u>, we <u>lie</u>, and do not the truth. But if we walk in the <u>light</u> as He is in the light, we have fellowship one with anodder and the blood of Jesus Christ His Son cleanse us from all our sin.*

> *But if we say that we have no sin, we <u>deceive</u> ourself, and the truth is not in us. If we confess our sins, He is faithful and just to <u>forgive</u> us our sins, and to <u>cleanse</u> us from all <u>unrighteousness</u>. If we say that we have not sinned, we made him a <u>liar</u>, and his word is not in us.*[67]

He looked up from the page. "That's how God is. You say you don't sin, you callin' God a *liar!*"

The Sabbath Day

I still felt duty bound to defend the human race. "Is there no way that people can change your mind, so you don't have to destroy us?"

He set his elbow on the table and rested his chin in his hand, perhaps considering mankind's remaining options. "Well, you don't have to speak no more against the people if they *join* with you," he said. "The hard feelings that come between the people and God is only when they don't want to serve God."

"Serve God?"

"The Sabbath day! The seventh day is the Sabbath day. And you're supposed to do no work on the Sabbath day at all."

"I see. Observe the Sabbath."

He nodded quickly. "From the time God create Heaven and Eart', that Sabbath day was there for every human bein' to keep, regardless whether he was an Israelite, whether a Jew, whether a Gentile. Whoever come in the world was to keep the Sabbath day. If you don't keep the Sabbath day, if you *work* on the Sabbath day, you sinned."

He held out a closed fist. "The Bible tell you that Sunday is the *first* day of the week," he said, extending the little finger of his closed hand. "Sunday, Monday, Tuesday, Wednesday, Thursday, Friday." He opened each finger in turn, then the thumb of his other hand. "That's six days. If you work them six days, you *don't* sin. But if you work on the seventh day, what God forbid you from workin' on, you *sin*. You see what I mean now? That is one thing strictly 'bidden, to keep the Sabbath day holy, and no man do no work on the Sabbath."

"And that's just one of many sins," I observed quietly.

"That's one of the *greatest* sins. That is one of the *laws*. You see what I mean now?"

"I see."

"You see. So in these categories, you are not innocent."

He reached across the table and covered my hand with his. "You got to always keep these words of God, because these are what is supposed to guide you." His features relaxed. "These are what God judge you for, at the end."

The Son Don't Sin

"Did you ever sin?" I asked him. "I mean, before the Spirit came to you?"

He glared at me indignantly. "*I* sinned? No!"

"Never?"

"God's Son don't sin at all!" he shouted. "You look right there in the Book of John, you're gonna see, <u>*They*</u> *that is born of God do not sin, for the seed of God is in <u>them</u>. And as long as the seed of God is in you, you do not sin.*[68] The Son *never* sin! Don't mind He called into repentance — He under the obedience of the Father to do His will. But when it come to sin, *the Son never sin*! The holy man don't sin. Now I take the Bible to read."

He angrily flipped through the pages of the black Bible, perhaps to find the quote that proved he had not sinned.

"It's okay," I said, "I believe you." I put my hand on his arm. "I just didn't understand."

"The Son don't sin," the Speaker repeated.

"I know," I said. "I'm sorry, I didn't mean to offend you."

He looked up from the Bible, his eyes moist, though no tears had flowed. "That's where the trouble come in," he said, his voice dropping an octave. "You cannot — Nobody can — The world's people cannot dictate for God." His voice grew cold, his mouth hard. "Because God dictate for every*body*. Because God made man, and God gave man no power to rule Him. Neither the Son. Because *nobody* gonna have power over *God*."

"I understand completely," I said.

God Put Good and Evil Before You

We sat for a minute. I listened to a bird's song, rare in this neighborhood, and felt a cool breeze brush across my face. Then I asked the age-old question of the spiritually naïve. "Why did God create a creature with such failings?"

"No!" the Speaker, said. "God made man *upright*. God made man to be *honest*. God made man to be *righteous*. Look in the Old Testament: *God made man upright.*[69] Read in the whole Bible, you will see God mention *righteous* people, *righteous* woman, *righteous* man. *Just* man, and *un*just."

"I see."

"God didn't pronounce *only* wickedness on man. When God come in the Book of Ezekiel, he said, *Trus, Son of Man, warn the wicked to turn from his wicked way, that he may live. For if he don't turn, he shall die in his iniquity and I require his blood at thy hand.*[70]

"He said, *When the righteous man turn from his righteousness and do that which is wrong, do iniquity, he shall die in his iniquity and his sin.*[71]

"He said, *When the wicked man turn from his wicked way and do that which is lawful and right, he shall not die, he shall surely live.*[72]

"So you see, God put good and evil before you," the Speaker said. "You do whichever one you please. If you want to be wicked, you do the wicked part, and if you want to be righteous, you do the righteous part. Choose or refuse, whichever way you want to go. If you do the *good*, you get the *good*, and if you do the *bad*, you get the *bad*."

As he cataloged our choices and our sins, I thought about my own decisions and transgressions, particularly today's. Ruth returned to the foreground. Had I upset the delicate balance between us? I glanced at my watch. Would she be home by now? I wanted to apologize, to repent, to turn from my iniquity.

"Look, I have to go now," I said. "But I'd like to talk to you again soon. Is there some special time when I should come?"

"No, is nothing special when I come out. I live here."

On the short walk home, I tried to set aside the heaviness in my heart. So often our meetings were conflictual, but "splitting ambivalence" notwithstanding, I loved Ruth, and it was hard to imagine life without her. Harder, even, than imagining the end of the world.

INTERLUDE FIVE

After her brief encounter with the Speaker, Ruth was distant. "I don't want to be a part of wherever it is you're going," she said. "I can't."

"I understand," I said. And now I had to ask myself whether continuing to talk with him was worth the cost.

I tried to imagine what it might have been like for the Speaker when he realized his calling. The more certain he became of his mission, and the more extreme his ideas, the harder it must have been for family, friends, and even for his own children, to stay connected. Had this, I wondered, also been the fate of the Apostles, and of Jesus himself, when they were called?

I'd seen friends swept away by the riptide of cults. My connection with the Speaker was, as far as I knew, a cult of only one. Was I homing in on something of unique value, or was I, too, drifting toward a severing from the people I held most dear? Could my own growing obsession — and I admitted, finally, that it *was* an obsession — with his story, and the widening rift it was causing between Ruth and I, lead me to stray, permanently, from the light of our relationship?

Yet the questions raised by my encounters with him continued to compel me. There had to be more to the Speaker's rage than mankind's violations of biblical commandments and covenants. I remained determined to uncover what that was.

For now, what mattered to me most was how much the puzzle he presented engaged me. When I'd retreated to Brooklyn, a vital aspect of myself had gone into hiding. Now, that part was back. In the end, why did it matter whether the Speaker was a madman, a visionary, or the Son of Man himself?

—

When I followed Ruth to New York, at first I was bewildered as to how to earn a living. I worked short-term jobs — salesman at a stock photo agency, clerk in a bookstore — before I found small renovation jobs to support my writing and photography habit. Briefly, I considered becoming a private detective. I took a crash course on how to access and interpret public records, follow people on foot or in a car without being seen, and pry from them truths they might rather conceal. This training was remarkably useful to me as a reporter.

When I interviewed people, I looked for consistencies and inconsistencies — what fit, what didn't, and what I may have missed. As they revealed the details of their lives, what intrigued me was the underlying patterns and the conscious and unconscious motivations that lay beneath them. I followed clues, gathering and analyzing bits of evidence until the pieces fell into place and a consistent whole emerged.

The process required patience and an open mind, and also what the poet John Keats called *negative capability* — the ability to dwell in "uncertainties, mysteries, doubts, without any irritable reaching after fact and reason." It was important to maintain that negative capability to prevent my own preconceptions from getting in the way.

Often, I had to work backwards from effects to causes — the methodology that led astronomers to discover Pluto years before telescopes could peer that deeply into space. From perturbations observed in the orbits of Uranus and Neptune, they predicted that another planet, or something like a planet, must be in the vicinity. These perturbations were the effects; the cause, still hidden, was the gravitational pull of Pluto.

Now I was applying this methodology to my conversations with the Speaker. My earlier interviews established these effects:

1. For the latter half of his life, the Speaker believed that his dreams were visions received from the Holy Spirit, and that correlating them to the words of the Bible could validate his identity as the Second Coming of Christ.

2. He acquired the "powers" of the prophets one by one, in order, by matching his dream content to biblical texts.

3. He vastly increased his dream matches by reading the words *Thus*, *Thou*, and *Thee* as the ubiquitous *Trus*, a neologism that identified biblical personages as incarnations of God.

4. He was called to Earth to warn mankind that we must stop sinning and obey the laws of God.

5. We persisted in sinning.

6. The time for mercy had passed, and we must be destroyed.

These were the perturbations in the Speaker's orbit. What, then, was his Pluto, the occult element that would bring his underlying motivations into sharp focus?

Like the Speaker's, my underlying motivations were also still unclear. Perhaps, I conjectured, my hope was that by uncovering his, I would find the cause of the perturbations in my own orbit.

THE FIFTH DAY: The Final Widgin

Letters to the nations. Seventy weeks. The final widgin. The end is now. The intruder. Recovering the kingdom.

Fish and Fowl

It is unlikely that the original Gospel writers were direct witnesses to the teachings and miraculous acts of Jesus of Nazareth. Because writing itself was not widespread, the authors most likely relied on orally transmitted tales. The best guesses of biblical scholars put the written form of the Four Gospels at nearly a century after Jesus' death.

I could do better with the Speaker.

I had a good memory for the spoken word, and practicing the Speaker's dialect made it relatively easy to remember our conversations nearly verbatim. When I arrived home after each encounter, I'd immediately regurgitate everything I recalled into a tape recorder for later transcription. But going forward, I wanted to streamline the process. Inspired, perhaps, by the Speaker's comment on "the pen of a ready writer," I started carrying a notebook and pen with me at all times, in case I chanced upon him while he was out in his yard.

One of the many aspects of the Speaker's narrative that confused me was whether, from his point of view, humanity was irrevocably doomed, or if there was a loophole in his thinking that might give us one last chance to be forgiven for our transgressions. I decided to test the waters, as I was evidently testing them with Ruth. (At the moment, I had more hope for success with the Speaker.)

If I had not come to see the Speaker as the Son of Man, I did regard him as more than a madman. He was the canary in the coal mine, the unwitting oracle who nevertheless accurately predicted humanity's fate. Though you would never have gotten me to say it out loud, a small part of me wanted to believe that somehow, by influencing the symbol bearer, I could shift the delicate balance between doomed and redeemed toward salvation.

I saw little harm in trying, anyway.

Letters to the Nations

I did not see the Speaker until a few days after the debacle with Ruth. On my way home from Fulton Street, I spied him at his table, Bible open, gold-tipped pen engaged in what I assumed was encoding messages to Heaven about his most recent dreams or miracles. He signaled me to join him.

Imagine us seated together on an early summer afternoon, he the authority, I the acolyte with notepad on the table and ready writer's pen in hand.

"After I was here with Ruth," I said, "you told me you had come to Earth as the teacher from God to tell us to obey His laws, and we had refused. I'd like to hear more about that."

He shrugged. "That's what caused the world to be lost," he reminded me.

"And when did that happen?" I asked.

"It started since 1959, from Eisenhower time," the Speaker said.

Nineteen fifty-nine. This was something new.

In 1959, I was eight years old. Although my understanding of world events was limited, the space race and the Cold War were within my sphere of awareness. I remembered Sputnik and Vanguard, the cartons of dried food in our school's improvised fallout shelter, cowering beneath my desk when the air raid siren sounded. What was it about that time that had tipped the balance?

I asked, "Why 1959?"

Anger flashed across the Speaker's face. In an exasperated tone, he explained, "These things is prophe*sized* from that time. It wasn't happenin' before."

"The Bible says that?" I asked.

"No, no, *I* prophesize," he said. "That is when I start sendin' letters to the nation."

"Letters to the nation?"

"Yes! Prophesizing to the government!" he exclaimed. "When*ever* a prophet come to the Eart', he's supposed to prophesize to the government. You didn't know that?"

I shook my head.

"The government is the *first* person a prophet is supposed to prophesize to. Or else when the people losing their life, they don't know who to call on."

He leaned on his forearms, closing the gap between us. "You see," he elaborated, "I only gotta send letters of dreams and signs and wonders of what would happen to *prove* that I was sent."[73]

And now another penny dropped. The doomsday countdown had begun not with the arrival of Jesus of Nazareth, but with the man seated before me. All this time he'd told me about the Son coming, he was talking about *himself*. How could I have missed that?

"What did the letters say?" I asked.

The Speaker's lips tightened into a rueful smile. "When I first prophesize to the nation, I tell 'em how I was not mentally ill. And I said, 'I am sent from God to gather all nations, lands, and people, and cleanse the Eart', to make His law honorable.'" He sounded out the syllables, his voice booming. "Ho-no-ra-ble. And, I said, 'Here are signs,' and I gave them the signs. I know what signs the Son of Man made."

"You told me about the signs: dreams and visions and miracles."

He grunted softly. "And I said, 'These signs bear witness to prove that I am the Son of Man. If these signs do not happen, then I am not what I say I am, but if it *do* happen, they prove that I *am.*'"

The Speaker laughed confidentially. "You can't go order no government man if you can't prove yourself from the Bible. From Genesis to Revelation mention *every way* how the Son of Man coming, and you got to be able to trace from this. That's about the only way a government man would listen to you. You see what I mean?"

It took me a moment to respond. In my mind's eye, I saw him sitting at an old-fashioned rolltop desk, composing his letters with his gold-tipped pen. "What did they do, when you proved yourself from the Bible?" I asked.

"They didn't listen!" the Speaker exclaimed. "And that *testify* against them. Because I didn't just tell them about my work. I had the Bible, and I have dreams, and I went in the Bible and show them it is written that these were God's works. All them things — the Son, and man, and times and seasons — was in the letters."

"And what happened then?" I asked.

"The government was noti*fied*, from the time Eisenhower was president. President Eisenhower, President Kennedy, President Johnson, President Nixon — all them presidents. I didn't send to President Ford. But all them odder ones receive letters in Washington, D.C. from *me.*"

Again I had to pause for a moment. "And how did they respond?"

"They woldn' answer!"

They hadn't even sent him an autographed portrait. What, I wondered, might have happened if they had?

"None of them answered?"

The Speaker nodded, and with a bitter smile he explained, "And the hardship come on the people, and they can't do *nothin'* about it." He leaned back, eyes narrowing. "If they don't answer, that don't make no difference to me. That's their hard luck. They gotta go the *same* way."

"Okay," I said. "So you sent these letters to the presidents of the United States, and they didn't answer you. What did you do then?"

He thrust out his hand in a stop-sign gesture. "No, no," he said. "I not only send to United States government. I send to *many.*"

"Many governments?"

He nodded. "To all the nations of the Eart'. Three hundred and nineteen different government receive it from my hands."

Again, for a moment I was flummoxed. "I didn't even know there *were* that many governments," I said.

He nodded several times, as if he were counting each letter in his mind. "I had to use as high as 41¢ stamp to get them letters mailed. Plus, my paper and *time.* Forty-one-cent stamp. And I send 319 of *them.*"

In my mind's eye, I watched him — now as Edward, my neighbor, not "the Speaker" — earnestly writing each letter, addressing each envelope, affixing each stamp, and sending each envelope to president after president, leader after leader, year after year, awaiting a response that was never to come.

"And *nobody* answered?"

He shook his head. In his God voice, he replied, "I turn and I said, '*Now* I am puttin' on judgement. Now I am puttin' on *judgement.*' Because I write it. And I don't forget what I write."

"And then?"

"If they don't listen, they be destroyed. They lose their *life.*" His eyes grew hard, his voice dropped almost to a growl. "And that's not *all* they lose. They also lose the opportunity for *everlastin'* life."

He sighed. "God don't always be strict and drastic on human beings. God say, *I will not cause mine anger to fall upon you, for I am merciful, and I will not keep anger for ever.*[74] He say, *The Gentile will live in a world without end.*[75] Because if the Gentile would come to the obedience of God by keeping the laws and commandments, then He don't have no need to destroy the people of the Eart'."

The Speaker breathed deeply, slowly. "I tell them all of that, too. But they wouldn't accept the law. And if they don't accept it, they gotta go. That's all. If you don't accept the law, even you don't make no response, you still gotta go. That's the meaning."

Seventy Weeks

He retrieved a thick white Bible from its resting place on the bird-bath lectern. "I show you where it is written that when God come to you, you must know what is his calling and do the law. See here?" He flipped to a bookmarked section. "This is where he say the seventy weeks:

> *Seventy weeks are becoming upon the people, and upon the holy city, to finish the transgressions and to make an* <u>end</u> *of sin and to make recrimination for* <u>iniquity</u>*, and to be in everlasting righteousness, and to seal up the widgin and prophesy, and to anoint it the most* <u>holy</u>*.*[76]

With his index finger he underlined the phrase *an end of sin*. "See there? You see that *end*, there? That is a dream."

I read the passage silently. "I see. What happened after the seventy weeks were up?"

"I show you that directly," the Speaker said. He moved quickly to another marked section. "See this here now? This is Daniel, near Hosea:

> *And from the time that the daily* <u>secrets</u>[77] *shall be taken away and abomination that make desolation set up, there shall be a thousand two hundred and ninety days. Blessed is he that waiteth, and cometh to the thousand three hundred and five and thirty days. But go Trus thy way till the* <u>end be</u>*."*[78]

"See where *till the end be* is?" he said. "That mean the end of the world."

Seventy weeks; 1,290 days; 1,335 days. What did these numbers mean?

"So, all this starts when?" I asked.

He shook his hands in frustration. "The law was extablished from the time I *send* them *letters* to the nation," he said. "When the time come that you were supposed to finish the transgressions and make an end of sin and you *don't* do it, it mean that the world collapse right *there*. You see there in the book?" He pointed again to the phrase *till the end be*. "That's where they lose their life."

The Final Widgin

The numbers still confused me. The Speaker may have been delusional, but he'd been strikingly consistent. "So when, *exactly*, did God close the door on mankind?"

"After the seventy weeks."

"Starting in 1959?"

"No. No, not 1959, 1975."

"1975?"

"Yeah, 1975. You see, God didn't close the door right when I prophesied. You have to show signs in order to prove the message was from God. It take time, and time, before God close the door on man."

At last I understood. He had been warning us, showing us his proof, for sixteen years, the time it took to write to Eisenhower, Kennedy, Johnson, Nixon. The time it took to write to all the nations of the Earth.

"So you wrote the letters to the presidents and the nations, and when they *still* didn't listen, that's when our time was up?"

The Speaker nodded. "That is how it is. The end of the nation is 1975 ABC. It end there. That's the fulfillment of the Bible. After the seventy weeks, they don't have no more right. Satan, or the Gentile nation's world power, end 1975 ABC."

"What do you mean, ABC?"

"ABC is the time when judgement supposed to come." His voice deepened once again. "That is Jesus Christ's final widgin on the nations. That's when the Armagodgen's War start," he said.

I ran more numbers in my head. If 1975 was the end time, then the doomsday clock started ticking at about the time of Nixon's resignation. Perhaps the Speaker hadn't bothered to write to Ford, after the former Vice President assumed office, because Armageddon had already begun.[79]

I prompted him for more. "What is the Armageddon War?"

"The Armagodgen's War is when man fightin' against the words of God," the Speaker said. "That is the war where God condemned man and cast him away. If they had come to obediency, they still would have remained to live out their days and had a right to everlastin' life. But they *wouldn'* do it."

Again, his voice dropped to a growl. "If you refuse the law of God, you don't have no more right in Heaven and neither on Eart'. *God* is first."

A flicker of anger illuminated his features. "Nobody can stand God anger forever," he said. "Not God's. If God get angry, the *fire* come from God, even without He openin' his mouth, and burn you up. Accordin' to the Scriptures."

The End Is Now

"What will bring about the final destruction?" I asked.

"It's happenin' now!"

"Now?"

"I see people missin' from off the street daily! Don't tell *me*! I know this judgement!"

"I'm not telling you, I'm *asking* you."

"That's how it is. The *judgement*."

"So when will everything *completely* collapse?"

"You don't have no definite time."

"But it's happening already?"

"It's in *process*. You see where I show you near Hosea, where it say *Trus, go thy way until the end be*? Well, the end is *now*. That's the end of the world. That is a dream, too. But you got to know where in the Bible to find it."

He paused. "See, the words of God is a Spirit. Whenever God come in a spirit and He tell you *until the end be*, that's it. There ain't no more going back. That's the *last* end. That's the final widgin in the Book of Daniel, the seventy weeks of Jesus Christ on the nation."

He smiled triumphantly. "That's when Jesus Christ become King of Kings and Lord of Lords, King of the Nations. If you do the law as He was commandin', you have a chance to live out your time. If you don't, when you end the seventy weeks, you gotta go."

As this piece of the Speaker's tale reached its crescendo, the boundaries between us briefly glitched, and for just a moment I experienced his exaltation. My world view yielded to his; I saw through his eyes and felt through his emotions. I remembered Carl Jung: I had finally made it to the moon.

I placed my hands on the table and pressed my palms against the smooth metal surface, willing this contact to reconnect me with myself. "There is no way man can reverse this process?" I asked.

"No, there's nothing. The seventy weeks already up. The time God gave for *repentance* is past."

The Intruder

The Speaker gathered up his papers, a signal that our meeting was nearing its end, too. As I picked up my notepad, I felt a tap on my shoulder and I turned to a skinny guy of about my age.

"What you doin' there?" he said. He was wearing a loose, bright blue shirt, black jeans, and black sandals. His narrow head was shaved, his face set in what appeared to be a perpetual sneer. His accent was Haitian.

Vaguely threatened by the question, I said, a bit defensively, "I'm talking with my neighbor."

"What you doin' with *that*, man?" the intruder asked, pointing to my notepad.

"I'm a writer," I told him. I gestured toward the Speaker, whose gaze was fixed ahead. "I want to write about him."

The intruder said to the Speaker: "You know he writin' about you?"

"It don't matter," the Speaker said, without altering his expression. "Don't matter."

As if I'd been caught in some illicit act, panic rose in my chest. "He *knows*," I said sharply. "He said it was *fine*."

"You gonna write a book?" the intruder asked.

"I don't know," I said.

The intruder scratched his chin. "Well, when you make some money, you gotta give him some, right?" He paused. "And you gotta give me some, too."

I laughed. "I've gotta give *you* some, too?"

"Yeah."

"I don't plan to make any money on what he says."

He persisted. "So, the book sell, right?"

"If I write a book and get it published," I conceded, "yes, I might make some money."

"Well," the intruder said, already moving down the block, "you remember me then, okay?"

"Sure," I said. "You'll be the first to know."

Recovering the Kingdom

I was no Judas. I told the Speaker, "I hope you don't think I'm talking to you just to try to make money."

"No, no," he said, waving my apprehension away. "It ain't good to create too much for money. Is good to *have* it, if it's conwenient. But don't put yourself out of the way to get it. Lots of thing in the world is just as much problem as money."

"Thanks," I said. "I have to make money to live on, of course, but that's not why I'm talking with you."

He laughed. "I, too," he said. "That's why I have to work so hard. And speak so loud."

It was an oddly relaxed moment. We were just two guys talking about work.

"I have to speak to recover the kingdom," he went on. "I have to keep watch until my kingdom is under control and I make laws and set up my own government."

"Your kingdom?"

"The kingdom is mine," he explained matter-of-factly. "I have the dream. I ask for something of the nation, from 1959. They wouldn't give me *nothin'*. So therefore I have to fight against the nation, so I don't have to keep doin' this work all day, or sit up all night. They got it coming. From 1959 till now is almost twenty *years*!"

He pointed to my notebook. "This is nothing to put in any newspaper, now," he said, "because the time is short. God stop pleading with you, you see? If God was still pleadin', if mercy was still open to you, you have a chance. But if God close the door of mercy to you, that is where you havin' the trouble."

INTERLUDE SIX

Fyodor Dostoevsky once wrote, "If someone proved to me that Christ is outside the truth and that in reality the truth were outside of Christ, then I should prefer to remain with Christ rather than with the truth."

It did not escape me that in recording the Speaker's words and deeds, I'd cast myself in the role of an apostle. I did not embrace him in that way. But if he was not my Christ and I his apostle, then perhaps he was my Don Quixote and I his Sancho Panza, sticking by my squire in spite of his delusions.

As I pondered my conversations with the Speaker, Don Quixote stayed with me.

Whenever I've been mired in uncertainty, it has been in books that I've sought refuge. In search of clarity, I found myself wandering through bookstores, scanning the shelves of libraries, even rummaging through piles of books left for the trash. It was in a recent publication by the French philosopher Michel Foucault that I came upon a key to understanding the underlying pattern of the Speaker's madness.[80]

In Cervantes' *Don Quixote*, the eponymous hero reads stories of knight errantry and, in them, finds the acts of chivalry and heroism he must perform to prove that he is a knight. Having done these deeds as best he can, he then points to his feats as demonstrations of his nobility.

Was the Speaker's reasoning the same? He claimed his dreams preceded their biblical validations, and though I believed this to be his remembered experience, I also wondered if, at some point, the order of dreams followed by biblical validation had inverted. Reluctantly, I admitted to myself that he may have constructed a literal self-fulfilling prophesy. His unique linguistic lens and his many editions of the Bible had given him ample material to draw from.

Seeing the Speaker through Foucault's eyes, I now posited that:

1. He read of the dreams and acts that foretold the Second Coming of Jesus Christ.

2. He systematically imitated the deeds the Son of God was said to perform upon his arrival.

3. He then pointed to these deeds as proof that he was Jesus come a second time.

I tested this theory in my mind.

Had he read in his Bibles that the Son must perform "works of miracle," and then performed his own works of miracle so he could establish himself as the Son? This seemed likely.

Had he read the Apostolic letters and concluded that the Son of God must also send letters? Now this, too, seemed likely.

I was pleased with my ingenuity but dismayed by the simplicity of this explanation, which rendered the Speaker's thinking pathetic in its circularity. Then I thought again. Hadn't the Apostles themselves done much the same when they saw, foretold in the Hebrew Bible, proof that Jesus of Nazareth was their Messiah?

Seen through this lens, the case for the Speaker's divinity was no weaker than that for Jesus, and, conversely, the case for the Speaker's madness no stronger. Had Jesus begun his ministry not in Galilee but in Brooklyn, wouldn't he, too, have been labeled insane, abandoned, left with only his dreams, his visions, and his words?

THE SIXTH DAY: What Cause the World to Be Lost

I been working from the time I gotta work. This Eart' is enough. You can't refuse your maker. Twelve offence. What cause the world to be lost. The government pretend to the people that I am crazy. Jesus Christ have a hour. The world cannot win Jesus Christ. You can't kill Jesus Christ now. Is no harm to come to me no more.

Beast and Man

Ruth and I were in a cooling-off phase, taking another "break." Historically, our breaks lasted no more than a month, though one had gone on for as long as six. Then we'd reconnect, and things would go well for a while, until our differences inevitably resurfaced.

Although I winced at the pain of our separation, I also saw it as an opportunity to catch up on work I'd been neglecting since I started talking with the Speaker, and I plowed into my book and the staircase project.

There was something satisfying about peeling off more than a hundred years of paint, each layer reflecting the technology of the time it had been laid down, until I broke through the final coat of casein-based paint and exposed the long-concealed knotty pine boards and cut nails. I worked one flight at a time, from the top down. When I rubbed the first coat of linseed oil into the topmost stair tread, the emerging grain patterns were as sinuous as a ballet performance.

The book project was less satisfying, with snags around permissions to quote from songs and disagreements with my editor over sentence structure and style, but packing the final draft into a cardboard box and mailing it off to her also gave me a substantial, if less tactile, sense of achievement. That night, I celebrated a job well done — and done with.

My hiatus from Ruth also freed me to continue visiting the Speaker without the constant chatter of her objections taking up space in my head. In the days that followed my fifth interview, I revisited, with renewed diligence, my collection of biblical concordances, harmonies of the Gospel, dictionaries of scripture and myth, and the Gnostic Gospels, searching more deeply for an understanding of the Speaker's theology.

Much of what I read, not only in biblical prophesies but also in the mythologies of other cultures, corroborated his notions. From Hindu texts, for example, I learned that we were at the end of the Kali Yuga, the last of four repeating stages of the universe, headed for final collapse. In the writings of contemporary cosmologists, I found parallels in the Big Bounce theory, which hypothesized cycles of expanding and compacting universes. How close were we now to the apogee of expansion, I asked myself, before the great collapse? According to the Speaker, very.

In light of these indications, as well as my subjective sense that things had gotten markedly worse even during my own short life, the

Speaker's claim that we had come to the collective end of our respective ropes didn't seem especially far-fetched, though of course I still found it hard to see *him* as the literal instrument of our imminent demise.

I Been Workin' from the Time I Gotta Work

A couple of weeks after my previous interview, while I was applying another coat of oil to the staircase, one of my housemates mentioned that he'd seen the Speaker holding court. I took the opportunity to get a little fresh air and sallied forth again.

With each visit, the Speaker had made me feel increasingly welcome, so this time, notepad and pen in hand, I walked straight up to him. He sat at his small table, working miracles or merely thinking, I couldn't say for sure. Without hesitation, he gave me a warm smile and a nod. I let myself into his yard and pulled up my usual chair.

In our last meeting, we had left off talking about the Speaker's efforts to regain his kingdom (in my mind, a metaphor), but I still had no idea how he made his earthly living. "The first time that Jesus Christ was here, he worked as a carpenter," I said. "What kind of work did you do?"

"No! Jesus Christ don't work," the Speaker said emphatically. "They say Jesus Christ was Joseph's son, a carpenter. But that don't say Jesus Christ *was* a carpenter."[81]

"No? What does that mean, then?"

"They were sayin' that he were the son of *Joseph*, who we *know* to be a carpenter. His *son*."

"The son *of* a carpenter. I see."

"That's the way it was."

"What about yourself? Have you worked? Not God's work, but regular work."

"Yes. I been workin' from the time I gotta work. I do work for years."

"What kind of work?"

"I do tailor, I do machinist, I do a little cabinet, I do a little work along mason, I work baker."

"Tailor, machinist, cabinet maker, baker ..."

"Yeah, and a sailor, too."

"A sailor? In the Navy?"

"No. Ordinary boats."

"Merchant marine, then?"

"Not even merchant. Where we come from, we have boats what ordinary people go sailin' on, that you could launch to steer by compass, etcetera. So, those are the things that I learned when I was there back home."

This Earth Is Enough

"Do you work now?"

"Now I don't have to work. I done with that. This Eart' is enough for I to live out," the Speaker said.

"Pardon?"

"This *Eart'* is enough for I to live out," he repeated. "I don't have to work again."

I waited expectantly.

"This *Eart'* is mine and so the *land* is mine,"[82] he explained. "You find that in the Book of Daniel: *Trus, O king, art a king of kings: for the God of Heaven hath given Thee a kingdom, power and strength and glory, and theresoever the children of men shall dwell.*"[83]

He smiled. "That's why I publish in the *Daily News* that I give every nation under the whole Heaven a dispossess from the land."

"A dispossess?"

"Yes. The dispossess mean the land is no longer theirs. And their dispossess up 1975 ABC, when the end of the Gentile nation was accomplished."

You Can't Refuse Your Maker

"What happened then?" I asked.

"I collect the tax," the Speaker said.

I imagined my pupils twisting into virtual question marks. "The *tax?*"

He swept his hand up and down the rows of brownstones on both sides of the street. "See the amount of three-family house here?"

"Yes."

"Now, I don't know how much exactly, but every one of them house pays out more than $50 a month for tax to the government. In twelve months, a three-family house pay $600, just for land tax."

"Okay."

"Well, if *you* could live out of it, *I* could live out of it."

"I'm still not quite following you."

"All right." He sighed and rested his hands on the table. "Listen what I tell you: The Eart' is mine. If *you* collect tax for the land, and the land is mine, don't you think *I* could collect? And if you collect and don't give me part of it, then it's *high time* I collect."

"I think I get it," I said. His point was difficult to refute. If you are the Creator, we are all, by definition, your tenants.

He smiled. "All right. They build millions of house in United States — in every nation — right?"

"Right."

"So if I ask for two million dollars a year from all the nations for my land, do you think I ask for too much?"

"No, when you put it that way, I guess not."

"I coulda asked for more — I got enough sense to ask for more — but I don't want to make so much hardship for the people."

How benevolent, I thought, perhaps unkindly.

"The nation was to do the law and pay the *money*. That's what was prophesized, *and* in the newspaper. But they wouldn't do it. So if they *refuse* God, God refuse *them*. You see how it is?"

"Yes, I think I do," I said.

Apparently I didn't sound convinced. He elaborated: "If you refuse God — if he call you and you don't want to come — he don't have to give you nothin'. You got no more comin' to you. You're on your own."

I nodded, recalling the stance Jesus had taken. In the canonical Gospels, He had said: *Render to Caesar the things that are Caesar's, and to God the things that are God's.*[84] And in the Gospel of Thomas, He had added, *and give to me what is mine.*[85]

"That's as far as it goes," the Speaker said. "You can't refuse your maker in everything He tell you. And if you can't do for God what He tell you to do, it mean you gotta be damned. Right?"

Twelve Offence

Another puzzle piece clicked into place. "So, we didn't do the law," I said, "and the governments ignored your letters, and we didn't pay the tax. Are these the reasons we have to be destroyed?"

He shook his head. "Not *only* those things." He pushed his chair back and stood, leaning forward, hands flat on the table. "Twelve *offence* United States government do to *God*."

He glowered. I took a breath. "Twelve offences?"

"*Twelve offence!* And God only give six or *seven!*"

And then I took another. "What were the offences?"

"All *right*," the Speaker shouted, rising to his full height. "Come and lock up the Son of God without commitin' a *crime*. I am the Son of *God*! United States government confine me nearly fourteen *years*."

And like the final coat of paint I'd stripped from the stair treads, a layer of the Speaker's story peeled away.

"See here?" he said. "I'm gonna show it to you now. I want you to see for your*self*. When I talk to a man, I quote. I don't go by hearsay." He swept his hand over his yard. "I got books. I study *these*. These are the words of *God*."

He fetched a large black Bible from one of the pieces of slate and paged through it furiously. "See here?" he said. "This is *Job*. Now, we gonna look *here* for the sixth struggle. I show you."

Nearby, two dogs barked incessantly, set off by the Speaker's outrage. He read silently, moving his finger along the page. He seemed to have difficulty finding his reference. "I want to show you where the Son supposed to be delivered of the sixth struggle. I had it marked off in one of the Bibles, but maybe I didn't take up the right one."

I tried to help. I knew the Book of Job well. "I think it comes after all of his friends speak to him."

He paid me no attention. "The odder Bible have it near to the first or to the second, third page, third chapter, and this don't have it here at all. Not so far."

He set the book down, visibly rattled by this setback. "I guess I have to go to anodder book."

He got up from the table and retrieved a smaller Bible from the center of the yard. Here, he met with success. "This is when God stop you from puttin' your hand on the Son," he said triumphantly. "See here? I read where it says *sixth* struggle, and *seventh*."

He shall deliver Thee in six troubles, even seven shall no evil touch Thee.[86]

337

"Here, see here?" He pointed. "*Thee* is the Son."[87]

In famine, He shall redeem Thee from death, and in war from the power of the sword. Trus shall be hide from the scourge of the town. Neither shall Trus be afeared of the destruction when it comes.[88]

His confidence restored, the Speaker tapped the Bible repeatedly. "You see I don't lie to a man. *Every word* that is in this is spoken by *God*! And if you *disobey* God's word, you pay the penalty."

What Cause the World to Be Lost

The Speaker closed the Bible and sat in silence, apparently lost in thought. I was, too. Like the mathematicians who computed Pluto's orbit, my mind flooded with numbers: the years 1959 and 1975, 1,290 and 1,335 days, 319 letters to the nations, seventy weeks, twelve offences, six troubles.

He broke the silence. "That thing that the United States government continue locking me up is what cause the *world* to be lost."

"Locked you up?" I asked. My heart raced as I sensed us closing in on the perturbations in the Speaker's orbit.

"Lock me up! From 1958. I was in ma house, and the government policeman — I didn't know whether he was from Washington or the state — come in my house and hold me, and handcuff me there without committin' a *crime*, and they lock me up."

And there it was. "In 1958 they did this?"

He nodded. "From 1958, the fifth of March. They take me to Kings County Hospital. When I get there, I tell the doctors that I had some dreams, and I am the Son of God. They took me from there and send me to Kings Park Hospital. And they lock me up there almost *eight years*, from the fifth of March to the eleventh of February, 1966."

"Eight years," I said, in as sympathetic a tone as I could muster.

"Before they take me, I have a four-room apartment house, clothes and furnitures, and cash money. And the government send me out without even no pocket handkerchief."

I struggled to find a response, but the magnitude of what he had just revealed momentarily overwhelmed me. It was impossible to stay neutral, to be just the interviewer.

I studied his face — his brow glistening, the lines around his eyes hard, his lips pressed together in some mix of anger and despair I couldn't decipher — and my heart broke.

The Government Pretend to the People That I Was Crazy

"The government want to pretend to the people that I was crazy," the Speaker said.

I took a breath, and then another, before I responded. "They didn't believe you were the Son of God?"

"Dr. Furnisher confess to me that he know I am not mentally ill," the Speaker said. "I ask him, 'What am I doing here? Why do I have to be lock up?' He say, 'I got to lock you up.' He say, 'I send you to the staff five times, and each time, I say you are improved, will they send you home? But they wouldn't send you home. It's not none of my fault.' He say, 'I will send you back as many times as I can, but I have to wait at least four or five months before I am able to present you to the staff. Otherwise, they are just gonna send you back.' That is what the government *do*."

"I'm so sorry, Edward," I said. I had seen people with histories like his on the Upper West Side and near the midtown train stations — released with vouchers to single-room-occupancy hotels and prescriptions they never filled, most of them ending up on the streets or in improvised shelters built from shipping crates and cardboard boxes.

But those people were strangers. This was Edward, my neighbor.

My eyes welled up. I wiped them with the back of my hand and forced myself to resume the interviewer role. "What did you do when you were in the hospital?" I asked.

"What I do? You mean like work?"

"Well, in your daily life."

"I read and I pray." He paused. "And I write."

"You wrote?"

"Yes! That's where I get to prophesize and send all the letters to the nation. That started in 1959. The head doctor give me permission to write. He tell the in-charge: 'Furnish prophet with stationary, let him write whatever he want, wherever he want.'"

I pictured the Speaker in the white pants and shirts I'd seen on patients in the psych ward I'd visited in Buffalo, sitting not at the rolltop desk I'd envisioned, but at a metal table similar, perhaps, to the one where we were now seated. He could have been the fourth Christ at Ypsilanti, had he lived in Michigan.

"They didn't make you do anything else?" I asked.

"Sometimes they put you to work, yes. They tell you that if you don't work, you won't get out of the hospital. They make patient scrub the floor and scrub dormitories, mop up, take clothes to laundry, *luggin'* all over the place. In the morning, you got to get your scrub brush and your mop and mop up the whole day hall. Half the time, they put patient in hospital to work just like the 'tendants work, even harder. The patient don't have no rest in the hospital."

I thought of the men I'd visited on the ward, all of them near release. How had their lives played out after they'd been freed from *their* bondage? I would never know. "What did you do when you got out?" I asked the Speaker.

"I come out and I work again in New Georgie until I get some money. When I leave from New Georgie and come here in Brooklyn, I buy a three-family house on East New York Street. But then the government come back and lock me up *again!*"

"So, they locked you up twice?"

"They lock me up twelve times!" He counted each incident out on his fingers. "Fifth of March 1958, Kings Park, that's the first. Then they take me out of Sheffield Avenue twice and put me in Pilgrim State. That's three. When I come out from Pilgrim State, I went to Wyandanch, in Huntington. They pick me up there three times. That's six. Three times again in Wyandanch make nine. And they lock me up in jail three times, too."

So these were the unforgivable acts of man against God, the twelve offences, each institutionalization another nail in humanity's coffin.

"Twelve times they lock me up! Without committin' a *crime*. And, they move everything out of my house. The government take what I have, and foreclose on my house, and put me on a disability."

I had gotten to the bottom of the Speaker's story, I was sure, but instead of the exultant glow I typically experienced when I arrived at the heart of things, all I felt was grief — for the immensity of his loss, and also for something more, something as yet ineffable.

"So they took everything from you?" I said.

He nodded. "All the offence that God forgive the world for, United States done committed," he said. "You see that yourself. That's why I showed you."

A wave of nausea passed over me. "I see. The six or seven troubles."

He nodded again. "You understand. There's no more forgiveness to them."

His eyes rested on me. "You might think I say it because I want you to lose your life, but it ain't that."

"Well, I didn't lock you up!"

"I know! I know!" He laughed. "I just tellin' you," he said, still chuckling, "that these are God's words, written words. That you cannot jump on God's son and do to Him as much as you want. God tellin' you that he *stop* you from puttin' your hand on the Son."

"I see."

"When I talk to you, I talk because I know you want your life like I want mine." His voice was soft, almost tender. "I don't want you to mess with mine. And I believe you would want to live out your days, too. But the government destroy your life. If the government had decided to do the law and call on the people and tell 'em it was God's work and not *his* work, the people might behave. But they wouldn't do it."

"I understand," I said. He had given us every chance, and then some. And we kept taking from him until, like Shel Silverstein's giving tree, he could give no more. His sadness palpable, I wondered if now he grieved for what he had lost, or for what he now must take away.

Jesus Christ Have a Hour

Still, one nagging question remained. "Why did you let them take you to the hospital?" I asked, "instead of using your power to stop them?"

"Jesus Christ have a hour," the Speaker explained. "Jesus Christ have a hour."

"I see." Like the crucifixion, I surmised, this, too, needed to play out. "And, what made them finally release you from the hospital?"

"What made them release me? *Power* make 'em loose me, power of God." He pointed to the sky. "You see the light shinin' in the cloud

341

in the air? In the night?" he said. "Look up. That's when Jesus Christ power turn loose. That's when the Son come in full *power*."

He paused, his body shaking. "You hear them get up in Washington on the telewidgin and tell you that the leading nation in a *disaster*? A disaster's trouble! And *destruction*!" He shook his head. "The government want to make the people believe that the time and the seasons just happen so." Again, he slapped his hand against the table. "They *lied*! *They* lead the nation in a disaster. From 1959, you see so much thing happenin' — earthquake, floods, storm comin' up, and you gonna say that just *happen* so? They mis*lead* the people. *I* create storm and flood and things that were hittin' United States, and I tell them that. *That's* why they loose me. They *better*, else then God woulda done destroyed the whole United *States*."

His voice dropped into its deepest register. "God *power*, boy. That's where I stand: my worst stand against the government. Power meet *power*! And the smaller power have to give in. That's how I get out."

The World Cannot Win Jesus Christ

We sat together quietly. My heart heavy, I glanced up the block, still unaltered by the cataclysms the Speaker had unleashed, and waited for his anger to dissipate and my sadness to subside.

I asked, "Do men have the power to do to you what they did to Jesus?"

"No. Not this time. Jesus Christ cannot lose to the world. The Bible tell you no. Man cannot fight Jesus Christ. Jesus Christ is the man who gave you the *Spirit*! He is the *head of every man*![89] As soon as Jesus Christ the Spirit get angry, you gotta run for your life, because that's the Spirit that control *yours*."

He leaned forward, shifting again to mentor mode. "You see, if you fight a man, he gonna take what he gave you. Right?"

"Of course," I said.

The Speaker peered at me fiercely. "The same go for Jesus Christ. Jesus Christ is the Holy Spirit. Well, you *create* by the Spirit. Nobody else can make no child. So if Jesus Christ don't want you to have His Spirit, you're *dead*."

I shuddered as I imagined him withdrawing his spirit from all mankind, then each of us winking out, one by one, like the stars in "The Nine Billion Names of God."

He tapped the smaller Bible. "Jesus Christ testify, *I have power to lay down my life, and take it up again. And none can take my life without I lay down.*"[90] As long as Jesus Christ fightin' back with power, the world cannot win Jesus Christ. Not Jesus Christ — Jesus Christ is God himself! Jesus Christ cannot lose. Not to man, not even to the *world.*"

He spread his hands wide, as if to encompass that world. "Jesus Christ is the Creator, Jesus Christ is the God in the Book of Corinthians. And Jesus Christ is Almighty God, too. Any time Jesus Christ come to fight the world with power, he destroy the world in less than any time."[91]

"I understand," I said.

"The Second Coming of Jesus Christ, he don't come to die at all," the Speaker said. "That is when he become King of Kings and Lord of Lords. That's the real Jesus Christ. That is in the Book of Daniel and," his voice deepening, "the Book of Revelation."[92,93]

He placed the smaller Bible on top of the larger one and covered both books with his hand. "God want to keep Jesus Christ alive. And if the words of God could create Heaven and Eart', you know he could keep a man alive." He continued in a harsh, magisterial register. "When Jesus Christ becomin' King of Kings and Lord of Lords, He come to reign forever and ever on this Eart'. You can't kill Jesus Christ now. It's not his time. Not as long as he is King of Kings. He live forever and ever and *never* die. So you don't fool yourself. It's an everlasting life. Believe it."

Is No Harm to Come to Me No More

I understood, now. I had read the Speaker from his Genesis to his Revelation. I had, I believed, drilled down to his core.

His gaze was serene. "Is no harm to come to me no more," he said. "All my sorrow and all my grief and all my persecution is gone. It's a time when I come in full possession and full power, and never again a man could put his hand on me, regardless of what it is. I am Chief and King. I am King of the Nations. And I am the King of Kings and Lord of Lords. And I am *Trus* and I am *Thee*. I am Jesus Christ, the Lamb of God."

In my mind's eye I saw him standing at his birdbath lectern wearing royal robes and a crown of thorns, untouchable and invincible. "Nobody cannot bodder me again," he said. "After I tell you 'no,' you cannot do it again. Nothing that I tell you 'don't do,' you can't do it. If you resist, I would kill you right there. Take your *life*. That's how God word is."

Again I felt tears welling. I couldn't say exactly why.

"You see, that's why you hear God tell you these things. Because you gotta know. You gotta know."

He stood. "God is holy. God is holy. God is holy," he said. "The Spirit is holy. And, that is how it will be."

INTERLUDE SEVEN

When I was an English Lit student, the novelist I was most drawn to was James Joyce, author of *A Portrait of the Artist as a Young Man* and *Ulysses*. The latter, Joyce once remarked, took him eight years to write, and he expected readers to take as many to read it. I spent only one. In that year, I also read a dozen critical studies and biographies. Somewhere in the mix, I stumbled on the phrase "ontogeny recapitulates phylogeny," the theory that the development of an embryo (ontogeny) parallels the evolutionary development of its species (phylogeny).

Now, reflecting on my meetings with the Speaker, I saw that, similarly, the succession of stages I'd traversed as I interviewed him had recapitulated my own evolution from kid scientist to nascent literary scholar to investigator, and that in both the interviews and my personal development, I had failed to actualize my full humanity.

With the Speaker, I'd worked from the outside in, peeling off what I perceived to be a sequence of layers, each of only transient interest and quickly discarded in my relentless pursuit of his "true" story. I'd begun with the most superficial — his gestures, movements, and delusions. When I'd had my fill of these, I'd moved on to his methodology, mythology, biography, psychology, and finally to the trauma of his repeated incarcerations. I'd documented the effects, uncovered the patterns, and penetrated to their cause. To paraphrase Einstein, I knew God's thoughts. The rest were just details.[94]

Mission accomplished.

What I had *not* done was relate to him as one authentic human being to another. I'd taken much and given little, my questions and responses merely prompts to keep him talking.

I thought back to my failed efforts to publish the street people stories. My agent, Harvey, had arranged a meeting with an acquisitions editor at one of the more prominent New York publishers. The editor had looked through my proposal and sample stories, but that's not what interested him in my work. In our meeting, he tapped the pale blue folder Harvey had sent him. "Your writing shows me you've got the chops," he said, "but what grabbed me was your pictures of the bag ladies."

He handed me a thin paperback. On its silver-toned cover was a black-and-white photo of a helmeted, bearded man in black leathers, a pair of handcuffs dangling from his belt. The book was a photo essay on the S&M leather culture, and he told me it was a model for the kind of book he saw me creating. I leafed through it as he described his vision: a virtual fashion show of the "bizarre," featuring bag ladies in their layered "costumes," with "colorful quotes" to complement the photography. For this, he was prepared to offer a sizable advance — more than enough to live on for the time it would take to crank out such a book.

I turned it down. "What he wants me to do turns my stomach," I told Harvey over lunch at a nearby café. "These are human beings. I'm not going to exploit them just to advance my career."

Harvey, of course, tried to dissuade me — the offer was more than generous, and of course fifteen percent is fifteen percent — but though it may have been smart to take it, I would not budge. "Okay," he said. "There are lots of fish in the sea."

Now I understood that in my indignation, I had failed to see how what I was doing was really no different; I, too, was a thief. I had "documented" these people, as I was now documenting the Speaker, as if the purpose of their suffering was to be objects of interest to my future readers. The Haitian guy who had intruded on my fifth meeting with the Speaker was right, I realized, to intervene. In my effort to give Edward and the others an audience, I had stolen a bit of their souls and provided little in return. My hypocrisy was, at last, self-evident.

—

My willingness to see people as "subjects" had deep roots.

As a boy I was so detached from my emotions that I didn't believe they existed. I saw feelings as rapid, subconscious processing of data — quicker, if less accurate, than rational thought.

I wasn't the kind of kid who tortured animals and wound up a psychopath (we had one of those in the neighborhood; I can still see him holding two severed rabbit's feet in one hand, a bloody knife in the other), but I didn't regard others as fully real. Instead, to me they were like the robots and aliens in the science fiction stories I incessantly read, distant and, sometimes, threatening.

In a family where emotions were largely suppressed, I found an alternative in logic and deliberation, the slower but surer course. My self-appointed mission was to become the perfect scientist: dispassionate, precise, and, if necessary, ruthless in my pursuit of Knowledge.

In retrospect, I see that this emotional distancing allowed me, in my own way, to play God.

I did terrible things to insects, as a child. In the name of Science, I loaded grasshoppers and crickets into model rockets and blasted them into the sky, caught flies and bleached them in hyper-chlorinated water until their bodies became translucent and their eyes glowed a piercing red, and incinerated pill bugs and spiders with the death ray of my disassembled telescope's parabolic mirror.

But my primary experimental subjects were ants. It was ants who were my first aquanauts, held under water on a leaf or twig, tiny bubbles of air clinging to their wriggling bodies, and ants I threw into jars filled with sulfur dioxide gas, and then attempted to reanimate with pure oxygen.

My experiments culminated in their electrocution.

As a school science project, I built a Tesla coil, an air-core transformer that generated enough energy to light fluorescent bulbs from across a room and interfere with the neighbors' television reception. With it, I had won the seventh-grade science fair.

While I experimented with the Tesla coil, I had also been cultivating an ant farm. I'd transplanted its inhabitants from an ant hill at the base of the swing set in our back yard into a large peanut butter jar, punched tiny holes in the lid, and covered the outside of the jar with black construction paper to keep out the light. Every few days, I spread bread crumbs and chopped-up raisins on the soil and added water to a bottlecap I'd set up as a trough.

One Saturday morning, these two parallel projects converged.

I turned on the Tesla coil, grabbed one of the steel poles that supported our house and, with my free hand, picked up the ant farm by the lid. Then I let the six-inch, blue-white spark discharge through the jar, the shock rippling through me as electricity arced along the black paper covering, which I'd left in place like an executioner's mask. A few seconds later, I set the jar down and switched off the power.

Later that day, when I stripped away the paper and unscrewed the jar lid, I found a few ants still scurrying through their tunnels and, neatly stacked at the entrance to one, a mound of dead ants. It had never occurred to me that only some of the ants would die, or that ants would respond meaningfully to the deaths of their compatriots. Survivors of their own miniature holocaust, they had dealt with the unthinkable as best they could, and moved on.

Stunned, I brought the ravaged ant farm back to the ant hill from which it had come and dumped out the contents, leaving it to the survivors and their kin to sort the dead from the living. I tossed the jar itself into the trash and, a few days later, moved the Tesla coil out to the garage.

On that day, my experiments with insects ceased and my understanding of what it is to live, and die, and grieve began.

—

My quest to become whole was more intentional in high school, and by college it had become the primary driver of everything I did.

I transferred out of engineering and filled my schedule with literature, philosophy, psychology, and creative writing courses. I sought guidance from mentors living and dead, among them fiction writers, poets, ancient Buddhist and Hindu sages, and modern-day gurus like Carl Jung, Fritz Perls, G.I. Gurdjieff, Ram Das, and Maharishi Mahesh Yogi. I skinny dipped at Woodstock, marched against the Vietnam War, hitchhiked across the U.S. and Canada, made friends and lovers laugh (and had friends and lovers!), learned the carpenter's trade and knife-maker's craft, played tennis, rode a motorcycle, wrote poems, took photos, dropped acid, meditated, and plumbed the depths of my psyche in therapy.

By the time I moved to Brooklyn, I had come a long way from the boy who electrocuted ants, but I had not come far enough. The illusion of detachment still permeated my life, and some of the deepest emotions still escaped me. Love was difficult to distinguish from lust. Joy was difficult to differentiate from excitement. And perhaps most importantly, true compassion was not yet fully within my grasp.

Detachment had cost me in the past, was costing me now with Ruth, and would continue to extract its fee, I realized, until I freed myself from the prison cell I had unwittingly erected around my heart.

I'd eaten of the Tree of Knowledge and, after my meeting with the Speaker, saw my own nakedness: I was a fraud, a simulacrum. All along I'd just been pretending.

While I professed to be an advocate for the street people I'd encountered — to give voice to the voiceless, visibility to the invisible — instead, I had appropriated their stories. "I think you have something important to say," I would tell them, and they would willingly reveal to me their hopes and dreams and intimate secrets. Only now, after wringing from the Speaker the heart of his suffering and loss, did I finally see that none of the people I photographed and interviewed were ever "subjects." They were human beings — more so, I feared, than I was.

With horror I saw that I had approached the Speaker with the same detached curiosity that had enabled me to torture insects. He was a nuisance, a madman, a subject, a puzzle, a story, a metaphor, a symbol. But not until our last talk, and then only fleetingly, had I seen him as a *person*. I still could not call him by his given name. He was not Edward; he was "the Speaker."

If ever there were a truly voiceless voice, it was his. Here was a man who, despite every effort to be heard, was ignored by his neighbors, laughed at by children, locked away by mental health workers — a man who had lost his earthly belongings and what life he had built not once, but a dozen times. Guided by dreams and visions, he had emigrated from his island to save us from ourselves, and in response we had shunned and shamed him.

I vowed, in our future encounters, to do better, not only for Edward's sake, but also for my own.

THE SEVENTH DAY: Ascension

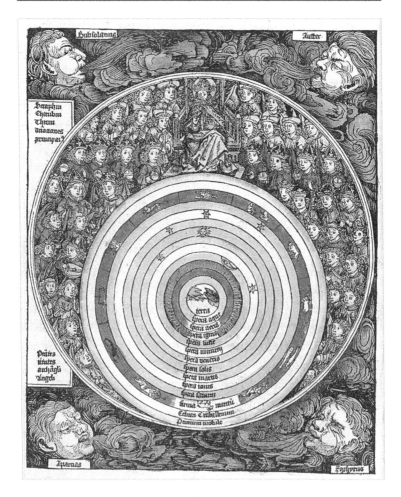

Rest

One night I had a dream about the Speaker. I'd never dreamt about someone I was interviewing before. And although Ruth and I were still "on a break," we were talking again now, sometimes late into the night, and I told her about it. She listened with interest, or at least with tolerance.

In the dream, I am both the Speaker's agent and his friend, a relationship not unlike the one I had with my own agent, Harvey. I'm in his apartment, a roomy two-bedroom in a tonier part of Brooklyn. He's slumped onto a sofa in the living room wearing a shiny, gold lamé outfit.

He has his own television show and it's playing in the background. From the TV comes music with a heavy beat and on the screen flash indistinct images. He's fallen on hard times, and I'm helping him locate a cheaper place to live. "You find anything?" he asks me. "No luck," I say.

The scene shifts to a café, where we're talking about cleaning out his spare room so a roommate can move in. "Or a woman," the Speaker says. "But," he adds, "the problem with a woman is that it is permanent." I say, "Not necessarily."

At a nearby table, three attractive Asian women are listening. One of them overhears us. "What's that?" she says, apparently offering herself as a candidate. Protectively, I wave her off. "Nothing. Never mind," I say.

The Speaker and I resume our strategizing about how to save him from financial ruin.

Landlord Mode

The next morning was a Saturday, and without giving it much thought, I went out looking for the Speaker, but he was nowhere to be found. Silly me. God doesn't work on the Sabbath day.

A next-door neighbor happened to be out sweeping her yard, and I asked about him. She leaned on her broom and shrugged. "I don't pay him no mind," she said.

A couple of days later, I saw the bald man who'd kidded the Speaker about his Bible.

"I haven't seen Edward for a while," I said. "Do you know how he's doing?"

He shook his head. "They came and picked him up about a week ago."

"Picked him up? Is he all right?"

"He's all right. He got into landlord mode again."

"Landlord mode?"

"Yeah, he goes knockin' on people's doors askin' for rent. I tell him to stop doin' that, but he don't listen to me. Somebody must've called the cops."

Collecting the tax. "Do you know where they took him?"

"Nah. Last time, I think it was somewhere on Long Island, but he's been in a lot of places. Could be anywhere. Anywhere they got a bed."

Response

My reaction was complex. Most immediately, I was concerned about Edward, once again locked up, again at risk of losing whatever life he had pieced together since his last incarceration. But, very quickly I thought of myself — the missed opportunities to capture the details I might never learn, and also the regret that my newfound determination to be more open with him would not be realized. Finally, I was disappointed. The part of me that was fascinated with puzzles no longer had anything to figure out, and the part attracted to the cult of one no longer had something to believe in.

All my efforts to imbue the Speaker's fantasies with meaning seemed foolish now, a failed attempt to imbue my own life with meaning, too. The analytical, the literary, the investigative, the symbolic, and the mythological had yielded, in the end, to the psychological. I had created a house of cards built on a foundation of delusion, the Speaker's no more so than my own.

The spell was broken and I awakened from that dream. It was quite a comedown. But also a liberation.

Over the next few weeks, I finished proofing the galleys for the folk music book and, with that behind me, started to re-think my relationship with writing, with Ruth, with everything.

Proposal

With the Speaker out of the picture, Ruth and I were able to knit our relationship back together again. And, in my newfound openness, I asked her to marry me.

I hadn't planned it. We were walking through the Brooklyn Botanical Gardens, and though the cherry blossoms were past their prime, it was still lovely to be there, and to be there with Ruth. In that moment, I felt closer to her than I had in months, possibly years. I realized *this, now,* was what I wanted.

I stopped walking and took both her hands in mine. My throat was tight, but my heart felt ready to burst.

"Ruth?" I said.

"Yes, David?"

"Let's get married. Let's just *do* it, this time."

She was quiet for a few moments, her eyes cast downward. Then she shook her head.

"Can't we just leave things the way they are?" she said. "I do love you. But I don't want to marry you and I don't want to live with you again. Not now, anyway."

An avalanche of feelings passed over me in an instant. I took a long, slow breath, then let one of her hands go. I wiped a tear from my eye, and then one from hers.

We resumed walking through the gardens, quietly, for half an hour or so. Later, at an Indian restaurant in Park Slope, we talked and even laughed, as if that conversation had never occurred. I could feel the clock winding down on our relationship. But honestly, I think we both felt some relief at the prospect of laying down the burden of our ambivalence, someday.

And life went on.

REVELATION

Apocalypse. Resurrection.

Apotheosis

We were in Manhattan when the lights went out.

It was a hot, sticky night in mid-July, the beginning of a projected heat wave, but neither Ruth nor I seemed to mind as we made our way down Broadway to the Columbus Circle station.

We'd played hooky from work and had met at The New Yorker Theater to see *Annie Hall*. The similarities to the mismatch between Alvy and Annie and our own misalignments were not lost on us, but that night our differences seemed more comical than contentious. Taking marriage off the table, unexpectedly, had freed us to enjoy them.

It was still early evening when we arrived at the subway station. We intended to ride the A train together until West Fourth, where Ruth would change to the train for Queens and I would continue on to Brooklyn. It was a work night for her and she had to get up early the next day. As we sat together on a bench, I pictured her riding alone on the train. Protectively, I said, "I can come to Queens."

She demurred. "I'm a big girl," she said, and squeezed my hand to signal that this was a preference, not a rejection.

I felt, more than heard, the train lumbering toward the station, its headlight casting a shimmering glow on the tracks. Ruth and I, along with a dozen others on adjacent benches, rose as one to greet it. I led her to a position just to the side of where I knew the doors would open, spilling their burden of travelers onto the platform.

Then the station went dark.

A glitch? The trains were still running. As ours pulled into the station and disgorged its passengers, Ruth stepped forward. I touched her shoulder, holding her back, stilled by a recollection.

I was in eighth grade in 1965 when a power surge blacked out most of the Northeast. Although the lights had gone out in Buffalo, I was mesmerized by what had happened in New York City, a mythical realm to me then. I read about people trapped in subways and elevators, babies born in taxi cabs, doctors who performed surgery under flashlights, ordinary citizens directing the orderly flow of traffic. A fan of superhero comics, I fantasized that I would have been among those catapulted to heroism by this crisis.

I was so captivated by this event that I wrote about it for my English class. In my story, I'm in a subway car when the lights go out. The train drifts to a halt. The car is crowded, men with newspapers and felt hats, women with groceries and babies, all of us plunged into sudden darkness. Girls scream, babies cry, grown men panic, but I remain calm. "We'll be all right," I say in a voice no longer impaired by adolescence. A Boy Scout, I am prepared: I have a flashlight. I turn it on. "Follow me," I say. "We can walk along the tracks back to the last stop."

But now, as I stood on the platform at Columbus Circle beside the waiting train, I was not feeling especially heroic. More than once I'd been stuck on sweltering trains stalled by some mishap. "Let's get out of here," I said. Against the flow of patrons still entering the station, we exited onto the street.

It was uncannily quiet. Disoriented by the darkness, the only light the glare of passing headlights, it took a full minute to take in the extent of what must have occurred.

With no clear path back to Brooklyn or Queens, we were unsure what to do. I flipped through a mental rolodex of people I knew who lived in Manhattan, and Ruth must have done the same, because when we broke the silence, we immediately traded names.

We settled on Paul, Ruth's roommate's boyfriend. Paul lived on the Upper East Side — crosstown, but a straight shot after that.

"I'll call Leslie," Ruth said.

I was relieved to find that payphones still worked in a blackout. Ruth got Paul's number from her roommate. Luckily, he, too, was home. She held her hand over the mouthpiece and turned to me. "He says we can stay there tonight, no problem. I've got directions."

"Okay," I said. I fished a pen from my shirt pocket and wrote Paul's address on my forearm.

Holding hands so we wouldn't get separated, Ruth and I made our way across the base of Central Park, drifting in the current of all the other ghosts.

I was surprised that traffic was still flowing smoothly, and impressed by the noble citizens who, as in my eighth-grade story, were already directing traffic. Everywhere I looked, people seemed to have risen to the occasion — startling, in a city where no one acknowledged you when you passed on the street, and each person was his own private island.

We made our way across town and up Third Avenue. This sense of orderly cooperation continued. I would later learn of widespread looting, fires, and arrests, but what I saw as we headed uptown was a party-like atmosphere: Bars were still open, and people had dragged their chairs onto the sidewalk. They sat with drinks in their hands, laughing and talking.

As we approached Paul's street, I wondered how, without power, we could signal him to let us in. But when we arrived, the door was propped open.

We made our way to the ninth floor, sweating in the damp heat. Paul, happy to see us, handed each of us a beer and led us to the roof, where we joined a party in progress. Similar festivities were happening on roofs all around us, where distant candles and flashlights flickered like fireflies. After a couple of hours, we went down to Paul's apartment and spent the remainder of the night camped out on his couch.

—

I'd expected the trains to be back online by morning, but when we arrived at the nearest station, a transit cop told us they were still down. Fortunately, the buses were running. Though neither Ruth nor I knew the routes, I had a map — still the Boy Scout — and we quickly determined the combination of buses that should get each of us within striking distance of home.

"Call me when you get there," I said, as her bus arrived.

We kissed quickly. "You, too," she said.

My trip took three hours and five buses.

I got out at the corner of Fulton and St. James. Looking around, I saw shattered shop windows and businesses emptied of their goods. Trash, broken glass, and abandoned merchandise littered the streets and sidewalks. Shopkeepers were nailing up plywood. Images of my father's furniture store on Buffalo's East Side after the sixties race riots flashed through my mind, overlaying the scene before me. The thick, steamy air added to the heaviness in my chest. There had been no parties here.

I glanced down St. James. The residential areas seemed unscathed. Had my house fared as well? I paused to orient myself, and in that moment heard a familiar burbling sound, a vocalization I'd know anywhere.

The Speaker stood on the corner opposite me, gesturing and declaiming. Despite the blistering heat, he wore his black suit and a white shirt. I stood, momentarily transfixed. It had been more than a

357

month since he'd disappeared from Grand Avenue. His forty days in the desert?

I crossed the street. "Hello, Edward," I said, smiling.

"Hello," he said, returning my smile.

"I haven't seen you around the neighborhood," I said.

"They come and take me again," he explained.

I nodded. "I heard."

"Now I live here, St. James." He gestured down the block to another brownstone not unlike his former home on Grand Avenue.

"How's it been, living here?"

His eyes brightened. "It give me more *power*," he said. His voice growing louder and deeper, he elaborated: "More power in Heaven and on Eart'." Much louder, in his God voice, he proclaimed, "More *power* in Heaven and on *Eart'*!"

And he was off, admonishing and prophesying, like I'd witnessed him do so many times before. After a minute or two, I waved goodbye, but he took no notice.

As I made my way down Fulton Street, I remembered an observation he'd made, one so obvious I hadn't thought much of it at the time.

"Prophe*size* mean to tell what will happen, the future," he'd said. "If a person is a prophet, when he speak, he speak by the power of the Holy Spirit, and the Holy Spirit is true. If he is *not* true, the thing is not going to happen. But as long as he *is* true, that thing will be fulfilled."

More power in Heaven and on Earth, he had said. More power in Heaven and on Earth.

The next day, I read in the *Times* that Con Edison attributed the blackout to an act of God.[95]

THE END?

NOTES

[1] Lacan, Jacques. "Propos sur la causalite psychique."

"[I]t is worth adding that if a man who believes he's a king is mad, a king who believes he's a king is no less so."

c.f. Lichtenberg, Georg Christoph, as quoted by Jacques Lacan in "The Function and Field of Speech and Language in Psychoanalysis."

"A madman who imagines himself a prince differs from the prince who is in fact a prince only because the former is a negative prince, while the latter is a negative madman. Considered without their sign, they are alike."

[2] The kudzu of the Northeast.

[3] Miller, George A., "Thirteen Maxims for the Mind."

"In order to understand what another person is saying, you must assume it is true and try to imagine what it might be true of."

[4] REVELATION 1:15.

"[A]nd his voice [was] as the sound of many waters."

See also 2 ESDRAS, 6:17.

"I rose to my feet and listened, and behold, a voice was speaking, and its sound was like the sound of many waters."

[5] *Gospel of Thomas,* 24.

"His disciples said: 'Show us the place where Thou art, for it is necessary for us to seek it.' He said to them: 'Whoever has ears let him hear. Within a man of light there is light and he lights the whole world. When he does not shine, there is darkness.'"

[6] *Gospel of Thomas,* 50.

"Jesus said: If they say to you: 'From where have you originated?', say to them: 'We have come from the Light, where the Light has originated through itself. It stood and it revealed itself in their image.'"

[7] MATTHEW 1:23.

"Behold, a virgin shall be with child, and shall bring forth a son, and they shall call his name Emmanuel, which being interpreted is, God with us."

8   Freud, Sigmund. "The Claims of Psycho-Analysis to Scientific Interest."
"If we reflect that the means of representation in dreams are principally visual images [Bilden] and not words, we shall see that it is even more appropriate to compare dreams with a system of writing than with a language."

9   Foucault, Michel. *The Order of Things.*
"In its original form, when it was given to men by God himself, language was an absolutely certain and transparent sign for things, because it resembled them. The names of things were lodged in the things they designated."

10   REVELATION 1:14.
"[H]is eyes were as a flame of fire."

11   Foucault, Michel. *The Order of Things.*
"There is no difference between the visible marks that God has stamped upon the surface of the earth, so that we may know its inner secrets, and the legible words that the Scriptures, or the sages of Antiquity, have set down in the books preserved for us by tradition."

12   MATTHEW 7:15.
"Beware of false prophets, which come to you in sheep's clothing, but inwardly they are ravening wolves."

13   Foucault, Michel. *The Order of Things.*
"There is no difference between marks and words in the sense that there is between observation and accepted authority, or between verifiable fact and tradition. The process is everywhere the same: that of the sign and its likeness, and this is why nature and the word can intertwine with one another to infinity, forming, for those who can read it, one vast single text."

14   JOHN 1:1-3.
"In the beginning was the Word, and the Word was with God, and the Word was God. The same was in the beginning with God. All things were made by him; and without him was not any thing made that was made."

15   1 CORINTHIANS 3:10-11.
"According to the grace of God which is given unto me, as a wise masterbuilder, I have laid the foundation, and another buildeth thereon. But let every man take heed how he buildeth thereupon. For other foundation can no man lay than that is laid, which is Jesus Christ."

16   ISAIAH 48:13.
"Mine hand also hath laid the foundation of the earth, and my right hand hath

spanned the heavens: when I call unto them, they stand up together."
HEBREWS 1:10.
"And, Thou, Lord, in the beginning hast laid the foundation of the earth; and the heavens are the works of thine hands."
PSALMS 102:25.
"Of old hast thou laid the foundation of the earth: and the heavens are the work of thy hands."

[17] REVELATION 1:16.
"And he had in his right hand seven stars: and out of his mouth went a sharp twoedged sword: and his countenance was as the sun shineth in his strength."
See also REVELATION 10:1-3.
"And I saw another mighty angel come down from Heaven, clothed with a cloud: and a rainbow was upon his head, and his face was as it were the sun, and his feet as pillars of fire: And he had in his hand a little book open: and he set his right foot upon the sea, and his left foot on the earth, and cried with a loud voice, as when a lion roareth: and when he had cried, seven thunders uttered their voices."

[18] Foucault, Michel. *The Order of Things*.
"The book is not so much his existence as his duty. He is constantly obliged to consult it in order to know what to do or say, and what signs he should give himself and others in order to show that he really is of the same nature as the text from which he springs."

[19] LUKE 7:21.
"And in that same hour he cured many of their infirmities and plagues, and of evil spirits; and unto many that were blind he gave sight."

[20] DEUTERONOMY 29:29.
"The secret things belong unto the Lord our God: but those things which are revealed belong unto us and to our children for ever, that we may do all the words of this law."

[21] PSALMS 45:1.
"My tongue is the pen of a ready writer."

[22] **Editorial note:**
The Speaker appears to be combining, in previously unrecognized ways, the concepts illustrated in DANIEL 2:22 ("He revealeth the deep and secret things") and DANIEL 2:27-28 ("The secret which the king hath demanded cannot the

wise men, the astrologers, the magicians, the soothsayers, show unto the king; but there is a God in Heaven that revealeth secrets, and maketh known to the king Nebuchadnezzar what shall be in the latter days.").

23   Spivak, Gayatri Chakravorty. Introduction to Jacque Derrida's *Of Grammatology.*

"If in the process of deciphering a text in the traditional way we come across a word that seems to harbor an unresolvable contradiction, and by virtue of being one word is made sometimes to work in one way and sometimes in another and thus is made to point away from the absence of a unified meaning, we shall catch at that word. ... We shall follow its adventures through the text and see the text coming undone as a structure of concealment, revealing its self-transgression, its undecidability."

24   EZEKIEL 26:19.

"For thus saith the Lord God; When I shall make thee a desolate city, like the cities that are not inhabited; when I shall bring up the deep upon thee, and great waters shall cover thee."

25   PSALMS 110:5-6.

"The Lord at thy right hand shall strike through kings in the day of his wrath. He shall judge among the heathen, he shall fill the places with the dead bodies; he shall wound the heads over many countries."

26   **Editorial note:**

Panpsychism proposes that consciousness is intrinsic to all matter throughout the universe, and that even the fundamental building blocks of reality have conscious experience.

27   DANIEL 7:13.

"I saw in the night visions, and, behold, one like the Son of Man came with the clouds of Heaven, and came to the Ancient of days, and they brought him near before him. And there was given him dominion, and glory, and a kingdom, that all people, nations, and languages, should serve him: his dominion is an everlasting dominion, which shall not pass away, and his kingdom that which shall not be destroyed."

28   DANIEL 2:19.

"Then was the secret revealed unto Daniel in a night vision."

29   1 CORINTHIANS 14:1-2.

"Follow after charity, and desire spiritual gifts, but rather than ye may prophesy. For he that speaketh in an unknown tongue speaketh not unto men, but unto God: for no man understandeth him; howbeit in the spirit he speaketh mysteries."

30 DANIEL 7:1.
"In the first year of Belshazzar king of Babylon Daniel had a dream and visions of his head upon his bed: then he wrote the dream, and told the sum of the matters."

31 JOHN 4:24.
"God is a Spirit: and they that worship him must worship him in spirit and in truth."

32 EZEKIEL 11:24-25.
"Afterwards the spirit took me up, and brought me in a vision by the Spirit of God into Chaldea, to them of the captivity. So the vision that I had seen went up from me. Then I spake unto them of the captivity all the things that the Lord had shewed me."

33 GENESIS 3:22.
"And the Lord God said, Behold, the man is become as one of us, to know good and evil: and now, lest he put forth his hand, and take also of the tree of life, and eat, and live for ever."

34 **Editorial note:**
The Speaker seems to be conflating "Adam" and "Edom" here, much as he saw "thyme" as another way to spell "time" and "Thou" and "Thus" as alternative spellings of "Trus." The conventional interpretation is that the Edomites were the descendants of Jacob's brother Esau.
See OBADIAH 1:1.
"Thus saith the Lord God concerning Edom; We have heard a rumour from the Lord, and an ambassador is sent among the heathen, Arise ye, and let us rise up against her in battle."

35 DANIEL 2:32.
"This image's head was of fine gold, his breast and his arms of silver, his belly and his thighs of brass."

36 REVELATION 2:18-19.
"And unto the angel of the church in Thyatira write; These things saith the Son of God, who hath his eyes like unto a flame of fire, and his feet are like fine brass; I know thy works, and charity, and service, and faith, and thy patience,

and thy works; and the last to be more than the first."

37   REVELATION 19:12-13.

"His eyes were as a flame of fire, and on his head were many crowns; and he had a name written, that no man knew, but he himself. And he was clothed with a vesture dipped in blood: and his name is called The Word of God."

38   ISAIAH 66:15-16.

"For, behold, the Lord will come with fire, and with his chariots like a whirl-wind, to render his anger with fury, and his rebuke with flames of fire. For by fire and by his sword will the Lord plead with all flesh: and the slain of the Lord shall be many."

39   JOHN 1:32

"And John bore witness, saying, I saw the Spirit descending from Heaven like a dove, and He remained upon Him."

40   LUKE 4:1.

"And Jesus being full of the Holy Ghost returned from Jordan, and was led by the Spirit into the wilderness."

41   **Editorial note:**

This appears to be an original interpolation of the Speaker's, and an elaboration of the text present in each of the Gospels that refers to the Spirit coming to Jesus in the form of a dove, during his baptism. Neither the image of the feeding with the spoon, nor the quotation from the Spirit about its identity, is present in the King James version of the Bible or in the Apocrypha. The passage does, however, bear slight similarity to JOHN 19:29, in which a sponge filled with vinegar is put to the mouth of Jesus on the cross, just before he dies, and also to REVELATION 10:9-10, in which the writer eats of the book brought by the angel. In addition, the notion of the Spirit and the man to whom he appears is often found in EZEKIEL.

42   ISAIAH 22:18.

"He will surely violently turn and toss thee like a ball into a large country."

43   EZEKIEL 28:15.

"Thou wast perfect in thy ways from the day that thou wast created, till iniquity was found in thee."

44   LUKE 1:31.

"And, behold, thou shalt conceive in thy womb, and bring forth a son, and shalt call his name Jesus."

45   HEBREWS 7:3.
      "Without father, without mother, without descent, having neither beginning of
      days, nor end of life; but made like unto the Son of God; abideth a priest con-
      tinually."

46   LAMENTATIONS 5:3.
      "We are orphans and fatherless, Our mothers are as widows."

47   JEREMIAH 1:6-8.
      "Then said I, Ah, Lord God! behold, I cannot speak: for I am a child. But the
      Lord said unto me, Say not, I am a child: for thou shalt go to all that I shall send
      thee, and whatsoever I command thee thou shalt speak. Be not afraid of their
      faces: for I am with thee to deliver thee, saith the Lord."

48   REVELATION 9:16.
      "And he hath on his vesture and on his thigh a name written, King of Kings, and
      Lord of Lords."

49   GENESIS 2:1.
      "Thus the heavens and the earth were finished, and all the host of them."

50   DANIEL 9:23.
      "At the beginning of thy supplications the commandment came forth, and I am
      come to shew thee; for thou art greatly beloved: therefore understand the mat-
      ter, and consider the vision."

51   Clarke, Arthur C. "The Nine Billion Names of God."

52   DEUTERONOMY 28:45-46.
      "Moreover all these curses shall come upon thee, and shall pursue thee, and
      overtake thee, till thou be destroyed: because thou harkenest not unto the voice
      of the Lord thy God to keep his commandments and his statutes which he com-
      manded thee; and they shall be upon thee for a sign and for a wonder, and upon
      thy seed for ever."

53   Foucault, Michel. *The Order of Things.*
      "As the archaeology of our thought easily shows, man is an invention of recent
      date. And one perhaps nearing its end. If those arrangements were to disappear
      as they appeared, if some event of which we can at the moment do no more
      than sense the possibility ... were to cause them to crumble, ... then one can
      certainly wager that man would be erased, like a face drawn in sand at the edge
      of the sea."

54   Zimmer, Heinrich Robert. *Myths and Symbols in Indian Art and Civilization.*
"During the Kali Yuga, man and his world are at their very worst. The moral
and social degradation is characterized in a passage of the Vishnu Purana:
'When society reaches a stage where property confers rank, wealth becomes
the only source of virtue, passion the sole bond of union between husband and
wife, falsehood the source of success in life, sex the only means of enjoyment,
and when outer trappings are confused with inner religion ...' then we are in
the Kali Yuga, the world of today."

55   JEREMIAH 7:16.
"Therefore pray not thou for this people, neither lift up cry nor prayer for them,
neither make intercession to me: for I will not hear thee."

56   GENESIS 3:9.
"And the Lord God called unto Adam, and said unto him, Where art thou?"

57   **Editorial note:**
Such practices were common in the ancient world. Many of our most sacred
texts are amalgams and reinterpretations of different mythologies told at different times. Multiple versions of the creation myth were combined in Genesis,
and these same stories also appear in the creation myths of earlier cultures.
Likewise, the flood story of Noah and the Ark was also central to the mythology
of other ancient peoples.

58   MARK 3:21–22.
"And when his friends heard of it, they went out to lay hold on him: for they
said, He is beside himself. And the scribes which came down from Jerusalem
said, He hath Beelzebub, and by the prince of the devils casteth he out devils."
JOHN 10:19–20.
"There was a division therefore again among the Jews for these sayings. And
many of them said, He hath a devil, and is mad; why hear ye him?"

59   1 CORINTHIANS 11:9.
"Neither was the man created for the woman; but the woman for the man."

60   EPHESIANS 5:22-24.
"Wives, submit yourselves unto your own husbands, as unto the Lord. For the
husband is the head of the wife, even as Christ is the head of the church: and
he is the saviour of the body. Therefore as the church is subject unto Christ, so
let the wives be to their own husbands in every thing."

[61] 1 TIMOTHY 2:11-12.

"Let a woman learn in silence with all submissiveness. I permit no woman to teach or have authority over a man; rather, she is to remain silent."

[62] DEUTERONOMY 26:16-19.

"This day the Lord thy God hath commanded thee to do these statutes and judgments: thou shalt therefore keep and do them with all thine heart, and with all thy soul. Thou hast avouched the Lord this day to be thy God, and to walk in his ways, and to keep his statutes, and his commandments, and his judgments, and to hearken unto his voice: And the Lord hath avouched thee this day to be his peculiar people, as he hath promised thee, and that thou shouldest keep all his commandments; And to make thee high above all nations which he hath made, in praise, and in name, and in honour; and that thou mayest be an holy people unto the Lord thy God, as he hath spoken."

See also:

DEUTERONOMY 28:1-14 (the blessings of obedience)

DEUTERONOMY 28:15-68 (the curses for disobedience).

[63] PSALMS 18:25.

"With the merciful thou wilt shew thyself merciful; with an upright man thou wilt shew thyself upright."

[64] JEREMIAH 3:12-3:14.

"Go and proclaim these words toward the north and say, Return, thou backsliding Israel, saith the Lord; and I will not cause mine anger to fall upon you: for I am merciful, saith the Lord, and I will not keep anger for ever. Only acknowledge thine iniquity, that thou has transgressed against the Lord thy God, ... and I will bring you to Zion."

[65] JEREMIAH 6:19.

"Hear, O earth: behold, I will bring evil upon this people, even the fruit of their thoughts, because they have not hearkened unto my words, nor to my law, but rejected it."

[66] JOB 1:21.

"Naked came I out of my mother's womb, and naked shall I return thither: the Lord gave, and the Lord hath taken away; blessed be the name of the Lord."

Or possibly ROMANS 11:26-27.

"And so all Israel shall be saved: as it is written, there shall come out of Sion the Deliverer, and shall turn away ungodliness from Jacob: For this is my covenant unto them, when I shall take away their sins."

67 1 JOHN 1:6-10.
"If we say that we have fellowship with him, and walk in darkness, we lie, and do not the truth: But if we walk in the light, as he is in the light, we have fellowship one with another, and the blood of Jesus Christ his Son cleanseth us from all sin. If we say that we have no sin, we deceive ourselves, and the truth is not in us. If we confess our sins, He is faithful and just to forgive us our sins, and to cleanse us from all unrighteousness. If we say that we have not sinned, we make Him a liar, and His word is not in us."

68 1 JOHN 3:9.
"Whosoever is born of God doth not commit sin; for his seed remaineth in him: and he cannot sin, because he is born of God."

69 ECCLESIASTES 7:29.
"Lo, this only have I found, that God hath made man upright; but they have sought out many inventions."

70 EZEKIEL 3:18-19.
"When I say unto the wicked, Thou shalt surely die; and thou givest him not warning, nor speakest to warn the wicked from his wicked way, to save his life; the same wicked man shall die in his iniquity; but his blood will I require at thine hand. Yet if thou warn the wicked, and he turn not from his wickedness, nor from his wicked way, he shall die in his iniquity; but thou hast delivered thy soul."

71 EXEKIAL 3:20.
"Again, When a righteous man doth turn from his righteousness, and commit iniquity, and I lay a stumblingblock before him, he shall die: because thou hast not given him warning, he shall die in his sin, and his righteousness which he hath done shall not be remembered; but his blood will I require at thine hand."

72 EZEKIEL 33:19.
"When the wicked man turn from his wicked way and do that which is lawful and right, he shall not die, he shall surely live."

73 JOHN 4:48.
"Then said Jesus unto him, Except ye see signs and wonders, ye will not believe."

74 JEREMIAH 3:12.
"I will not cause mine anger to fall upon you: for I am merciful, saith the Lord, and I will not keep anger for ever."

75 EPHESIANS 3:20-21.
"Now unto him that is able to do exceeding abundantly above all that we ask or think, according to the power that worketh in us, unto him be glory in the church by Christ Jesus throughout all ages, world without end. Amen."
Or possibly ISAIAH 45:17.
"But Israel shall be saved in the Lord with an everlasting salvation: ye shall not be ashamed nor confounded world without end."

76 DANIEL 9:23:24.
"At the beginning of thy supplications the commandment came forth, and I am come to shew thee; for thou art greatly beloved: therefore understand the matter, and consider the vision. Seventy weeks are determined upon thy people and upon thy holy city, to finish the transgression, and to make an end of sins, and to make reconciliation for iniquity, and to bring in everlasting righteousness, and to seal up the vision and prophecy, and to anoint the most Holy."

77 **Editorial note:**
In DANIEL, the text reads "daily sacrifice." See DANIEL 12:11-13, below.
But see also DANIEL 2:47.
"The king answered unto Daniel, and said, Of a truth it is, that your God is a God of gods, and a Lord of kings, and a revealer of secrets, seeing thou couldest reveal this secret."

78 DANIEL 12:11-13.
"And from the time that the daily sacrifice shall be taken away, and the abomination that maketh desolate set up, there shall be a thousand two hundred and ninety days. Blessed is he that waiteth, and cometh to the thousand three hundred and five and thirty days. But go thou thy way till the end be: for thou shalt rest, and stand in thy lot at the end of the days."

79 REVELATION 16:14-16.
"For they are the spirits of devils, working miracles, which go forth unto the kings of the earth and of the whole world, to gather them to the battle of that great day of God Almighty. Behold, I come as a thief. Blessed is he that watcheth, and keepeth his garments, lest he walk naked, and they see his shame. And he gathered them together into a place called in the Hebrew tongue Armageddon."

80 Foucault, Michel. *The Order of Things*.
"[I]n his reality as an impoverished hidalgo he can become a knight only by listening from afar to the age-old epic that gives its form to Law. The book is

not so much his existence as his duty. He is constantly obliged to consult it in order to know what to do or say, and what signs he should give himself and others in order to show that he really is of the same nature as the text from which he springs. The chivalric adventures have provided once and for all a written prescription for his adventures. And every episode, every decision, every exploit will be yet another sign that Don Quixote is a true likeness of all the signs that he has traced from his book."

[81] **Editorial note:**

The gospels disagree on this. The Speaker favors Mathew. Compare:

MARK 6:3.

"Is this not the carpenter, the son of Mary, the brother of James, and Joses, and of Juda, and Simon?"

MATTHEW 13:55.

"Is not this the carpenter's son? Is not his mother called Mary? And his brethren, James, and Joses, and Simon, and Judas?

[82] PSALMS 24:1

"The earth is the Lord's, and the fulness thereof; the world, and they that dwell therein."

[83] DANIEL 2:36-38.

"This is the dream; and we will tell the interpretation thereof before the king. Thou, O king, art a king of kings: for the God of Heaven hath given thee a kingdom, power, and strength, and glory. And wheresoever the children of men dwell, the beasts of the field and the fowls of the heaven hath he given into thine hand, and hath made thee ruler over them all. Thou art this head of gold."

[84] MARK 12:17

"Render to Caesar the things that are Caesar's, and to God the things that are God's."

[85] *Gospel of Thomas*, 100.

"They showed Jesus a gold coin and said to him, 'Caesar's men demand taxes from us.' He said to them, 'Give Caesar what belongs to Caesar, give God what belongs to God, and give me what is mine.'"

[86] JOB 5:19.

"He shall deliver thee in six troubles: yea, in seven there shall no evil touch thee."

[87] **Editorial note:**
In the text, "thee" refers to Job, but in the Speaker's reading, all biblical personages referred to as "thee" or "thou," or preceded by the word "thus," are actually *Trus*, the hidden name for the Son of God. See the "Trus is God" section of THE THIRD DAY in this text.

[88] JOB 5:20-21.
"In famine he shall redeem thee from death: and in war from the power of the sword. Thou shalt be hid from the scourge of the tongue: neither shalt thou be afraid of destruction when it cometh."

[89] 1 CORINTHIANS 11:3.
"But I would have you know, that the head of every man is Christ; and the head of the woman is the man; and the head of Christ is God."

[90] JOHN 10:17-18.
"Therefore doth my Father love me, because I lay down my life, that I might take it again. No man taketh it from me, but I lay it down of myself. I have power to lay it down, and I have power to take it again. This commandment have I received of my Father."

[91] LUKE 21:22-28.
"For these be the days of vengeance, that all things which are written may be fulfilled. But woe unto them that are with child, and to them that give suck, in those days! for there shall be great distress in the land, and wrath upon this people. And they shall fall by the edge of the sword, and shall be led away captive into all nations: and Jerusalem shall be trodden down of the Gentiles, until the times of the Gentiles be fulfilled. And there shall be signs in the sun, and in the moon, and in the stars; and upon the earth distress of nations, with perplexity; the sea and the waves roaring. Men's hearts failing them for fear, and for looking after those things which are coming on the earth: for the powers of Heaven shall be shaken. And then shall they see the Son of Man coming in a cloud with power and great glory. And when these things begin to come to pass, then look up, and lift up your heads; for your redemption draweth nigh."

[92] DANIEL 2:47.
"The king answered unto Daniel, and said, Of a truth it is, that your God is a God of gods, and a Lord of kings, and a revealer of secrets, seeing thou couldest reveal this secret."

93   REVELATION 17:14.
"These shall make war with the Lamb, and the Lamb shall overcome them: for he is Lord of lords, and King of kings: and they that are with him are called, and chosen, and faithful."
REVELATION 19:15-16.
"And out of his mouth goeth a sharp sword, that with it he should smite the nations: and he shall rule them with a rod of iron: and he treadeth the wine-press of the fierceness and wrath of Almighty God. And he hath on his vesture and on his thigh a name written, KING OF KINGS, AND LORD OF LORDS."

94   **Editorial note:**
"In 1925, Einstein said to a young student, Esther Salaman, "I want to know how God created this world. I'm not interested in this or that phenomenon, in the spectrum of this or that element. I want to know His thoughts; the rest are just details.""

95   **Editorial note:**
But also see *The New York Times*, July 15, 1977.
"Later, Paul O'Dwyer said that whatever caused the blackout, it definitely was not an act of God."

A Letter from My Father

I received a letter from my father today. After thirty years, he's closing down his store, and at least in theory he's going to retire. It's a warm letter. For reasons neither of us has ever figured out, letters, and doing things for one another from time to time, are the only ways we know to show that we love each other.

I grew up thinking I was pretty much like my mother. We're both nearsighted, have the same brown curly hair, cut of face, delicate temperament; each of us is an oldest child and has those kinds of problems. But as I get older, I come to see more of my father in me, and also in my brothers. Although growing up we saw little of him except on Sundays, he seems to have left his mark.

When we, his children, get together, and we talk about him, we acknowledge how he has always been an anchor for us, there to be depended on, even after his two heart attacks. But inevitably we also acknowledge how none of us can really talk with him, as we have always been able to talk to our mom. It has been an ambition for each of us to get through the barrier before he dies and it's not passable anymore.

—

My father had two stores, one after the other, each with the same name: Brothers Furniture. The second one, the one that's closing now, is near the teachers' college, in the Italian part of town. The other was in what, by the time of my childhood, had become the center of Buffalo's Black ghetto. My father ran that store for twenty-five years, first with his brother Phil and then, after my uncle died, with my mother's help. He left because he felt, finally, that it would kill him to stay there much longer.

The store — we always called it that, as we called the big street near where we lived "the Boulevard" — had been broken into dozens of times over the years. But they never stole much (my father always took the cash box, his tools, and the really valuable things home each night), and he adjusted to his losses.

Following the race riots of the mid-sixties, though, a new, more militant element moved in, and things got tougher for white business-men. Some shops went under; others were torched, by whom was sometimes difficult to tell. Still, my father stayed. His was the only used furniture and hardware store around, and he had a loyal clien-tele. Though business fell off, it was what he knew to do, and in a way he loved it. He could, he believed, endure.

Even during the week of the riots itself, he and my mother had kept the store open, leaving each day only when the police radio announced a break-in elsewhere on the East Side. "We didn't think about it," my mother told me later. "It seems crazy, but we didn't think anything would happen to us, and nothing did."

Until the evening following the mayor's announcement that the riots had ended, the store itself also remained unscathed. The win-dows of all the businesses surrounding my father's store had been shattered earlier in the week; his glass, though the big panes had mostly been divided into smaller ones from earlier break-ins, was still intact. But just after supper, we received a call from the police saying a boy had tossed a brick through the last undivided panel. It was as if the riots themselves had been the major statement, and this a kind of afterthought, a reminder to my father that he was not exempt. The next day, he boarded up his windows for good, eliminating the expense of replacing broken glass, and soldiered on.

Then the man who owned the grocery store across the street was shot in the chest and killed in a robbery. My mother — and us kids, too; we were old enough by then — began to worry, and to press Dad to consider another way to make a living. There was some talk of his going into business with my cousin, but my father knew they would never see eye to eye, and I suspect he worried that the offer was one of charity. He still hoped, I think, the trouble would blow over. But soon they held him up, too: twice, with knives, within a couple of weeks.

My father bought a gun from one of his regular customers, a small, pearl-handled thing smuggled up from the South. He felt uneasy about it, though — it wasn't right, wasn't honest — so after a couple of months he got a police permit, bought a more substantial pistol legally, and went through the proper training. He carried the new gun in a shoulder holster beneath his vest, and at home he kept it in the top drawer of the nightstand by his bed. Sometimes, after school, when my parents weren't home, my brother Mike and I would open the drawer to look at it, wrapped in dark red velvet, though we would never take it out.

Things quieted down, and for a couple of years nothing consequential happened. Then one rainy afternoon, two men came in, one of them carrying a sawed-off shotgun. They took the cash on hand and did not, thank God, check my father for his gun, nor did he try to draw it on them. They wore stockings over their faces. My father couldn't identify them from the mug shots the police showed him, but he told me more than once that he would never forget the deep, coarse voice of the man who held the gun. "Get outta here, white man," he had said. "You better get out."

—

As a boy, I was ashamed that my father had to earn his living the way he did. I knew that the fathers of my friends at school didn't come home with their hands dirty, the nails and calluses black, and their pants torn and stained with grease. I hope he never suspected. It is to this day a source of some pain to me that he might. And yet I could not help the way I felt.

He would need us, sometimes, my brother Mike and me, on Saturdays, to help with a delivery or to stay with my mother while he went out to look at merchandise. I hated going there so much that the only memories I have are furtive, shadowy: my brother and I carrying some appliance too heavy for my hands, the sharp metal edge digging through my gloves, the houses we entered warm and humid, fogging my glasses; inside, a blur of small children running naked, torn linoleum floors peeling up at the corners and edges, an old chair repaired with tape or a fat red sofa with the stuffing coming out, a feeling of intrusion; and then the man of the house, bigger than possible in his torn white T-shirt, looking up at us from the ball game on TV; or my-self trying to listen politely while an old woman with gold in her teeth and liquor on her breath squeezes my arm, tells me about her daughter in a language so unlike the one I am used to hearing that, while I recognize some of the words, I can only nod, and pray for my father to come and, with his laughing, friendly voice, rescue me.

It was no better in the store itself, except when there wasn't much business and I could occupy myself with cleaning a refrigerator or helping my father fix an old TV. I remember hearing the belled door ring, and hoping before I looked that it was an aunt or uncle dropping in, and then seeing it was not, forcing myself down the narrow aisle between the tables heaped with faucets and dishes and porcelain fig-urines, all the while sensing my ineptitude, dreading the moment I would have to say, "Can I help you?" I remember feeling the shame, but also the relief, that came when a regular customer called out to my father for assistance.

"Hey, brother?"

"Yeah?"

"This your boy?"

"Sure is."

"When you gonna teach him? He don't know what to *do!*"

And I remember feeling, as well, how my father and the customer chuckled, each of them maybe a little annoyed, but neither of them meaning any harm, I see now, as I could not have seen then.

I believe at first my parents thought I was selfish when I would object to working at the store, but it soon became apparent, to my mother, anyway, that I was genuinely afraid. Within a year, spending Saturdays there was no longer expected of me, and although I remem-ber feeling envious of my brother Mike (who by then earned $10 or more for his day's work) and ashamed of my own fragility, I also knew I was better off at home.

I was shy, anyway, even among my peers, and the work with my father often threatened to push me past where I could safely go. Once, when I was quite small, my father had tried to make me swim in water above my head. At his insistence, I jumped in, but I'm certain I would have drowned had he not leapt in after me, even though I knew, in the shallows, how to swim. I was not a particularly courageous child, I suppose.

—

When I was young, my father would tell stories at the dinner table of the *schvartzes*: of their dirty houses, the payments they would miss, the big cars they would drive, the excuses they would make; and of their boyfriends and mistresses and the crimes of their illegitimate children, some of whom he employed from time to time as helpers on pick-ups and deliveries. I accepted what he said, then, but as I got older, his statements about the Black people of the East Side began to annoy me, and by the time I was a senior in high school and fancied myself — bearded, long-haired, and wearing John Lennon glasses with gold wire rims — a radical, his comments at the dinner table often triggered arguments between us. I would call him a racist; he would accuse me of ignorance and impudence. What right did I have to talk? he would ask me. As a boy, I couldn't stand to be anywhere near his customers, he would accurately point out.

I went away to college but transferred back to Buffalo after a year. At first, I shared an apartment with Anna, my high-school girlfriend, and when that fell apart, I moved in with a couple of roommates. I visited my parents only every two or three weeks, for dinner. I hoped to get to know them better, and I wanted to show them that their fears about what would become of me were unwarranted. I would not "wind up a junkie in a gutter" because I'd smoked grass or dropped LSD, nor would I languish in prison because I'd gone to demonstrations against the war, nor would I father unwanted children just because I'd lived with Anna, nor become a failure in life because I'd quit training to be an engineer.

As time passed, and I saw more of my parents, our relationship did relax somewhat. My mother and I began to grow closer, but with my father, things were more difficult. He still condoned neither my academic choices nor my "hippie" lifestyle, though when I started working construction, we at least had a neutral topic we could talk about. Dinner with my family became, if not pleasant, more bearable for us all.

It was at one of these dinners that I learned what had passed between my father and Raymond Johnson, my father's helper.

—

My brothers were only available to work at the store on Saturdays, and even then they were not enough help if a pick-up or delivery was particularly large or heavy. My father's business couldn't support a regular helper, so he found men or boys who, for a couple of bucks, could help him out from time to time. They seldom stuck around for long, but when one vanished, there was usually someone else ready to take his place. Sometimes, they were men on welfare or disability, but most often they were kids. Raymond Johnson was one who worked with my father a good deal longer than most. Raymond began to work with my father when he was just 13, and he stayed with him for the next two years.

Raymond was the youngest son of one of my father's oldest and most reliable customers, one of the few, my father said, who had an intact family, in the sense in which I had grown up thinking of family: Raymond's father, Bill Johnson, still lived with Raymond's mother and their passel of kids, all of whom, as far as I knew, Bill had fathered.

I'd met Raymond a couple of times. I remember him as broad and tall, and tough-looking for 13, but shy and good-natured all the same. Raymond and my younger brother Mark, built like me, often worked together on the truck; my brother seemed pale and skinny beside the Johnson boy, though he was a year or so older. My father, in time, came to regard them as a team, and he showed more fondness for Raymond than he had for most of the other helpers he'd hired over the years.

He treated the boy as a sort of foster son. Though he could pay Raymond, he said, only a dollar or two each time he used him, my father taught him to read street signs and tell time, and he always had my mother pack an extra sandwich, in case Raymond was around at lunchtime. When he took my brother out for ice cream, he would treat Raymond, too. I think Mark resented the attention my parents paid Raymond; he's told me, since, that he never liked the Johnson boy. Still, it was Mark, not Raymond, who at the end of the day drove home beside my father, and it was in Mark's wallet that three $5 bills were carefully folded.

I hadn't seen Raymond for at least a year — I rarely visited my father's store, even then — and it had been nearly as long since I'd heard his name around the house. When I came to dinner that evening, my father was already seated at the kitchen table, near the phone, where he had sat for meals as long as I could remember. He ran a "Furniture Wanted" ad in the evening paper, and people with something to sell would often call at supper time.

He was reading the newspaper. He didn't look up when I walked into the room. "You know that Johnson kid," he said, setting down his paper, "the one you said I ought to hire on a regular basis?"

My mother set a bowl of thick pea soup with ham and barley in front of each of us. The smell of it made me hungry, but my stomach was tight. I knew I was being goaded, and tried, with less success than I might have hoped, to keep the hard edge out of my voice. "Yeah?" I said.

"I fired him yesterday," my father told me. He turned his face to his bowl of soup and spooned some into his mouth.

I said nothing. Still chewing on a bit of ham or carrot, my father went on: "Caught him stealing. He's been stealing from us for *months*." My father put the spoon back in the bowl and stared at me over the top of his reading glasses, as if to say, What do you think of *that*? "I told him he couldn't come to the store anymore," my father said.

My mother sat down at the end of the table, the three of us forming the points of a narrow triangle. I fiddled with my soup spoon. I remembered how, as a kid, I had stolen change from the lunch money drawer in the den, and I knew how I would have felt if I'd been caught. Did you have to fire him? I wanted to ask. Don't you understand why he was stealing from you? I wanted to say. But I knew my footing was shaky. "You're sure he was stealing?" I asked instead.

"We caught him red-handed," my father said, *I told you so* in his tone.

I ate a spoonful of my soup, felt the barley slippery against the roof of my mouth. "What happened?" I asked.

At first parceling out his words, and then warming to the telling, he explained. He did most of the talking, while my mother filled in details.

—

My mother was the first to notice something strange, he said. She was in the habit of wearing a blue smock, and kept some change in the pockets so she wouldn't have to return to the register if a customer at the front of the store needed a nickel or a dime. She never bothered to keep track of it, but she did notice, from time to time, that it seemed a little light. She figured my father had put the change back in the register, and it irritated her, though she didn't complain.

She put up with it for months, until she finally got annoyed enough to say something. "Al, why do you keep taking the silver out of my apron?"

"What? I never touched the silver in your apron."

"Well, I don't know," my mother said. "Every couple of days, I'm waiting on a customer and I go to my pockets for change, and it isn't there."

"Well, I didn't touch it," my father told her.

It was the end of the day, and they were getting ready to close up for the night. My guess is they drove home angry with each other, but it couldn't have taken them long to figure out who the culprit really was.

From time to time, my parents would leave Raymond alone in the store. They trusted him to watch things and tell any customers who happened in that they would be back soon, though they never let him make an actual sale. "He doesn't know how to make change," my mother explained.

The day after the argument about my mother's apron, Raymond came by after school to see if my father had anything for him to do. My father told the boy he had a delivery in half an hour, and he could use a hand. My mother offered him a can of root beer and some cookies, and he stuck around.

"Ray," my mother said, as the boy was finishing up his pop, "Al and I have to go next door for a couple minutes. Can you mind things for a while?"

"Sure, Mrs. Brothers," Raymond told her. Like all my father's customers, Raymond called my father by the name of his store, and my mother was always "Mrs. Brothers," never Mrs. Bookbinder.

"If anybody comes in, tell 'em I'll be right back," my father added.

They left Raymond and went across the street, keeping just out of the boy's view. When they returned a few minutes later, my mother picked up her smock from the chair behind the register, where she had draped it, and put it back on; then she checked the pockets. She nodded to my father, as they had prearranged, and showed her empty hands.

Raymond was sitting at the workbench, watching a soap opera on TV. My father walked over to him and put his hand on the boy's shoulder. "Ray," my father said, "you've been stealing from us."

"What!" Raymond said. "Not me, Mr. Brothers! I like you! I wouldn't steal nothin' from you!"

"Well, Ray," my father said, "I know you just took 49¢ out of Pearl's smock, because we put it there, and it isn't there now. And I don't think this is the first time you've done it."

"I didn't take no 49¢, Mr. Brothers. Honest I didn't!" Raymond said. My father told me Raymond was crying, then. But he was not persuaded by the boy's tears.

"Ray, you're the only one that's been in the store — we were across the street the whole time and we didn't see a customer walk in. I know the money was there when we left. It's not there now."

Raymond continued to cry, and to deny his guilt, but my father had hard evidence, now, and he'd made up his mind what to do. "From now on," he told the boy, "I want you to stay out of the store. You're not gonna be my helper anymore."

Later that week, my father talked with Jack, who ran a convenience store across the street. Jack told him that for the longest time, Raymond had been paying him for cans of pop, candy bars, and sandwiches with change — nickels, dimes, and quarters, sometimes still in their paper rolls. He assumed my father had been paying him this way.

"No, I always gave him a buck or two in bills," my father said, shaking his head at the extent of his loss. The register was always locked when they left the store, but he had kept the rolls of coins in a "secret compartment" in the desk and it had never occurred to him that Raymond might know where that was, and how to open it.

—

My father found another helper fairly easily, an older guy "on the welfare." From time to time he would notice Raymond hanging out on the corner, a cigarette dangling from his mouth (that surprised my father, who had never seen the boy smoke around the store), but they never talked. Sometimes, my father said, he would see the boy while he was on a pick-up or delivery and give him a beep.

Two months after the smock incident, my father got a call from the police at three or four in the morning. The cop on the beat had noticed the rear door of the store ajar and suspected a break-in. My father hurried down. This kind of thing happened a couple of times a year, but it always shook him up — made him question, I imagined, why he kept on, though he never admitted that to me, even when he called on me to help him fix a smashed-in door or better secure a window.

When my father got to the store, he discovered someone had crawled in the bathroom window, breaking off the rusty grate and cutting through three layers of screen and mesh. The change in the register and the extra change my father had hidden away in the desk was gone, and so were a number of small items — transistor radios, lamps, knickknacks, "things a person could carry away easily, without a truck," my father told the cop who made out the report. Also missing was the recipe box that contained the store's accounts receivable slips.

The next morning, when he went out back to see what damage had been done, my father found the box on the ground, two-thirds of the slips still in it, the rest scattered around the yard like autumn leaves. The slips formed a trail, and my father followed it over the back fence, out onto Ferry Street, and down the block, picking them up as he went. The trail petered out near 51 Ferry Street, where the Johnsons lived.

After my father returned to the store, he alphabetized the slips and checked them against his memory. There were several missing, and one was Mrs. Johnson's.

He'd figured right off that the thief must have been a kid, because none of the really valuable things, the collectibles, had been taken, and because the bathroom window was too small for an adult to crawl through. Now, he was sure it was one of the Johnson boys, and fairly certain it was Raymond.

As my father told it, later that day, he saw Raymond passing in front of the store. He called him over.

"Ray, you broke into my store last night," he said.

"No, I didn't, Mr. Brothers," Raymond told him. "I didn't!"

"You did, Ray. It had to be you," my father said, grabbing the boy by the shoulder. "Nobody else knows where we keep the silver."

"I didn't touch your silver, Mr. Brothers," Raymond said. He stepped back, trembling, out of my father's grip, and ran toward the corner, not stopping until he was half a block away. My father watched him for a minute, then, shaking his head, returned to the store.

Mrs. Johnson was one of half a dozen customers my father "trusted"; that is, she would get what she needed from him, he would add the price to her account, and she would pay him after the first of the month, when the welfare checks came in. He knew that Mrs. Johnson owed him about $110 for items she'd bought over the past few months. He decided to send her a bill for $50 more. When she got it, she came (as he put it) "screaming that she didn't owe me that kind of money."

"Well," my father said, "your slip got lost when they broke into my store last week, but in my mind that's what you owe me."

"Well," Mrs. Johnson told him, huffing and puffing, "I got the slip at home to show I don't owe you that." My father said she shut right up as soon as she said that. They both knew he never made duplicate slips.

He talked to a detective who worked the neighborhood and seemed to have an interest in trying to rehabilitate kids who'd gotten into trouble. My father didn't want to press charges. "That isn't going to do him or me any good," he said. "Ray's not really a bad kid," he added. But he wanted to get his merchandise back if he could, and he wanted Raymond to know he couldn't get away with what he'd done.

The detective knew the Johnson family. At that time, one of Raymond's brothers was in jail for stealing a car, and two of his sisters had been picked up for streetwalking. He said he'd talk to the boy and see what he could do.

In time, Raymond came on by. He confessed to having broken the window. He hadn't, he said, actually committed the robbery — he'd sent a smaller kid in, and had told him where the change was and what to steal, and they had split the take between them. Raymond refused to identify his partner, but he gave back most of the change and half the merchandise; the rest, he said, they'd sold. The Johnsons remained regular customers of my father's, but Raymond never came around again, and my father and Mrs. Johnson avoided talking about him for the two or three more years my father remained on Ferry Street.

My father believed Raymond probably came to no better end than his brother or his sisters. He was philosophical about the robbery, though. "Ray turned against me," my father told me, not long afterward, "but, you know, after he brought the stuff back, Mom and I talked about it. She couldn't understand why Ray did it. And I remember telling her that even our own kids might be tempted if they didn't have a nickel in their pockets, and they saw other people walking around with more than they had. Even I might be tempted," he said.

—

I moved to Fort Greene, adjacent to Bedford-Stuyvesant, in February of 1977 and lived there nearly two and a half years. I'm still not sure why I stayed as long as I did, but I am coming to understand why I was able, finally, to leave.

I had been apprehensive, at first, when Janet, a friend of Ruth's, invited me for dinner for a mutual meet-and-greet. Although in time the neighborhood would grow familiar and plain, when I arrived that first evening, I confess I was wary.

I was keenly aware that by the time I got to my stop, I was the only white person left in the subway car. Exiting onto Fulton Street, I found myself passing through an atmosphere reminiscent of my days at my father's store. The streets were paved with ice six inches thick, the signature, I found out over dinner, of a fire three nights before. A wino squatted half-frozen in the doorway of a boarded-up hardware store. Two women I suspected were prostitutes, though I may have been mistaken, fought, tearing at one another's clothes. A burned-out trailer lay in the corner of a lot strewn with trash. Even the colors of the buildings seemed, somehow, discordant.

However, the block where my would-be home was located was peaceful and pleasant. My future landlady, Doc, was open about telling me that the house had been broken into a couple of months before, but now it was wired with an alarm, and she and my future house-mates all said they felt more or less secure. If she had it to do over again, Janet told me, she would. The next-door neighbors, Edwardo and Bernice, who stopped by for coffee and desert, were long-term residents who spoke with enthusiasm of the neighborhood. Everyone seemed welcoming, even excited about the prospect of my joining them.

Although I waffled for a few days before I said yes, really, I'd made up my mind halfway through dinner.

Somewhat to my surprise, Fort Greene soon became home. I spoke to people on the street, played with the neighborhood kids, got to know the keepers of most of the local stores. I felt my father's presence, there, in the competence of the plumbing supply man, and in the scattered bric-a-brac in the windows of the little shops near the bank.

—

Late one evening I spoke with a young woman on the street. I had come upon a man out cold, drunk, in front of the house next to hers. I'd tried to shake him awake, and when he wouldn't stir, I headed up the block, intending to ask Edwardo for advice. Standing inside her gate, she'd been watching me. She called to me as I passed by.

"Hello," she said, her voice ringing round and full. I stopped and tried to make her face out in the dim glow of the distant streetlight. "How come you never talk to me?" she asked. I couldn't remember having seen her before. "I see you all the time," she went on, "and you never so much as look my way."

I stammered for a moment. "I'm sorry," I said. "I don't mean anything by it. I never saw you. I get preoccupied, sometimes. I'm in my own world, you know?" I tried to smile.

I couldn't see her expression, but then she laughed. Was she laughing at me, or just laughing? "That's okay," she said. "I'm just foolin' with you a little." She laughed again, deep and hearty, and this set me more at ease.

Her name, she told me, was Loris. I told her mine was David. She said she'd seen me try to wake the man on the ground, and that I needn't have bothered. "He's okay, in his own way." She explained how he was the husband of the woman who lived in the basement apartment, and how he had come home drunk, and his wife, who was Loris's aunt, kicked him out; and how he returned, hours later, and the aunt had kicked him out again, and how he had sat outside the gate and drunk more whisky, and sobbed, and even sang a little before he passed out cold; and how this was not unusual for him or them to do, nor was it strange, Loris said, to her. Her own father had been a drunk, as best she could remember, and her first husband had been a drunk, as well.

She broke off at this point. "That girl I seen you walkin' with — she your wife?"

"No," I said. "Just someone I know." A college friend had come to visit for a few days.

"She your girlfriend?"

"No," I told her, feeling a little uneasy about where this might be going, "she's not my girlfriend, either. I don't have a girlfriend now," I said.

"You still married?" I asked, deliberately turning the conversation back to her.

"No," she said, and she looked toward the bottom of the black, iron fence posts before turning back to me. "Yeah, my husband, he used to drink. That wasn't so bad. But he was *mean*."

"Mean?"

"He used to hit me. And the last time, he cut me, and he beat my baby black and blue, and after that happen, I said to myself I wouldn't take no more of that kinda treatment. That was when we were livin' in the projects. We been a number of places since then. Now we're here."

She had a daughter, who was three — "She's a little doll. You have to see her." — and she was pregnant once again. We stood and talked for maybe half an hour about her family, about my job, and about her hopes of getting educated and finding some way to make a decent living, and not having to depend on a man, or on the welfare. I tried to encourage her but felt foolish doing so. She was only 23, and I was 27, but I felt younger than her by half a century.

As I was leaving, we made vague plans to get together sometime. At that moment, I thought we would, but passing her on the street in the daylight, I found I was reluctant to say more than hello — as friendly a "hello" as I could muster, but still just hello — and as the days passed, even that came uneasily, until finally I went to Fulton Street another way, so as not to pass her house. I kept that up for several weeks, until enough time had elapsed so I was sure that "hello" was all it would ever come to.

Over the next few months I would see her, sometimes, standing at the gate as she had that night, or sitting on her stoop, round and swollen. Once I saw her daughter, who in her pigtails and pink dress really was the "little doll" Loris had described. Months went by, and once, while working on the roof, I saw her again, standing by the fence, and I supposed she'd had the other child, because she looked much thinner. And then she must have moved, because after that, I never saw her again.

—

Most of my work on the house consisted of general repair and renovation, but I also completed two major projects, for which Doc paid me a little extra. One of these was the central staircase, which I restored and refinished. The other was a Chinese-style porch I built from scratch that extended out from the kitchen into the backyard. Doc designed it to go with the rock garden she'd set up three years before. When it was done, it was a sturdy, handsome thing of redwood, cedar, and yellow pine, with an enclosure below, sheathed in reed fencing, for storing bicycles and garden tools. It was during the construction of this porch that I met Dwayne and Rodney.

This was in my second summer in Fort Greene, one more than I'd reckoned on. Temperatures hung near a hundred for close to two weeks, difficult weather for digging footers, setting posts, and cutting and planing the pine boards for the deck so they fit tightly together. But I was nearly out of cash. I worked, drank quarts of water, and ate bags of pretzels and peanuts to make up for the salt I gave up in sweat. It was heavy work in that heat, and though I kept at it, I also welcomed any interruption. So I was pleased when I noticed, peering at me from behind the roof peak of the neighbor's garage, two small sets of eyes.

"Hello!" I said, "you interested in carpentry?" I smiled at the two young owners of those eyes, but they stayed where they were, half hidden. I waited another minute for a response, and when neither boy said anything. I shrugged and went back to the task at hand. Still, their presence made the work seem, somehow, more important, my movements more precise and sure. Within a few minutes they were gone, and I worked the rest of the day without an audience.

The next day, though, they were back, hanging their heads over the edge of the garage roof upside-down, giggling and snickering. They covered their ears when I started the circular saw. "Hey! What's that thing makin' all that noise?" the smaller of the two boys shouted, displaying a wide, thin smile.

"It's a saw," I said. I held it up to show them. "The blade goes around and around, real fast, like a bicycle wheel, and these teeth cut the wood." I flicked the blade with my fingernail; it made a hollow, ringing sound. "Watch!" I picked up a scrap of two-by-four and sheared off a corner. "See?" I held up the part still in my hand, then grabbed the corner I'd cut off. I tried to toss it to the garage roof, but the wind caught it, and it clattered against the side of the building, splitting in two. The boys, apparently frightened, vanished again.

The following day, they came up to the gate and into the yard — unannounced, as far as I could tell, though it's possible they'd called to me and I hadn't heard. I was planing the edge of a plank, the pungent scent of resin mixing with the omnipresent odor of ailanthus that permeated the neighborhood. I didn't see the boys until they were right in front of me.

"Hey!" I said, "where'd you guys come from?" I set down my plane and wiped off the wood chips that clung to my face and arms. The taller of the two boys hung back, his hands in his pockets. The one who had asked me about the saw stood with his arms crossed in front of him, smiling that wide, thin smile. "So," I said, "how're you doin'?"

"Fine," the smaller boy said.

"That's good." I went to pick up my plane again, but changed my mind. I liked these boys. They had *chutzpah*. So I sat on the sawhorse and asked, "Who are you guys, anyway?"

They told me their names: Rodney, the smaller and more talkative one, and Dwayne, the quieter and obviously older boy. Rodney lived a block over and was, I'm certain (though I let on I believed him when he denied it), one of two kids who had broken up a barbecue the summer before by throwing rocks at us from that same roof. He introduced Dwayne as his cousin. They were seven and nine, respectively.

Rodney had been doing all the talking so far, but just as I was about to announce that I had to get back to work, Dwayne spoke up. He pointed to my tool belt. "What's that?" he said.

I patted the metal tape clipped to the left side of the belt. "This?" I asked, displaying it on my palm. "It's a measuring tape. You use it to see how long things are. I'll show you."

I backed Dwayne up against one of the posts of the porch deck. "Stand there," I said.

I got Rodney to hold the bottom of the tape near Dwayne's foot, then I extended the tape up to his chin and held it there. "How long have you been around?" I said, briefly embarrassed when I realized that neither boy had gotten the joke.

I pulled the tape up to the top of Dwayne's head. "You lock it with this button," I explained, slipping the mechanism down to their eye level, pointing with my thumb. "This is how tall you are: 54 ½ inches — that's four feet, six and a half inches."

Dwayne smiled, looked at Rodney, and then both of them laughed, as if at some private joke. I laughed, too. I released the lock and the tape was sucked into its container like spaghetti.

"Lemme see that!" Rodney said, grabbing for it.

"Hold on a second!" I said, raising it above his head. It was a good tape — a ¾", sixteen-foot Lufkin — and it belonged to Doc. I'd have a hard time paying for a replacement, but I didn't want to disappoint them. "Let me show you first," I said.

I taught them how to pull the tape out without kinking it, how to draw it back into the case without pinching their fingers, and how to hook the end onto corners and edges, so they could measure something longer than their reach. They set to wandering around the yard, measuring trees and wood and parts of walls, naming improbable figures and giggling all the time. They couldn't read the numbers.

After a few minutes, I began to worry about the time, and the tape. "Okay, guys, I've gotta get back to work," I said, and held out my hand. I had to ask several times before Rodney handed it back to me.

The boys stood together, waiting. My immediate plan was to plane a few more planks, then drill them out and nail them into place with copper-plated nails. "It might not be too interesting to watch, but you can stick around if you want to," I said.

While I went back to work, they sat on the large stones in the rock garden and watched. I looked up to them from time to time to explain what I was doing, but the task was repetitious and they soon grew bored. "I'm sorry I don't have something more exciting-looking today," I said.

Rodney got up first. "Well," he said, "we be goin' now."

"Okay, you guys," I told him. I set my hammer down and wiped the sweat from my forehead. "C'mon back any time. I'll be here."

Thus began a routine we three repeated several times over the next week. I taught them what I could of measuring and numbers in the few minutes they stayed with me, and I let them try out a few cuts with the handsaw and hit (and bend over, and try to straighten) a few nails.

Sometimes things got a little hairy. Once, Dwayne asked me if he could keep the measuring tape, and he resisted giving it back to me when I told him no, I needed it for my work. Rodney got hold of the circular saw and started it up. The kick of the motor knocked it out of his hand. It scared him, but I think I scared him even more when I hollered at him. "Those tools are really *dangerous*," I exclaimed. "I've seen guys with their fingers cut off by saws like this." I wasn't exaggerating — my first construction boss was missing a digit and a half. "I don't want anything like that happening to you." Basically, though, we got along. The kids added something to my day, as I did, it seemed, to theirs.

The following week it rained and I stayed inside, grateful for the extra time to write. But by the end of the week, the weather had cleared and the rain had cooled and sweetened the air. I brought out the tools and again commenced working on the porch.

Doc was out for the day, and toward noon two of my housemates headed down to the Village for a movie. They invited me along, but I thought I ought to take advantage of the weather. Later that afternoon, I heard the phone ringing on the third floor. I let it go a couple of times, and then had a strong feeling the call was important — I got those feelings sometimes and never knew what to make of them. I dropped my tools and ran through the kitchen, took the stairs two at a time, and arrived out of breath on the sixth and, I hoped, not final ring. Wrong number. Ours must have been a digit or two off from one of the two whorehouses in the neighborhood, because we were always getting calls for women, always from men, and the callers were usually embarrassed or annoyed when they found out it was one of us on the other end of the line.

I was already down one flight of stairs when the phone rang again, and this time it was Ruth.

We hadn't talked since she'd started seeing another guy. I tried to keep her out of my thoughts, and I wasn't sure how happy I was to hear her voice. Now, standing in the third-floor hallway, where the wall phone was mounted, all the old sadness and resentment, and a little of the joy, came flooding back to me. As we felt out our new relationship, I gazed out the window at the desolation of my neighborhood, feeling the grit and sweat between the tool pouch and my belly, aware of the gulf between what she'd wanted me to be and what I was, and what I'd hoped for us, and how little we had together now.

Twenty or thirty minutes into the conversation, I heard the front gate swing open and saw below me two small, dark bodies walking alongside the house toward the back yard. I considered yelling down to the boys that I'd be there in a few minutes, but I didn't want to disrupt the fragile connection Ruth and I were trying to create. A minute later, I heard the gate groan again. They'll be back, I thought.

After the call, I dragged myself downstairs, carrying the weight of the conversation and the fatigue of another day's work with me. I stopped in the kitchen for a glass of iced tea. When I got out to the porch, I stood there for a while, trying to remember where I'd left off.

Absentmindedly, I patted my tool pouch. No tape.

I scanned the railing I'd been working on. Not there, either.

A little frantic, I checked everywhere I might have put it — tool apron pockets, beneath the deck, even in the basement, thinking I might have left it there that day — before I concluded that the boys must have stolen it. More hurt than angry, my first thought was, Why did they do that? And my second, What should I do, now that they had?

I knew I shouldn't let them get away with it, but also that it was unwise to go knocking on doors, the white guy in a Black neighborhood, making accusations. I decided to wait till Doc came home before

I did anything. It was her tape, and she who would be living in the neighborhood long after I was gone.

When we talked about the theft at dinner, Doc said she was willing to let it go, if that's what I wanted to do. "It's up to you. You know these boys."

"Not as well as I thought," I said.

The next day, Sunday, I wandered around the neighborhood, asking kids if they knew Dwayne and Rodney. Eventually, another boy told me where Rodney lived.

Rodney's mother was a heavy, tired-looking woman, older than I'd expected. She didn't know what I was talking about when I said something about Rodney and his cousin. "I know Dwayne" she said, "but he's no cousin." She said Rodney wasn't home, but she'd talk to him, and I should come back at supper time.

"I just want the tape back," I explained. "I don't want to get the kids in trouble."

I returned at six, and she was waiting there with Rodney. "He said the other boy took it, and he still got it." Her eyes shone. "I gave him a good lickin' anyway," she said, as if that would satisfy me. Rodney stood in the corner, glaring at me.

Rodney's mother told me Dwayne lived in the hotel down the block from me, with his uncle. I thanked her, wishing for Rodney's sake and my own that I had not come, but at the same time compelled to follow through; I had taken things this far.

I'd never been inside the corner hotel. The outside doors hung open like a slack mouth. Inside, it was even gloomier, darker, and shabbier, than I had imagined. Behind the streaked brown door of apartment 1-B, where I hoped to find Dwayne, I heard a radio, and also a baby crying. I pressed the doorbell, painted and dirty. When I got no response, I knocked several times.

The radio noise ceased and the crying grew more muffled. I heard footsteps, and took a deep breath, then a short one, to calm myself. I wanted, somehow, to put everything right.

A stocky man with a thin mustache opened the door. Behind him stood a boy about two, naked except for a dirty white T-shirt. I cleared my throat, but stood speechless, the script I'd rehearsed on the way wiped clean.

I cleared my throat again. "Hi," I said. "My name's David. I live up the block?"

The man said nothing.

"I just came from Dwayne's cousin Rodney's house. His mother told me Dwayne lived here."

The man nodded.

"Is he home?" I asked.

"Dwayne's around the corner. What do you want with him?"

In broken sentences, I told him about the tape measure and how Rodney's mother had told me Dwayne, not Rodney, had stolen it. "I'd just like it back," I concluded.

"Dwayne don't have any cousin Rodney," the man said.

"Uh, look," I said. "I don't know whether he's Dwayne's cousin or not, but he's a kid Dwayne plays with, and his mother told me Dwayne had my tape. I just want it back" I repeated. "Do you know anything about it?"

The man looked me over carefully, now. "What's it look like?" he said. I described it. He'd seen Dwayne playing with it. "He said he found it," the man said. "I'll talk to him. Come back tomorrow."

But as we were talking, Dwayne entered the building. My back was to him, and he must have backed off when he saw me, because the man called to him, "Dwayne! You get over here!"

I turned. Dwayne took a couple of steps in our direction.

"This man tol' me you took his — what'd you say?"

"Tape. Measuring tape."

"His tape machine. He wants you to give it back."

Dwayne retreated, his hands stuffed into the pockets of his ragged cutoffs. The expression on his face was awful to behold. "I don't have it!" he cried. "A man got it! I sold it to a man!" he said.

"What man you sold his tape machine to?" his uncle asked. Now there was an edge to his voice.

"Just a man!" Dwayne cried. "He give me $2 for it!"

Neither Dwayne's uncle nor I said anything for a few moments. Then his uncle asked Dwayne, "Can you get this man's tape machine back for him?"

Dwayne's eyes searched the floor. "I don't know," he mumbled. I took in his bare feet, his skin smeared with dirt and sweat, the cigarette butts near the doorway. What am I doing here? I thought. What am I doing to this boy?

"How much that tape machine of yours cost?" Dwayne's uncle asked me.

I thought somewhere between fifteen and twenty dollars; "Ten," I said. "Ten dollars." But I knew even that was too much.

"Well," the man said, "how about you give Dwayne and me a couple days to see if we can get it back, and if he can't find that man I'll give you the $10. Okay?"

"That'd be fine," I told him, eager to let it drop. I had taken it plenty far enough.

—

The boys, of course, never came by again. It was their company, more than the tape, I'd hoped to salvage, and I had failed terribly. I did see Dwayne once more, about a month and a half later. I was walking down Fulton Street toward the subway, preoccupied as usual, and in something of a hurry. Coming toward me, kicking a beer bottle along the curb, was Dwayne.

"Hey!" I called to him, smiling the smile I reserved for kids, "Hey, Dwayne!"

He took another step, then his whole body stiffened.

"Hey, how're you doing?" I said. In my excitement, I had almost forgotten the terms we'd parted on. Dwayne hadn't. He said nothing. Stupidly, remembering, I asked, "Hey, whatever happened to that tape?"

"I'm gettin' it back," Dwayne told me. He looked both furious and about to cry. "I'm still tryin' to get it back."

"Okay, Dwayne," I said quietly, sickened by my own actions. "Okay, you bring it by when you get a chance. Don't worry about it," I said, knowing it was way too late to reassure him.

—

In the sense that I hardly ever questioned it, I got used to living in Fort Greene, though occasionally — walking past the burned-out shell of Thriftees Super Market and Grocery, where the numbers runners used to have coffee, or talking with Sandy, who at 18 had already aborted her third child, or passing the bottle caps embedded in the asphalt and knowing from them the habitation of the corner, or listening to crazy Jessie sing gospel outside the abandoned garage she lived in — I would start at the fact that I was still there, this was my life, my home. I never stopped being aware of how alien I was here, as much a foreigner as I would be if another language were my native tongue. It was much more than my white skin.

Still, I stayed, even after I could reasonably, from a strictly monetary point of view, have left. I found, always, some reason to linger, much as my father, perhaps, had found reason to stay on East Ferry Street for so many years. I can remember him, after he'd closed down his first store, telling me he wished he'd been the kind of man who was more willing to take risks, to give up what he had to try for something more. I remember observing to myself, then, the risks he took in remaining where he was.

—

My father's store was just a few blocks from where he was born. I wondered how he must have felt when the neighborhood started to change, the old Jews moving out or dying, the Blacks moving up from Georgia, the Carolinas, Alabama, and spreading out from the city's south side. He had spent his childhood in that neighborhood, among his kind. When he opened his store with my Uncle Phil, the neighborhood must have been mostly Jewish, judging from the remnants of that culture which, in my childhood, still remained. Now, the old stone temples were churches with rummage sales and bingo on Saturdays, our Sabbath.

I envisioned my father persisting, adapting to the changes and their implicit threat, more by failing to acknowledge them in his heart than by any other means. And yet he could not have kept all of that in check: his fears, his sense of something lost.

It was my mother, in the end, who persuaded him to leave. I still visited my parents infrequently, but even so, I witnessed their arguments more than once; or more precisely, my mother's railing at my father, and his decreasingly effective defense.

He would sit at the table, eating, and at some point in the meal offer a justification for an unpleasantness of that particular day, or make a remark that indicated his intention to remain. My mother, who had convinced herself that they'd already agreed to move the store, would fume.

"We've been through this already," she would say. "We decided."

My father's face would grow hard and a beleaguered tone would come into his voice as he spoke my mother's name, "Pearl ..."

Within minutes she'd be crying. "You and that stupid *store*," she would say. "What am I going to do if they come in and decide to *shoot* you?"

My mother would sob and accuse while my father alternated between fighting back and pacifying her. My brothers and I would keep quiet, as we had done when we were younger, and their arguments were about us.

—

During one of the winter months in the year before I left Fort Greene, a 14-year-old Black kid was shot to death by a transit cop. The boy had jumped a turnstile. The cop who killed him claimed he had to shoot because the boy came at him with a knife, but no weapon of any kind was found near the body. The cop was never charged.

That spring, a Black priest was choked to death in a struggle with several police officers, his larynx crushed by a billy club. The papers reported it as an accident, but my next-door neighbor, Edwardo, had been a friend of the dead man, and he told me witnesses described it as murder.

When it became clear no charges would be brought against any of the cops involved, angry Blacks from the neighborhood organized a demonstration that shut down the Brooklyn Bridge. The story made headlines in the *Daily News*, half the front page taken up by the photograph of the great stone structure, the technological marvel of its day, clotted with angry faces and raised fists.

For weeks thereafter, in their windows, Black storekeepers on Fulton Street hung portraits of the dead priest, blown up from a snapshot. As I walked along the street, his cool, sad eyes stared at me from half a dozen locations, accusing.

By the time muggings became a regular topic of conversation among the few white people in my neighborhood, I'd been there close to two years. At first, I attributed these muggings largely to their victims' inexperience, rather than to any change in the neighborhood itself. I'd lived with students on and off since I'd come to the area, and I knew them to be somewhat cavalier — as I had learned not to be. But after one of my housemate's friends, a third-year painting student at Pratt, was robbed and stabbed as he was leaving the subway, I gave more weight to the smaller troubling events I'd experienced. He'd been stabbed several times in the gut and was in the hospital for weeks before anyone could say for certain whether he was likely to survive.

When he came to, he said he hadn't put up a struggle. They had cut him, as far as he could tell, for kicks.

A few incidents stood out as personal warnings.

One cold, gray, autumn evening, on my way home for supper I noticed a couple of guys on the stoop of a Fulton Street hotel. I was almost upon them before I heard the chanting. At first I couldn't quite make it out, but after I'd taken a few more steps, it came through clearly: "Wring that honky's neck," one of the young men was saying; "Wring that honky's neck! Wring that honky's neck!" he sang, as if performing an incantation.

I was the only honky around.

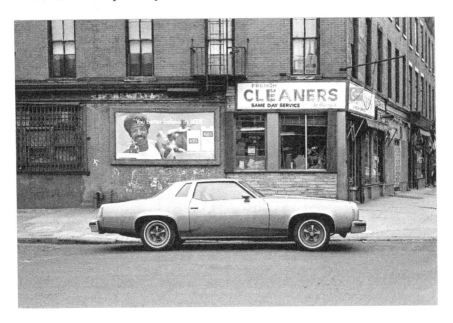

Some months later, on a summer-like, spring afternoon, I was walking home from the hardware store on Myrtle Avenue with some curtain rods and nails. I'd taken the back way, past the beverage center. Although this route was shorter, I usually avoided it, but that afternoon I was fed up with zigzagging from safe block to safe block, and besides, there were people out on the street.

Not far from my corner, I saw two bare-chested kids chasing each other in the roadway, their slick bodies gleaming in the sun. The smaller of the two looked about 13; the other was a few years older.

They stopped as I drew nearer and stood together in the middle of the street.

"Lotta *white* motha*fuckers* movin' in here these days," I heard the young one sing out, the sound almost musical. "Hey, whaddaya *say* let's *rag* that motha*fucker*," his high-pitched voice rang.

I pretended not to hear. I shifted my grip on the curtain rods I was carrying, and wished I had bought something with more heft.

"What motherfucker?" a deeper voice asked.

"That white mothafucker, over there," the first one said.

I was by then past them. I began to measure in my mind the distance from the corner, and to listen for the fall of footsteps from behind.

"Him?" asked the deeper voice. "That motherfucker don't got no more money than I do," he said.

When I reached the corner, I let out the breath I had not realized I'd been holding. Later, telling the story to my housemates, I had to laugh, though even then I knew that laughter was not an entirely accurate response.

About two months after the painting student was stabbed, a white shopkeeper from Queens who had worked in the neighborhood for nearly thirty years was shot to death by two 16-year-old kids while he waited on the subway platform for his train home. My housemate Elliot moved out shortly after that. Noel, a theater major, soon replaced him, but a few weeks later he came in, breathless, and reported that he'd almost been knifed. Within a month, my other housemate, Drew, was mugged. He'd just stepped out of the liquor store on Fulton Street and was on his way to a friend's house for dinner. One guy blocked him from the front while two more came up from behind. They dragged him around the corner and pushed him to the ground, face down. One held a knife to his throat while the others went through his pockets.

"I couldn't see their faces," he told me, "but I got a good look at the knife. It was about eight inches long, shaped like a triangular file."

"A stiletto, I think that's called," I told him.

"They call it a pig sticker around here," he said.

After Drew was mugged, I made it a point to keep off the streets after dark. If I was going to be out late, I'd stay with friends whenever

I could. I also started to look for apartments in the Village or Park Slope, though even there, I knew people who'd been hassled. I thought about leaving New York altogether, but where would I go? And I bought a knife, though I seldom carried it.

Walking home on those few evenings when I did end up returning late, I fought a thousand muggers in my imagination. I could never tell, in advance, which way the battle would go.

one:

> *I am turning the corner from Fulton to Washington and it is dark and warm, nobody on the street. But leaning against the wall of the grocery on the corner, skulking in the shadows, is a man with a knife. He leaps into the open and I can see the gleam of the street lights in his blade. He is fast, but I am faster, and have taken the corner wide enough to leave myself room to move. I carry an umbrella with a weighted handle. I have been holding it like a club, and in one motion, I whirl and swing hard and fast across my attacker's face, breaking his nose. As blood trickles down his face in thin, black lines, I kick him in the groin. He doubles over, dropping his knife. I ram him with my shoulder and knock him to the ground, then stomp on his wrist when he reaches for the knife; hear it snap. I leave him on the sidewalk, groaning, as I slowly walk away.*

two:

> *I am coming home and at the corner of Fulton and Washington there are two of them waiting, and I don't see or hear them till they are upon me. Although I have my knife, each of them has one, too. They rush me. I am slow, hesitant, and when I reach for it they grab it easily. I feel the steel pierce my gut, a coldness. I am suddenly weak, and sink to the ground, and now it is warm where they have cut, and the warmth oozes down my side. My head hits the pavement but I do not feel it. I hear them laughing, sense them rifling my pockets while my body begins to cool and the sky goes dim. I hear their voices talking far away.*

> *"Fucker pulled a knife," one says. "You don't pull no knife on me!"*

There is no pain but I cannot move. "Hey, let's split," I hear another voice say. "I think you hurt him bad!" And then I feel a boot smack against my head, the concrete scraping the flesh from my cheek as my head is jerked across the pavement. The first voice, far away though at the same time close enough so I smell his breath, growls: "Mothafucker, you don't pull no knife on me!"

—

Linda and I met several months back, in Buffalo, where she worked as an elementary school teacher. Since then, we had tried without much success to get a romance going through letters and long-distance telephone calls. When she came to New York for a week-end conference, we seized the day. We met in Little Italy for dinner, and I wound up escorting her back to her aunt's, near Coney Island, and staying there for several hours. We succeeded in advancing the romance, but it was after 2 a.m. when I finally started home.

Though it was still early summer, the weather had turned cold and wet. I considered taking a cab, but was short on cash, and, anyway, dubious of being able to find one at that time of night. I took the F train to downtown Brooklyn, then caught the A train home.

Two or three people got off at my stop. I stayed close as we climbed the stairs to the outside. Breathing in the familiar scents of piss and stale tobacco, I told myself that in ten minutes I'd be home, and what fears I had now would seem ludicrous to me then.

Fulton Street was quiet up and down its length, and the bright, pink lights gave it an eerie feel, like a movie set for a horror film. It had stopped raining, but there was still a heavy mist in the air. I hoped one of my fellow passengers would be going my way, but they all headed off in different directions, quickly absorbed by the mist. I walked to the corner and tried to pick the safest route home. I zipped my leather jacket and stuck one hand in my pants pocket, remembering the knife I'd left behind, feeling for anything else I might use as a weapon in what I convinced myself was the unlikely event I'd need one.

I heard somebody suck his teeth. To my right, I saw a woman swaying her hips as she walked down Fulton. Between me and her were two men slouching in a doorway, smoking cigarettes. I decided to cross the street to avoid them.

Halfway, I heard one of them shout, "*Hey you!*" I didn't look back. I remember trying to walk tough, though what I felt was awkward and stiff. When I reached the other side of the street, I picked up speed, trying to put some distance between me and the two guys on the corner.

I hadn't taken ten steps before I heard a tandem patter from behind. I glanced over my shoulder and saw the two men from the doorway trotting toward the curb. They reminded me of a team of horses, their movements were so neatly paired.

I could feel the texture of the pavement through my boots, and hear the beat of their footsteps keeping pace with mine. The mist left a taste like metal in my mouth and my body felt buoyant and sluggish, as if I were moving through water. The two men's footsteps grew louder, faster. I forced myself to quicken my own pace, and moved closer to the curb.

It was four blocks to my house, and three to the turn off Fulton and onto Grand Avenue. I wasn't confident I could outrun them all the way home, and I knew that trying would give me away, so I walked even with them for another block, trying to devise a strategy. When I heard them gaining on me again, my chest tightened. Short of breath, I fought to make myself understand this was *really happening*, there was something that I really *had* to do. I veered off the sidewalk and into the street itself and opened my jacket to let in some air.

Walking in the middle of the road, I felt, for the moment, safe, but my turn was coming up and the two men were nearly parallel with me, now; I could see them from the corner of my eye. I sensed they knew that they could afford to wait.

I had only half a block to go before the turn, and I didn't know yet what to do. I remember actually praying for a cop, begging God for a cab to happen by or a car I could flag down, but the street was quiet and empty as far as I could see. I scanned the sidewalk, but saw only a couple of drunken men and giggling women near the after-hours club across the street, and, barely visible in the mist, a man in a white raincoat walking toward me from a couple of blocks away.

Moving at a clip just shy of a run, I took the corner sharp, cutting directly across the two men's path. I saw them clearly for the first time, not half a dozen feet away: tandem specters, hooded, one in army green, the other in iridescent blue.

Immediately, I heard their footsteps round the corner, too.

I crossed the street. It was my last evasive tactic, and it put me on the side opposite my house, but it also created a little distance between us.

I was nearing the entrance of the hotel on the corner when I saw the taller of the two men motion to his partner with his thumb. I watched them start across the road. For a moment, I indulged the thought they weren't after me at all, they lived in the hotel, they were just heading home. I almost laughed. Then I saw how they had gauged their path to intersect with mine. I felt in my pockets again. All I found were my keys and a penknife I'd had since I was a kid. My sweaty fingers slipped on the worn plastic of its handle.

It was, I thought, too late now to run. When they were hardly more than a car's width from me, I stopped short. "What's happening?" I asked.

They took another step or two and stopped, as well. "What's happening?" the taller of the two, in his army green jacket, repeated. Their rain hoods hid their faces in shadow, but I could still make out their teeth and eyes. "Whaddaya mean, 'what's happening?'" he asked me. They each took another couple of steps, blocking the sidewalk in front of me. We were no more than three or four feet apart.

The tall one giggled, and slapped his partner on the shoulder. "'What's happening?' he says." He spoke in falsetto. He laughed again, then turned cold eyes on me. "*Do you know me?*" he asked. I didn't know what to say. "You don't know me," he went on. "Whaddaya mean, tellin' me 'what's happening?'" They spread apart slightly and took another step forward. I retreated in lockstep, edging toward the hotel's iron fence.

I tried to assume a casual air. "You know," I said, "that's just something you say to people when you pass 'em on the street." I could hear the failure of my tone. "Sort of a friendly greeting," I went on. "I live just up the block." I tipped my head toward my house. "I see somebody on the street in my neighborhood, I'm gonna say hello."

407

The tall one bared his teeth again. "Yeah?" he said. "Well, we live around here, too. That don't mean nothin'. What're you tryin' to say?"

I could feel them circling, calculating. I nudged forward just a little to see if they would let me pass. The short one jerked his hand out of his jacket pocket and took a half step backward. "He's got a knife," he whispered, then pulled his own blade out part way.

The taller one kept his footing. "Hey, you don't got a *knife*, do you?" he said. I could see his teeth again, shining through his snarl.

I took a step back and bumped into the fence. The rigid iron pressed against my spine. "What is this, huh?" I said sharply.

The tall one took up the space between us. His head was silhouetted against the street light, and in the mist, it seemed to have a halo around it. "Okay, now," he said slowly, "whaddaya got in those pockets?" Their circling, I understood, had come to an end.

My right hand still in my pocket, I stood there for what might have been a full minute, trying to think of something to say, something else to stall or appease. But I'd exhausted everything I had. Then, from behind, I heard a quiet voice say, "Don't shoot him yet," like a waiter in some comedy calling out, Hot soup! Hot soup!

The man in the white raincoat I'd seen walking down Fulton Street some minutes before stepped into our midst. "Hey, anybody got a dollar?" he said. "I sure need to borrow a dollar."

The two muggers and I exchanged a look that said, What the fuck? And then I saw he might be my ticket home.

I took one step forward.

The four of us began to move up the block, the man in the raincoat in the lead, I following a foot or two behind him, and the two muggers bringing up the rear. I felt — abruptly and incongruously — elated.

"Hey, now," the tall one repeated, "what you say you got in those pockets?"

I wasn't thinking, but I was moving, inching around the man in the white rain coat, trying to position him between me and the other two. "My keys," I answered, "my wallet" — should I have said that? Of course they would know that — "a packet of Kleenex, and a Boy Scout knife I've had since I was a kid."

"A knife! See, I told you!" the short one said.

"Oooooh, gimme some Kleenex, I gotta wipe my nose," the tall one taunted. They started to fall back. I fumbled in my pocket for my keys. "Watch it," he warned. But I realized I didn't have to listen to him, anymore.

When I was within easy reach of the house, I made a break. I ran hard across the street, vaulted over the gate, and leapt up the front stairs. I heard the tall one calling after me, "Lookit him run! Look how scared he is!" I didn't turn around until I was almost through the door. They started toward me, then stopped in the middle of the street.

"You wanna know what's happening?" the tall one asked me. "I'll tell you what's happening," he said. He pulled back the hood of his rain jacket, revealing in the light of the corner street lamp a cap made from a nylon stocking. He pulled it down over his face. "This!" he said. "This is what's happening, m-a-a-an!" He feigned another dash toward me, then aborted it.

I slipped inside and locked the door. Leaning against it, I could still hear their quick, derisive laughter.

—

There is an argument my father and I have repeated, with variations, for many years:

Dad: Ever since you were 16, you've been telling me, 'Dad, I'm 16, I have my own life, I know what I'm doing. Dad, I'm 17, I have my own life, I know what I'm doing, Dad, I'm —

Me: Okay, Dad.

Dad '18, I know what I'm doing, Dad I'm 19 — '

Me: I said okay! I get your point! I said that then, and I'm saying it now, and I still mean it. It's my life, and I wanna live it my own way. I'm sick of fighting with you about it. I don't tell you how to live *your* life.

Dad: Can't I talk to you like a father talks to his son? You say I don't talk to you. Every time I've ever given you advice, you turned around and did the opposite. And where's it gotten you? It's always worked out bad.

Me: What do you mean, it's always worked out bad?

Dad: Look at you! Would you call your life a shining success?

Me: Would you?

But with each repetition, the arguments get less severe, and the gap between them lengthens; it has been several years, now, since the last time we spoke this way to one another. Whether this is because my life is more to his liking — I have a job, and live in a neighborhood he would find acceptable, and have long since cut my hair — or because he has grown more tolerant of the choices I make, or just because he is tired of trying to change me, I don't know.

Regardless, I have enjoyed the way things have been, these past few, quieter years.

—

I left Fort Greene and New York City a few weeks after my encounter with the muggers.

I didn't know, then, where to go, so I packed up my things in cardboard boxes from the beverage center up the street, rented a U-Haul truck, and headed for Buffalo, to my parents' house. I remember feeling, as I headed over the bridge and onto Route 17, that I was leaving something behind, had given up. I could feel the weight of all my belongings stacked behind me, the accumulation of five years in the city, letters and books and so many uncompleted projects. Most of all, I felt the growing distance between Ruth and me, now also physical and likely irrevocable.

As I eased off Route 17, I skidded slightly — I'd grown unused to driving four-wheeled vehicles — and had a vision of the truck overturning, all I owned catching fire, burning quickly to nothing. I immediately recovered control, but the image stayed with me for a while. As I eased onto the highway and was, at last, beyond the city's bounds, I understood that I did not need the fire to release me.

—

In his letter, my father talks about his reasons for retiring. "As you know," he says, "we are in the process of closing down the store, after thirty years of good times and bad times. I haven't told Dr. Glick yet, because he advised me not to retire unless I had plenty of money and wanted to travel and do things I couldn't do when I was working. He said I'm much too young.

"I guess he's concerned that I'd just sit around and do nothing but eat, get fat, and wreck all the good things that surgery, work, exercise, and keeping busy have done to put me into the shape I'm in today. However, after working most of my life since graduating from High School, I think I can stand loafing for a month or so, especially the cold, snowy, blowing winter months, and then look for something to do later on.

"Mom has also worked hard, right alongside me, and many times, even harder, especially since my surgery, when she had to practically run the business all by herself. To this day, she still does a lot of the buying, selling, taking care of the bills, plus running the household, which is almost a full-time job itself. So for Mom's sake as well as my own, we both decided to call the store quits. Two more broken windows since you were home, and calls from the Police Department in the early morning hours, have helped us make that decision."

My father does not know that from my mother I have already heard a somewhat different version of this story. I imagine them sitting up in bed together after the second police call about the broken windows:

Mom: We're closing down the store.

Dad: What?

Mom: I said we're closing the store.

Dad: What do you mean, closing the store?

Mom: We're closing down the store. Two calls in the middle of the night is too much.

Dad: We can't close the store!

Mom: Yes, we can.

Dad: How can we close the store? We'll never get rid of all that stuff.

Mom: We'll get rid of it. You said we couldn't move off Ferry Street, and we did. We'll have a going-out-of-business sale. We'll put ads in the paper. We'll call Morrie. Other people go out of business. We'll manage.

Dad: We can't close down the store.

Mom: Yes, we can.

Dad: What're we going to do? We can't live on Social Security.

Mom: We'll figure something out. I'll get a job. We'll take care of kids. We'll do what Rose and Molly do, with the auctions and the flea market. We'll manage.

Dad: We're not closing the store! Don't be ridiculous!

(short silence)

Mom: Al, we're closing down the store. If you don't want to close it, you can run it yourself, because I'm not coming in anymore.

(long silence)

Dad: All right. Can we wait till the first of the year?

But my father's version, too, has meaning to me. In his letter, he describes how they're liquidating their merchandise.

"As it is," he writes, "I've been slowly bringing home all the good stuff, things that are new and that I hate to sell at a loss, so I can just about stock a small store right now with what I have in my closet and basement." (He exaggerates, I'm sure.) "Mom has also been bringing a lot of the good dishes and collectibles home. We spray everything real good, so we don't bring home a few of our friends, the *cockaroachillas* — that's the affectionate word for cockroach."

He goes on about what the rest of the family has been up to since I was last in town. My brother Mark is "skinnier than ever and working very hard and long hours. I'd like to see him put on some of the weight he lost and work less hours, but there again, just like you and I and Mike and Paul and Mom, we Bookbinders just don't settle for mediocrity. I personally think we can be proud of our attitudes. I hate the poor workmanship and salesmen's attitudes I come across every day."

Like I say, it's a warm letter. Underneath, there is a message of support, and though I know we still have more arguments ahead of us, I believe him when, in closing, he says he wants me to succeed in whatever it is I do. "I love you, son," he says. "Remember that — always."

We still don't see eye to eye, and perhaps we never will. But I'm not sure it really matters anymore.

414

Afterward

The story of *Street People* begins with a photograph.

It was the summer of 1969, I was 18, and I'd just hitch-hiked into New York City from "three days of peace and love" at the Woodstock music festival. This was my first visit to the city. Strolling on the Bowery, I saw human beings sprawled along the curb and lying beside buildings like so many sacks of garbage. I shot this photo of a man passed out in a doorway, his arms extended like Christ on the cross.

The image stayed with me long after I left the city.

—

Fast forward six years to the summer of 1975.

I was living in a cockroach-infested railroad flat on the corner of West 98th and Broadway, a neighborhood that was literally falling apart around me. Big cities were not new to me by then, but New York was still a shock to my system.

Much of that jolt came from its street life. I saw and sometimes interacted with people I had rarely encountered before, among them prostitutes, bag ladies, derelicts, drug dealers, beggars, small-time thieves, and con artists. What disturbed me was not the people themselves; it was their apparent invisibility to everyone but me. While most New Yorkers kept their gaze fixed ahead with eyes that warned, "Don't approach me," mine went everywhere.

In the movie *The Sixth Sense*, Haley Joel Osment sees dead people. I saw street people. I struggled to understand this attraction. Was it their novelty? Did I identify with them? Was I a voyeur? None of these explanations rang completely true. Only years later did I realize that I was an empath: Like one tuning fork resonating with another, I felt their presence and, often, their pain.

It was not empathy, however, that motivated me to start to write about street people. It was opportunity.

New York was likely the worst city in America for someone with virtually no experience in the field to begin a career in journalism, and after a year, I'd made little progress. I lived a hand-to-mouth existence, writing articles and taking pictures for neighborhood newspapers, working odd jobs, collecting unemployment.

The way forward was unclear. Yet I was determined to forge a path as a writer, so I decided to take a less traveled road: to follow in the footsteps of authors whose masterful works had inspired me, such as the stark portrayal of southern tenant farmers in James Agee and Walker Evans' *Let Us Now Praise Famous Men*, the "as told to" interviews in Studs Terkel's *Working*, and the searing vision of street life in Hubert Selby's *Last Exit to Brooklyn*.

This was a high bar. I was willing to start low.

My first efforts were short vignettes and character sketches (some of them woven into "Manhattan Notebook"). These came easily to me and from them grew an idea.

Police routinely rounded up Upper West Side prostitutes as part of Mayor Beame's push to clean up the city. Like me, my roommate Henry, a portrait photographer, was struggling to establish a career. I proposed that he and I team up. We would create a book of portraits and profiles of the local streetwalkers and do for this disenfranchised group of workers what Agee and Evans had done for the sharecroppers. Incidentally, we hoped, we would also write our own ticket, if not to fame and fortune, then at least to visibility.

—

Henry and I first spotted Margie as she sauntered down Broadway some twenty feet in front of us, wiggling her hips invitingly. From that distance, she looked like any of the other prostitutes on the Upper West Side: bright-red platform shoes, a flimsy red blouse, tight mini-skirt, torn stockings, and an ill-fitting dirty-blonde wig.

At the corner of West 96th Street and Broadway she stopped, and we soon caught up with her.

"Good evening. Can we talk with you for a moment?" Henry said.

She gave us a once-over and flashed a smile. "They call me Margie," she said.

Her five o'clock shadow, not quite concealed by pancake makeup, revealed her to be no ordinary streetwalker. She was one of a dozen drag queens Henry and I had seen roaming the streets of our neighborhood.

Henry explained that he was a *professional* photographer and I was a writer. I added, "We'd like to talk with you about your life and take some pictures. We can pay whatever you usually charge for your time."

Margie clapped her hands together. "Oh, you can do a whole *book* about me, darling! I could make Xaviera Hollander *this small*," she said, giggling as she made a knee-high gesture with her hand. "Or Linda Lovelace. Linda Lovelace is a *nothing*, and she wrote *her* book. So if you write something like that, you hit it."

"Well," I said, "that depends on what we talk about."

"I guess, in my line of work, honey," Margie said, "we won't talk about church. And that's for sure."

—

417

As I got to know Margie, Romeo, Muñeca, and others, my interest broadened to include representatives of every type of person who lived or worked on the street, from bag ladies, bums, and prostitutes to vendors and traffic cops. Meanwhile, Henry's took a different tack. Fascinated by the transvestite world, he envisioned a book of studio portraits that ran the gamut from streetwalkers like Margie to the well-known drag queens who performed in the Village and beyond. As he developed this idea, the place for my writing in the project dwindled to little more than extended captions.

Henry and I stopped working together. But I kept writing, and I started to take my own photos of the street. By chance, I met an editor who was excited about my book idea, and also my photography. "You can do this yourself, David," she said. "You don't need to work with anyone else."

For the next two years, I wandered the streets and subways of Manhattan carrying with me a steno pad, two cameras, and a tape recorder. I thought of myself as a correspondent to the middle classes, able to step into this invisible realm and return with something of value. I hoped, even if I did not possess their genius, that if I persisted, I would become a writer and photographer worthy of standing in the company of those I most admired. I stopped writing newspaper stories and, freed from the pressure of deadlines, sought out the heart of my subjects.

I called what I was attempting "slow journalism."

Such a book should never be published

My first proposal for *Street People* came together in the spring of 1976, about the time I started hanging out with Morris Kavesh's street corner society. In it, I outlined a book consisting of twenty to twenty-five profiles, no more than ten pages each, that depicted in words and images the different categories of street people I had identified.

The editor who had encouraged me to go solo introduced me to a literary agent who was also just starting out. I was, I thought, on my way.

Over the next year, Harvey circulated *Street People* to his contacts at New York publishers. But what began as a validating — at times even thrilling — process soon took a disappointing turn. An editor at one press said she liked the idea and my writing, but that I needed to team up with a sociologist. Another editor said he'd only consider a book about bag ladies. Yet another was prepared to advance me a respectable sum, but only if I would write, as he put it, "about the more bizarre and eccentric inhabitants of our streets who perform their wonderful brand of street theater, which, for a lot of us, makes a city a more interesting place to be." Most of the others returned my materials with a short note stating that although they found the idea intriguing, the subject was too "downbeat" to be salable.

Street People came heartbreakingly close at Scribner's, the publishing house that was home to F. Scott Fitzgerald, Thomas Wolfe, and their equally legendary editor, Maxwell Perkins. The editorial board was prepared to offer me a $10,000 advance — about $45,000 today. There was just one little hitch: They needed a final okay from the firm's president, Charles Scribner IV, who was in London at the time. It seemed like a sure thing, my big break, the payoff for living on brown rice and peanut butter and jelly omelets while I stayed true to my vision and ideals.

Harvey prefaced the bad news with, "Into every life, a little rain must fall." Mr. Scribner had reviewed the book proposal and declared, "Such a book should never be published." The editor-in-chief returned my manuscript. Digging through my notes, I found her accompanying letter:

February 8, 1977

Dear Harvey,

This is a great disappointment. As you know, I'd very much wanted to do STREET PEOPLE at Scribner's, as did a lot of us here.

With regret,

Patricia

The trajectory of my life would likely have been very different had Mr. Scribner come back from London with a more compassionate attitude.

By the twenty-second rejection, Harvey's contacts had run dry. I set *Street People* aside and moved to Brooklyn, where I completed a book on American folk music. There, I also met Edward, the subject of "My Interviews with God."

A few months later, I left Brooklyn and headed for Buffalo with all my belongings packed into a U-Haul truck.

—

For the next year, I was in motion. I traveled through Europe and then, back in the U.S., jumped from one artist colony to another. The colonies supported my writing and asked for nothing in return. I wanted more of that.

I believed that a teaching fellowship would extend the artist colony experience, but to distinguish myself as a candidate, I needed to demonstrate that I had range. The coming-of-age novel I was working on was very different from the street people stories, and that was good, but all the graduate-level programs I'd found were for *fiction* writers. Could I, in good faith, submit a street people story?

At the Virginia Center for the Creative Arts, one of my fellow colonists, fresh from the prestigious Iowa Writer's Workshop, read

"Margie" and provided an answer. "Send it!" she said. "How do you know what's fiction and what's fact in here?"

Her comment nudged me in a new direction. By the following fall, I'd landed in a Master's program in creative writing at Boston University, where I continued to work on *Street People*, now re-imagined through the framework of fiction. There, I wrote early drafts of "Morris Kavesh, Newsstand Man" and "A Letter from My Father."

The stories began their migration from slow journalism to their present, more ambiguous form.

—

Fast forward another decade.

After a dismal ten years as a tech writer for Boston-area computer companies, I moved to Albany, NY, to begin a doctoral program in English, with a specialty in creative writing.

Street People still nagged at me, and after a few months I gave in to their entreaties and began work on "My Interviews with God." By then, I fully embraced straddling the boundary between fact and fiction. Distance from the actual street people I knew had loosened my attachment to literal accounts of their lives and imbued the writing with new energy.

Serendipitously, the summer after my first year of grad school, an unexpected opportunity emerged. A Parisian friend visited for a few weeks, and he left for home with a copy of the street people stories to read on the plane. Within a week of his return, he connected me with an editor looking for books to populate a new series the editor called *Périphérique*, named after the highway that divides Paris from its sub-urbs and signifying "outsiders." He quickly offered me a contract; I was to be his American *découverte*.

Remembering my disappointing experience with Scribner's, I resisted getting my hopes up. My motto had become, "Don't count on anything until the check clears."

The check (in *francs*) cleared. Visions of a book tour in Paris danced though my head.

With great energy and enthusiasm, the editor began to translate my stories into French. Midway through, however, he abruptly vanished. It took the publisher a year to find a successor, and the new editor discarded most of his predecessor's choices, including *Street People*.

The ghost of Charles Scribner IV intoned, "Such a book should never be published."

I put *Street People* away, set aside the PhD program, and returned to Boston, where I eventually became a psychotherapist. I've written two books in that field, as well as dozens of short, self-help pieces. I thought I'd left *Street People* behind for good. But these people, these images, and this project have stayed alive inside me, like a secret I cannot tell but also can't forget.

Fact or Fiction

Take a deep breath and fast forward another thirty years.

In a recent move, I unearthed the unfinished books and unprinted negatives and contact sheets I'd created over the course of a lifetime and consolidated them all into six large file drawers. For a year, the file cabinet sat just to the left of my desk — a black-and-gray monolith glaring at me each time I sat at my computer. Then one day, *Street People*, the firstborn of these books-in-waiting, called to me again. The result is the book you have just read.

Much as the man I am today differs from the much younger me who roamed the streets of New York, on the lookout for whatever story opportunity might come his way, so *Street People* differs from the book I outlined in the 1970s. Then, I planned to go broad; now I have gone deep. Then, the genre was clear; now it is ambiguous. Then, the subject was topical; now it is history.

The distance of several decades has separated me from prior expectations and allowed the material to assume what I believe is its truest form. And yet, despite these years and differences, *Street People* has also come full circle, back to its roots in the books and photographs that first inspired it.

—

Over the years, people have asked whether the street people stories are nonfiction or fiction.

For the photographs, the answer is simple. I've adjusted contrast, brightness, and sometimes cropped for composition and repaired defects in the negatives, but the images are otherwise unaltered. For the writing, the answer is more complex.

In the seventies, I was heavily influenced by what was then called "New Journalism." Pioneered by writers such as Truman Capote (*In Cold Blood*), Norman Mailer (*The Armies of the Night*), Tom Wolfe (*The Electric Kool-Aid Acid Test*), and Hunter S. Thompson (*Fear and Loathing in Las Vegas*), New Journalism blurred the line between fiction and nonfiction. No longer was the teller of a real-life tale the neutral, invisible recorder of events. Nonfiction writers could be subjective, their writing styles eclectic, and they could at last claim the fiction writer's tools as their own.

When I arrived in Boston, the New Journalism approach was where I stood with the street people stories, but as I made my way through graduate programs in creative writing and immersed myself in fiction projects, even New Journalism, at first a liberation, began to feel constraining. In this new environment, I grew more willing to experiment with using fictionalized elements to clarify or enhance the work, and I also became intrigued by the blurry boundaries between fiction and fact.

On the whole, I have stayed close to the facts as I recorded and remember them, but I've made changes, too. Sometimes I've substantially restructured conversations and scenes. What appears to be a single, linear speech such as Margie's monologue, or Morris's, may have taken place over multiple interviews across several days or weeks. Scenes are sometimes literal depictions of what I observed, but many are constructed from notes, bits of dialog captured on tape, memories, my imagination, or a combination.

The narrator is both me and not me, as if we are two versions of the same person living in parallel, but slightly different, universes. The basic fabric of my remembered life is imprinted on him, but his personality and his voice have become his own. Likewise, minor characters may be partly invented. The biggest departure from autobiography is Ruth. Though she is loosely based on women I have known, Ruth's identity, history, and personality are distinctly hers.

As I sifted through raw materials and early drafts, I realized that fiction and fact are also blurred in a more intrinsic way.

Although my intention to help the people I interviewed was earnest, I was also pursuing an ambition, and I shaped what I said to them so I could gain their confidence. I told them I believed they had a point of view different from what I'd read about in books and magazines, and that it should be heard. I sometimes added that I thought the straight world had the wrong idea about them — they'd gotten a bum rap — and telling their side of the story could help to put things right. They confided in me, I think, because I seemed genuinely interested in what they had to say, and also, I suspect, because I seemed naïve and, therefore, harmless. I have wondered how sincere and harmless I really was.

If it is true that in my interactions with the people in this book I was sometimes not completely frank, it is also true that they were sometimes less than honest with me. Some of these fictions were intentional: I saw no benefit in showing all my cards and they had no reason to fully trust me. Others are intrinsic to all storytellers. Memories are malleable. And as my friend at the Virginia artist colony implied, unreliable narrators are as close as our own thoughts.

If *Street People* were to be assigned to a high school English class, an essay assignment might read something like this:

Answer two of the following questions:

1. Did Margie actually know the famous drag queens she admired? Was it truly her desire to seduce her brothers?
2. Did Romeo actually have a daughter? If so, was she killed?
3. Was Morris "the happiest man in the world"? Or did he ward off despair by convincing himself he was?
4. Who was this boyfriend for whom Cookie was willing to take a walk on the wild side? Was Cookie pregnant?
5. What were the real motivations of *Street People*'s narrator?

Support your argument with at least three citations from the text.

The most honest character in this book is likely Edward, who truly believed he was who he claimed to be and spent half a lifetime trying to prove it.

Norman Mailer's *The Armies of the Night* is subtitled "History as Fiction, Fiction as History." *Street People* could similarly be subtitled "Biography as Fiction, Fiction as Biography."

Lessons

The street people project has shaped me more profoundly than I could ever have foretold. When I contemplated writing this Afterward, I asked myself what I have learned in the years since I began it. Three life lessons occur to me now:

1. Then, I felt that a writer with no support had to choose between creating art and living life, and that the true artist must always choose the former. Now, having gone to both extremes, I've learned not to sacrifice life to art, nor to trade off art for a safer life.

2. Then, I often wondered what, if anything, separated me from the people I wrote about. Now, I know I have always been on *this* side of the line, and that what keeps me here owes as much to the luck of the draw as to any effort on my part.

3. Then, I saw myself as an anthropologist. Now, I see that all of us share more than our DNA, and that we each deserve — though seldom get — equal time in the limelight. Perhaps in this way I am still naïve, but it's a naivete I hope never to lose.

About writing, there has really been only one lesson, but it's a big one.

Then, I believed that books could "change the world," that writers wrote to expose falsehoods and to reveal overlooked truths, and that these exposures and revelations would help us become better people in a better world.

Now, I see that books seldom change the world in any enduring way and that a writer's influence is scattershot at best. But I have also seen how, through books, we can vicariously experience the lives of others and see their points of view from the inside.

This is no small thing.

A supervisor from early in my psychotherapist career periodically posted quotations on his door that he hoped would inspire us in our work with clients. The one I still remember comes from Gandhi: "Whatever you do in life will be insignificant, but it is very important that you do it."

This is how I see a writer's role today. I understand that the effects of what I write may be felt in unknown ways, and at great distances in time and space.

I ask myself: Did James Agee, Studs Terkel, or Hubert Selby know they had set me on the path to *Street People*? Of course they did not. Nor did the hundreds — by now, likely thousands — of authors who enlightened me in as many ways have even an inkling of their impact on me.

And yet they did have an impact, and maybe, since you find yourself here, on this last page of *Street People*, so have I.

After the Afterward

For most of the past four-plus decades, I had no way of knowing what became of the people I've written about here. But thanks to Google, I've found some details about two of them, and possibly also a third.

On the way back to our apartment for her first interview, Margie told me that she had been the scream in an Andy Warhol film. At the time this seemed improbable, though not impossible. But a 2020 exhibition of Warhol's work reveals that Andy Warhol made use of Margie's talents in more ways than she or I could have imagined.

Margie was one of fourteen drag queens Warhol met through the Gilded Grape, a club frequented by bisexual, gay and trans people including Margie, Romeo, and Muñeca, among many others. Warhol took about 500 Polaroid photos of these drag queens and from them created some 250 screenprints and paintings. He called the series "Ladies and Gentlemen." Though less well known than his images of soup cans and Marilyn Monroe, it was his largest body of work.

Fifty-five of the 250 pieces in the series are of Margie. Warhol photographed Margie in two sittings and paid her $50 per sitting. Since its re-release in 2020, "Ladies and Gentlemen" has been exhibited worldwide at prestigious venues that include the Tate Gallery in London and the Metropolitan Museum of Art in New York.

Warhol is said to have observed that in the future, everyone will have fifteen minutes of fame. Few can attest that theirs came from Andy Warhol himself.

About Morris all I know is that he died in 1985 at the age of 82 and is buried in Queens. I never made it to the 50th anniversary celebration of his newsstand, if it took place. I can't confirm that it did; I was unable to find any mention of him in the digital archives of the *New York Times*, the *Daily News*, or the *New York Post*.

I never knew Cookie's or Frankie's real names, or Edward's last name, so learning about their later lives has proved to be impossible. However, I am almost certain I know something about Romeo's.

In a recent Google search using his real name, I found an obituary from 2021. The deceased was the age Romeo would have been, and in subsequent searches I found that for most of his life he lived in the Bronx. The brief summary of his life in the obituary reveals that he had served in the military and raised a family.

The man who gazes at me through the photographer's lens in the obituary photo has Romeo's knowing smile, and his sharp eyes are those I remember well. He's lounging on a stone bench, dressed with casual elegance, a gold stud in one ear. Even as an older man, as Romeo once put it, he "ain't ugly." In the photo, he looks happy.

A Note on the Illustrations

Except for a magazine cover and the Hotel Cumberland photo in "Morris Kavesh, Newsstand Man," the photographs in this book are mine. They are a selection from the roughly 4,000 images I shot during five years of roaming the streets and subways of Manhattan and Brooklyn. You can view larger versions of these images on my photography website, phototransformations.com. The photographs in this book, as well as others from this period, are also in the companion to this book, *Street People: Portfolio*.

The illustration for the Revelation section of "My Interviews with God" is from *The Apocalypse*, a series of fifteen woodcuts by Albrecht Dürer published in 1498.

The eight remaining illustrations in "My Interviews with God" are derived from woodcuts created by Michael Wolgemut. They are included in *The Nuremberg Chronicles* (1493), Hartmann Schedel's account of the Judeo-Christian God's works from the Creation through the end of time. These images depict the seven days of Creation described in the Book of Genesis. They begin with the division into day and night on the First Day and increase in complexity as the days progress. To distill them to their simplest form, I have taken the liberty of removing the Hand of God depicted in seven of Wolgemut's original paintings.

You can view the original illustrations here:

https://www.faena.com/aleph/7-days-of-creation-and-their-most-beautiful-illustrations-o

Dear Reader

Dear Reader,

Please stay with me one minute longer.

First, thank you for reading *Street People*. I know you have many choices and that your time is limited, and I'm grateful you've taken this journey with me.

If you've found this book meaningful, I have a small favor to ask of you.

I believe every writer's hope is that his or her work touches readers in ways that resonate beyond their words. If the stories and images in this book have spoken to you, you'll understand why I have brought these people, and this much younger version of myself, out of the shadows of the past and into the light of today.

I'd like to share *Street People* with as many readers as possible and I can only do so with your help. I will be forever grateful if you would consider letting other readers hear about your reading experience. You can do this by writing just a few words about *Street People* and posting them on Amazon. If you are on Goodreads, your response to *Street People* posted there would also be deeply appreciated.

With gratitude,

Acknowledgements

This book would not have been possible without the generosity of many people. I'd like to express particular thanks to the following:

Linda Kuehl, who led me in a new direction in my writing, and without whom *Street People* could never have been born.

Dan Porges, for his help in the early stages of the street people project.

Hayes Jacobs, who gave me the confidence to forge ahead on my own.

Mary Foskett O'Connor, Jerry Bornstein, and Florence Isaacs, for their invaluable critiques in the early years.

Harvey Klinger, for his diligent efforts to place an early version of this book with New York publishers.

Herbert Mason, who helped me keep on with the project in the face of significant self-doubt.

Geoffrey Wolfe, who encouraged early attempts to shape nonfiction materials with fictional techniques.

Laurent DeBonnerive, who connected me to a French editor and collaborated on a screenplay based on some of the stories in this book.

Eugene Garber, for his incisive comments on multiple iterations of these stories and his unflagging support over many years.

Barrie Levine, for her steadfast interest and encouragement, and for her keen proofreader's eye.

My beta readers, for their generous assistance with the final drafts.

The writers and photographers who inspired me.

And, of course, the people I have written about here, who entrusted me with their stories. Thank you for letting me into your lives. I hope I have done justice to them.

My apologies to those whose names I no longer recall, or whom I have neglected to mention. It's been a long, strange trip. I'm grateful to you all.

About the Author

David J. Bookbinder is a writer, photographer, and life coach. In addition to *Street People*, he is the author of *Street People Portfolio: Invisible New York Made Visual*, *Paths to Wholeness: Fifty-Two Flower Mandalas*, *The Art of Balance: Staying Sane in an Insane World*, *What Folk Music is All About*, two coloring books for adults, and three books about computer software.

He is the recipient of teaching fellowships from Boston University and the University at Albany, and of writing residencies from the Millay Colony for the Arts and the Virginia Center for the Creative Arts. His Flower Mandala images were awarded a Massachusetts Cultural Council grant in photography.

David recently retired from a long career as a psychotherapist. He lives and writes north of Boston and is a native of Buffalo, New York.